TRAVEL, MODERNISM
AND MODERNITY

To H.T.

Travel, Modernism and Modernity

ROBERT BURDEN

Routledge
Taylor & Francis Group

LONDON AND NEW YORK

First published 2015 by Ashgate Publishing

2 Park Square, Milton Park, Abingdon, Oxfordshire OX14 4RN
52 Vanderbilt Avenue, New York, NY 10017

Routledge is an imprint of the Taylor & Francis Group, an informa business

First issued in paperback 2019

British Library Cataloguing in Publication Data
A catalogue record for this book is available from the British Library

The Library of Congress has cataloged the printed edition as follows:
Burden, Robert
  Travel, modernism and modernity / by Robert Burden.
    pages cm
  Includes bibliographical references and index.
  ISBN 978-1-4724-5286-3 (hardcover: alk. paper)
  1. Expatriate authors—Criticism and interpretation. 2. Authors, English—History and criticism. 3. Authors, American—History and criticism. 4. Travel in literature. 5. Cultural awareness. 6. Modernism (Literature) I. Title.
  PN495.B87 2015
  823'.9120932—dc23

2014042348

ISBN 978-1-4724-5286-3 (hbk)
ISBN 978-0-367-88099-6 (pbk)

Contents

Acknowledgements

I would like to record here my thanks to former colleagues and friends who kindly agreed to read drafts of chapters as work-in-progress: Ben Knights, Bruce Ingraham and Stephan Kohl. Bruce Ingraham also generously read an early version of the whole manuscript. Their comments were invaluable in my moving the text towards greater coherence and cohesion. With the encouragement of Ann Donahue at Ashgate, the comments of the publisher's anonymous reader, the sharp scrutiny of the text and argument by my wife, Hildegard Träger, and the thoroughness of the editorial team at Ashgate, I was able to get the book into its final shape. Any remaining faults are, of course, the sole responsibility of the author. Thanks also go to Charles Kenwright for the design of the cover image.

Cover image: Image of Edith Wharton: © The New York Times/Redux/laif.

Images of Joseph Conrad, E.M. Forster, D.H. Lawrence and Henry James: © Wissenmedia, Gütersloh, Germany.

Italian landscape: © Charles Kenwright, www.openmind-images.com.

Introduction

Aim

This book is a study of the significance for modernist writing of travel. The writers selected as representative are Joseph Conrad, E.M. Forster, D.H. Lawrence, Henry James and Edith Wharton, since they travelled and produced travel writing to one degree or another and in some form or another. I look in some detail at the place of travel and travel writing in their respective work, work broadly conceived as modernist. For there is an effect of travel and travel writing on their fiction as narrative paradigm and as recurrent trope for questions of identity and otherness in the encounter with places and cultures. Perspectives gained from travel at home and abroad or simply the desire for expatriation spill over into the deep-seated concern with the emergent crisis of national cultural identity, Englishness or the new American identity. Thus the perceived depredations of modernity, together with the question of imperialism – the older British and European, and the emergent American from the late nineteenth century and into the early twentieth – frequently arises as a focus on tourism, which each of these selected writers disparage as the ruin of real travel, a problematic attitude at best, and one which stands for another sense of superiority to add to that of nationalism in the competitions of modernity. Indeed, it is sometimes as if the battle ground for the emergent collective feelings of racial superiority and its critique is the aesthetics of western High Culture against the ancient forms of so-called primitive cultures – extreme positions that distinguish Henry James from D.H. Lawrence. The 'racial encounter' is at the heart of modernity, and travelling modernists reconceived the dramas of encounter in the imperial field in, at best, an ambivalent perspective (Armstrong, 136–9).

Key Concepts

Modernism

In discussing modernism, I join those who have been calling for a broader synthetic conceptualization (Armstrong, *Modernism: A Cultural History*; Levenson, *Modernism*). While recognizing the complexities of the critical formations of modernism both in its self-understanding and in the belated readings of critical approaches, I also insist on the variety of modernisms and the force of residual aesthetic discourses and codes of representation even while newer forms are emerging. Peter Gay writes about the ways in which modernist novelists 'enlisted long-established techniques for radical ends' – Henry James is his example who works within 'literary orthodoxy' to achieve newer complexities in the 'exploration of consciousness' (*Modernism*, 190–94); and I would add Conrad's impressionism in narratives that rework the codes of the adventure story deconstructing their ethical implications.[1] Impressionism is then a radicalized realism, as the real is what is visible to the gaze and is subject to a specifically characterized perspective. As Levenson claims, realism 'followed out a shadow history alongside modernist formalism' (*Modernism*, 230). The relationship between older representational typologies and modernist narrative needs to be looked at in some detail, as it demonstrates that the opposition between realism and modernism as such is reductionist. Indeed, Jameson insists that there are modernist novels that are 'not at all to be understood as some opposite number of realism', but instead can be 'perfectly well interrogated with the categories and within the limits of realism'. His example is, provocatively, *Ulysses*: 'certainly a prime example of a stubborn and hard fought attempt to hold onto the absolute being of the place and day, the untranslatable reality of a specifically limited secular experience' – although, of course, residual realism may also be subject to a modernist defamiliarization (*The Antinomies of Realism*, 215–16).[2]

Where modernism is generally divided between early, high and late periods,[3] I shall now add the concept of 'late realism', which begins with Conrad's impressionism and continues in the ironic uses of the limited points of view of characters and character-narrators in Forster, Lawrence, James and Wharton where priority is given to character consciousness first accessed through the use of the gaze, so that subject and object are placed in a problematic relation fitting for the changed realities of modernity and the epistemological scepticism of modernism. In Eysteinsson's words, modernism is 'seeking reality at a different level of human existence, reality as it is perceived by the human consciousness' (*The Concept of Modernism*, 184).[4] This is not just critical comment on modernist writing in scholarship now but what was consciously promoted by the modernists themselves, for example by Virginia Woolf in her essay 'Mr Bennett and Mrs Brown'.[5] Levenson has recently added his voice to the call 'to restore a place for

---

[1]   Fredric Jameson reads in *Lord Jim* 'the trace and the remnant of the content of an older realism now displaced and effectively marginalized by the emergent modernist discourse'. *The Political Unconscious*, 207. See also Michael Levenson, *A Genealogy of Modernism*, 34–6.

[2]   'It is thus instructive to read *Ulysses* as a compendium of these residual realist narrative lines and as an extraordinary new combinatory play with such residues. The presence of the *Bildungsroman* is the most obvious ...' Jameson, *The Antinomies of Realism*, 150.

[3]   See, for example, Armstrong's 'mapping modernism' in *Modernism: A Cultural History*, 23–41.

[4]   This study is particularly instructive for its thorough discussion of the critical formations of the concept in different national traditions. Peter Gay writes of the literary modernists as 'Realists' whose 'redefined reality now mainly consisted in thoughts and feelings, domains of life that earlier writers had neglected or felt unable to capture and express'. *Modernism*, 229.

[5]   In this essay, Virginia Woolf famously announced that 'in or about December 1910 human character changed ... [and] All human relations have shifted' (320), so that the novelist has to find new convincing ways of representing character.

realism in the history of modernism' (*Modernism*, 225). And in this discussion of residual aesthetic or representational codes in modernism, there seems to be another shadowy presence, especially in the description of landscapes and ruins in travel writing, and that is romanticism – which was also marked by attempts to set the aesthetic realm against the conditions of modernity.[6]

Modernity

It is generally agreed that any study of literary modernism requires an understanding of the concept of modernity: 'The notion that modernism involves a critique of the self-understanding of modernity construed in terms of the enlightenment project is, of course, essential to any theoretical understanding of modernism' (Giles, 'Afterword' in *Theorizing Modernism*, 178).[7] The general response to modernity in the late nineteenth and early twentieth centuries was twofold. In the one camp, it was celebrated as a great advance in man's control over nature in technology and science (Futurism, Vorticism); in the other, it was condemned as a greater loss to the culture: a life empty of meaning as the instrumentalities, mass cultural formations and standardization of modernity were perceived as having swept away the traditional values that had given the self its senses of identity. However, a problem arises when modernity is understood as the liberation from 'tradition and prejudice', as David Punter defines it (*Modernity*, 210). Being modern has something to do with emancipation, greater freedom of movement (social mobility and travel) and opportunity; and questions of gender and sexuality are famously addressed by the modernists, more directly than their Victorian predecessors.

The modernist critique of modernity is represented by the writers examined in this study. Frisby quotes Siegfried Kracauer as representative of the anti-modernity position: the human being 'is a cog in a powerful soulless machine which rests upon the interlocking of countless little wheels. The goal that is striven for vanishes from the inner gaze' (*Fragments of Modernity*, 113). Kracauer's description is reminiscent of Mark Gertler's 1916 painting, 'The Merry-Go-Round', which impressed D.H. Lawrence because it articulates the mechanization and spiritual emptiness of modern existence.[8] The greater efficiencies of modern life have been at the cost of dehumanization, and modernist cinema portrayed this effect in Fritz Lang's *Metropolis* (1926) and Charlie Chaplin's *Modern Life* (1936).

---

[6]   Jàs Elsner and Joan-Pau Rubiés remind us that 'Romanticism reveals a disenchantment with the process of Western civilization'. Introduction to *Voyages and Visions: Towards a Cultural History of Travel*, 4. Carl Thompson writes about travel 'off the beaten track' as 'driven partly by a Romantic desire to visit sites of unspoilt natural beauty, and/or cultures seemingly untouched by modernity' (54).

[7]   See also Harvey, *The Condition of Postmodernity: An Enquiry into the Origins of Cultural Change*; Armstrong, *Modernism: A Cultural History*; and Punter, *Modernity*.

[8]   The painting is reproduced on the back cover of Mark Kinkead-Weekes's biography, *D.H. Lawrence: Triumph to Exile 1912–1922* (Cambridge: Cambridge University Press, 1996).

This characterization of modernity through the trope of the machine has had a long history. Alain Supiot writes:

> Industrial society's imaginary represented the world as a clockwork mechanism, subject to the laws of Newtonian physics, and turned workers into the cogs of a giant productive machine. Following Taylorist precepts, they were subject in both capitalist and communist countries to a so-called 'scientific' organization of labour, whose first principle was to prohibit them from thinking ... the dehumanization of labour was seen as the price of progress. (*New Left Review* 83, 110–11)

There is a general consensus that modernity in its modern understanding originated in Baudelaire's slogan from the mid-nineteenth century that modern life was characterized by the 'transitory, the fugitive, and the contingent' (Frisby, 2). Society had become unstable, traditional values were being questioned, conventions seemed an empty shell and social relations were subject to instrumental reason and reification. These are the terms of the critique of modernity argued for variously in the work of Weber, Simmel, Kracauer and Lukàcs. The loss of traditional beliefs and community – the displacement of *Gemeinschaft* by *Gesellschaft* (Tönnies) (Frisby, 13)[9] – also led to the disappearance of the traditional storyteller, according to Benjamin;[10] and modernist literature is characterized by its radicalizing of storytelling.

Modernist Responses to Modernity

Modernist solutions to the chaos, decadence and instrumentalities of modernity were to assert the aesthetic order as the only alternative. Fragmentation and loss of value would be overcome by aesthetic and formal values.[11] Conrad, Forster, James and Wharton all lament the loss of value in modern life, and attempt to recover a sense of value in the aesthetic realm. Lawrence, however, objected to a purely aestheticist doctrine – especially the autonomy of art promoted by his contemporaries, Clive Bell and Roger Fry.[12] Lawrence did, though, try out experiments in writing to rival those of Joyce – parody and self-parody, self-conscious authorial intrusion, broken text and collage – in *Mr Noon* and *Kangaroo*. Sometimes modernists turned to mythic solutions for the cultural crisis. As Jameson put it, modernism

---

[9]   Raymond Williams discusses the gradual loss of community in *The English Novel from Dickens to Lawrence*, beginning with the premise that traditional novels are 'knowable communities' (14), and that the confidence in this knowledge – of persons and relationships – breaks down with the growth of modern urbanization.

[10]   Walter Benjamin: 'The art of storytelling is reaching its end because the epic side of truth, wisdom, is dying out' (*Illuminations*, 87). 'A great storyteller will always be rooted in the people, primarily in a milieu of craftsmen' (101).

[11]   What Jameson calls 'aestheticizing strategies' (*The Political Unconscious*, 230) or 'strategies of containment' (242), when describing Conrad's stylistic impressionism.

[12]   For a discussion of Lawrence's relationship to the aesthetics of Clive Bell and Roger Fry see Anne Fernihough, *D.H. Lawrence: Aesthetics and Ideology*, chapter 4.

can be read 'as a Utopian compensation for everything reification brings with it' (*The Political Unconscious*, 236). Examples range from Lawrence's valorization of peasant cultures and primitivism, Conrad's nostalgia for the adventure of the sea, and Forster's wish to recreate the queer space of the English 'Greenwood', to James and Wharton imagining an American culture without the tastelessness of modernity along the lines of a gentrified England or an old Europe. Yet, at the same time, these writers reveal a greater ambivalence about modernity in their fiction and travel writing, the greater freedoms to travel and the better transport to facilitate their journeys being an obvious point.

In Conrad, Forster, Lawrence, James and Wharton, place, monument, landscape or seascape are aestheticized by the gaze of the traveller. Moreover, the sublimation of desire into the aesthetic – 'a desire for artistic enjoyment' (Dwight, 187) – gives an order to desire: either that of the compositional principle of the recurrent leitmotif which creates a rhythm of symbolic associations across the text, as it does in musical composition – reminding us of Walter Pater's dictum: 'All art constantly aspires to the condition of music' (*Studies in the History of the Renaissance*, 124), the 'condition of music' derived from Wagner; or the classical principles of proportion, symmetry and harmony. Furthermore, the aesthetic gaze enables the picturesque or sublime object. Celebrating the joy of perception of the Italian villa and its gardens or the Tiepolo fresco enables Wharton's *jouissance*, which is by definition outside the law of the Father. There is here a correlation between demand and *jouissance* – as we see also in Lucy Honeychurch's moment of joy in Florence in Forster's *A Room with a View*. But the aesthetic has a moral value too, and moral imperatives have an ideological function because appreciation of art and the virtues of classical harmony are paradigms for civilized living. Terry Eagleton has called this the 'ideology of aesthetic' (see *The Ideology of the Aesthetic*), and we should not overlook the class privileges and financial independence of Forster, James and Wharton which enable them to prioritize the aesthetic realm of high culture against mass culture, materialism and tourism, and as a way of life.[13]

The modernist critique of modernity was given a greater focus by the effects of the Great War. As Harvey puts it:

> The trauma of world war and its political and intellectual responses ... opened the way to a consideration of what might constitute the essential and eternal qualities of modernity that lay on the nether side of Baudelaire's formulation. In the absence of Enlightenment certitudes as to the perfectibility of man, the search for a myth appropriate to modernity became paramount ... But it also seemed possible to build metaphorical bridges between ancient and modern myths. (30)

---

[13] I would also add that despite their rejection of modernity – often understood as Americanization – James, Wharton and their contemporaries benefitted from the new technologies that enabled mobility, luxury travel and expatriation – dollars and pounds went a long way abroad.

One thinks immediately of Joyce's *Ulysses*, T.S. Eliot's *Waste Land* and Lawrence's *Phoenix*, as well as the influence of Frazer and Weston on the mythic imaginary of the modernists.

However, the mythic is just one representational code alongside impressionism, symbolism and expressionism in a radicalized, residual realism that marked its modernist intent by shifting away from the omniscient moralizing of the Victorian novel to a representation of modern consciousness that would be able to account for the newer understanding of subjectivity, gender and sexuality. To quote Harvey again:

> The articulation of erotic, psychological, and irrational needs (of the sort that Freud identified and Klimt represented in his free-flowing art) ... had to recognize the impossibility of representing the world in a single language. Understanding had to be constructed through the exploration of multiple perspectives. (30)

Unfixing limited perspectives to problematize the relationship between language and truth, and question worn-out values are central to the project of literary modernism, a project represented variously by the writers studied in this book. Jameson encapsulates the representational crisis of modernism in a way that may be applied pertinently to all the writers in this study:

> By this suspension, in which representation undermines itself, Modernism hopes to preserve and keep open the space of some genuine Experience beyond reification, the space of the libidinal and Utopian gratification of which the Frankfurt School speaks, a space in which the failure of the imagination, cancelled by the form itself, can then release the imaginary to some more intense second-degree fulfilment and narrative figuration. (*The Political Unconscious*, 171)

Approaches to Modernism

Richard Sheppard has suggested that the critical formation of the concept of modernism may be traced to the explosion of interest in the 1960s. Since then, national academic traditions have approached the concept in such different ways that it is now impossible to come to terms with modernism 'as a total phenomenon' ('The Problematics of European Modernism', 1). Eysteinsson also argues that modernism is the object of different critical formations (*The Concept of Modernism*, 48). For Roland Barthes it is '*écriture*' (the problematics of language); for Lukàcs it is decadence, for Ortega y Gasset the dehumanization of art; for Adorno a radical attack on modernity in the realm of the aesthetic, while for Jameson aestheticizing strategies are a compensation for reification; for Shklovski it is defamiliarization and for Brecht '*Verfremdungseffekt*'; for T.S. Eliot in his reading of Joyce's *Ulysses* it is 'the mythic method' which gives order to the chaos and futility of contemporary history ('"Ulysses", Order and Myth', rept. in Kermode, 177–8). The German academic tradition, following Habermas, reads modernism as a continuation of the Enlightenment tradition, and one that has still not completed its project; while some American and British scholars still argue for a clear separation between the modernist and the postmodernist. The difficult and subversive novels of modernism are now, of course, classics on the university curriculum; and Raymond Williams argued that the radical nature of the early-twentieth-century avant-garde modernists had been commodified by the very business community it was attacking: radical art techniques have become the common currency of the advertising companies (*The Politics of Modernism*).

In the light of this multiplicity of approaches, Sheppard usefully suggests three strategies for answering the question: what is modernism? First, look for the common traits of relativism, anti-democratic ideology, nihilism, alienation and the use of myth. But, as he points out, the weakness here is that generalized common ground pays scant attention to the details of specific contexts, and is therefore reductionist. Thus there is the need 'to reconstruct the dynamic, not to say cataclysmic context which generated them [the common traits] in their specifically modernist *combinatoire*' (2). The second strategy is to approach modernism through a more broad-based historical, literary historical or sociological context. Thus modernism is a continuation of romanticism, a rejection of realism or a precursor of postmodernism. All these positions depend on the examples selected. But this approach tends to concentrate exclusively on aesthetic considerations – like Barthes's celebrated claim that the whole of modern literature since Flaubert is concerned with the 'problematics of language' (Sheppard, 3).[14] The third strategy is a 'matrix approach', which compares ostensibly disparate works by demonstrating their responses to a common underlying problematic. For instance, for Adorno the problematic is imperialism, while for Lukàcs it is reification (Sheppard, 4–5).[15] Sheppard endorses this third strategy; and it is one I adopt too in looking at the various responses to modernity as cultural crisis, because it enables a comparison of writers while acknowledging their differences. For example, after the war, Lawrence's apocalyptic response was Spenglerian, while sharing Forster's critique of British imperialism in India, a critique already seen in Conrad's Africa and Malay fiction. Also Forster's condition of England stories and novels are comparable to James and Wharton's critique of the American abroad and the state of American modernity.

Travel and Modernism

What my study now adds to the discussion of modernism and modernity is the significance of travel for literary modernism, as narrative paradigm and trope, and one that leads to a greater topographical insistence. As David Farley argues, travel and travel writing 'transformed literary modernism as they were transformed by it' (*Modernist Travel Writing*, 1). Travel was important to the 'creative consciousness of the period' (Farley, 2). Indeed, a new consciousness of mobility and borders,

---

[14] For Roland Barthes's famous claim see *Le degré zero de l'écriture* (Paris: Seuil, 1953). Translated as *Writing Degree Zero* (London: Cape, 1967).

[15] I would add that the latter is reworked by Jameson in his reading of Conrad's 'will-to-style'. See *The Political Unconscious*, chapter 5: 'Romance and Reification: Plot Construction and Ideological Closure in Joseph Conrad' – which I discuss in Chapter 1.

of difference and otherness, and of the limits of western ways of seeing and representation characterize the period of modernism.[16] For Farley the greatest impact of travel was on the late modernism of the 1930s. I insist, though, that the metaphor of travel and the structure of the journey and the significance of topography are emergent already in early modernism – in the travel fiction of Conrad, and the stories and novels of Forster, Lawrence, James and Wharton. Moreover, it should be no surprise, as Helen Carr has argued, that given how many novelists and poets were 'travelling writers', imaginative literature and travel writing had 'shared concerns' (Carr, 73–4). Largely displacing the moralizing and didactic styles of Victorian travel writing, modernist travel writing became 'a more subjective form, more memoir than manual … a more impressionistic style with the interest focused as much on the travellers' responses or consciousness as on their travels' (Carr, 74).

Thus, in investigating how far modernism transformed travel writing, a point of departure is to investigate the formal connections between travel and storytelling, between residual codes and styles, and formal and epistemological questions that represent degrees of modernist deconstruction of conventional travel writing. Travel has always generated stories; and narratives are structured like journeys, with beginnings and departures, incidents and arrivals, endings and homecomings. As Peter Hulme and Tim Youngs claim, 'the traveller's tale is as old as fiction itself' (2).[17] The forms of travel have become narrative archetypes like the odyssey or the pilgrimage, the quest or the voyage of discovery and the Grand Tour.[18] These archetypes are residual in the literary tourism of the writers discussed in this study, where a travel itinerary contains the sites of famous artists and writers, places first commodified as sights by the developing tourist industry during the eighteenth and nineteenth centuries as part of the Grand Tour – Classical and Renaissance Italy, for example; or as part of the growing cultural nationalism in the nineteenth and early twentieth centuries – Hardy or Bronte country where the fictional landscapes are topographies for a literary geography. Nicola Watson tells us that 'Walter Scott was the first British writer around whose works a national literary map was constructed' (*The Literary Tourist*, 14). The writers selected for my study have themselves also become the object of such tourism. For example, late in life E.M. Forster became an object of literary tourism in Kings College Cambridge;[19] and

---

[16]   Alexandra Peat in *Travel and Modernist Literature* (New York: Routledge, 2011) also argues that modernist travel fiction 'began to subvert the framework of imperial relations' (133) provoking 'new ways of seeing that transform both foreign and familiar spaces' (170).

[17]   Jameson reminds us of Walter Benjamin's claim that the origins of storytelling 'lay in the intersection of travelling seamen and merchants with the sedentary life of the villagers'. *The Antinomies of Realism*, 20 note 7.

[18]   The principal claim of Peat's book, *Travel and Modernist Fiction*, is that the pilgrimage as a 'sacred and ethical' journey is a defining trope in modernist travel fiction.

[19]   'Now that he was known to reside in Cambridge, many people were burning to meet him. He was an object of pilgrimage particularly for visiting Indians.' Furbank, *E.M. Forster: A Life, vol. 2*, 277.

there is a 'memorial chapel' said to contain the ashes of D.H. Lawrence in Kiowa, New Mexico (Ellis, *D.H. Lawrence: Dying Game*, 534).

The planned tour was conceived as educational before mass tourism as such packaged travel into an itinerary of sights – tourist attractions – for easy consumption. The paradigm for writers travelling to develop their sensibilities was Goethe's *Italian Journey*, which was first published in 1786. The wanderlust Goethe expresses in his travel writing and literature – a northern longing for the south, its colours and light, the land where the lemon-tree blossoms – is the destination for a journey of self-discovery and a rite of passage for the young writer. Italy as destination and as scene for cultural encounters and aesthetic experience plays an important part in the travel writing and fiction discussed in the following chapters; but so do other European destinations like France, Germany and Switzerland, in a common scheme of values as sites either for travel proper or tourism. However, some of the writers travel further afield: Conrad to the Malay archipelago or Central Africa; Forster to Egypt and India; Lawrence to Australia, Mexico and New Mexico; and Wharton to Morocco – places that become the focus for reactions to imperialism and primitivism which sometimes challenges the nationalist or romantic mindsets that underpin them.

All the writers studied insist on the distinction between travel and tourism, where mass tourism becomes a principal example of all that has gone wrong with modernity. Caren Kaplan claims that 'the tourist acts as an agent of modernity' (*Questions of Travel*, 58). Carl Thompson explains that the tourist had been blamed for much since guided tours began:

> [T]he tourist represents the very worst aspects of modern travel and, indeed, of modernity generally. He or she is assumed to practise a lazy, timid, and superficial version of travel, in which everything is safely pre-arranged by the supervisory apparatus of the tourist industry. A genuine encounter with an alien culture or environment is thus replaced by a commodified, staged and inauthentic simulacrum of such encounters, with the result that tourists do not gain any significant insight into either the Other or themselves ... Tourists, it is frequently alleged, ultimately destroy the places and cultures they seek out; their laziness creates an infrastructure that spoils previously pristine landscapes, whilst their cultural insensitivity and boorishness works to vulgarise the traditional communities they visit. (122–3)

Travel stories, though, are not the same as tourist guides, even when some writers attempted guides – like Forster's book on Alexandria,[20] or Conrad's plan for a popular travel guide to Italy for English and American tourists.[21] Conrad insisted the tourist could never tell such good stories as the 'real traveller' (*Last Essays*, 88–90), stories of adventure to remote places often in the form of

---

[20]   *Alexandria: A History and a Guide* and *Pharos and Pharillon*, first published 1922 and 1923, respectively (London: André Deutsch, 2004).

[21]   Zdzisław Najder, *Joseph Conrad: A Life* (New York: Camden House, 2007), 351, quoting a letter to Pinker. The book was never written.

the voyage narrative with archetypal resonances of the mythic wanderers across the seas, or the quest characterized by the focus on a single enigmatic character whose actions and motives are the subject of the narrative – Almayer and Willems, Nostromo, Kurtz or Verloc – even when for deconstructive effects. Kasia Body asks 'what stories can possibly be sent back by tourism?' Her answer: a tourist sends 'parodies of authentic experience in the fragmentary forms of snapshots and messages designed to fit on (half) the back of a postcard' of already designated 'tourist attractions' (Elsner and Rubiés, 237). Real travel for Conrad is an adventure for real men; for Lawrence travel is a quest for places where the old relationships between man and the natural environment still exist, a quest which takes him to remote places in southern Europe before the even remoter and primitive places of the world, far away from the reach of the organized tour. Sometimes the search for the remote places is attempted on foot. Forster and Lawrence do walking tours which belong to the tradition of literary men romanticizing the landscape, whether at home or abroad, because, the real England like the real Italy or the real India, is to be found, if at all, off the beaten track, even when it will disappear once tourism had discovered it – an idea common amongst the writers studied in this book about the incursions of modernity on the traditional places.

But finding the real apart from perception of the object is a problem. Characters in the fiction studied in the following chapters appear to find the real elusive. Lacan asks: 'Where do we meet this real?' We have 'an appointment to which we are always called with a real that eludes us' (*The Four Fundamental Concepts of Psychoanalysis*, 53). In this sense, if the encounter with the real is an object of the traveller's desire, then it might be subject to misrecognition, which Lacan defines as what represents 'a certain organization of affirmations and negations, to which the subject is attached'. Therefore if the subject 'is capable of misrecognizing something, he surely must know what this function has operated upon. There must surely be, behind his misrecognition, a kind of knowledge of what there is to misrecognize' (Lacan, *Seminar Book I*, 167). Homi K. Bhabha redeploys Lacan for the concept of cultural difference:

> The subject of the discourse of cultural difference is dialogic and transferential in the style of psychoanalysis. It is constituted through the locus of the Other which suggests both that the object of identification is ambivalent, and, more significantly, that the agency of identification is never pure or holistic but always constituted in a process of substitution, displacement or projection. (*The Location of Culture*, 162)

Being abroad is often experienced as a lack at home. Italy or India or New Mexico is England's other, just as Italy and France – even England – will be America's other for James and Wharton, places for them of the High Culture and History lacking in the New World of American modernity. Can there ever be a direct and unmediated relation to the object or the other if the gaze is driven by demand and desire?[22]

---

[22]   For Lacan lack is the name of desire. He writes: 'Desire is a relation of being to lack …' *The Seminar Book II*, 223.

The demand for the sight of the real is pre-constructed by the tourist guidebook, or the reading of architectural history, or any of those other conditions of the gaze that characterize the object, like the picturesque or the sublime encoding the object and enabling the sublimation of desire in the now aestheticized object. The aesthetic demand of travel, in Forster, James and Wharton, transport the subject out of the mundane and superficial pleasures of tourism into the *jouissance* of travel. Thus place, like works of art, has a contemplative value. Like the tranquil cathedral close – a recurrent location in James – or the vista seen alone from a vantage point, or the ancient ruin as an object of the picturesque imaginary so favoured by James and Wharton, or the remote landscape haunted by an ancient spirit in Forster, and in Lawrence's moonlit scene; or Lawrence's admiration for the peasant farmer or the Native American Indian instinctive relation to the land, before the advent of modern self-consciousness or the 'tourist gaze' – places may be sought as refuge from the crowds of sightseers and the commodifications of modernity. But does feeling bring you closer to the object than thought? Or is feeling, the sensual apprehension of the object, mediated as thought in the form of contemplation? Questions about the real and the imaginary are fundamental to the modernist critique of tourism and the encounter with the other, and the writers in this study are representative of that critique in their travel writing and fiction.

Sightseers have a shared, preconditioned way of looking. John Urry writes that 'the tourist gaze' has a 'mass character', and it is opposed to the 'individual character' of travel. Tourist sightseeing is a reductive semiotics of the typical, 'tourism involves the collection of signs', which can be reproduced as postcards and photos (*The Tourist Gaze*, 5). It is superficial because it focuses on the signs of the typical: '[T]he typical English village, the typical American skyscraper, the typical German beer-garden, the typical French château, and so on. This mode of gazing shows how tourists are in a way semioticians, reading the landscape for signifiers of certain pre-established notions or signs derived from various discourses of travel and tourism ...' (12–13). Tourist semiotics has affinities with literary realism, both insisting on the transparent access to the real while effectively working with a selective metonymics. Thus realism in the novel and tourism in travel writing share the drive for a semiotics of the typical. However, just as there is a residual realism in the modernist fiction of the selected writers, so there are sometimes aspects of tourism in their travel writing – even when 'conscientious' tourism as James called it (*Collected Travel Writings: The Continent*, 86); and other times when there is a recurrent insistence that the tourist gaze is an inferior mode of observation, just as the literal and transparent representations of realism are inferior to the figurative, symbolic or mythic for literary modernism. Through mass produced images the tour guide can reinforce, at worst, a superficial and reductive view of the other culture. But reading place through literature can also make it difficult to differentiate the real from the pre-constructed. There will always be a slippage between seeing and sightseeing, between the local character and the stereotype, between art and kitsch. Thus the problem of seeing extends to what I would call 'the literary gaze' or 'the art gaze' for those who reject tourist sightseeing for the educated travel of the connoisseur – as we see especially in the travel writing of Forster, James and Wharton, where the art museum, palazzo, castle, ruin or Mediterranean landscape are so many sites of aesthetic experience.

Leaving home, exile and rootlessness are characteristics of the modernist writer and artist. Expatriation or self-exile is a feature of modernism. Gabriel Josipovici claims rootlessness and exile to be endemic to modernism by definition: 'at some deeper level Modernism and the diasporist imagination go together', which implies making real or imagined journeys into exile from the home culture (*Whatever Happened to Modernism*, 187). Terry Eagleton argued that the modernist exile or émigré was better positioned to see the cultural crisis whole and in its universal significance, and thus get beyond the parochial limits of conventional English culture (*Exiles and Émigrés*). Caren Kaplan suggests that exile becomes 'a vocational imperative' for modernist writers who are thus 'prototypes of "deracination", examples of the "artist as displaced person"' (*Questions of Travel*, 38–9). If questions of identity are tied up with place, with where one comes from and where one belongs, then identity itself is destabilized by the travelling modernist.

The opposition between the nomadic and the sedentary formed an underlying tension in the lives and writing of the literary modernists. Getting away from the constraints of home is a common theme; it is the personal story of expatriation for Conrad, Lawrence, James and Wharton; it is expressed in the themes of their travel writing and fiction. It also belongs to Forster's life and work – the Alexandria and India sojourns; the search for a congenial English home or woodland out of sight of the condemning public gaze; Forster in old age ensconced in his rooms at Kings in a sort of internal exile. Lawrence's writing records a life of travel that could be understood as the quest for the lost home after his self-exile. In Edith Wharton's life and work there is a tension between travel and residence: an energetic traveller with her own designs for houses, she had the contrary impulses of the traveller and the settler; expatriate writer settled in a house of her own in France to write fiction about the repressive side of the sedentary life especially for women who find themselves encaged in the domestic sphere; and about the woman of her class in flight from her marriage-destiny. Henry James is the classic case of the American expatriate writer, at home first in Europe and then settling in England, as only there, he believed, could he save the western cultural heritage from Americanization – like that other expatriate American who made England his home and saw himself as the keeper of the classical European cultural heritage, T.S. Eliot.

Travel, Place and Space: Beyond the Colonial Mindset

Histories of modernism have mapped the places of exile as locations of artistic communities, the different metropolitan centres of modernism – Paris, London, Berlin, New York and Chicago.[23] It is no surprise that the experience of travel and expatriation has lead to a new sensitivity to place in modernist writing. What links

---

[23]   See Bradbury and McFarlane, part 3: *A Geography of Modernism*.

the selected writers studied in this book is the significance of topographies with symbolic and aesthetic values in travel writing and fiction. Places have deep associations; places have stories to tell – *lieux-récit*: literally places of narrative, archives of the culture's past and its history; and also in the senses of Pierre Nora's *lieux de mémoire*, collective acts of memory as living witness that goes beyond the institutionalizing of the past as the past in the museum or State archive. To these senses we should add the narratives of place in guide books, travel writing and fiction. Indeed, the selected writers in this study have themselves added to the stories and descriptions of places that have become part of their archive.[24] Thus cityscapes or landscapes are cognitive maps.[25] Places and spaces are represented by different cultural formations of narrative and generic typologies: the dystopias of the dark places of the earth, the utopias of the Promised Land or the Celestial City. Landscapes are pastoral, georgic, exotic, picturesque or sublime. But to what extent do the selected writers discussed in the following chapters challenge limited, reductive views of the commodified places of tourism and official heritage?

To begin to answer this question we might try and distinguish land from landscape – as indeed do Forster and Lawrence. Land suggests something physical and tangible, a place worked upon, and a resource for farming or mineral extraction, or for settlement. But it may have greater associations that go beyond itself: emotional and imaginative with implications for nationalism and identity, territorial rights, roots or ancestral sites where ritual ceremonies are still performed – like the Native American Indian dances observed by Lawrence in New Mexico. However, land is not always easy to separate from landscape as the former is transformed into the latter becoming thus a cultural construction with collective ideological implications – as in essentialist-organic claims about race and the soil (*Blut und Boden*). Landscapes, forests or mountains have been immortalized as symbolic places, *Heimat* or Holy Land, sometimes memorialized in Diasporas as the lost homeland, a mythic imaginary whose emotional impact is kept in circulation by an expatriate language community.[26] Landscape might be represented symptomatically as 'psychic topography', as it is sometimes in Lawrence's writing.[27] Moreover, geographies of conquest and territorial struggle which have been central to the geopolitics of imperialism include *terra incognita*, the unmapped regions of land and sea.

---

[24] For further discussion of *lieux de mémoire* see Pierre Nora, ed., *Lieux de mémoire* 3 vols; and for a useful commentary see Jonathan Bordo, 'The Keeping Place (Arising from an Incident on the Land)'.

[25] For a discussion of cognitive mapping in literary modernism see Thacker, *Moving through Modernity: Space and Geography in Modernism*, 1. Thacker draws on the work of Henri Lefebvre, *The Production of Space*.

[26] For further discussion see the introduction in Christine Berberich, Neil Campbell and Robert Hudson, eds, *Land and Identity: Theory, Memory, and Practice*, 17–37, which I have drawn upon for some of these ideas.

[27] An example is the Australian bush in *Kangaroo*. For further discussion of 'Eschatological Landscape' see Kirby Farrell's essay in Berberich, Campbell and Hudson, eds, 117–39.

Travel writing has played a key role in the colonial mindset and its critique, and the travel writing and fiction discussed in the following chapters is representative of that critique in the late nineteenth and early twentieth century – the period of modernism where boundaries were being redrawn in more than one sense: '[M]obility, travel and global migration mark the period in a way that signals its significance for imperial eclipse in terms of the incursions of cultural hybridity made inevitable by the multiple contact zones created in those decades. After the confidence of the Victorian travellers, many modernists experienced the world with a different perspective' (Childs, *Modernism and the Post-Colonial*, 5). Travelling modernists have a kind of oedipal relationship with their Victorian 'colonial fathers' (Childs, 26), so that the emergence of the critique of imperialism in modernism – brought on by travel and encounter – appears as a generational conflict: 'because it took them away from the culture of the father and his law, the journey into the world of the primitive was conceived as a form of transgression; if the fathers had created and valorized the culture of modernity, the sons would seek their *dédoublement* from this culture by striving – through narrative – to possess its radical opposite' (Gikandi, qtd in Childs, 42). And this critique of the colonialist mindset includes the tourist gaze which was so often predicated on the residual nationalist, even jingoist, imaginary. The writers in this study are not always immune from a deep-seated Eurocentrism. What marks their travel writing and travel fiction as modernist, however, is the presence of a critical attitude to home seen from abroad. As Alexandra Peat explains, '[t]he journeys depicted in modernist travel fiction are always conducted in negotiation with the idea of home that has been left behind. It seems almost a truism to suggest that travel fiction is as much about changing conceptions of home as it is about the experience of the journey, as much about a sense of belonging as it is about a desire for change' (9).

The encounter with the other and the foreign places is approached through an ethics of difference. If many of the modernists were not only travelling writers but exiles and émigrés, expatriates who lived in other cultures – and the writers selected for this study are representative – then it is not surprising that cultural difference is a central concern of theirs. Helen Carr has argued for this greater awareness of cultural difference as a defining feature of modernism: 'Modernist texts register a new consciousness of cultural heterogeneity, the condition and mark of the modern world ...' (74). The newer consciousness of cultural difference, beyond diversity, lead to questioning the ethnocentric project of empire – and this questioning distinguishes modernist travel writing from much of Victorian travel writing.[28]

Tensions between modernism and imperialism in the forms of cultural difference and national cultural identity are played out symptomatically in the exiled and travelling artist. Novelists who travel further afield than Europe or North America – Conrad, Forster and Lawrence, for example – express a greater

---

[28]   Where 'cultural diversity' implies the liberal acknowledgment of multiculturalism, 'cultural difference' in Homi K. Bhabha's words 'focuses on the problem of the ambivalence of cultural authority: the attempt to dominate in the *name* of a cultural supremacy'. *The Location of Culture*, 34.

awareness of cultural heterogeneity in their fiction and their travel writing. Where James and Wharton argue for the limitations of the modern American identity, at once materialist and culturally shallow, while remaining within a Eurocentric ethos, Lawrence, Forster and Conrad sometimes establish the terms for a critique of British imperialist attitudes – in what could be read as proto-post-colonialist. In his appreciation of *A Passage to India* Lawrence clearly spoke for the liberal-minded reader in 1924 when he wrote that 'the repudiation of our white bunk is genuine, sincere, and pretty thorough' (Boulton, *Selected Letters*, 286). Like *Heart of Darkness*, *A Passage to India* was a novel of its time, a time when the superiority of the western model of civilization was being questioned even more: 'a questioning of attitudes to the "other" and to colonialism ... Modernism, and its philosophical underpinning, had ... found ways of producing texts that allowed for multiple voices and respectful relations to alterity and difference' (Booth and Rigby, *Modernism and Empire*, 2–5). But to what extent does the recognition of cultural difference enable the western traveller to get beyond seeing foreign places and peoples only through 'imperial eyes' (Pratt)? Do Conrad, Forster, Lawrence, James and Wharton *consistently* get beyond the common tendency of the period to see the other from a superior western perspective? The 'imperial gaze' is a pre-condition of misrecognition, like the tourist gaze – indeed it often underpinned Eurocentrism.

Whether imperial gaze or modernist mindset, topography as its object has always had a significant presence in travel writing and travel fiction. Michel de Certeau claimed that such stories 'traverse and organize places; they select and link them together; they make sentences and itineraries out of them. They are spatial trajectories'. (*The Practice of Everyday Life*, 115) The study will focus on topographical representations: the sea, the landscape and the land, the forest, and the modern metropolis – remote places and familiar places. Narrating place brings writing and topography, trope and topos together so that 'narrative structures have the status of spatial syntaxes'. Thus it is that, 'Every story is a travel story – a spatial practice' (Certeau, 115). The main chapters that follow this introduction address several 'spatial practices' understood as the cultural uses and meanings of place and space.[29] As we will see, moreover, the study of place and space blurs the distinction between travel writing and fiction – both sharing descriptive and narrative codes, styles and registers,[30] both drawing on the traditions of the travel imaginary that conflate the factual and the invented, memory and desire.

Places like journeys are also haunted by the ghosts of past dwellers and travellers. Besides following in the footsteps of Goethe to Italy, and indulging in literary tourism by pilgrimages to birthplaces and tombs of Petrarch, Dante and Balzac, or the places already immortalized in literature and art, place as archive

---

[29] For further reading in the study of place and space see the *Spatial Practices* series edited by Chris Thurgar-Dawson and Christoph Ehland (Amsterdam and New York: Rodopi).

[30] For example the similarities of style in James's early and late travel writing and fiction: a growing syntactical complexity, which I discuss in Chapter 4.

is prioritized by writers who prefer the past to the present – a conservative force that marks them as anti-modern modernists. Forster's Alexandria is haunted by the extinct civilization of its Golden Age, and the stones themselves that remain, the ruins and the archaeological sites, have to reveal their secrets. The 'Marabar Caves' in *A Passage to India* have a haunting echo that unhinges Mrs Moore.[31] The image of the silent earth that has a certain aura in its ancient rocks was attractive to Forster, especially the uncanny places of the English landscape. Lawrence was sensitive to what he called the spirit of place, whether in the ruins of an English monastery or the 'savage' landscapes of the Australian bush or New Mexico. Lawrence captured the post-war haunting of Europe in the story 'The Borderline' (1924),[32] where the journey across the ruined landscape of the Marne country to the 'city of the dead' becomes a ghost story that ends in German mythology as if trying to keep the memory of the race alive – an unwitting foreshadowing of worse things to come in Europe. Conrad described the 'dark places' of the earth – either the African forest, or London where the Thames is Styx 'the dark river', 'the river of dead' (*The Nigger of the 'Narcissus'*, 107); and the sea contains is own terrors and 'wandering corpses' (*Lord Jim*, 115). Exotic places up-river are approached in shrouding mist or gloom – 'A straight edge of vapour lines with sickly whitish gleams'; 'A brooding gloom lay over this vast and monotonous landscape' (*Lord Jim*, 74; 192). Like the white mist that hinders Marlow's navigation up-river in *Heart of Darkness*, there is gothic haunting here as there is in the seedy night-time streets of London where Verloc walks in *The Secret Agent*. In *The American*, Henry James turns old Europe into a Gothic place. Christopher Newman, the aptly named self-made man from the New World wants to marry the French Countess, Madame de Cintré, but her family is fundamentally opposed to the commoner without significant patrimony. The novel begins in the mode of Balzac, but the marriage plot is told as gothic romance encoded through the topoi of family residences in Paris and in the country, dark old houses with the hidden secrets of a feudal past, evil-looking places for Newman. He is defeated in his quest for the countess; and true to genre, to save the family name rather than marry the American businessman she prefers to enter a convent – a Carmelite convent which for Newman is a dark and horrible grotesque entombing (*The American*, 355). The Old World may be the location of History; but it is a feudal, aristocratic and undemocratic place. Its old ways persist in the present, resisting modernity and modernism. It is attractive to Americans, even when they appear out of place there. James himself preferred to settle in England, while continuing to travel in Europe and enjoy its high cultural heritage – a heritage he saw threatened by the war and one that he felt America did not appear to want to save.[33] When the American heiress Isabel

---

[31] 'Civilization strays about like a ghost here, revisiting the ruins of empire.' Forster, *A Passage to India*, 236.

[32] In Finney, ed., *Selected Short Stories*.

[33] James felt strongly that obsessive money-cultured America no longer had any 'aesthetic responsibility'. Cit. in Meissner, 270. In 1915 he gave up his American citizenship in protest, becoming a British subject.

Archer in *The Portrait of a Lady* first arrives in England at the country residence of Gardencourt she hopes the place has its lord and its ghost – figures out of her literary imaginary. But the location of the gothic and sinister will once again be in old Europe where she will be tricked into marrying the cold-hearted expatriate American Gilbert Osmond. If for James, and Wharton, Americans are searching for history, culture and sophistication in old Europe, it seems that they will not always get what they came for. Wharton may have believed France was the ideal place for civilized and cultured living, but some of her American fictional characters leisure-travelling in Europe are often exposed for their arrogance and ignorance.

The house as a locus of haunting is Forster's Howards End, an evocation of ancestry and the ghost of its previous owner, the first Mrs Wilcox. It is *heimlich* and *unheimlich,* homely and uncanny at the same time as Forster's novel ends in home comfort and a return of the repressed family secret. But it is also the end of a journey back to the tranquil English countryside, an image of stasis after the hectic motion of the modern urban world, a utopian vision of an English civilization that is no longer in movement, 'because it will rest on the earth' (*Howards End*, 290). We are reminded of that other utopian English vision when the rainbow appears over the cleansed earth in Lawrence's 1915 novel *The Rainbow*: 'She saw in the rainbow the earth's new architecture, the old brittle corruption of houses and factories swept away, the world built up in a living fabric of Truth, fitting to the over-arching heaven' (459). It is one version or another of a rejection of modernity that we see in all the writers in this study. Here in Lawrence the closing vision takes on Biblical, prophetic dimensions; in Forster it is quietly pastoral.

Travel and Transgression

If landscapes at home are estranged places those abroad visited by the travelling authors and their fictional characters are objects of projected desires. Conrad, Forster, Lawrence, James and Wharton take their characters abroad to challenge their received views. Such stories reflect the nomadic habits of modern life. Indeed, the restless traveller is a common trope in the travel writing and literature of the period. Freud argues that the desire to travel begins in dissatisfaction with home: 'My longing to travel was no doubt also the expression of a wish to escape from that pressure, like the force which drives so many adolescent children to run away from home. I had long seen clearly that a great part of the pleasure of travel lies in the fulfilment of these early wishes – that it is rooted, that is, in dissatisfaction with home and family' ('A Disturbance of Memory', 247).

Travel abroad promises transgression and the fulfilment of desires frustrated at home. As Dennis Porter argues: '[M]ost forms of travel at least cater to desire: they seem to promise or allow us to fantasize the satisfaction of drives that for one reason or another is denied us at home. As a result, not only is travel typically fuelled by desire, it also embodies powerful transgressive impulses' (*Haunted Journeys*, 9). In this reading, travel offers a resolution for the Oedipus complex in more ways than the rejection of the 'colonial father' discussed above. But I suggest two further points: first, travel may be a search for the lost home – it is one way of understanding the writing life of those discussed in this study as a life of travel and expatriation. Second, the interest in ancient civilizations demonstrated by so many educated travellers was one already rehearsed by Freud who then claimed archaeology as a metaphor for psychoanalysis itself: 'There is, in fact, no better analogy for repression, by which something in the mind is at once made inaccessible and preserved, than the burial of the sort to which Pompeii fell a victim and from which it could emerge once more through the work of spades' ('Delusions and Dreams', 65). Travel abroad is a device for the exposure of desires. Transcending the limits of home by a freer expression of desire abroad is a common theme in modernist travel writing and fiction: travel has a transgressive and transformative value. The traveller is supposed to come home changed; the ability to do so is a test of character, and failure a mark of class and cultural limitations. For example, in Forster's fiction English middle-class characters are taken on a journey that promises experiential challenge, and where difference challenges their arrogance and received opinions. Only the exceptional character manages to respond positively. In his fiction set in England, in stories about life as a journey, archetypal landscape or the 'greenwood' or the country house become refuges from modernity and the growing intolerance towards otherness at home, in the public forms of sexual repression, where Englishness itself becomes a pathology expressed in what Forster understood as the hetero-normative sham (most explicitly in *Maurice*, but underpinning all Forster's writing). It is a sham that Forster wants to expose both in society and in the dominant plot of the happy marriage as the closing device of the English novel – a closing device questioned in Lawrence, James and Wharton too.

The transgressive promise of travel abroad is also a question of gender. For Conrad, the ultimate test of manliness is the ship's captain in the storm at sea. Travel is a matter for men. At best there will be a bonding of men on board a sailing craft – the 'bond of the sea' (*Heart of Darkness*, 15) – a comradeship to battle the elements, an intimacy with nature. The sea has a significant presence in many Conrad stories as the space for the proving of courage, as the testing of character, and the expression thus of older values of masculinity. Being at sea is liberation from the problems on land, the ship providing a secure and stable environment. The problems on land are implicitly blamed on women who are not, of course, meant to be allowed on board, because then they are suspected as the source of unrest, as we see in *Chance*. The sea is also the location of solitude and tranquillity in a vast expanse that acts as a counterweight to the speed and chaos of the degenerate city – a trope that carries the full weight of Conrad's case against modernity. When not crossing the ocean Conrad's men might be sailing between islands in the Malay Archipelago, or up-river into the African interior to some trading post, an 'outpost of civilization'; or other exotic places like the Placid Gulf in *Nostromo* where Decoud and the Capitaz have to save the silver. Thus in Conrad place appeals strongly to the adventure imaginary. The hero is as often as not a figure out of Victorian boys' colonial fiction: 'the dug-out, four paddling savages, and the lone white man turning his back suddenly on the headquarters, on relief, on thoughts of home' (*Heart of Darkness*, 57). But, as we shall see in

Chapter 1, the adventure story is both narrative paradigm and substance, and an object of deconstruction, as the protagonist seems unable to live up to the demands of heroism; indeed, such ideas are seen to be illusions in a brutal and ruthless world of competing colonialists or insurgents.

The gender question in Forster is focussed primarily on men who should accept their sexuality even when it goes against the heterosexual norm and the pressures of class. It proves a difficult test not just for his fictional characters but for himself: gay sex either takes place abroad, or in some imagined future in an England where the men can be free again in the 'greenwood' out of sight of the normative gaze. Moreover, it seems that middle-class men will only find their lover in the working class. Lawrence's travel is predicated on a search for places were men have not succumbed to the New Woman's dominance, especially from 1918 when his journey is to ever more remote places where old patriarchal relations still pertain. For James the loss of cultural integrity is also a loss of masculinity. The new man of modernity is the businessman, an inferior character without culture. Wharton's women are either destroyed by the demands of the marriage market place of the rich, leisured class, or they learn to work it to their advantage – the difference between Lily Bart in *The House of Mirth* and Undine Spragg in *The Custom of the Country*. Place and travel are fundamental to the stories Wharton tells and the production of a critique that, like Henry James, problematizes American cultural identity as a crisis of modernity. The importance of place to gender is seen in the domestic space that entraps women and the public space that limits their mobility in the sight of the gaze of convention and the demands of conformity. Thus place defines senses of being; Wharton freed herself from the limits of conventional femininity through her expatriation and her writing. Indeed, her own achievement of independence as a woman was tied up partly with her successes as a writer, and her class and financial privileges. But they are circumstances not available to her female characters, though ones that afford her a critical perspective.

For all their interests in masculinity, Forster, Lawrence and James have famously created a series of memorable female characters. Lucy Honeychurch in *A Room with a View* manages only fleetingly to escape the reins of her chaperone in Florence; it is then that she tastes pleasure beyond control in 'one ravishing moment'(*A Room with a View*, 39). Lilia in *Where Angels Fear to Tread*, though, misreads Italy through her romantic imaginary and pays a high price. In the same novel, Caroline Abbott does return from Italy more aware of the difference between the life of the body and the life of the mind – an important distinction in Forster's work, as it is in Lawrence's where it forms the basis of a critique of the New Woman and the burgeoning feminism. From the 'dreaming woman' of the first fiction, through the active agencies of Ursula and Gudrun Brangwen in *The Rainbow* and *Women in Love* with quite different effects on the male characters in the battle of the sexes, to the travelling women of *The Lost Girl* and *The Plumed Serpent*, and finally to the woman with the determined quest for her own self-destruction in the late story 'The Woman Who Rode Away', Lawrence engages with the key debates of his day about the sexual emancipation of women. But where he sometimes supported a limited form of liberation, he also tended at other times to insist on male leadership in the gender relation – and even more so once travel became his dominant narrative paradigm.[34]

The 'Woman Question' is central to Wharton's writing. She was critical of modern sexuality because, instead of liberating women at last from being objects of exchange in the marriage market-place, it commodified them even more into misdirected objects of desire without passion and genuine emancipation – a view in Lawrence too. Her trapped women in New York are not much better off than the women she sees in the harem in Morocco: passive, languid and apathetic, these are women whose femininity is caged and stagnated by domesticity. The 'Woman Question' is also a key theme in James's novels. In *The Portrait of a Lady* it underpins the relationship between Isabel Archer and Henrietta Stackpole – the former led astray by her romantic imaginary; the latter a determined force for the independence of women, and a critical female voice recurrent in the story. Moreover, as Martha Banta claims, in James, 'every issue is ultimately gendered', as it underpins the relationship between men and women and shapes society ('Men, Women, and the American Way', 21). But I would add that gender relations once taken abroad – to France or Italy – characterize the differences between the cultures, and are thus significant in both James and Wharton's 'international theme'. The customs of countries are different even within a narrow class perspective. Christopher Newman in *The American* or Lambert Strether in *The Ambassador* – as we will see in Chapter 4 – struggle in their different ways to understand those customs, while learning more about their own masculinity and American identity.

The Archetypal Journey and the Condition of Culture

Beyond the gender and sexual implications, the journey may also have archetypal and mythic overtones – as it does in some of the writing of Conrad and Lawrence – where pre-civilized instincts are exposed as the expression of unconscious primitive drives. In *Heart of Darkness* we read that 'Going up that river was like travelling back to the earliest beginnings of the world' (59); and that modern man has a 'distant kinship' with the 'primitive savage' (85) – an idea deriving from the Darwinian evolutionary biology popular by the late nineteenth century, and promoted also by Freud as mankind's phylogenetic memory.[35] But the relations of the jungle are also re-imagined in the modern city. Conrad's London is

---

[34] 'The Woman Who Rode Away' takes travel as a story paradigm to its extreme conclusion. The unnamed woman leaves the familiar, comfortable, but boring existence of home, and rides abroad into the unknown and unfamiliar alien culture, as if unconscious of the danger that awaits her. It is the story of travel as liberation but also as death drive – and for Lawrence not just that of the modern, self-conscious American woman, but the culture itself.

[35] Freud discusses the 'phylogenetic acquisitions of the Id' in *The Ego and the Id* (1923), reprinted in *The Penguin Freud Library vol. 11*, 390; see also 376–9. In Conrad we read: '... what thrilled you was just the thought of their humanity – like yours – the thought of your remote kinship with this wild and passionate uproar.' *Heart of Darkness*, 63.

a 'monstrous' and 'dark' place; and forms of 'savagery' or degeneration are present in the mercenary relations of the smart set in Wharton's New York. For Lawrence, however, primitivism sometimes takes on a positive gloss as he is attracted to the perceived simpler lives of peasants and native peoples who have not yet been spoilt by modernity. He travels around the world in search of surviving older cultural forms, not though to return to a state of nature but to see what could be learnt from the instinctive relations between man and the natural world that may still exist in the more remote places. In his fiction he works out the consequences for western subjects of contact with such older life forms.

Darwinist thinking underpinned Victorian and Edwardian belief in Civilization and Progress. This discourse was used to confirm the superiority of the white races, and thus legitimize imperialism. However, a counter discourse emerged out of Darwinism and it was used as a critique of modernity. It argued that life had become brutalized by a struggle between the haves and the have-nots, in a struggle for survival of the fittest. It is a discussion developed by Thorstein Veblen in *The Theory of the Leisure Classes*, which was first published in 1899. Veblen's influence can be seen in Edith Wharton's New York fiction and Henry James's critique of American money culture in the early twentieth century in *The American Scene* (1907). Veblen's satire on the American leisure class for their conspicuous display of wealth – what he calls 'conspicuous consumption' – spills over into what we might call conspicuous travel: the luxury yachts and grand hotels and casinos on the French Riviera that are so many signs of the American leisure class at play abroad. Another effect of this new money – and we see it in the novels of James and Wharton about the American abroad – is the attempts of American money to marry French aristocracy, as if the New World needs to acquire history in the form of Old European families, and as if the loss of traditional values in modern America (lamented by both James and Wharton in remembering the New York of their own early lives) might be compensated for by the adoption of such values abroad. It is a story told by both James and Wharton. In this world women are reduced to trophies, valued for their fashionable appearance only, with sometimes destructive results. Those who do not fit into the new ethos, or cannot afford to, will not survive. As Veblen put it: 'The evolution of society is substantially a process of mental adaptation on the part of individuals under stress of circumstances which will no longer tolerate habits of thought formed under and conforming to a different set of circumstances in the past ...' – which is what it meant to be modern, and which is critiqued in Veblen, James and Wharton for its processes of conformity that empty life of value and history (128).

A similar analysis of the state of the culture was made by C.F.G. Masterman in *The Condition of England* (1909), a book that was also widely read at the time. Its influence can be seen in novels like Forster's *Howards End* (1910). Masterman belongs to a tradition of questioning the effect of industrialism and modernity on the national culture, a tradition which includes Carlyle, Arnold and Ruskin in the Victorian period, and which is also taken up by D.H. Lawrence in the modernist period. Like Veblen, Masterman argues that modern capitalism has had a brutalizing and dehumanizing effect. Modern England is now characterized by the 'monstrous inequalities of fortune', and made worse by the conspicuous display of wealth without 'social obligation' (25–8). England has gone the way of America where the rich flaunt their life of luxury, tearing about the countryside in motor cars – in fact Masterman sees the new upper-class motor-car generation as symptomatic of the 'speeded-up' life (22). Essentially taking up a moral position, Masterman idealizes the rural past of country-house England – estates that were now being bought up by wealthy Americans or South African millionaires (35). But worse still is the development of the suburbanization of the middle classes – 'the monotonous streets of Suburban England', its houses with 'pseudo-Georgian edifices' and 'well-trimmed gardens' (presumably opposed to the landscaped grounds of the gentry, or the wild untouched nature of the countryside; 64–5). There is here a yearning for the vanished 'yeoman class', lamented and also re-imagined by Forster and Lawrence, a class at once healthy and manly because of the 'life in the fields' before the mass migration to the 'life in the city' (Masterman, 77). The new life of busy crowds and mechanical labour has created a condition that is making the nation unhealthy. The worst urban existence, though, is in the industrial north, and Middlesbrough is singled out to illustrate the 'degenerate' life of the working class;[36] and contrasted to 'the jolly fisherman of the South coast', and the best of England: 'the beauty of its garden landscape, the refined kindly life of its country houses' (123).[37] Now clearly this reads like pure antiquarianism, yet it rhymes well with the writers discussed in this study. Indeed, as a reaction to modernity it represents a conservative mindset in crisis – a crisis that often characterizes the anti-modernity modernist position of Conrad, Forster, Lawrence, James and Wharton. Such views continue to be expressed throughout the early twentieth century in popular books like H.V. Morton, *In Search of England* (1927) with its easy nostalgia and the promotion of an old village Englishness. Morton seeks out the last old places and practices untouched by modernity – as Lawrence does in Italy and records in *Twilight in Italy*. Morton searches for the old pre-industrial craftsmen off the beaten track like 'the last bowl-turner' he finds in a fairy-tale place, 'a tumble-down hut on a green knoll' (7–8). Similarly, Masterman discusses 'George Bourne's' *Memoirs of a Surrey Labourer*, the peasant farm worker who 'stands for the last relic of a vanishing race', resourceful and vigorous with a 'slow-moving, deliberate mind' (152–5). He reminds us of the Brangwen farmers in the opening scene of Lawrence's *The Rainbow*. Masterman's apocalyptic conclusions about the decline of civilization and the coming of the war are reiterated by Lawrence.

If modernity is responsible for the decline in authentic being, there is also a worsening problem of class in English society. Indeed, the demands and inhibitions of class in society further constrain authentic being and genuine friendship. And the travelling classes are sometimes the worst, now extended from the aristocracy of the Grand Tour to the new wealthy middle class. Masterman is scathing about the

---

[36] Masterman, 81ff. See page 70 for his eugenic solution.

[37] Lawrence has a similar view in 'Nottingham and the Mining Countryside' (1929).

Englishman abroad – as are Conrad, Forster and Lawrence: 'when the Englishman goes abroad, the customs of the country, the opinions of the people amongst whom he lives, count for nothing' (48). What he calls 'the imperial citizen' – at home or abroad – 'despises the foreigner' (66). It is an arrogance born of the belief in the superiority of the British Empire; it is reduplicated in the Americans abroad in the fiction of James and Wharton – and clearly it was a serious discussion in the period of modernism.

Veblen and Masterman represent the terms of a debate current at the time of the state of the respective national cultures; a debate that achieves its most reactionary form in Oswald Spengler's *Decline of the West* (1918). It is an important context for the following chapters, as travel provokes home thoughts from abroad – itself a long tradition of assessing the merits and defects of the home culture by foreign comparison. As David Punter argues, 'modernity will very often have a complex relation to the "foreign"' (*Modernity*, 9), not least because in a global perspective modern developments are uneven.[38] But, moreover, Punter continues, 'there will always be something uncanny about modernity, some sense that it is in opposition to the *heimlich*, that with which we feel "at home"; modernity challenges us, as it were, in our own homes, it reminds us of other, frequently more disturbing possibilities of perception and it decentres and destabilizes our everyday domestic assumptions' (9). Modernity 'recognizes transience', challenging all senses of stability, including tradition (59). Yet modernity also broadens horizons, breaks down barriers, enables border crossings, and new senses of otherness. The writers discussed in the following chapters react to modernity by seeking solace in expatriation where they might in fact escape from modernity; or in the quest for other forms of life that correspond to their idea of a pre-modern world that has already disappeared at home.

The critique of modernity in the period of modernism was commonly argued in terms of the opposition between the mechanical and the organic, where the modern metropolis – London or New York – is now devoid of the organic relations of the older *Gemeinschaft*. This is Henry James's picture of the New York of the early 1900s in *The American Scene*. The past, like tradition, is organic, the present mechanical – an opposition we see in Lawrence too; and its most popular version is found in Spengler.[39] At its worst, this vision expressed fears about the future of the white race, a crisis provoked by the encounter with other cultures through travel, exploration and ethnographies; but also through immigration in America.[40]

---

[38] Eric Hobsbawm also writes about the uneven progress of modernity polarizing countries and nations in terms of racial and cultural superiority and inferiority. And he reminds us that many at the time questioned the benefits of continual progress. See *The Age of Empire 1875–1914*, 1–33.

[39] Spengler writes that a culture 'blooms on the soil of an exactly definable landscape, to which plant-wise it remains bound' (*The Decline of the West*, 73). Thus a culture is an organism, and for Spengler the migratory and nomadic tendencies of modern life are destroying the species.

[40] James's experience of Ellis Island – the point of entry for immigrants to the US – in *The American Scene* is discussed in Chapter 4.

The growing belief in eugenics from the late nineteenth century – and one espoused by many otherwise radical thinkers and writers in the period of modernism – is a symptom of such fears.

As the spokesman for anti-modernity high modernism, T.S. Eliot called 'tradition' the whole of classical western High Culture, which he wanted to preserve against the onslaught of modernity (mass culture). As he puts it in 'The Waste Land': 'These fragments I have shored against my ruins' (*Collected Poems*, 79). In this light, a set of key oppositions in Eliot's cultural theory are shared by the writers in this study: civilization and barbarism, classical and modern, harmony and chaos, the past and the present, Europe and England or America, the South and the North, light and dark, plenitude and closure. The greyness of home is challenged by the bright sunlight and colourful flora and fauna of the Mediterranean places – the location for the origin of Culture expressed by Fielding in Forster's *A Passage to India*: 'the Mediterranean is the human norm', because it is the place of 'harmony', and going further east the traveller approaches 'the monstrous and extraordinary' (266). It is a cultural norm promoted in literary modernism by Eliot and shared by the writers discussed in this book.

However, the experience of the Mediterranean or the Orient still requires turning into writing and this is a complex process, whether in the jottings of the diary *in situ* or the measured account belatedly – *nachträglich* – or the fictional recreation. Conrad's or Forster's 'colonial' fiction derives from their own travel experiences, yet they only manage to finish the respective novel later back home where critical distance and reflection enable fictional reconstruction. Lawrence, however, needed the influence of place – the spirit of place as he called it – to inspire his story, writing at least early drafts where he was. Indeed, travel for him was necessary as he wrote fictions of place: *Aaron's Rod* in Italy, *Kangaroo* in Australia, *The Plumed Serpent* in Mexico. James and Wharton judge their countrymen and women at home or abroad by the distance they themselves have travelled once settled in their expatriation. Moreover, it is in the travel writing that the novelists work out the importance of being abroad for themselves and the development of their writing. Writing about journeys became a paradigm for telling stories. Descriptions of places, buildings, gardens, landscapes and seascapes established a set of values that would form the cornerstone of a cultural critique of modernity, and one these writers shared in many ways in their practice of literary modernism.

Method

The following chapters will discuss in some detail the thematic and formal modernism of the selected writers. The focus will be on the similarities and differences in writing styles and narrative strategies played out in the texts of the five writers; and the extent to which residual codes of realism or romanticism are defamiliarized by those strategies thus challenging reader expectations – in the forms of delayed decoding, refusal of closure, free indirect discourse and implicit irony unsettling stable truth-values; and the uses of character projection indirectly revealing unconscious desire, in the form of the misrecognized other or the symbolic landscape. The aim is to ascertain the extent to which modernist travel narratives have destabilizing effects on cultural identities. Methodologically, the close textual readings engage with current discussion of each of the canonical writers' work, while also raising issues in modernism and travel writing theories; yet not losing sight of the travelling or expatriate lives of the writers in the contexts of modernity – a crisis of culture as the problematic shared by Conrad, Forster, Lawrence, James and Wharton. The study begins with Joseph Conrad, then E.M. Forster and D.H. Lawrence as representatives of the condition of England, then Henry James and Edith Wharton for the 'American scene' in the period of late-nineteenth and early-twentieth-century modernist travel writing and travel fiction.

Chapter 1
Joseph Conrad:
Stories of the Sea and the Land

Introduction

This chapter will discuss a selection of Conrad's travel fiction, to look at the ways in which narrative and travel are closely connected in a number of ways in his writing. There is the story of a journey by sea, of departures and arrivals where narrative itself takes on the structure of a journey, and where the reader is taken on a journey to exotic places. There are stories that travel through space and time, as in tales of hearsay, rumours, legends, histories. A recurrent narrative archetype in Conrad's writing is the quest, often in the form of a journey in search of someone, which may be read in mythical or psychoanalytic terms as encounters with the other or a process of self-understanding in a journey towards enlightenment. In the adventure quest paradigm a protagonist is often driven by idealism and ends in disappointment or disillusion. Conrad, like his character Jim in the novel *Lord Jim*, may have longed to go to sea after being steeped in adventure travel reading, but the reality of the journey and the encounters tend to deconstruct the paradigm. In the details of the readings that follow, scepticism and doubts in Conrad's travel stories mark the extent of his modernism.

There is probably no better writer for a study of travel and storytelling in the age of modernism than Joseph Conrad. As a boy his dreams of travel and adventure were inspired by his reading. When first seeing the sea at the Venice Lido on a trip with his tutor – a trip that took in Munich, Vienna and Northern Italy – he knew he wanted to go to sea. He spent several years crossing the oceans or working coastal trading routes in the merchant marine, eventually becoming a certified master seaman in the British merchant navy. After he gave up the sea for the sedentary life of writing he was a restless dweller in a series of English houses, taking regular trips abroad for health reasons – the Mediterranean being a preferred destination – and once his finances permitted it in later life, returning home to Poland to make his peace with the culture he once abandoned and the late father he never appreciated. He crossed the Atlantic on the invitation of his American publisher in the early 1920s there to be celebrated as the great writer – fame and appreciation largely denied him in his adopted country, England. Thus Conrad travelled extensively, as a profession and for leisure. A list of the places visited would be long, and would include Australia, India, Malaysia and the Congo as seaman; France and Italy as tourist. Conrad reminisced in his last essay, 'Geography and Some Explorers' that as a young man he read with passion the travel writing of the great discoverer-explorers. He was, he tells us, an early addict of 'map-gazing', stimulating his imagination with 'the great spaces of the earth'

(*Last Essays*, 13), which had him announcing already in 1872 that he intended to go to sea (he was 15). And at the end of his life he could say: 'Thus the sea has been for me a hallowed ground, thanks to those books of travel and discovery which have peopled it with unforgettable shades of the masters in the calling which, in a humble way, was to be mine, too' (*Last Essays*, 21). His life of travel really began in 1874 when he got on a train in Cracow and headed for Marseilles via Vienna, Zurich and Geneva – and he would later return (1914) by train from Berlin with his family as the respected writer of English novels and stories.

The story of his life is now well known, after several biographies, not least Zdzisław Najder's *Joseph Conrad: A Life*, translated from Polish, which places Conrad in the details of a cultural history, as well as a history of Conrad's own cultural hybridity at once Polish by origin, French by education and English by adoption.[1] When he gave up the sea to write, his sea voyages and the places he visited and the stories he heard from those he met naturally became the raw materials for a series of novels and stories; supplemented, as so many Conrad scholars have shown, by his extensive reading in the literatures of the cultures he could understand. A recurrent figure in his novels and stories is the storyteller, the mariner as *homme-récit*, the most renowned being Charles Marlow who appears in four narratives. Using Marlow as narrator gave the stories a specifically defined English voice, and one that gave Conrad a distance to the material which so often had autobiographical origins. Najder writes that 'Marlow, a model English gentleman, ex-officer of the merchant marine, was the embodiment of all that Conrad would wish to be if he were to become completely anglicized. And since that was not the case, and since he did not quite share his hero's point of view, there was no need to identify himself with Marlow.' The distance to his narrator-character is especially visible in *Lord Jim* (Najder, 267). Yet at times Marlow's life resembles Conrad's: Marlow also admits in *Heart of Darkness* to having had 'a passion for maps' as a boy (21);[2] Conrad recalls 'when nine years old or thereabouts, that while looking at a map of Africa of the time and putting my finger on the blank spaces then representing the unsolved mystery of that continent, I said to myself with absolute assurance and an amazing audacity …: "When I grow up I shall go *there*"' (*A Personal Record*, 13, emphasis in original). And like his character Jim, who also read adventure and travel literature as a boy,[3] and who 'saw himself saving people from sinking ships, cutting away masts in a hurricane' (*Lord Jim*, 5),[4] for Conrad the sea was the 'accomplice of human restlessness'; and as he explains in *The Mirror of the Sea* (1906), being at sea reflects his boyhood desire for adventure and danger, impulses that will be imaginatively recreated in his fictional travel narratives (*The Mirror of the Sea*, 135–6). For, like the mythic

---

[1]   For another account of Conrad's early life and travels see Andrzej Braun, 'Cracow in the Life of Joseph Conrad' in Gene Moore, ed., *Conrad's Cities*, 49–56.

[2]   Subsequent page references abbreviated as *HD* in text.

[3]   Najder (264) tells us that as a boy Conrad's favourite writers were Frederick Marryat and James Fenimore Cooper.

[4]   Subsequent page references abbreviated as *LJ* in text.

seafarer Ulysses, voyages consist of adventure, romance and wonder (151). And, just as the young Conrad longed for the beginning of his 'own obscure Odyssey' (54), once he had 'turned [his] back upon the sea' he hoped to find 'in an inland valley the silent welcome of some patient listener' (183) for his stories of travel and adventure in far-off places.[5] What started as a need to get away from home, (*A Personal Record*, 122) to be nomadic, ends with a desire to find a place to write – a sedentary occupation. The traveller's imaginary is a vital source for Conrad the writer of fiction.

Travel, Travel Writing and Fiction

Why, though, did Conrad write fictional stories and novels derived from his experiences in the Malayan Archipelago or the Congo some years later, and not simply travelogues? Why, for example, does the 'Congo Diary' become *Heart of Darkness*? We can turn to Conrad's autobiographical writing for some answers: 'One's literary life must turn frequently for sustenance to memories … every novel contains an element of autobiography' (*A Personal Record*, xv–xvi). However, this does not mean an open display of feelings; he is not writing confession in the style of Rousseau: 'The matter in hand, however, is to keep these reminiscences from turning into confessions' (*A Personal Record*, 95). Nor does he believe that simply recording facts or simply inventing them is the answer. 'Imagination, not invention' is the key, 'an imaginative and exact rendering of authentic memories' (25). The Conradian aesthetic is based on imaginative reconstruction, and this goes for the Congo journey too. Conrad believed the best form of imaginative reconstruction was the novel: 'itself a form of imagined life clearer than reality and whose accumulated verisimilitude of selected episodes puts to shame the pride of documentary history' (15). Travel is turned into fiction after the fact enabling 'the exact understanding of the limits traced by the reality of his time to the play of his invention' (95). Thus fiction is better than travelogue because travel is best as source and trope for the imaginative play of fiction.

However, the text also travels. Conrad records how he took the manuscript of his first novel, *Almayer's Folly* in his luggage to the Congo; indeed he carried it around with him on his travels for three years. He nearly lost it as the canoe he was in almost capsized on the river Congo; and again later leaving it on a train in Berlin (14–19). As he declares at the beginning of *A Personal Record*: 'Books may be written in all sorts of places' (3). On a ship stuck fast in ice in Holland, Conrad begins writing his first novel. If the text travels, so does the first reader: a travelling reader, 'a man of few words' who will not live long enough to 'know the end of the tale', confirms that the story makes perfect sense 'as it stands', and Conrad is encouraged to continue writing despite the imminent death of the reader (15–18).

In 1905 Conrad thought he might in fact do a travel book about Italy, 'places visited every year by the English and American tourists'. Such a book,

---

[5]   He would though have a largely disappointing reception and readership until the more popular later novels, *Chance* and *Victory*.

in his opinion, would have 'a better chance of popularity' (Letter to Pinker in Najder, 351). The book, however, was never written. Most of his travel accounts are in his letters. They contain observations from his travels, as we see from his critical comments about the English tradition of Italophilia: 'It's all very well for Englishmen born to their inheritance to fling verse and prose from Italy back at their native shores. I, in my state of honourable adoption, find that I need the moral support, the sustaining influence of English atmosphere even from day to day' (Letter to Gosse in Najder, 355). Nevertheless, he is able to feel more at home in Montpellier: 'I am better in this sunshine. The landscape around is magic all subtle, all of colour alone. The villages perched on conical hills stand out against the great and sweeping lines of violet ranges as if in an enchanted country. The beauty of this land is inexpressible and the delicacy of colours at sunset and sunrise beyond the power of men to imagine ...' (Letter to Ford in Najder, 372). His Polish journey of 1914 became 'Poland Revisited' (1915), a record which included a hazardous return to England as war broke out. However, its accuracy has been doubted, as, according to Najder, it 'underwent a significant change in the telling' (Najder, 469).[6] After the war, Conrad with wife and son travel by car through France for a holiday in Corsica. They first visit the battlefields to share Borys's war stories, then drive on south through the French countryside where Conrad is able to admire the view of the land and the villages: 'falling dusk on this plain with a horizon like a sea in perfect stillness and solitude', he writes lyrically to Pinker on 26 January 1921 (cit. in Najder, 533). A longer description Conrad sent to Pinker of their drive to Montélimar, and then by boat to Ajaccio begins: 'We found a magnificent sunset over these wild and barren peaks' (cit. in Najder, 534). This is the stuff of travel writing that was more extensively practiced by Forster, Lawrence, James and Wharton. There are even disparaging comments about English tourist groups, already making a distinction implicitly – and one that will be reiterated in the other writers in this study – between travel and tourism as part of his critique of modernity.

In his contempt for the comforts of modern travel resulting from his Atlantic crossing, and published as the essay 'Ocean Travel' Conrad insists that the 'whole psychology of sea travel has changed':

> Formerly a man setting out on a sea voyage broke away from shore conditions and found in the ship a new kind of home. This applied even to such comparatively short passages as across the Atlantic. But now a man (especially if setting out for the United States) brings the conditions of shore life with him on board, and finds in his ship the usual sort of hotel ... It was otherwise with the old-time traveller under sail ... (*Last Essays*, 35–6)

'The days of heroic travel' with their 'spirit of adventure' are over ('Travel' in *Last Essays*, 89–90). Travel has become commonplace in the forms of tourism.

---

[6]   Published in the *Daily News* in four instalments: 'The Shock of the War', 'To Poland in War-time', 'The North Sea on the Eve of the War' and 'My Return to Cracow' (Najder, 660 note 4).

Conrad's attitude to modern tourist comforts should be taken in the same spirit as his attitude to the change from sailing to steam-powered ships because they are fundamental to his case against modernity. Real sea voyages for Conrad were on the old sailing ships. In *The Mirror of the Sea* he indulges in nostalgia for his own seafaring days: 'He who loves the sea loves also the ship's routine' (7). Life on board has a bonding effect between men: 'the bond between us was the ship ... that sort of faithful and proud devotion' (19–20)[7] which is his idea 'of fidelity as between man and ship' (29) – a common effort against the elements especially seen in the technique and discipline required for manning the sailing ships (as distinct from the modern steamships), and resulting in a 'quality of intimacy with nature'. Moreover, this technique is 'like all true art' (31).

Writing the Sea

> '[T]he unsettled and exploring, sea-crossing Conrad.' (Raymond Williams, *The English Novel from Dickens to Lawrence*, 154)

> 'The sea has been good to me.' (Charles Marlow, *Lord Jim*, 33)

The concept of 'the bond of the sea' recurs in several Conrad texts, and brings together the idea of the crew surviving the hardships of the sea by working together despite differences, and masculinity.[8] For example, in the first Marlow tale, 'Youth' (1898) we read: 'Between the five of us there was the strong bond of the sea, and also the fellowship of the craft' (*Heart of Darkness and Other Tales*, 71). Then the first narrator reminds us at the start of *Heart of Darkness* that the group of men who are gathered to listen to Marlow's story also have the bond of the sea between them; and here he means they are 'tolerant of each other's yarns' – the very audience Marlow requires (*HD*, 15–16). Sticking together helps the crew of the 'Narcissus' survive the storm at sea, as it does the crew under the single-minded captain MacWhirr in the story 'Typhoon', as the adverse weather is a test of character (*The Nigger of the 'Narcissus'*, 5; *Typhoon and Other Tales*, 3–74).[9] In *Lord Jim* Marlow becomes a listener as well as a teller of stories; but his sympathy for the plight of Jim cannot prevent Jim from suffering the consequences of being 'a seaman in exile from the sea' (*LJ*, 4), alienated by his failures and trying to find ways of re-establishing his reputation. And when Jim cannot face returning home because he could not explain himself to his father in the parsonage, Conrad illustrates a principle behind travel. As Marlow puts it in *Lord Jim*: 'We wander in our thousands over the face of the earth ... but it seems to me for each of us going home must be like going to render an account ... one must return with a

---

[7]   In *Heart of Darkness* the narrator says, 'Between us there was ... the bond of the sea' (15).

[8]   Clearly a woman on board will disrupt the male bonding as we see in the novel *Chance* (1914).

[9]   Subsequent page references abbreviated as *NN* in text.

clear conscience'. Jim 'would never go home now' (*LJ*, 160–61). Marlow returning from the heart of darkness has to hide the truth about the horrors of the Congo and Kurtz from his fiancée in Brussels, even while he tells the full story to his like-minded male audience in London – these are stories amongst men and for men, at least for Marlow, because as he says in *Heart of Darkness* 'It's queer how out of touch with truth women are' (28), a claim that takes on a positive if ironic gloss later: 'They – the women I mean – are out of it – should be out of it. We must help them stay in that beautiful world of their own, lest ours gets worse' (80). Marlow represents the old masculine values of the sailor in more than one sense.

The topos of the sea is as central to Conrad's fiction as it was to his life. It has an important presence in the travel imaginary for the enactment of journeys, adventure, encounters; the testing of courage, individual and collective – as we see in the story 'Typhoon' and the novella *The Nigger of the 'Narcissus'*; a challenge in times of storm or becalmed for the preferred ships under sail; or collisions in the dark as we see in *Lord Jim* as the crew misjudge the situation and abandon ship, and in *Nostromo* where the lighter loaded with the silver is run down by Sotillo's troop-carrying steamer in the utter darkness of the Gulfo Placido with complicated consequences for the story. Already in Conrad's first novel, *Almayer's Folly*, we read: 'It was a very long time since he had seen the sea – that sea that leads everywhere, brings everything, and takes away so much' (152).[10] As a practice, the space of the sea is crossed for trade, as are coastal routes or inland rivers for the establishment of trading posts. Fredric Jameson argued for the sea in Conrad as the focus of a double function, at once an imaginary and an ideological space: 'Thus the non-space of the sea is also the space of the degraded language of romance and daydream ... but is also, just as surely, itself a place of work and the very element by which an imperial capitalism draws its scattered beachheads and outposts together' (*The Political Unconscious*, 213).[11] Marlow refers proudly to the merchant service where 'the craft of the sea' is practiced, a profession for which Jim has been trained, even when a combination of exacting standards of the service in 'devotion to duty' and a desire for heroism on his part prove too much for him (*LJ*, 33; 5). Moreover, the principles of the merchant marine have a long history going back to the heroic voyages in the seventeenth century for the spice trade of 'Dutch and English adventurers' in the East Indies, risking their lives 'for a slender reward' and leaving 'their bones to lie bleaching on distant shores, so that wealth might flow to the living at home'. Marlow, however, laments the passing of the 'glory' (*LJ*, 164–5); and his attempt to tell Jim's story is characterized by the more ruthless and less heroic seamen whose actions are anything but heroic as we see in the episode on the 'Patna'. Some of Conrad's best known novels and stories also take us upriver into dangerously remote places – like *Almayer's Folly* or *An Outcast of the Islands* in the Malaysian Archipelago, or 'An Outpost of Progress' and *Heart of Darkness* in Central Africa. In these stories trade is a focus for the

---

[10]   Subsequent references abbreviated as *AF* in text.

[11]   The sea is thus a spatial practice as well as a location for adventure and romance.

competing colonialist powers – the Dutch and British in Malaya, the Belgian and the British in Africa.

The sea is a trope for freedom from the problems of life on land. Life on board the ship is the microcosm for a simple and effective societal order as well as the ideal of male bonding. In 'The Secret Sharer' the narrator 'rejoiced in the great security of the sea as compared to the unrest of the land', for the life at sea was 'invested with an elementary moral beauty by the absolute straightforwardness of its appeal and by the singleness of its purpose' (*Typhoon and Other Tales*, 183). In *Chance*, Marlow explains that the sea 'was there to give them [Flora and Captain Anthony] the shelter of its solitude free from the earth's petty suggestions' (230–31). 'Shore people' (landlubbers) are always troublesome and 'demoralizing', whereas at sea: 'You hear no tormenting echoes of your own littleness there, where either a great elemental voice roars defiantly under the sky or else an elemental silence seems to be part of the infinite stillness of the universe' (*Chance*, 242–3). Captain Anthony's thoughts 'turned to the sea which had given him so much of that congenial solitude' (*Chance*, 257) – the lonely figure on board ship being a recurrent trope. The ship is a sort of refuge from the complexities and confusions of life on land; on the ship's deck the individual can contemplate his place in the immense cosmos. And there are many examples in Conrad's writing of the perspective of a ship as a mere speck on a vast ocean dwarfed by the immensity of nature, with 'the eternal serenity of the Eastern sky overhead and the smiling peace of the Eastern seas possessing the space as far as the horizon' (*LJ*, 9).[12] Once outside the harbour, as the Narcissus starts its sea voyage from Bombay to London, 'the measureless expanse of smooth water lay sparkling like a floor of jewels, and as empty as the sky' (*NN*, 16). In such descriptions the sea is a non-space only delimited by the ever-receding horizon or the sight of land. Sailors become conscious of its power during the storm, in 'Typhoon' and again in *The Nigger of the 'Narcissus'* ('the roar of the seas', 56); but also in the heat of the equator as the ship is floating becalmed 'upon a smooth sea' (63), a condition nearly as bad as the storm for a sailing vessel. The first sight of land for the crew of the Narcissus is given a negative gloss by Donkin for whom the land 'draws life away' (90) as it ends the bond of the sea (96), and the motif continues as the ship docks in London, 'the sordid earth', where it 'ceased to live' (102). The land is prefigured as a non-place for the sailor; it is the death of the sailor because he is not at home there. As the ship sails up the river Thames at the end of its voyage, it is 'the dark river', a mythic place of death (*NN*, 107) – a motif reiterated at the start of Marlow's narrative in *Heart of Darkness* as he refers to London as 'one of the dark places of the earth' (18), a topographical symbolism with implicit associations to the 'dark satanic mills' of Blake, and the 'darkest England' of William Booth's take on Stanley's *In Darkest Africa* (1890)[13] – thus bringing together significant contemporary allusions to both the critique of imperialism and the critique of capitalism – allusions which underpin Conrad's

---

[12] Another example in *Lord Jim*, '... the circular stillness of water and sky with the black speck of the moving hull remaining everlastingly in its centre' (13).

[13] William Booth, *In Darkest England* (London: Salvation Army, 1900).

critique of modernity. The Dickensian sooty, grey London Docks at the end of Conrad's novella are hardly a home to compare to the magnificent sailing craft that has just successfully crossed the oceans.[14]

The placeless space at its most enigmatic is the Placid Gulf in *Nostromo*. As Decoud and Nostromo are entrusted with the silver to keep it out of the hands of the invading Monteros, they are on the lighter in 'the tremendous obscurity of the Placid Gulf'[15] in the 'featureless night' where they cannot see anything (*N*, 210; 240). The utter darkness is like nothingness itself, a void that drives the sensitive Decoud to despair and suicide once left alone by Nostromo (246). On the becalmed sea the darkness becomes a condition of being, or non-being, a recurrent signifier echoing the symbolism of *Heart of Darkness* where there is also 'a weirdness', 'a death-like stillness' surrounding the boat (*N*, 253–5).[16] In both texts there is an uncanny effect, an unsettling of identity through the severe restriction of perception: 'No intelligence could penetrate the darkness of the Placid Gulf' (*N*, 252). It is even difficult to know whether they are moving without Decoud feeling the water 'slip though his fingers' (253). He can though hear Sotillo's boat approaching even when he cannot see it, until even that sound is suddenly extinguished before the collision (266). And then, as Decoud and Nostromo try to keep their boat afloat to save the silver, Conrad can return to an older storytelling paradigm: 'they were merely two adventurers pursuing each his own adventure, involved in the same imminence of deadly peril' (269), inspiring both of them to survive. But Decoud's problems really begin once he finds himself 'solitary on the beach like a man in a dream' as a 'sudden desire to hear a human voice once more seized upon his heart' (275). With a characteristic Conradian delay, we return to Decoud's story for the final act of his suicide. After the despair brought about by three days of solitude Decoud starts to doubt his own sense of identity (451). By the tenth day alone he appears to have lost all sense of agency, driven 'as if accomplishing some sort of rite', and like 'a somnambulist' (453) to shoot himself, and weighted down with the four silver ingots he slips overboard into the waters of the Placid Gulf, 'whose glittering surface remained untroubled by the fall of his body' (455). Decoud had lost his hold on life once he 'believed in nothing', and nature responds with an 'immense indifference' (455). Nature (the sea) in *Nostromo* – the Placid Gulf – has a metaphysical force as the void filled by Decoud's nihilism.

In addition to these recurrent moments of metaphysical implication there are the mythical allusions: the sea or upriver journey as quest or odyssey testing man's

---

[14]   The image of London and its allusions are indebted to the excellent paper by Robert Hampson, '"Topographical Mysteries": Conrad and London' in *Conrad's Cities*, 159–74. I return to this paper later in the chapter.

[15]   Subsequent page references abbreviated as *N* in text.

[16]   Examples from *Heart of Darkness* are: 'What we could see was just the steamer we were on ... and that was all. The rest of the world was nowhere ...' as Marlow gets closer to Kurtz shrouded in mist (68–9). Marlow describes Kurtz as 'an impenetrable darkness', and hears him say that he was 'lying here in the dark waiting for death' (111), thus keeping the signifier darkness in play.

ideals, with its Conradian twist of disillusion. As Marlow travels further up the Congo in *Heart of Darkness*, the interior becomes a mythic place whose centre is the heart of darkness, a play of signification on the colonialist image of Africa in the nineteenth century and a trope for the breakdown of civilizing principles, and much more besides. Haunted by the 'wandering corpses' of 'the terrors of the sea' and his own professional disgrace, Jim once a 'seaman in exile from the sea' travelled the islands like a nomad in search of a home, a place 'where he could withdraw', and finally journeying upriver to the remotest trading outpost in the Malay Archipelago – like Almayer before him – to seek his fortune and recover his reputation (*LJ*, 115; 5; 122). But as Almayer in *Almayer's Folly*, Willems in *An Outcast of the Islands*, Kurtz in *Heart of Darkness* and Kayerts and Carlier the 'two white men in charge of the trading post' in the ironically titled story 'An Outpost of Progress' all prove, the colonial white man may not be able to maintain his sense of cultural and moral superiority in those places. Jim becomes 'Tuan' (Lord) Jim to the native people but dies when other white men come and disturb the precarious order he has established in Patusan, as if his past finally catches up with him; Kurtz becomes a demi-god to the natives whom he wants to 'exterminate'; Almayer degenerates into opium addiction, while earlier in his story's chronology he judges Willems as someone who is 'disturbing the harmony of the universe by robbery, treachery, and violence' (*An Outcast of the Islands*, 160). Kayerts hangs himself when he realizes how far he has degenerated. Thus the sea is also the location for a series of travel fictions that undermine the values of imperialism.

Conrad's Impressionism

Setting the episode that ends in Decoud's suicide in the Placid Gulf in *Nostromo*, or the enigma of the journey up-river in Africa or Malaya, Conrad draws on a descriptive impressionism that transforms a symbolic topography into a metaphysical condition, itself a dominant characteristic of the Conradian style from the concrete to the abstract. Here are two examples from *Heart of Darkness*: 'Watching a coast as it slips by is like thinking of an enigma' (29). 'The great wall of vegetation, an exuberant and entangled mass of trunks, branches, leaves, boughs, festoons, motionless in the moonlight, was like a rioting invasion of soundless life, a rolling wave of plants, piled up, crested, ready to topple over the creek, to sweep every little man of us out of his little existence' (*HD*, 54). The description is impressionist in its sensory perception and symbolist in its larger implications. As I argued in the introduction to this book, impressionism as a modern art form attempted to capture the world as subjectively perceived, and thus limit the real to what is seen. Thus perception has psychological implications, and Conrad is an impressionist writer in this sense, and this defines him as a modernist writer. The 'as if' in the text marks the transition from the object to the trope, and assures its fictional value. Description in Conrad's text has the effect, in Jameson's words, 'to derealize the content and make it available for consumption on some purely aesthetic level' (*The Political Unconscious*, 214). Walking the city Marlow in *Lord Jim* describes streets, 'full of jumbled bits of colour like a damaged kaleidoscope: yellow, green, blue, dazzling white' (*LJ*, 149); and recalling leaving Jim in Patusan, 'all this dropped out of my sight bodily, with its colour, its design, and its meaning, like a picture created by fancy on a canvas ... It remains in the memory motionless, unfaded, with its life arrested, in an unchanging light' (240). And as ever in Conrad the sea is the descriptive focus of poetic and symbolic resonance: 'at last Jim looked astern ... He saw a silent black squall which had eaten up already one-third of the sky ... A straight edge of vapour lines with sickly whitish gleams ... its shadow flies over the waters, and confounds sea and sky into one abyss of obscurity' (*LJ*, 74).[17] The exotic place is also an object of descriptive evocation:

> They could see below them in the declining light the vast expanse of the forest country, a dark sleeping sea of sombre green undulating as far as the violet and purple range of mountains; the shining sinuosity of the river like an immense letter S of beaten silver; the brown ribbon of houses following the sweep of both banks, overtopped by the twin hills uprising above the nearer tree-tops. (*Lord Jim*, 188)

And: 'A brooding gloom lay over this vast and monotonous landscape; the light fell on it as if into an abyss. The land devoured the sunshine; only far off, along the coast, the empty ocean, smooth and polished within the faint haze, seemed to rise up to the sky in a wall of steel' (*LJ*, 192). Sometimes topographical description has a more resonant symbolism as when nature seems to foreshadow Jim's death: 'The sky over Patusan was blood-red, immense, streaming like an open vein. An enormous sun nestled crimson amongst the tree-tops, and the forest below had a black and forbidding face' (301). The light reflected on the water or the landscape, the stark and contrasting colours, and the evocation of the exotic – these are the characteristic features of impressionist art (Gauguin's greens, violets and purples); and they are subjectively perceived (Conrad is always precise about who is doing the seeing). Moreover, there is something excessive about the exotic that belongs to the colonial field. As Padmini Mongia puts it, 'the colonial context allows for the presentation of remote and alien regions created as spaces of excess, spaces which threaten engulfment and a loss of demarcating boundaries' ('Ghosts of the Gothic', 159).

In the preface to *The Nigger of the 'Narcissus'*, Conrad insisted that his art is concerned with the 'visible universe', with its forms, colours, light and shadows. The preface could be read as a sort of manifesto for his stylistic impressionism. Writing should be 'an impression through the senses'; it should try to emulate 'the colour of painting' and 'the magic suggestiveness of music' – recalling Pater's dictum: 'All art constantly aspires to the condition of music' (124). Conrad defines his task, with half an eye on Pater's aestheticism without committing himself to 'Art for Art itself': 'by the power of the written word, to make you hear, to make

---

[17]   Further examples of the symbolic seascape: 13, 89, 242.

you feel – it is, before all, to make you see'; and not just for art's sake, but 'that glimpse of truth for which you have forgotten to ask' (*NN*, 145–8). As a modernist, Conrad wants the reader to look at the world anew, not as some superficial sight for easy consumption, but as a challenge to the senses as the object is thickened by poesis, and – this is crucial – is located in the consciousness of the character or narrator's gaze. Conradian impressionism is then a radicalized realism, because the real is what is visible to the gaze and is subject to a specifically characterized perspective – which has a defamiliarizing effect on the reader.

Jameson wrote of Conrad's 'stylistic passion' where 'reality became image'. The episode on the Placid Gulf in *Nostromo* foregrounds the senses 'as a theme in their own right', and here 'registering auditory perceptions' (*The Political Unconscious*, 239). Jameson, moreover, insists that this 'displacement of reading attention toward the image' has an ideological function in a 'great historical drama' that unfolds within the non-place of the sea. Indeed that function allows Conrad 'to register history itself' (*The Political Unconscious*, 242). But while Conrad expresses the resentment of Nostromo, Old Viola and others in the novel, including the Montero brothers who want to wrestle their country and its wealth (the silver mine) back from the foreigners, his own political attitudes towards revolutions and democracy are 'presupposed, and reinforced by ethical and melodramatic markers', so that at best history repeats itself in the cycle of revolutions and counterrevolutions that brings chaos to the fictional South American banana republic – 'the fallen history of Costaguana' – while order is maintained by the material interests of the American and British investors. Thus it is that the Latin American world is 'externalized into Otherness by the Anglo vision' (276),[18] as Conrad maintains his belief in the impossibility of what Jameson calls 'genuine historical change' (277).[19] As a historical novel, *Nostromo* focuses on the 'individual passions and values' of a range of characters from the Goulds to Old Viola to Decoud and Nostromo, which for Jameson demonstrates that Conrad cannot narrate the 'dimension of collective reality' (279).

---

[18] Jameson wonders what a Latin American novelist would do with this material (270). We now have an answer in Juan Gabriel Vásquez, *The Secret History of Costaguana* (London: Bloomsbury, 2010), a postmodern Latin American response to Conrad's modernist novel.

[19] For Conrad's views on state power and repression see his essay, 'Autocracy and War'. Here he celebrates the defeat of Tsarist Russia by Japan in 1905, and foresees the new threat of Pan-Germanism to the peace of Europe. With the repression of his homeland, Poland, in mind, Conrad expresses his strongly felt view that imperialism is driven by material interests (a slogan recurrent in the novel he was writing at the time, *Nostromo*), and that the global rivalry between the dominant nations has created the present condition of war. Conrad makes his ideological position clear: 'The trouble of the civilized world is the want of a common conservative principle … to form a rallying point of international action tending towards the restraint of particular ambitions' (54). The failures of revolutions and anarchy, and abuses of state power are worked through in *Nostromo*, *The Secret Agent* and *Under Western Eyes*. Conrad's radical aesthetic should not be confused with his conservative politics.

In the attempt to collate the different storytellers' versions of events and their origins, the novel foregrounds the processes of textualization, which for Said means that this novel is 'no more than a *record* of novelistic self-reflection' (cit. in *The Political Unconscious*, 279). But I would object to that 'no more than': it is reductionist of a complex modernist writing, and one that finally gives the highest value to the aesthetic (impressionism) over the categories of history and politics. I think we should acknowledge Conrad's insistence on the real as image, and the object as trope and symbol which should not allow critics to reduce writing to the 'no more than' formula. It is a feature of modernism – rightly or wrongly – to prioritize the aesthetic over history. Yet for Conrad the aesthetic is the way to a greater truth about the modern world.

Narrative as a Journey

In Conrad's writing, older seamen – like Marlow – tell stories about journeys to remote and exotic places and the characters they encountered. Later in this chapter I look at Conrad's storytelling men – his *hommes-récit*. This section will address the idea that narrative itself has the structure of a journey, and that the best example is the story of the sea-voyage from departure through the passage across the ocean and to the arrival, and the hazards of the changing weather and the conflicts between the crew members that threaten the harmony or bonding required on board. A classic example is *The Nigger of the 'Narcissus'* (1897).

In a letter to Edward Garnett about the progress he is making Conrad writes, 'I shall make sail with the "Narcissus" and expect to make a quick passage. Weather fine, and wind fair' (21 November 1896, rept. in *NN*, 176).[20] Notwithstanding the humour, for Conrad writing is a sea voyage, too, and he is reporting his progress like the captain's log. The novella begins with the arrival, and introduction of the captain and crew, the 'new hands' (the characters, including the 'nigger' James Wait), the preparations for departure from the harbour in Bombay as the ship 'was for sea' (1). There is a reminder of the need to stick together (5), of the kinship of 'the brotherhood of the sea' (18) – 'the bond of the sea', that key concept which recurs in 'Youth' and *Heart of Darkness*; but also a sense of longing for home before the long and hazardous ocean voyage ahead:

> Young Creighton stood leaning over the rail, and looked dreamily into the night of the East. And he saw in it a long country lane, a lane of waving leaves and dancing sunshine. He saw stirring boughs of old trees outspread, and framing in their arch the tender, the caressing blueness of an English sky. And through the arch a girl in a light dress, smiling under a sunshade, seemed to be stepping out of the tender sky. (13)

Conrad establishes a strong sense of place, of land, home and abroad; of the leaving and the destination; but also the idealized English countryside inscribes

---

[20]   All further page references in text are to the Norton Critical edition of *The Nigger of the 'Narcissus'*.

a desire that will keep such men going through the long voyage, even when the London at their arrival will be nothing less than a dystopia.

The chapters of the novella follow the sequence of the voyage, with the raising of the anchor at the end of chapter 1, the 'Narcissus' 'went to sea' as it leaves the harbour at the start of chapter 2 (16) on 'the homeward passage', and the crew are described as 'sinking into the peace of a resumed routine' (17). The story begins at the start of the ship's passage; and the strong sense of place shifts from the land to the sea with its immense space marked by the overarching sky: 'and the ship, a fragment detached from the earth, went on lonely and swift like a small planet. Round her the abyss of sky and sea met in an unattainable frontier. A great circular solitude moved with her, ever changing and ever the same, always monotonous and always imposing' (18) – another example of that reiterated feature of Conrad's writing the sea voyage of the ship dwarfed by the immensity and indifference of nature;[21] a perspective with the double function of admiring the sight of the magnificent vessel sailing the ocean – Captain Allistoun's ambition is 'to make her accomplish someday a brilliant quick passage which would be mentioned in nautical papers' (19)[22] – and what Conrad calls 'the sordid inspiration of her pilgrimage' (18), implying the greed of trade for which the ship is being used, where time is money and the new steam-powered ships were competition. Moreover, the switching of perspective from the cosmic view to the narrow internal one of the ship's crew and their conflicts enables the sometimes critical distance. As Singleton puts it: 'Ships are all right. It is the men in them!' (14).

The narrative of the voyage becomes the story of the men, and it is James Wait, the eponymous 'nigger', who will be the catalyst for the attitudes and actions of the crew. He is an ambivalent figure, 'calm, cool, towering, superb' (10) yet described also as having 'the tragic, the mysterious, the repulsive mask of the nigger's soul'; and when we read that 'the nigger's eyes rolled wildly, became all whites' (11) it would be difficult today, at least, not to react to the racist implications.[23] But even here there are moments of mitigating ambivalence: the crew sometimes see him as 'this obnoxious nigger', yet the narrator insists that 'we all lovingly called him Jimmy' (22). The problem is less one of the colour of his skin and more of his playing sick and refusing to work: 'from the first he was very slack at his

---

[21] Further examples: '... she remained lost in a vast universe of night and silence ...' (64). 'The sun, rising lonely and splendid in the blue sky, saw a solitary ship gliding close-hauled on the blue sea' (82).

[22] The Norton Critical edition has a picture on the front cover of the real 'Narcissus' sailing through the waves in colour and a set of drawings to illustrate the masts, sails, rigging and accommodation. It is not difficult to appreciate what Conrad admired about this sailing ship.

[23] Conrad changed the title for the American publication to *The Children of the Sea*, thus telling us that the racist interpretation was also an issue then. He did though regret it and changed it back to the original title in a later edition. See 'Textual History' in the Norton critical edition, 111–13. The text is though largely off the syllabus, and is usually only referred to because of Conrad's famous preface.

work' (27); he keeps to himself, and even though he is an object of fascination he was 'disturbing the peace of the ship' (28). In the storm he is trapped in his cabin and the crew risk their lives to rescue him, but he is not grateful; and although Captain Allistoun thinks he has been 'shamming sick' (74), Wait dies and is buried at sea, but not before dividing loyalties and requiring the captain to impose his authority (83). After his death, the effect Wait has had on the crew is summed up: he was 'nothing but trouble' and nearly caused a 'mutiny' (99–100).

There is, therefore, a disjunction between the dignified image of the magnificent sailing ship in the vast and indifferent ocean and the indiscipline of the crew who attempt to defy the captain's absolute authority. The bond of the sea is threatened by the dysfunctional James Wait and the reaction of the crew to him. However, it is the storm at sea that brings the men together as a single force for survival, and this is the focus of chapter 3. 'It was bad weather off the Cape that year' (30), and the narrator tells us that the men 'knitted together aft into a ready group by the first sharp order of an officer coming to take charge of the deck in bad weather' (31). Conrad takes the ship the long way round the Cape when the Suez Canal was already the shorter preferred route. Why? Perhaps because he wants to give us the storm episode as a test of crew's courage.[24] And even though the age of sail was gradually coming to an end, and the merchant marine dominated by the new steam-powered ships, Conrad, like Herman Melville's *Moby Dick* (1851), sets his story on a large sailing ship – presumably for reasons of nostalgia – and with all his technical know-how shows how the captain and his crew survive the storm at sea.[25] Denis Murphy calls the third chapter of *The Nigger of the 'Narcissus'* 'one of literature's enduring descriptions of men trapped in a storm at sea' (136). It is not just a matter of what to do with the different masts and sails, but also whether the cargo has been carefully loaded because, as Murphy explains, 'any shifting of the cargo in heavy seas could be fatal' (136–7). Moreover, the shallower and lighter keels of such sailing ships compared to their modern counterparts made them less safe (Murphy, 137). Meeting a monster wave in a big sea, and after taking water on board the ship cannot straighten up and therefore 'has reached a point of precarious equilibrium', and is in danger of capsizing (Murphy, 39). The crew wants the

---

[24]   'By 1869, when the Suez Canal halved the maritime distance between London and Bombay, Peninsular & Oriental Line steamers could do the journey in four weeks ...', although Britain did not obtain a controlling interest until 1875. But this is still 23 years before the publication of Conrad's novella. See Brendon, 142–3.

[25]   Mark D. Larabee claims that 'the historical record indicates how changes to trade patterns wrought by the opening of the Suez Canal were not quite as abrupt and extensive as some of Conrad's narrators claim; consequently, voyages like that depicted in this novella were not archaic final episodes in the dying age of sail transport. Even as this story incorporates rich symbolic, mythic, and other psychological dimensions that assist any romanticization of the maritime tradition, *The Nigger of the "Narcissus"* also portrays historically specific commercial transaction typical of those central to the maintenance of Britain's trading empire' (55). I would add that Conrad's ships in his fiction are not all sailing ships, as the chart in Larabee's paper shows (51–2): the Patna in *Lord Jim* is a steamship as is the Nan-Shan in 'Typhoon'; while the Ferndale in *Chance* is a sailing ship.

captain to cut the masts down, but he refuses without explanation (asserting his absolute authority); the ship continues practically on her side after a wave hits her broadside. The captain demonstrates his skill (and Conrad's knowledge of such situations) by eventually steering the ship into such a position that the wind will help right her: 'The ship trembled, trying to lift her side, lurched back, seemed to give up with a nerveless dip, and suddenly with an unexpected jerk swung violently to windward, as though she had torn herself out from a deadly grasp' (*NN*, 54). The men are ecstatically relieved, while the captain remains distant and focused. The final scene, as Murphy points out (141), leaves us with the image of the white-bearded sea dog, Singleton with 'steady old eyes' and 'attentive face' steering the ship 'with care' (*NN*, 55). The men survive, and have a greater sense of bonding, which is then put to the test when they realize that 'Jimmy' is trapped in his cabin. He is rescued but ungrateful, and Conrad implicitly sets Wait's death drive against the 'desire for life which kept them alive' (50). Under blue skies and sunshine, and relieved for having survived, they feel reborn: 'Yet from that time our life seemed to start afresh as though we had died and had been resuscitated' (61). The motifs of life and death drives continue to recur for the rest of the story, as James Wait appears to give up on life and dies, and the sailors themselves appear to die once they reach home. Near the Azores, becalmed, the ship itself is like a ghost ship, echoing the long dying of Wait (89–90); and his death reminds the crew of the importance of 'a common bond' because he was no 'shipmate' (96). Eventually the breeze comes and 'the waking sea began to murmur sleepily of home to the ears of men' (99). The narrator expresses pride in the 'mighty ship' that had proved 'stronger than the storms!' (101) – echoing Conrad of *The Mirror of the Sea* who wrote of 'the contests of mankind with the sea' (*The Mirror of the Sea*, 141). The homecoming, the end of the journey, is a kind of death for crew and ship: 'The *Narcissus* came gently into her berth … She had ceased to live' (*NN*, 102). The voyage over, the narrator has a last view of the rest of the crew in London: 'they were like castaways, like mad castaways making merry in the storm and upon an insecure ledge of a treacherous rock' (107) – as if home on land they need rescuing. Conrad keeps the tropes of the sea, the storm and the dangers to mankind in play, but here the land appears more treacherous than the sea, and 'the dull roar of the busy earth' (106) has replaced the howling gales at sea: 'Land draws life away' (90). The death motif attains mythological implication with the Thames as 'Styx', 'the dark river' (107), the 'river of the dead'.[26]

The end of the narrative is the arrival of the ship at its destination, after the story of a voyage from Bombay around the Cape and up through the tropics where the sunset is always sudden – 'and the sun, as if put out, disappeared' (46) – and across the equator where 'the ship, in close heat, floated upon a smooth sea that resembled a sheet of ground glass' (63). The sea is ever present as topos, and as trope sometimes anthropomorphized as 'the great sea' that held the life of man 'in its immense grip … the sea that knew all, and would in time infallibly unveil to each the wisdom hidden in all the errors' (85) – proving the old adage that wisdom

---

[26] See 107 note 4 in the Norton Critical edition.

comes from travel.[27] Finally the sea will test the masculinity of the crew as it is 'real men' who 'stand by one in a tight place' (77).[28]

In Conrad's fiction, then, voyage narrative has archetypal resonance of the mythic wanderers across the seas. A recurrent trope in Conrad is the sea as a mirror, which has associations with the myth of Narcissus, and the self-absorption of lonely seafarer.[29] Voyage narrative aligns itself with a long tradition of travel and adventure fiction. Yet Conrad also destabilizes that tradition. In Andrea White's words: 'While profoundly influenced by the travel writing and the adventure fiction of his time and by many of the ideals revealed and espoused in those works, he would challenge the convention's assumptions … the very sea-going tradition he had admired … was questioned and placed into jeopardy' (*Joseph Conrad and the Adventure Tradition*, 108–9). It is fundamental to Conrad's modernism that there is a tension between adventure travel and its deconstruction.

Adventure Travel and its Deconstruction

> 'The estuaries of rivers appeal strongly to an adventurous imagination.' (Conrad, *The Mirror of the Sea*, 100)

The values of solidarity, courage and seamanship that are proposed and tested as manly ideals in *The Nigger of the 'Narcissus'* are finally seen to be possible only on board the well-run sailing ship. The image of degenerate London at the end of the story, the powerhouse of modern industrialization, puts everything that has gone before into a new light. It seems that the sea voyage has been a strategy of nostalgia, which makes this novella the fictional expression of *The Mirror of the Sea* (1906), that personal eulogy to the art of sailing ships. For it is here that Conrad lays bare his critique of modernity in the opposition between the sailing and the steamship, where the former brings the seaman closer to nature (38), and demands all his resourcefulness and courage (62). The steamship has destroyed the old instinctive relations with the force of nature (71), because the machine – the dominant trope of modernity for its critics – now stands 'between man and the sea', and the modern ship is no longer 'the sport of the waves' (72). Conrad's novels and stories, however, show the frailties of men in the face of such demands.

It is in *Lord Jim* where Conrad brings together best his belief in the values of sea travel and adventure and the ways in which they can create impossible demands on those who espouse the romanticism inherent in them. Marlow claims

---

[27]   'In leaving home one learns life. You travel. Travelling is victory! You shall return with much wisdom.' *An Outcast of the Islands*, 101.

[28]   Further examples of the narrative of sea voyages are 'Typhoon' (1902), 'The Secret Sharer' (1909); but also episodes in *Lord Jim* (1900), 'Youth' and *Heart of Darkness* (1902) and *Chance* (1914).

[29]   For further discussion see Gerald Morgan, 'Narcissus Afloat' reprinted in the Norton critical edition of *The Nigger of the 'Narcissus'* (262–75). And of course *The Mirror of the Sea* works the trope in Conrad's autobiographical reflections.

that Jim lived 'in his mind the sea life of light literature. He saw himself saving people from sinking ships, cutting away masts in a hurricane ... He confronted savages on tropical shores' (*LJ*, 5). Coming from an English parsonage, his reading in travel and adventure literature – like the author's – helped him to decide early on for the sea as his vocation. When he first appears to Marlow he is 'spotlessly neat, apparelled in immaculate white' (3), and 'always an example of devotion to duty' (5). Significantly because of what happens on the Patna, Jim is convinced that when 'all men flinched ... he alone would know how to deal with the spurious menace of winds and sea ... he exulted with fresh certitude in his avidity for adventure, and in a sense of many-sided courage' (7). He trains for a career in the merchant marine and becomes a chief mate. However, he remains relatively inexperienced, untested in the demands of courage at sea. The cocktail of romanticism and the maritime codes of honour and devotion to duty will be his undoing when put under pressure on the Patna. Jim, and others like him, suffers from what Marlow calls, 'a high-minded absurdity of intention' (142).

Conrad had prepared the ground for the exposure of the contradictions of the adventure story tradition in his early fiction – *Almayer's Folly*, *An Outcast of the Islands*, 'An Outpost of Progress' and *Heart of Darkness*, as well as the sea stories like *The Nigger of the 'Narcissus'*, 'Youth', 'Typhoon' and 'The Secret Sharer'. Andrea White discusses Conrad's early fictional works in the light of their critical relationship to the adventure tradition in travel writing and fiction that was more popular than ever in the late nineteenth century – and which, as we know, Conrad had read with enthusiasm as a boy: 'He was influenced from an early age by the legends about and writings by the heroic figure of the day, the explorer-adventurer, and he wrote appreciably about the civilizing work of Captain James Cook, Sir John Franklin, Francis Leopold McClintock, R.N., Rajah James Brooke, and David Livingstone – all English explorers' (2). Although Conrad's reading of adventure fiction was formative of his young mind, as an adult his reading was more demanding and more influential on his modernism, and it was this reading formation that influenced his deconstructive use of the popular genre.[30]

The problem with the intrepid heroes of Victorian popular fiction in the late nineteenth century – in Ballantyne, Marryat, Rider Haggard and Kipling – is that they reflected the dominant attitudes to empire. Conrad's attitude, however, can be seen in those characters in his fiction that adopt such pro-imperialist views uncritically and are undone by their naivety. Jim is a case in point. As White argues: 'Choosing to write from within the fiction that had traditionally celebrated an unqualified kind of heroism, Conrad achieved a critical irony, but also announced his regret that the dream of pure, disinterested adventure was no longer

---

[30] As Najder tells us, not only was Conrad well read in Polish Romantic literature, but also Russian, English and French literature, which he drew on for his own writing – although Najder defends Conrad from the accusation of plagiarizing 'impressions, phrases and images' from Flaubert and Maupassant (236). For further discussion see Najder 456–7. For Conrad's French influences see Yves Hervouet, *The French Face of Joseph Conrad* (Cambridge: Cambridge University Press, 1990).

possible' (White, 5). I would add, of course, that the figure of Marlow, as world-weary British sea captain, enables that critical voice at a distance from the author – that is without the responsibilities of an autobiographical omniscience. Yet Marlow the rampant British patriot of *Heart of Darkness* appears in *Lord Jim* as having a much more critical attitude to all high-mindedness including that of British superiority. In *Heart of Darkness* Marlow comments on a large map of Africa that there was 'a vast amount of red – good to see at any time, because one knows that some real work is done in there, a deuce of a lot of blue, a little green, smears of orange, and, on the East Coast, a purple patch, to show where the jolly pioneers of progress drink the jolly lager beer' (*HD*, 25).[31] In *Lord Jim*, admittedly Marlow still admires the immaculately dressed white-suited British colonialist – a racial signifier; but Jim fails in his duty, even when he is never as bad as the so-called Gentleman Brown, described as 'a latter-day buccaneer' (*LJ*, 256) whose arrival in Patusan precipitates Jim's death. Brown represents the ultimate imperialist mindset for Conrad: 'with grim impatience of plunder … the land already seemed to be his to tear to pieces, squeeze, and throw away' (269). Marlow insists that Jim is 'one of us' (gentlemen-mariners); but then Gentleman Brown is too – and both of them go wrong although to different degrees. Jim becomes the 'white lord' to the natives of Patusan, and where Kurtz in *Heart of Darkness* became a tyrant Jim believes he has achieved something in bringing stability to the place (196, 282). But there is more to say, because Marlow recounts Brown's own version of Jim (later on Brown's death-bed): 'he was a hollow sham' (250); and in the light of Marlow's own dim view of any form of greatness, we too are left thinking Jim a sham, or at best a self-deceiver: 'And yet is not mankind itself, pushing on its blind way, driven by a dream of its greatness and its power upon the dark paths of excessive cruelty and of excessive devotion?' (254). Such pessimism could never underpin the heroism of adventure in the imperial field. Conrad's refusal of heroism is signalled early on in the novel. The Arab pilgrims being taken to Mecca on board the Patna may trust the courage and wisdom of white men, but the crew of the Patna 'did not belong to the world of heroic adventure' (18).

After his experiences of the excesses of imperialism in the Congo (dramatized in *Heart of Darkness*), Conrad found himself in a difficult position. As an adopted British subject he tried to avoid being openly critical of the work of the British Empire (and Marlow proved useful here),[32] while having a fundamentally pessimistic view of the grand values that underpinned imperialism (and revolution), and of course having experienced Imperial Russia's repression of Poland.[33]

Imperial travel and adventure stories evidently required a blind acceptance of white racial superiority, and one which Conrad's work challenges. There is,

---

[31]   Such maps were colour-coded according to the nation's colonial territory with red representing the British Empire.

[32]   Conrad celebrates British naval history in the last section of *The Mirror of the Sea* as an example of 'the national spirit' (194).

[33]   For Conrad's attitude to Imperial Russia, see 'Autocracy and War' and the novels *The Secret Agent* and *Under Western Eyes*.

though, a sometime opposition between white and black in Marlow's gaze: 'In the midst of these dark-faced men, his stalwart figure in white apparel, the gleaming clusters of his fair hair ...' (166); and also: 'Their dark-skinned bodies vanished on the dark background long before I had lost sight of their protector. He was white from head to foot, and remained persistently visible with the stronghold of the night at his back, the sea at his feet, the opportunity by his side ... For me that white figure in the stillness of coast and sea seemed to stand at the heart of a vast enigma' (244).[34] The white man's gaze is pre-constructed by the imperial real that can classify what is seen into known types, as we see *in extremis* in Henry Morton Stanley, *In Darkest Africa*, representing the Darwinian evolutionary view of race in the 1890s:

> We had four women and a boy, and in them I saw two distinct types. One evidently belonging to that same race described as the Akka, with small, cunning monkey eyes, close, and deeply set. The four others possessed large, round eyes, full and prominent, broad round foreheads and round faces ... and certainly deserving of being classed as an extremely low, degraded, almost a bestial type of human being. (vol. 1, 313)

As Stanley demonstrates, racism gives priority to the visible. Kalpana Seshadri-Crooks argues that in 'wholly racialized' societies like the European and the North American in the imperialist era, 'the fundamental significance of physical attributes remains constant ... we read certain marks of the body as privileged sites of racial meaning' (*Desiring Whiteness*, 1–2). Racist ideology has a psychic investment in appearance because race is fundamentally a regime of looking for the details of difference that inform the model of visibility. The master signifier, Whiteness, 'the inaugural signifier of race', establishes 'a structure of relations, a signifying chain that provides subjects with certain symbolic positions such as "black", "white", "Asian", etc. in relation to the master signifier' (Seshadri-Crooks, 4). Teresa Brennan suggests that the dominance of the visual is a symptom of social psychosis, 'the imaginary process of fixing the other is not only confined to *seeing*; it involves naming' (*History after Lacan*, 60, emphasis in original). Seshadri-Crooks further explains that race identity 'is about the sense of one's exclusiveness, exceptionality and uniqueness ... Racial difference ... has no other reason to be but power ...' (7). Racial difference reproduces itself as common sense for Stanley's readers, as culture turns itself into nature or biology – the primitive state from which civilized man has evolved. Moreover, Western culture is superior because it has developed sophisticated symbolic means of representing itself and its history beyond totemism. In Stanley's words, '[t]hese people, having no literature, and undisturbed by the advent of superior influences among them, have only learnt what has been communicated to them by their parents' – the 'evil

---

[34] See also: 'The group of vivid colours and dark faces with the white figure in their midst' (*Lord Jim*, 276); 'he appears no longer to me as I saw him last – a white speck catching all the dim light upon a sombre coast and the darkening sea' (287).

eye', omens and witchcraft instead of literature: this is the measure of the advance of Western civilization (vol. 2, 351–2).[35]

But before we accuse Conrad of racism,[36] we should acknowledge the signifiers of white and black as Marlow's, and that the stability of the white imperial subject implicit in the foregoing discussion is questioned in Conrad's novel; and, additionally, that Conrad has from his earliest fiction included the views of the native other. Already in Conrad's first novel Nina Almayer chooses her mother's Malay culture after disillusion with her white education. She rejects 'the hateful finery of Europe', as 'after all these years, the savage and uncompromising sincerity of purpose shown by her Malay kinsmen seemed at least preferable to the sleek hypocrisy, to the polite disguises, to the virtuous pretences of such white people as she had had the misfortune to come into contact with ... and so thinking she fell more and more under the influence of her mother' (*Almayer's Folly*, 22; 38). Nina prefers to marry 'the ideal Malay chief of her mother's tradition ... a man totally untrammelled by any influence of civilized self-discipline' (55); a desire which will not be without its difficulties. The novel ends with Muslim prayers being offered after Almayer's death, as if in defiance of the Christian mission of Western colonialism. In *An Outcast of the Islands*, Babalatchi tells Lingard: 'You whites are cruel to your friends and merciful to your enemies – which is the work of fools' (185). As Andrea White puts it: 'Like *Almayer's Folly*, *An Outcast of the Islands* tells more than the white man's story; in fact, here the native telling takes over' (146). About Dain Waris, Doramin's son in *Lord Jim* who was 'the first to believe in him [Jim]', Marlow comments: 'Such beings open to the Western eye, so often concerned with mere surfaces, the hidden possibilities of races and lands over which hangs the mystery of unrecorded ages' (*LJ*, 190). Christian westerners are known by Moslem locals as 'the Nazarene' (*LJ*, 206). The voice of the local ruler is heard questioning colonial power: 'Were the Dutch coming to take the country? Would the white man like to go back down the river? What was the object of coming to such a miserable country? The Rajah wanted to know whether the white man could repair a watch'; and it is the white man who in the remote island of Patusan is 'shunned by some, glared at by others, but watched by all' (183) – indeed, Jim has become the other, the object of the collective native gaze.[37]

For fiction located in the colonial field, Conrad's writing has a subversive effect. The irony implicit in the title and worked through in the letter of the story 'An Outpost of Progress' is symptomatic. Working within the imperial adventure

---

[35]   A critique of this position would begin with a discussion of the rich tradition of oral storytelling.

[36]   As Chinua Achebe and others have done. Levenson (2011) writes of 'the racism in Conrad's rendering of the Congo and Southeast Asia', and insists that 'Chinua Achebe has made it impossible to ignore the racism of Conrad's *Heart of Darkness*'. *Modernism*, 100–101. For a critique of Achebe's argument see Burden, 'Conrad's Heart of Darkness: the Critique of Imperialism and the Post-Colonial Reader'.

[37]   There is this kind of a switch of focus to the gaze of the other at times in Forster and Lawrence, offering a challenge to the dominance of the western gaze in travel fiction.

tradition Conrad deconstructs its basic tenets: heroism, white supremacy and imperialism (the agency of capitalist greed). There is, however, one other subversive element in Conrad's writing that destabilizes the adventure story. As White puts it, in Conrad's fiction, 'the nature of the telling itself made the tale suspect; it lent instability rather than authority. The method involved the reader in moral judgments that were no longer simple and depicted situations without offering conclusive interpretations' (7). The next section of this chapter discusses the attention given to travelling storytellers and their tales.

Travellers and Storytellers: Conrad's *Homme-Récit*

Travel stories are not the same as tourist guides. Comments on the difference between the traveller and the tourist appear occasionally in Conrad's novels. The hotel where Marlow will meet Jim 'was more than half full of people with a hundred pounds round-the-world tickets in their pockets. There were married couples looking domesticated and bored with each other in the midst of their travels'; and these tourists behave exactly as they do at home, and are 'just as intelligently receptive of new impressions as their trunks upstairs. Henceforth they would be labelled as having passed through this and that place, and so would be their luggage' (*LJ*, 56). In *Nostromo*, there is the image of lonely American women 'sketching all day long' in an 'old German historic town' (62); and in the same novel, Captain Mitchell becomes the tourist guide of Sulaco in an ironic narrative strategy where the future of the turbulent place is commodified into a tour destination and history collapses into heritage with its legends and monuments (*N*, 430ff.). Clearly, the tourist is not the 'real traveller' described in Conrad's essay, 'Travel' (in *Last Essays*). The difference between tourism and travel, as I explained in the introduction to this study, plays a significant part in the travel writing and travel fiction of the period, and the writers studied in this book are representative to one degree or another, where tourism is a prominent focus for a critique of modernity. However, even when travellers tell better stories than tourists, storytellers are a focus in Conrad for narratological and epistemological questions that belong to his modernist credentials.

In *Lord Jim* Marlow makes one thing very clear: 'He [Jim] existed for me, and after all it is only through me that he exists for you. I've led him out by the hand; I have paraded him before you' (162). The narrator and the narratee are specifically characterized in *Lord Jim* as they are in *Heart of Darkness*, both placed in a storytelling situation with its historical context which establishes a like-mindedness, a shared set of beliefs – in both 'Youth' and *Heart of Darkness* it is the 'bond of the sea' that the addressees share with Marlow; but also he represents a particular Victorian English attitude undermined by doubts characteristic of the *fin de siècle* which challenges their fixed ideas.[38] Yet Marlow questions the values of

---

[38] As we see in 'Youth' and *Heart of Darkness* too, Conrad occasionally reminds us of the addressees when Marlow pauses in his storytelling thus drawing attention to the

capitalism and imperialism, the strict code of the merchant marine, the superiority of Englishness and the white man in the colonial field; but also the romanticism that drives Jim to leave home and go to sea. What this section of the chapter now adds to this critique at the level of content are the doubts about the ability to tell the story, to capture the whole truth about the protagonist.[39]

Conrad goes further in *Lord Jim* than he does in *Heart of Darkness* with the quest paradigm: finding Kurtz is a goal with a single journey upriver and a few rumours along the way; but there are a number of encounters with Jim in different places and several sources of his story for Marlow to piece the whole story together. Sometimes these are stories by those who met Jim and had dealings with him, like 'Gentleman Brown' who much later on his deathbed talks to Marlow; sometimes they are simply tales of hearsay. Sometimes a story itself will travel: 'Next day, talking casually with the people of the little native court of the place, I discovered that a story was travelling slowly down the coast about a mysterious white man in Patusan' which constructs a 'Jim-myth' (203). The identity of Jim relies for the most part then on Marlow, as traveller and as storyteller: 'And later on, many times, in distant parts of the world, Marlow showed himself willing to remember Jim, to remember him at length, in detail and audibility' (24) – indeed, recalling the voice as well as the words spoken is a feature of Marlow's portrait of Kurtz too: 'Kurtz discoursed. A voice! A voice! It rang deep to the very last. It survived his strength to hide in the magnificent folds of eloquence the barren darkness of his heart' (*HD*, 110). Jim's speech, however, is more hesitant at times (*LJ*, 23), and what he has to say coloured by what Marlow calls, 'the impossible world of romantic achievement' (*LJ*, 60).

Marlow is used, then, not only as storyteller but to draw attention to the difficulties of getting the story told. Although he insists in *Lord Jim*, like he does in *Heart of Darkness*, that we need to hang on to 'some crumb of belief in a few simple notions' (*LJ*, 32),[40] he is determined to get at the deeper truth of Jim. But this turns out to be a difficult task: 'All this happened in much less time than it takes to tell, since I am trying to interpret for you into slow speech the instantaneous effect of visual impressions' (35). Even after hearing Jim's version of events, Marlow claims he does not understand him: 'I wanted to know – and to this day I don't know, I can only guess' (57). Narrative authority and epistemology are part of the same problematic: the plausibility of traditional storytelling and the knowability of the other – key concerns in Conrad's modernism. Conrad's refusal of omniscient narration enables a dramatization of the crisis of the modern subject. The sources of the story are multiple. As well as the different characters who

---

narrative frame: 'Marlow sat up abruptly and flung away his cheroot with force … Nobody stirred' (*Lord Jim*, 83–4). Or: 'Some of you may know what I mean …' (125), directly speaking to the addressees. Further examples: 158, 162–3, 216, 233, 236, 255.

[39]   Jim himself tells Marlow that the natives who put their utter trust in him, 'Tuan Jim', can 'never know the real, real truth' (*Lord Jim*, 221).

[40]   'There was surface-truth enough in these things to save a wiser man' (*Heart of Darkness*, 63).

give Marlow their version, there is the written text handed over to the 'privileged man', which contains Jim's surviving version of the end of the story, and which itself includes the text of a letter from his father with its 'easy morality and family news', a reminder of what Jim went to sea to get away from, and to which he feels he could never return because he could never explain himself because the distance is too great from the other side of the world, in more than one sense (248).

In addition to the attention drawn to storytelling as a destabilizing force, critics have often pointed to the discontinuity in the text itself between the events surrounding the Patna episode and the events in Patusan. There appears to be a shift between the Patna incident and the Patusan romance which Jameson has described as 'a shift between two distinct cultural spaces, that of "high" culture and that of mass culture' (*The Political Unconscious*, 207),[41] and that this discontinuity is symptomatic of a tension within modernism itself. Conrad is representative of this tension where the adventure tale and sea narratives derived from mass culture are contained in a novel characterized by self-conscious narrative production and other forms of scepticism characteristic of modernism. For Jameson, the first half of the novel is modernist textual production (*The Political Unconscious*, 219), self-conscious narrative and metaphysical speculation; the second part melodrama,[42] with Jim's Patusan adventure, his romance with 'Jewel' and the effect of Gentleman Brown. But do we need to read the text as discontinuous? As Stape rightly argues, the second part is 'far from being a simple tale of romantic love and heroic adventure in an exotic setting', because there is continuity between the parts in its 'thematic coherence', its 'formal hybridity' and Jim's continued failure (*LJ*, 75–7). It seems to me, additionally, that all Conrad's stories and novels have plots which draw on the popular paradigms of adventure, quest romance, and exotic travel;[43] and that they often resort to the narrative structure of enigma and revelation which underpins mystery stories and melodrama. But as White rightly argues, Conrad works from within the popular forms of writing to subvert their formal assumptions, and thus implicitly to destabilize the imperial subject. Like the great Victorian adventurer-travellers in the imperial field, Jim leaves England to gratify a personal desire for the adventurous life he had read about. But his story is not the same as those fictions. White calls Jim 'a fictional victim of this fiction' (White, 65); and Conrad achieves a double subversion: storytelling loses its naivety in his modernist text; and the fictional character is no longer capable of fulfilling

---

[41]   For F.R. Leavis *Lord Jim* was a partial failure because of its perceived discontinuity: 'The presentment of Lord Jim in the first part of the book, the account of the inquiry and the desertion of the *Patna*, the talk with the French lieutenant – these are good Conrad. But the romance that follows, though plausibly offered as a continued exhibition of Jim's case, has no inevitability as that; nor does it develop or enrich the central interest, which consequently, eked out to provide the substance of the novel, comes to seem decidedly thin' (*The Great Tradition*, 218).

[42]   See Jameson, *The Political Unconscious*, 267–9, on the metaphysical and the melodramatic in *Lord Jim*.

[43]   Even in the later fiction, *Victory* (1915), the tale resembles more and more a thriller.

the demands of the imperial subject to endorse the 'ideology of patriotic heroism' (White, 81), and maintain the putative superiority of the white man over the 'savage'. Subversion of the genre's expectations, however, was already emerging in Stevenson and Rider Haggard in their questioning the dangers to indigenous peoples of the white man's ignorance, the commercial exploitation, the right to export civilization at home to the colonies when morality was breaking down, and the recognition of the 'essential kinship with savagery' of western imperialists – an idea that we also see in *Heart of Darkness*, and one developed by Freud.[44] As White puts it: 'While profoundly influenced by the travel writing and the adventure fiction of his time and by many of the ideals revealed and espoused in those works, he [Conrad] would challenge many of the convention's assumptions, affording and necessitating new ways of viewing the imperial subject' (White, 107–8). And it is here in his philosophical and formal interrogation of the colonial field and its representation that Conrad goes further than his Victorian predecessors.

However, to what extent does Conrad achieve ideological resolution in his critique of the subject? For it appears he is not working through a political discourse but instead – as modernist – displaces the issue onto the aesthetic level. Conrad's fictional narratives, like those of Henry James, are characterized by shifting perspectives that limit the real to what is seen or subjectively perceived. And this is fundamental to Conrad's writing, where, as in impressionism, 'reality became image' (*The Political Unconscious*, 239). Moreover, description and narration are consonant. As Peters explains: 'narrative methodology emphasizes the subjectivity of knowledge and the impossibility of knowing anything for certain' (*The Cambridge Introduction to Conrad*, 65–6). While attempting to tell Jim's story, the novel undermines the heroic potential of the content through problematizing storytelling itself at formal (its achronology and different versions) and epistemological levels (what can really be known).[45] Jim may want his romance adventure, and Conrad his nostalgia for the simplicities of the travel and adventure story tradition or the challenge of sailing ships; but the novel speaks against their possibility in the age of modernism.

The Land and the Places

Writing about journeys also entails writing about places. Writer-travellers focus on place in their travel writing and topography plays a significant role in their fiction – as all the writers in this study demonstrate. Paul Kirchner wrote of 'Conrad's topographical eye' (224), and clearly Conrad's work has a strong sense of place. His stories have specific locations, places Conrad himself knew during his life as seaman. Principally, the Malay Archipelago in *Almayer's Folly*, *An Outcast of the Islands*, *Lord Jim* and *Victory*; the Congo in 'An Outpost of Progress' and *Heart of Darkness*; South America in the 'Costaguana' of *Nostromo*.

---

44   See White, chapter 4.

45   The last paragraph of the novel significantly poses the question: 'Who knows?'

And then there are the cities: London in the last chapter of *The Nigger of the 'Narcissus'*, and in the frame narrative of *Heart of Darkness*, in *The Secret Agent*, and in *Chance*; 'Sulaco' in *Nostromo*; and St. Petersburg and Geneva in *Under Western Eyes*. Although Conrad also went to India, there is no 'Indian novel' as there is in E.M. Forster's work (discussed in the next chapter).[46] Nevertheless, Conrad's novels and stories are rich in the evocation and symbolism of place; and where I focussed on the uses of the sea and the sailing ship in an earlier section of this chapter, it is now time to discuss stories of the land and the places – the coasts and estuaries, tropical forests, islands and remote places upriver, mountains and harbours; and also cities – in the next section – whose streets are mapped by characters walking, and where Conrad locates the degeneration of western man much discussed at the *fin de siècle*.

Conrad's first reviewers praised the new worlds that his stories presented to 'the untravelled reader' (cit. in White, 117). Such a reader was fascinated by travel stories with exotic locations. For the reader today, there are editions of the novels with maps to supplement Conrad's topographical descriptions. Sometimes these descriptions are evocative:

> The coast of Patusan ... is straight and sombre, and faces a misty ocean. Red trails are seen like cataracts of rust streaming under the dark-green foliage of bushes and creepers clothing the low cliffs. Swampy plains open out at the mouth of rivers, with a view of jagged blue peaks beyond the vast forests. In the offing a chain of islands, dark, crumbling shapes, stand out in the everlasting sunlit haze like the remnants of a wall breached by the sea. (*Lord Jim*, 176)

This is landscape empty of agency. It is given priority in Conrad, as if place itself has character enough. And Conrad's insistence that nature is immense and overwhelms or crushes man brings him closer to naturalism than romanticism. The motif of nature's powerful presence is recurrent as Marlow imagines Jim's upriver journey: 'At the first bend he lost sight of the sea with its labouring waves for ever rising, sinking, and vanishing to rise again – the very image of struggling mankind – and faced the immovable forests rooted deep in the soil, soaring towards the sunshine, everlasting in the shadowy might of their tradition, like life itself' (*LJ*, 177). Topography becomes metaphor, lending nature a greater significance than mere setting or geography. Moreover, the character of place is clearly signified as exotic, like the tropical climate ever present in *Almayer's Folly*: 'motionless there in the oppressive calm of the tropical night she [Nina] could see at each flash of lightning the forest lining both banks of the river, bending before the furious blast of the coming tempest' (*AF*, 19); or the sudden sunset in the tropics: 'the sun

---

[46]   Eloise Knapp Hay also raises the issue of the absence of Conrad's India novel: 'I wondered why it was that Conrad never once wrote about India, the jewel in the crown of his adoptive homeland ... We know from letters Conrad wrote in Calcutta between November 1885 and January 1886 that he was there during the very months of the Berlin Conference, when England signed on as a party to trade agreements "opening up" the Congo to fourteen Western nations, including herself' (127).

dipped sharply, as if ashamed of being detected in any sympathizing attitude, and the clearing, which during the day was all light, became suddenly all darkness' (*AF*, 137); and the flora and fauna: 'There, on the edge of a banana plantation, a clump of palms and mango trees formed a shady spot' (*AF*, 54). Sometimes the topography is the location for anthropological observation: 'There is a village of fisher-folk at the mouth of the Batu Kring branch of the estuary' (*LJ*, 176); and here in this remote place in the Malay Archipelago the story of Lord Jim will continue.

However, the descriptions of place are not simply guides for the untravelled reader, but function as deictic indicators, precise locations for character, thought and action. There is also a tendency to anthropomorphize nature already in Conrad's first novel: 'the merciless creepers clung to the big trunks in cable-like coils ... hung in thorny festoons ... and ... carried death to their victims in an exulting riot of silent destruction' – this forest is an anti-Arcadia, a place where only parasites lived, and where the smell of decay prefigures a place of natural corruption, as Conrad works the motif of the grove of death (*AF*, 134–6). As with Conrad's seascapes, the tropical forest is not the consoling or symbiotic force, but a hostile threat to man which stands at the opposite pole to Dain's affirmative allegorical-romantic imaginary: 'Yes, when the next day broke, they would be together on the great blue sea that was like life – away from the forests that were like death' (*AF*, 137). The oppositions are first an indication of the native mind's tendency towards allegory, a version of the primitive mind so widespread in late nineteenth-century thought; but we should notice the ways in which Conrad's work reiterates such oppositions as the sea and the land, life and death, in his work – examples in *The Nigger of the 'Narcissus'* and *Chance* have already been mentioned above.

Topographical symbolism is a feature throughout Conrad's fiction. In his second novel, *An Outcast of the Islands* the location is the islands of the Eastern Archipelago, one of those 'out-of-the-way nooks of the world' (181). Conrad wrote in his 'Author's note' to the 1919 edition of the novel: 'It is certainly the most *tropical* of my eastern tales. The mere scenery got a great hold on me as I went on' (282, italics in original). Here nature is once again hostile to man's ambitions: 'oppressed by the hot smell of earth, dampness and decay in that forest which seemed to push him mercilessly back in the glittering sunshine of the river. And he would recommence paddling with tired arms to seek another opening, to find another deception' (*An Outcast of the Islands*, 52). Even the 'big trees' are 'indifferent in the immense solidity of their life, which endures for ages, to that short and fleeting life in the heart of man who crept painfully amongst their shadows in search of refuge from the unceasing reproach of his thoughts' (53).

Although Conrad draws on tropical settings and exotic images familiar from the travel and adventure story tradition – Lingard 'loved it all: the landscapes of brown golds and brilliant emeralds' (*An Outcast of the Islands*, 154) – place and landscape are at first independent of the characters, and then form significant objects of perception evoking frames of mind and emotional states. In this sense nature allows Conrad to go beyond the generic limits of adventure travel writing by refusing the setting as pliant playground for the intrepid explorer-adventurer, just as he allows encounters between westerners and indigenous characters to the disadvantage or detriment of the white man in a place where 'strength and resolution, body and mind alike were helpless' (67) – themselves key western values. Sometimes Conrad takes things much further by getting Willems trapped in a tropical storm of apocalyptic proportions where the 'mighty downpour' transforms the world into 'a deluge', bringing together the native mindset and the western with references to 'a wrathful and threatening discourse of an angry god' and the allusion to the Biblical Flood (218). And towards the end of the novel the sunset itself implies a sense of ending, a reading encouraged by Willems himself: 'he would look at the glow of gold passing away amongst the sombre clouds in a bright red flush, like a splash of warm blood. It seemed to him ominous and ghastly with a foreboding of violent death that beckoned him from everywhere – even from the sky' (257). The death motif recurs throughout the pages leading up to Willems being shot.

From the start, then, Conrad's travel fictions are subversive of the uses of place in traditional adventure writing because the Gauguin-like exotic locations allow him to render savagery, as Chris Bongie argues, as 'a state of nature, more or less empty of its cultural content' (135). It is here, far away from home, where the white man is exposed and degenerates into a state beyond restraint. In *Heart of Darkness* we read of the African forest: 'The great wall of vegetation, an exuberant and entangled mass of trunks, branches, leaves, boughs, festoons, motionless in the moonlight, was like a rioting invasion of soundless life, a rolling wave of plants, piled up, crested, ready to topple over the creek, to sweep every little man of us out of his little existence' (*HD*, 54). Here the landscape is a kind of rough sea, and the metonymies of place overwhelm the reader, too – what F.R. Leavis famously criticized as Conrad's 'adjectively insistence' (*The Great Tradition*, 204). Nature itself is out of control; it is not the English landscape or garden of the pastoral tradition. In *Lord Jim*, Marlow is going home, 'to meet the spirit that dwells within the land, under its sky, in its air, in its valleys, on its rises, in its fields, in its waters and its trees'; a landscape and a land to which he is 'rooted', whose 'spirit' begins 'above the white cliffs of Dover' (*LJ*, 160–61). In this opposition of landscapes lies the cultural difference with which the traveller has to come to terms in the exotic places of the colonial field – an opposition in Forster's representation of India too, discussed in the next chapter.[47] However, in Conrad's fiction alien places are sometimes nearer home. The city is a place of moral depravity and degeneration; and it is to Conrad's cities that I now turn.

Conrad's Cities

The cities in Conrad's fiction range from Amsterdam as a focus of Almayer's and Willems's longing for 'civilization' in Conrad's first two novels; to Sulaco in *Nostromo*, that 'exemplary Hispano-American city' (Berthoud, 147), and its

---

[47] For further discussion of Conrad's exotic places as colonial archive see Christopher GoGwilt, 'Joseph Conrad as Guide to Colonial History' in John G. Peters, ed., *A Historical Guide to Joseph Conrad*, 137–61.

implicit counterpart, San Francisco from where Holroyd's finance comes; and then St. Petersburg and Geneva in *Under Western Eyes*. But I will focus on London, because it has a significant topographical presence in a number of Conrad's novels, and is a relocation of his critique of modernity from the African to the urban jungle.

When Marlow begins his story in *Heart of Darkness*, he challenges the first narrator's triumphal history of conquest: 'the great knights-errant of the sea' sailed from London, 'the adventurers and the settlers', down the Thames to build empires (*HD*, 17). For Marlow instead, London 'has been one of dark places of the earth', where the Romans brought their civilization to a savage place, a place of 'darkness' (*HD*, 158–9). History repeats itself, as the contemporary imperialists are now the conquerors of the earth. But the darkness persists in London, and this motif will return in Conrad's other fiction, like *The Secret Agent*, where the centre of the Empire, London, is a seedy, run-down place of murky backstreets and dubious characters, of ineffectual secret agents and a web of anarchists and police informers. Moreover, where Africa was commonly understood as the place of primitive tribes and savage customs, Conrad's London is now itself a place of depravity and degeneration – and here he represents key debates in the late nineteenth century which had begun to question the state of the 'race' and its fitness to rule the world.[48]

London first appears in the last chapter of *The Nigger of the 'Narcissus'* as a death-haunted place, a counterpart to the life-force of the sea for the crew; the Thames as 'the dark River', a mythic river of the dead (*NN*, 107). The docks are smoky and sooty with black barges drifting on 'the murky stream', and a 'jumble of begrimed walls loomed up vaguely in the smoke, bewildering and mournful, like a vision of disaster' (101–2). Images of sooty, 'grimy houses' (*NN*, 107) recall the London of Blake and William Booth. Similarly, in the London of *Chance* there are poor people rushing about 'with the continuous dreary shuffling of weary footsteps on the flagstones. The sunshine falling on the grimy surfaces …' (*Chance*, 159) in the novel that sets the 'shore people' (vulnerable, gullible, cynical and predatory) against those who go to sea (242–3). However, Conrad's most sustained depiction of London, what Robert Hampson calls, 'an exactly conceived topography' (174) of one of those 'dark places' is in *The Secret Agent*.

Hampson writes: '*The Secret Agent* is Conrad's most wide-ranging engagement with London: a quick enumeration of locations gives some sense of the mapping of London that is implicit in the narrative' – a range from Vauxhall Bridge Road to Piccadilly, and on to Soho (Verloc's shop) to Islington through Whitehall and Westminster; then on to Greenwich, and the Old Kent Road; Knightsbridge, Charing Cross; Westminster Bridge, and Waterloo Station, Victoria, and Sloane Square, in a mapping of a city 'that shades from specificities

---

[48] 'Perhaps we could say that for Conrad city life is, at best, trivial and de-humanizing; in worse aspects, it is ugly, squalid, even chaotic … Cities as centres of "gracious living" do not figure in Conrad's work' (McLauchlan, 57).

to indeterminacies' (Hampson, 169). From the start London is its dark, foggy and rain-soaked streets.[49] Verloc lives in 'one of those grimy brick houses' (*SA*, 3) hidden away in 'the shades of the sordid street seldom touched by the sun, behind the dim shop with its wares of disreputable rubbish' (29), behind which his house was 'nestling in a shady street … where the sun never shone' (189). London is depicted from its streets as a place of 'topographical mysteries', yet Verloc knows his street map well (11); as does the anarchist Professor who walks the streets with a bomb strapped to him, 'lost in the crowd' (61); and later 'Comrade' Ossipon walks London mapping it street by street, passing Westminster Abbey, Victoria, Sloane Square and on Waterloo bridge his attention is caught by the river, 'a sinister marvel of still shadows and flowing gleams mingling below in a black silence' (*SA*, 219), as Conrad keeps the motif of darkness in circulation, with 'perspectives of shadowy houses' seen in the dull yellow light of gas lamps. Ossipon walks on 'through monotonous streets with unknown names where the dust of humanity settles inert and hopeless out of the stream of life' (220). The novel ends with the image of potential suicide bomber, the Professor, an unsuspected terrorist walking amongst 'the odious multitude of mankind' prepared to blow himself up in a gesture of destruction – a figure of anarchy from whom Conrad distances himself through irony.

The London of *The Secret Agent* – like the Geneva of *Under Western Eyes* – is mapped through its streets. Conrad's walkers in the city transform the streets into geometrical spaces focalized through the gaze of specific characters with all the implications of desire and misrecognition as the other comes into view. Topographical symbolism lends the urban landscape meaning with a mythic or universal implication in the Conradian thematic that this chapter has been elucidating.[50] Conrad's narratives thus have what Michel de Certeau calls 'spatial trajectories' – whether in the representation of the topographies of the sea, the landscape of the African forest, the remote trading post upriver in the Malay Archipelago, or the modern metropolis – they are in each case 'a spatial practice' (115).

The city has replaced nature as the oppressive force, suffocating its inhabitants, indifferent to its ideals and plans. It is a symbolic topography for a world in the grip of modernity, which Conrad, like many of his contemporaries, sees as a cultural crisis. This particular setting creates an atmosphere of mistrust and threat through the play of tensions, silences, deceptions, impulsive actions, fears

---

[49]   The Assistant Commissioner, one of many walkers in the streets in this novel, 'advanced at once into an immensity of greasy slime and damp plaster interspersed with lamps, and enveloped, oppressed, penetrated, choked, and suffocated by the blackness of a wet London night, which is composed of soot and drops of water' (*The Secret Agent*, 110). Further page references abbreviated as *SA* in text.

[50]   For example, there is in the contrast of streets that allude to a wider Conradian symbolism, as Malcolm Bradbury put it: 'the city of light and of darkness, the facades of order in the harsh light set against the underlying anarchy and exposure in the dark shades of the East End' ('London 1890–1920', 182).

and anxieties. Moreover, the narrative and its descriptions are precisely located in characters whose gaze and point of view are the source of the text, without any direct authorial intrusion. Conrad's position is always only implicit because enabled by the subtleties of irony located in the interplay of character thoughts and misunderstanding; and the disjunction between event and narrating, where the reader is apprised of knowledge while characters remain ignorant. The whole story of the bombing and Stevie's death is a case in point. There is also a disjunction between mental and clock time in the scenes when Winnie murders Verloc, and its after-effect on her state of mind. In all this, Conrad is modernist in theme and form, even when playing on the expectations of the popular sensationalist and detective fiction. Once again Conrad's modernism is characterized by narrative experiment with residual discourses. If, in *The Secret Agent*, London is a seedy, disturbing and dangerous place; it is familiar in its detail yet unfamiliar in the shifting perspectives that rely on characters' estranging psychology for their truth. Framed by Conrad's irony, these shifting personalized truths have hardly any solidity to them. Indeed, Conrad uses the characters' unusual perspectives – an ensemble of hysterias, paranoias and a whole range of other pathologies – to further estrange the topography, thus effectively defamiliarizing London.

An important context for the story about criminality, anarchy and revolutionary ideas for the first readers of Conrad's novel is the widespread fear of 'degeneracy'. One of the key figures in the degeneracy debate mentioned in *The Secret Agent* was Cesare Lombroso[51] whose belief that delinquency and degeneracy were biologically hereditary and would be visible in the physical features of the person was widespread in the late nineteenth century. After Lombroso it was commonly believed that physical appearance and irrational or antisocial behaviour prove degeneracy, and that this was a threat to the health of the race. In Conrad's novel, Ossipon recognizes Stevie and later Winnie Verloc as 'degenerates'. Significantly, Stevie's semi-autistic and obsessive drawing of circles represents an abstract and enigmatic modern art, itself seen as symptomatic of degeneracy. Representative of this view is Max Nordau, who in his popular book *Degeneration* (1895) wrote: 'Our epoch of history is unmistakably in its decline and another is announcing its approach. There is a sound of rending in every tradition ... Forms lose their outlines, and are dissolved in floating mist ... And in the artistic products of the age we see the form in which dreams become sensible' (5–6). In the last chapter Ossipon and the anarchist Professor offer their own proto-fascist solution to this state of the culture: to exterminate 'the weak, the flabby, the silly, the cowardly, the faint of heart, and the slavish of mind', to exterminate the 'great multitude' (*Degeneration*, 222) who represent conventional morality and the general mediocrity. This kind of extreme solution to the decline in the perceived purity of the race would lead to the deadly serious ideas of eugenics and genocide. Such extremism was also expressed

---

[51]   Cesare Lombroso (1836–1909), who between 1862 and his death in 1909 had held professorships in mental diseases, forensic medicine, psychiatry and criminal anthropology. Lombroso argued in his study, *Delinquent Man (L'uomo deliquente)* (1875) for the existence of a criminal type, clearly recognizable and distinguishable from the normal person.

by Kurtz in *Heart of Darkness* who wished to 'exterminate all the brutes!' (*HD*, 84) But now we are in the heart of London. The Professor's destructive act is meant to be regenerative. But in the closing words of *The Secret Agent* Conrad leaves us in no doubt where he stands: 'Nobody looked at him. He passed on unsuspected and deadly, like a pest in the street full of men' (*SA*, 227).

By the end of the nineteenth and throughout the early decades of the twentieth century, as Lyn Pykett explains, 'social, literary and psychological debates were dominated by the language of degeneration and by the question of whether modern European society was progressing or declining' (*Engendering Fictions*, 27).[52] The discourse of degeneration is an important context for the literature of the late nineteenth century and the Edwardian period. It derives from a popularized form of Darwinism which gave scientific credence to the superiority of the so-called advanced civilizations, and was called upon to legitimize the colonization of the so-called primitive peoples. But by the end of the nineteenth century doubts and fears were being voiced. As Frank Kermode explains:

> There were signs of a more critical attitude to the past, a developing habit of national self-examination. The fragility of Empire had become more evident after the Boer War. The educated conscience had discovered the poor, whose plight, like that of women, troubled the liberal mind as much as the low standard of national health disturbed those whose property might, before long, be dependent on the country's ability to find fit men for the army. There was a powerful sense of transition, accompanied as always by mixed reactions to all the new evidence of decadence or of renovation, according to how one interpreted such signs of relaxation as the criticism of capitalism, the questioning of conventional sexual morality, and the treatment in literature of previously forbidden subjects. (*Essays on Fiction*, 33–4)

Conrad's diagnosis of the cultural crisis was common enough at the time in popular fiction. Erskine Childers, *The Riddle of the Sands* (1903) expressed worries about degeneration, while still showing some confidence in the racial superiority of the British. More alarmist was H.G. Wells's *The War of the Worlds* (1897), and *The War in the Air*, a fiction about the inevitable coming of world conflict that was serialized in 1907 (the date of publication of Conrad's novel). In these condition-of-England fictions some of the crisis was blamed on foreigners. The widespread Germanophobia can be seen in a casual comment by Winnie Verloc: 'We aren't German slaves here, thank God' (*SA*, 44). And the Assistant Commissioner tells the ruthless Mr Vladimir at the Embassy that he wants to use the affair of the Greenwich bombing to start 'clearing out of this country all the foreign spies' (166).

Conrad's depiction of the more squalid side of the social environment, the places of the seamier aspects of human existence, the impoverished and the

---

[52] Contemporary studies of aspects of degeneration beside Nordau's included Lombroso's *Criminal Man* and *The Female Offender*, Lankester's *Degeneration*, Krafft-Ebing's *Psychopathia Sexualis*, Carpenter's *Civilization: Its Cause and Cure*, Havelock Ellis's *The Criminal* and *The Problems of Race Regeneration* and Freud and Breuer's *Studies in Hysteria*.

underprivileged in this novel is close to the naturalism of Emile Zola. Moreover, as in Zola, there is in Conrad's novel much melodrama and sensationalism, as well as other elements of popular fiction – the detective novel, spy thriller, clandestine meetings and shady dealings, in so much misty, gas lit night-time activity. However, the urban spaces of London, its streets and buildings, offer more than just a sinister backdrop to the machinations of the characters: 'Then the vision of an enormous town presented itself, of a monstrous town more populous than some continents and in its man-made might as if indifferent to heaven's frowns and smiles; a cruel devourer of the world's light. There was room enough there to place any story …' (*SA*, 231). But Conrad puts all that to work for a more ironic purpose. The attempt on the Observatory, for example – that centre of mean time – is, in Kermode's words, 'all the more nihilistic in that it is carried out by an idiot at the instigation of an informer whose master is a corrupt and foolish politician' (*Essays on Fiction*, 49).

Clearly, in *The Secret Agent* Conrad is neither on the side of the revolutionaries and anarchists, nor does he accept the paranoia of those who were obsessed with decadence and degeneration. His irony gives the reader a perspective or distance to these extremes. And the ironies permeate the whole novel. If the City of London is 'the very centre of the Empire on which the sun never sets' (*SA*, 157), and 'the lofty pretensions of a mankind oppressed by the miserable indignities of the weather appeared as a colossal and hopeless vanity deserving scorn, wonder, and compassion' (74), the characters themselves are unheroic, shabby and seedy figures, whose idealism is undermined by their low-life status, or their physical and moral ugliness – especially the three fat men, Verloc, Michaelis and Sir Ethelred. A key word in the text is 'indolence', and this is frequently applied to Verloc, who is described early on as having 'a sort of inert fanaticism' (10).[53] The Professor is described (through Ossipon's gaze): 'the flat cheeks, of a greasy, unhealthy complexion, were merely smudged by the miserable poverty of a thin dark whisker. The lamentable inferiority of the whole physique was made ludicrous by the supremely self-confident bearing of the individual' (46). Irony is also produced by the multiple views on the same event. The bombing incident is investigated by Chief Inspector Heat who suspects the wrong man, which creates dramatic irony because the reader already knows he is mistaken. Winnie continues to believe that Verloc was 'a very good husband' (128), and that Stevie 'would go through fire' for him (135); she even encourages Verloc to 'take that boy out' with him (136), thus unwittingly colluding in his tragic death. 'Comrade' Ossipon

---

[53] 'Indolence' is a key word in the colonial archive, but one usually applied to the natives. In *Heart of Darkness* Marlow appears to collude with the colonialist mindset in the attitude towards the black African native when endorsing the Company's Chief Accountant's attitude to the native's 'distaste for the work' (washing and ironing his clothes) (36–7); an attitude seen everywhere in Marlow's descriptions of 'Black shapes' that 'crouched, lay, sat between the trees' (34), blaming the 'lazy' natives for what he calls 'the great demoralisation of the land' (36). However, once again, I would insist that this attitude is not simply attributable to Conrad himself.

continues to suppose that it is Verloc who has been blown up, until he stumbles across his body after Winnie has stabbed him. And her suicide is reported as an anecdote in a newspaper read out by Ossipon in the last chapter, thus reducing its significance to a sensationalist anecdote.

Conrad wrote in the 'Author's Note' to the 1920 edition: 'Even the purely artistic purpose, that of applying an ironic method to a subject of that kind, was formulated with deliberation and in the earnest belief that ironic treatment alone would enable me to say all I felt I would have to say in scorn as well as in pity' (*SA*, 232). The irony, but also the psychological realism, the unconventional narrative structure, and the larger moral and philosophical concerns belong to the modernist credentials of *The Secret Agent*. Conrad's London may have been 'prompted in part by Dickens' creative achievement in *Bleak House*', as Cedric Watts claims (27),[54] but it also belongs to the context of Conrad's critique of modernity and imperialism, not least with the bombing attempt on Greenwich, the centre of 'mean time', 'the first meridian' (26), indeed, the symbol of Britain's 'chronological imperialism' (Watts, 28).

Conclusion

The study of place and space in the city leads inevitably back to the critique of the modern subject in the colonial field of Conrad's narratives of the sea and tropical places, travel stories in the wider sense whose narrative structures correspond to the trajectory of the journey, as in *The Nigger of the 'Narcissus'* or in *Heart of Darkness*; or the traveller's tale with its meanderings and digressions, as in *Lord Jim*. Moreover, as this chapter has shown, real travel is meant to be an adventure to remote places – places representing the colonial archive, and where the subject is challenged in the encounter with the other. The dominant paradigm for the narrative of the journey is the quest; a paradigm at its most evocative in the novella, *Heart of Darkness* with Marlow's search for Kurtz; but also in the search for the whereabouts of Jim in *Lord Jim*. In both cases, journeys towards the other give the narrative the structure of travel stories, supplemented by stories about the sought-for protagonist which themselves travel – circulating rumours, tales of hearsay or legends. Conrad's storytelling is frequently characterized by the focus on a single enigmatic character whose actions and motives are the subject of the narrative – from Almayer and Willems in the first two Malay novels, to James Wait on the Narcissus, the illustrious 'Capitaz de Cargadores' Nostromo, Verloc in *The Secret Agent*, and Razumov in *Under Western Eyes*, Flora de Barral in *Chance* and Axel Heyst in *Victory*.

---

[54] For further discussion of the uses and revisions of Dickens's London in Conrad's novel see Hugh Epstein, 'A Pier-Glass in the Cavern: The Construction of London in *The Secret Agent*' in *Conrad's Cities*, 176–82. See also Terry Eagleton, who comments that: 'The naturalistic style of the novel presents us with a slimy, foggy Dickensian London populated by grotesque, slow-moving, object-like figures …' (*The English Novel*, 252).

This chapter has looked at Conrad's uses of the popular tradition of adventure and travel writing – his residual realism – for a modernist critique of the imperial subject. *Heart of Darkness* is probably his most well-known narrative, and a summa of the complexities of the Conradian storytelling, which produces a critique of imperialism while at the same time deconstructing the processes of getting the story told. Moreover, the process of reading is mirrored in Marlow's journey upriver with its hazards and snags, its disorientation and the force of its quest for the meaning of Kurtz. The difficulties of storytelling spill over into problems of knowledge and truth, which align Conrad with other modernist writers. In this respect *Heart of Darkness* might be compared to that other end-of-an-era story, Thomas Mann's *Death in Venice* (1912). Yet, Conrad's work seems to correspond to two phases of modernism: early modernism characterized by its philosophical critique of modernity; and late modernism characterized by the problematic of representation as Conrad tried to capture the instability of the subjective apprehension of the world, and in the framed narrative which demonstrates, as David Harvey puts it, 'the impossibility of representing the world in a single language. Understanding had to be constructed through the exploration of multiple perspectives' (30).[55] Conrad's work, like other modernists, belongs to the Nietzschean debate about transvaluation of values, a cultural crisis of modernity and one often expressed in the apocalyptic Spenglerian terms of cultural decline.[56] Culture in this sense is synonymous with civilization. There is in the early twentieth century nihilist tendencies in a whole series of fictions: *Heart of Darkness*, *Death in Venice* and *A Passage to India* – all travel narratives.

The collapse of the Victorian values of Civilization and Progress was seen through the lens of social Darwinism, and represented in Conrad's ironic take on degeneration in *The Secret Agent*. However, thinking through the perceived crisis of civilization has broader implications in Conrad. The journey itself has archetypal overtones – a journey from civilization into pre-civilized instincts, or the primitive drives of the unconscious. 'Going up that river was like travelling back to the earliest beginnings of the world' (*HD*, 59). The 'distant kinship' (85) with the 'primitive savage' represents for Marlow a deep primordial memory that reminds the civilized world of its ancestry, seen in the story about the deterioration of European man in the wilderness of Africa – the western evolutionary idea of primitive ancestry that became popular by the late nineteenth century.[57] Moreover, although some modernists celebrated primitivism (D.H. Lawrence in particular), and anthropology exposed ethnocentricity, Conrad, like Freud, supported the growing belief that savagery was beneath the surface of western 'civilization'.

---

[55]   I discussed the idea of early and late modernism in the Introduction.

[56]   Oswald Spengler, *The Decline of the West* (1918). I return to Spengler in the discussion of D.H. Lawrence's *Twilight in Italy* (1916) in Chapter 3.

[57]   '… but what thrilled you was just the thought of their humanity – like yours – the thought of your remote kinship with this wild and passionate uproar'. *Heart of Darkness*, 63. Freud discusses the 'phylogenetic acquisitions of the Id' in *The Ego and the Id* (1923), reprinted in *The Penguin Freud Library* 11 (London: Penguin, 1984), 390; see also 376–9.

Unconscious destructive drives had destabilizing effects on the confidence in the colonialist subject-object relationship, an effect represented in modernist art and literature (and one in Forster too, discussed in the next chapter). Moreover, Homi K. Bhabha's 'mimic man', a colonized subject-position as transculturated hybrid identity, has undermined the unity of the other which was so important to the coherence of imperialist ideology.[58] The drive to civilize the 'dark continent' manifests itself in the fear of degeneration at home: 'going native' insinuates itself in the popular imagination through literature and travel tales, threatening widespread miscegenation and the degeneration of the race. Eugenics is the outcome of this fear – as we saw in *The Secret Agent.*

If degeneration is an effect of travel in the colonial field, the only restraint left in the text is the aesthetic one: all those devices of distancing, indeterminacy and epistemological doubts, that enable the reader to be provoked by the text; a decisive, extra layer of critique that functions predominantly on the aesthetic plane, making questions of representation part of the text's surplus of meaning.[59] The text establishes an internal interrogation of its colonialist ground, whereby, as Benita Parry explains, 'moral confidence and certainty (hymned by Kipling as Law, Order, Duty and Restraint, Obedience and Discipline) are disrupted by the ambiguities, doubts, anxieties and alienations of a stylistic modernism' (55). If Marlow at times seems to be Rudyard Kipling, he does not evade the irony of the implied author. As Robert Hampson put it: 'Conrad's objectification of Marlow's narrative, his distanced representation of Marlow's representations, opens *Heart of Darkness* on to a critical reading of its range of late-Victorian discursive practices and creates the possibility for the reader of going beyond the narrator's conceptual and ideological limitations' (Introduction to *Heart of Darkness*, xxxvii–xxxviii). The complexity and undecidability of *Heart of Darkness* is situated somewhere in the relationship between the colonialist work and the modernist text. Conrad signals his critical intent by exposing the discourses that define the historical limits of Marlow's first addressees who represent the British colonial establishment, and either give up listening to Marlow's tale or refuse to accept his criticisms.[60]

Heart of Darkness has a counter-hegemonic potential because its modernism deconstructs imperialism. The writing and the narrative strategies undermine certainties, which include the values and truths that are called upon to legitimate the imperialist project while unwittingly revealing its racist implications: 'Instead of affirming the opposition of darkness and light, civilized and savage, Marlow's narrative works to destabilize it: darkness is located at the heart of the civilizing mission' (Hampson, xxxiv). But even the descriptive style of impressionism – and

---

[58] Anne McClintock writes of 'the savage who was fireman', the man who works the ship's boiler in *Heart of Darkness* as an example of a 'hybrid mimic man'. See *Imperial Leather: Race, Gender and Sexuality in the Colonial Conquest*, 65–6. For Homi K. Bhabha's discussion of hybridity and mimicry see *The Location of Culture*, 85–92.

[59] See Edward Said, 'Intellectuals in the Post-colonial World'.

[60] When Marlow gets carried away one of the listeners interrupts him: 'Try to be civil, Marlow' (*Heart of Darkness*, 60).

one that dominates Conrad's several novels and stories as we have seen in this chapter – is only a 'surface truth', an attention to the shine and texture of things at first sight. It is not concerned with depth, but like the perception of landscape locates the gaze on the object so that the impression remains in the imaginary and does not get through to the real itself: 'When you have to attend to things of that sort, to the mere incidents of the surface, the reality – the reality, I tell you – fades' (*HD*, 60). The implication here is that the western gaze is preconditioned through its own perception codes (impressionism as an art form that challenged realism), and like the totems essential to Marlow of 'devotion to efficiency' (20), 'backbone', 'keeping up appearances' (36), and 'restraint' (71), they cannot in the end conceal the fact that they are constructions that are unable to save a man from himself, and are only effective by fiat.

The details of close reading have confirmed the character of Conrad's modernism. In a letter to William Blackwood (31 May 1902) Conrad himself claimed: 'I am *modern*, and I would rather recall Wagner the musician and Rodin the sculptor who both had to starve a little in their day – and Whistler the painter who made Ruskin the critic foam at the mouth with scorn and indignation. They have arrived. They had to suffer for being "new"' (cit. in Najder, 321, emphasis in original). And yet, as Patrick Brantlinger argued, Conrad also 'mourns the loss of true faith in modern times, the closing down of frontiers, the narrowing of the possibility for adventure, the commercialization of the world and of art, the death of chivalry and honour' (*Rule of Darkness*, 274). We know that Conrad lamented the modern development of steamships: 'The taking of a modern steamship about the world ... has not the same quality of intimacy with nature ... the single-handed struggle with something much greater than yourself' (*The Mirror and the Sea*, 30–31). Conrad appears to demonstrate what David Punter has described as a paradox in 'the complex structure of modernity', namely 'a certain kind of nostalgia, a moment of regret for that which is superseded ... within the onset of the new' (*Modernity*, 6).

As I have been arguing in this chapter, Conrad exposes the doubts and contradictions in the convention of travel and adventure stories for the modern reader. Conrad's travel stories signal a change that was already occurring in the paradigmatic travel-adventure-discovery tale: a loss of confidence in its heroic substance. Admittedly, in *Heart of Darkness* Marlow imagines his hero, Kurtz as an adventure-traveller: 'It was a distinct glimpse: the dug-out, four paddling savages, and the lone white man turning his back suddenly on the headquarters, on relief, on thoughts of home – perhaps; setting his face towards the depth of the wilderness, towards his empty and desolate station' (*HD*, 57). In the end, though, this turns out to be a boy's adventure story that is far from the truth of Kurtz. It is nostalgia on the part of the author for the simpler tale. Marlow insist that the best that one can hope for is 'some knowledge of yourself' (*HD*, 113). This dictum might also stand for the goal of travel in Conrad's sceptical world; a world where the older ways of travel and the older ways of storytelling are, for him, regrettably no longer possible in the age of modernism and modernity.

Chapter 2
E.M. Forster:
The Heuristic Value of Travel and Place

Introduction

In 1895 Forster travelled abroad for the first time. Equipped with his reading of Ruskin on church architecture, he toured the churches of Normandy, accompanied by his mother, and kept a travel journal of his impressions – impressions not just of the sights but of the fellow-tourists, those awful English abroad he would satirize in his fiction. However, his very first writing, at 15 (a year before his first trip abroad), was a memoir of the house where he spent his childhood, 'Rooksnest', which would be the model for Howards End, and which he later called the house of 'my childhood and safety' (cit. in Furbank, vol. 1, 16). A quintessentially English place, the garden running into a meadow and a neighbouring farm where Forster played as a child, 'its very ordinary Englishness', as Wendy Moffat put it, 'made it mystical, tied as it was to a past that was rapidly being eroded by the growth of suburban London. The walk to the village was about a mile. In the meadow beside the house was an ancient wych-elm' (*A Great Unrecorded History*, 28). Always remembered with a sense of loss, the house would be replaced by a series of surrogate homes, from a villa at Tunbridge Wells – where he would experience 'oppressive English suburban life' recaptured as Sawston in the novel *Where Angels Fear to Tread* (Furbank, 57) – to 'Harham' in Weybridge, and from 1924 Abinger House, West Hackhurst in rural Surrey; until finally after the death of his mother in 1945, he was offered rooms in Kings College where he spent the rest of his days and accepted the idea of being 'homeless'.

This chapter addresses the tension in Forster's life and work between home and travel, between a longing for a house of his own in the English countryside and wanderlust – a tension characteristic of the modernist writer, where leaving home, exile and rootlessness lead to a critique of the home culture, but also a sense of loss. The perspective gained from being abroad positioned Forster – and the other writers discussed in this study – to see the cultural crisis of modernity at home with critical distance. The modernist identity problematic comes into greater focus by the reflection on place and belonging brought about by travel and displacement. In Forster's fiction houses are important; but so are landscape and the land as the roots of a culture, both ancient and enduring.[1] The English landscape in Forster's writing acts as a measure of value for the description of landscapes in other countries. One

---

[1]   Forster owned Piney Copse, a piece of woodland in the Surrey countryside, which he bought with the money made from sales of *A Passage to India*. See 'My Wood' (1926), in *Abinger Harvest*, 21–4.

such iconic landscape is Figsbury Rings, the Iron Age earthworks in Wiltshire, which he visited for the first time in September 1904 on a solitary walking tour. Such remote parts of the English landscape were the destination for his several walking tours – Dartmoor, the Chilterns or the Sussex Downs are other examples. Through them Forster develops a sense of the land beneath the landscape, its ancient rocks and the history that lies in them as the location of the 'real England', where there is evidence of a once close relationship between man and nature, and a countryside unspoilt by modernity. Sometimes these places are magical or uncanny, like an isolated copse or woodland. The Forsterian landscape is a focus in the discussion of the stories and novels in this chapter, Figsbury Rings playing a key role in *The Longest Journey*.[2] Landscapes are important as topographical symbolism for all the writers discussed in this study. For Forster, however, the Wiltshire landscape 'remained haunted by my fictional ghosts' (cit. in Furbank, vol. 1, 149). There is a tradition of literary men romanticizing the countryside in long walks, from Wordsworth to A.E. Houseman (Moffat, 72). On one of his walking tours Forster goes on 'a personal pilgrimage, following the route of rural place-names in A.E. Houseman's elegiac *A Shropshire Lad*' (Moffat, 91). Literary tourism is a feature of his travels in England and abroad and also plays a role in his stories and novels, as it does in the other travel writing and travel stories discussed in this study.[3]

Despite Forster's deep interest in the English landscape, once enchanted by Italy, or India, the return home was always at first a depressing experience. After his second tour of India (1921), 'he felt no enthusiasm at seeing the cliffs of England again' (Furbank, vol. 2, 105). His travels abroad always made him more critical of England, which would seem 'tighter and tinier', and he would long to leave home again and 'sprawl over continents' (Furbank, vol. 2, 18). This is in 1915 when the idea of the limits of home are, of course, made worse by the war, and the restrictions on travel – a situation that Lawrence would also experience. Italy, by contrast, was from the first visit (1901–1902) a liberating place: 'The beautiful country where … things happen.[4] Forster was concerned about the limits of England and the English national character from the very start of his writing

---

[2]   The ancient English landscape is also important to D.H. Lawrence, as we will see in the following chapter. Interestingly, Lawrence accompanied Forster on a walking tour of the Downs in 1915. Forster would return there once more in June 1964 with William Golding. For further discussion of Forster's development of a 'passion for the English landscape' see Furbank, vol. 1, 116–17.

[3]   See Nicola J. Watson's *The Literary Tourist*. Late in life Forster himself becomes an object of literary tourism in Cambridge: 'Now that he was known to reside in Cambridge, many people were burning to meet him. He was an object of pilgrimage particularly for visiting Indians' (Furbank, vol. 2, 277). Literary tourism, however, is not always a positive development. In Forster's story 'The Eternal Moment' the writer Miss Raby has made Vorta's reputation by fictionalizing the place and the subsequent literary tourism has destroyed the town's former pastoral community.

[4]   As he wrote in the early draft of *A Room with a View*, cit. in Furbank, vol. 1, 96.

life, a concern which goes beyond a contrast of landscapes to a critique of class and sexuality – including the force of the heterosexual norm – as limitations on the nature of being English.[5] Travel, in his life and fiction, is heuristic – a chance to broaden horizons and to experience life-changing senses of being for himself, and for his fictional characters in stories and novels that test the limits of realism and the-condition-of-England genre.

This chapter will first address Forster's travel writing, before going on to discuss the significance of travel in his stories and novels – especially travel to Italy and India; but also in and around England. There are three non-fictional travel books, *Alexandria*, *Pharos and Pharillon* and *The Hill of Devi*, which record his time in Egypt and India respectively. Other travel sketches exist in diaries, letters and journalism; some of this is collected in *Abinger Harvest* with particular focus on his India sojourns, and his characterization of England and Englishness.

Forster's Travel and Travel Writing

Forster's Italy

Much of his early Italian travel writing was published in the new *Independent Review*. There is no single Italian travel book; but there are stories and novels with Italian settings, so that we get Forster's Italy largely in his fiction. Letters and diaries, however, contain travel sketches, and I will be referring to some of them in what follows. It was his tutor at Cambridge, Nathaniel Wedd, who first encouraged Forster's interest in Italy, its art, architecture and literature. In October 1901 Forster left England with his mother for a year's travelling, touring Italy, Sicily and Austria. The troublesome journey was soon compensated for by 'the dazzling scenery' around the Lago di Maggiore, when 'Italy began to declare itself' (Furbank, vol. 1, 81). Travelling across borders, long delays and mislaid luggage did not make the journey easy. Once arrived at the destination, it would always take a while for the informed and sensitive English tourist to be able to respond to the place.

Forster prepared the tour well, reading up beyond necessity about the art, architecture and history; but this also created the problem that he would find it difficult to see anything that he had not expected to see.[6] But when the place

---

5   Complaining about the over-valuation of physical health through sport in English public school education Forster wrote: 'They go forth into it [the world] with well-developed bodies, fairly developed minds, and undeveloped hearts. And it is this undeveloped heart that is largely responsible for the difficulties of Englishmen abroad ... it is not that the Englishman can't feel – it is that he is afraid to feel.' 'Notes on the English Character' (1926) in *Abinger Harvest*, 4–5.

6   'I have got it up so well that nothing comes as a surprise', Forster, cit. in Furbank, vol. 1, 82.

eventually 'declared itself' he expresses the rapturous effect in the style of the Romantic Sublime:

> The scenery so magnificent I could hardly believe myself alive ... There was not only an enormous torrent in a gorge, & snow mountains in the far distance, but all the nearer hills were covered with chestnuts, acacias, and heather in flower, and the sun which was brilliant but not too strong, spread a kind of purple bloom over them. Also little villages, spread one above another in every direction, all with graceful campaniles. (Letter to his mother, 14 September 1908 in Furbank, vol. 1, 168)

The scenery is one part of the tour, as in the tradition of Italian journeys since Goethe. Another part is the pilgrimage to the tomb of the famous writer, like Dante's in Ravenna – and Forster was a literary tourist all his life;[7] and Italy he visited several times in his life, even in old age (Furbank, vol. 2, 316). Moreover, he learnt early on that one could also venture a little off the beaten track to discover 'Italian Italy' – the 'real' Italy – recommended by the better tour guides; he even considered 'writing a book on some Italian town'.[8]

Being abroad is always a mark of cultural difference in a critique of Englishness, both in terms of the repressive force of class at home and the sheer arrogance of the English abroad, witnessed in the British in India or the 'pensione' in Italy full of elderly English ladies, where he thought it no different to being in Tunbridge Wells.[9] For him, though, Italy was a place of awakening and transgression, first imagined on seeing young men walking arm in arm in public with a physical ease not possible in Edwardian England. Forster's Italian journey inspires him to work out the transgressive potential of being abroad in his fiction. Italy, and Greece, teaches Forster, as it did so many sensitive Englishmen, the classical, Southern ethos that you should 'cherish the body' as opposed to the puritanical Northern idea of penance. In Italy, as Moffat explains, Forster found that even 'the tourist venues were admirably unprudish and practical' (Moffat, 60). Italy brings his imagination alive, inspiring his writing. In Furbank's words, 'Italy, which he had been slow to love, had at last done a great thing for him. It had told him that one could live in the imagination; and he knew now for certain that he was a writer' (vol. 1, 93).

---

[7]   Goethe's *Italianische Reise* was first published in 1786 and became the paradigm of such journeys for ambitious writers. As well as meeting or being acquainted and corresponding with many of his contemporary writers, Forster made a point of visiting places of literary interest at home and abroad, like the places in Italy mentioned in Virgil, reading the lines *in situ*; or Voltaire's Ferney; or even seeing the New England landscape through Edith Wharton's *Ethan Frome*.

[8]   Furbank, vol. 1, 94. Instead a trip to San Gimignano in the Tuscan hills gave him the idea for 'Monteriano' in the novel, *Where Angels Fear to Tread* (1905).

[9]   'The hotel seemed entirely inhabited by elderly ladies ... he might have been back in Tunbridge Wells' Furbank, vol. 1, 82. These impressions of tourism are reworked in *A Room with a View* (1908).

Alexandria Past and Present

Forster's stay in Egypt during the Great War inspired no fiction as such, but a book on Alexandria, and a series of short, sometimes satirical sketches of the life there.[10] What is unusual about the Alexandria book as travel writing is that Forster insists on mapping the streets only to recreate the lost ancient city. He guides the visitor along its contemporary streets, Baedeker fashion, pointing out where the great library or lighthouse – wonders of the ancient world – once stood. The Alexandria book is a journey back in time, because Forster valued the culture and civilization of the past over and above the modern city – nostalgia for past civilizations is an index of Forster's case against modernity, as it is in the other writers in this study.

But why is ancient Alexandria a special place? To answer this question Forster distinguishes it from the rest of Egypt – 'The Alexandrians have never been truly Egyptians' (18) – founded as it was by Alexander the Great, and looking out from the beginning to the Hellenistic culture of the Mediterranean, which reached its Golden Age under Ptolemy – 'the greatest period that civilisation has ever known ... Mathematics, Geography, Astronomy, Medicine, all grew to maturity in the little space of land between the present Rue Rosette and the sea' (40). It was the coming of Christianity from 45 CE that ended the Golden Age (53). The Temple of Serapir was 'the last stronghold of Paganism against Christianity', as no one religion was deemed exclusive or superior (27–8). The Christian era is marked by 'hatred and misery', and schisms (49); and even at the time of writing Forster notices the different Churches in cosmopolitan Alexandria: Catholic, Armenian, Anglican and Coptic, as well as the Synagogue and the Mosque. However, not only is Forster accusing the early Christians of ending the Golden Age of Alexandria, but the Arab conquest from 641 CE of allowing the place to fall into ruin (54–5). Moreover, the 'physical decay that crept on her [Alexandria] in the 7th century had its counterpart in a spiritual decay' (68). The city never recovered from the thousand years of Arab rule; nor did Turkish occupation from the sixteenth to the eighteenth centuries, or the modern period from Napoleon and the subsequent British rule do anything to restore the city to its former glory. The current city authorities during Forster's stay are equally as irresponsible, for with the exception of the public gardens and the museum, 'the Municipality has scarcely risen to its historic responsibilities ... and the links with the past have been wantonly broken'. What does remain is 'the north wind and the sea ... as pure as when Menelaus, the first visitor, landed upon Ras-el-Tin, three thousand years ago' (81–2).

What the book on Alexandria reveals is Forster's attitude to history. History is a recreation from archive documents and literature. In his preface to the 1922 edition, Forster insists that his history is 'after the fashion of a pageant' (7) – 'a pageant of people and events' as Miriam Allott writes in her introduction (xl). Moreover, what makes this 'History' and 'Guide' travel writing is that it is a tour

---

[10]   In what follows I shall be referring to the single Abinger edition of *Alexandria: A History and a Guide* and *Pharos and Pharillon* first published 1922 and 1923, respectively (London: André Deutsch, 2004).

of the past with the aim to 'understand and bring alive its ancient inhabitants' (Allott, xxxvii). The 'imaginative sketch' is favoured over 'accuracy of fact' to bring 'the past to life' (Allott, xxxix). Indeed, Forster's motto is 'only through literature can the past be recovered' (38). And the figure behind this claim is the poet Constantine Cavafy – whom Forster met in Alexandria, and was then responsible for promoting in the English-speaking world. At the end of *Pharos and Pharillon*, Forster introduces Cavafy's poetry which he reads as poetry of the city and its ancestry, a literature that recovers the past. Cavafy is Alexandria's link with the past. He it is who is 'a man worthy of such a city',[11] and who has in Allott's words 'a special feeling for the city' (xv). I would add, though, that Lawrence Durrell – another writer of the city – made similar claims about Forster's book: 'In its way it is a small work of art.'[12]

It is though the 'Guide' section of the book that meticulously charts the topography, as geography becomes the key to history by creating a sense of place – a place haunted by the ghost of the ancient city. Modelled on Baedeker, Forster aims to produce a Guide for the educated tourist. Looking back later at his Alexandria book Forster made his interest in Guide Books clear:

> I have always been interested in Guide Books. For me they constitute a branch of literature which follows its own laws ... The pre-1914 Baedekers are the best Guide Books I know ... I began to think I should like to write a Guide Book to the complex city. It would have to be a History as well as a Guide, for there is not much to see at Alexandria: the past has to do full-time work if the present is to work at all.[13]

In the Guide he takes us on a walking tour through the streets, starting at the Square, indicating where to turn right or left, describing what we would see now, and what we would have seen there in ancient times. Like Joyce's Dublin in *Dubliners*, Forster's Guide is a walker's street map: 'We start from the northwest corner of the Square ... the district is picturesque ... The best way of seeing it is to wander aimlessly about' (103) – although there is nothing aimless in the directions given for getting to that part of the city. Sightseeing is carefully located;[14] yet the important sights themselves have to be imagined: 'This battered and neglected

---

[11]   Cavafy's own words cit. in Forster, 82, from the poem 'The God Abandons Antony' and referring to Mark Antony.

[12]   Words from his introduction to the British edition (1982), quoted in Allott, xli. Durrell's *Alexandria Quartet* was published 1957–1960. The American edition of Forster's book was published in 1961 to coincide with Durrell's. Allott (liv) tells us that Durrell 'carried the Guide with him as he went about the city streets', and one of Durrell's volumes makes significant reference to Cavafy. For further discussion of Forster's relationship to Cavafy see Peter Jeffreys, 'Cavafy, Forster and the Eastern Question' in *Journal of Modern Greek Studies* 19/1 May 2001, 61–87.

[13]   Reprinted talk from 1956 in Appendices, Forster, 356.

[14]   In *A Room with a View*, Lucy Honeychurch tries to use Baedeker to navigate the streets of Florence. I return to the effect of the place on her later.

little peninsula is perhaps the most interesting spot in Alexandria, for here, rising to an incredible height, once stood the Pharos Lighthouse, the wonder of the world' (111). Or: 'The walls of the Arab city used to reach the sea at this point' (134); 'Traces of ancient roads and drains have also been found here ... burial places, Ptolemaic and Roman' (135). Here as elsewhere the Guide indicates the archaeological sites, even when they are not being excavated. Some places, though, are reached by tram or train; or like the Libyan Desert on horseback: 'Half a day over the desert southward brings the rider to the Wady Natrun' (161).

Pharos and Pharillon, the final section of the book, collects Forster's Alexandrian journalism. Here he uses even more licence in his historical sketches by fictionalizing scenes; and then satirizing modern Alexandrian life. For example, in the short essay, 'Between the Sun and the Moon' he writes about the three most important streets in contemporary Alexandria, now gentrified and modernized, especially the Rue Rosette with its 'cleanliness, and the refined monotony of its architecture'; it is residential where other streets are 'tainted with utility; people use them to get something or somewhere' (243). But, as we should expect, the streets of the modern city are no match for the 'vanished glory' of their ancient counterpart which was 'lined with marble colonnades from end to end' (244). In another short piece, 'The Solitary Place', he captures the spirit of a remote place, and in so doing draws attention to the limits of Western descriptive codes:

> Delicate yet august, the country that stretches westward from the expiring waters of Lake Mariout is not easy to describe. Though it contains accredited oriental ingredients, such as camels, a mirage, and Bedouins, and though it remounts to a high antiquity, yet I cannot imagine our powerful professional novelists getting to work at it, and extracting from its quiet recesses hot tales about mummies and sin. (240)

Here Forster insists, through irony, on the otherness of the landscape, and its essential resistance to western description beyond orientalist stereotypes. It is an insistence reiterated in the novel he was working on at the time, *A Passage to India*. He continues: 'It has beat a general retreat from civilization, and the spirit of the place, without being savage, is singularly austere' (240). Forster acknowledges the limits of his own language, referring to the opposition of 'civilization' and the 'savage'; and then comparing the landscape and the climate with the Sussex Downs – a comparison of landscapes, which Forster returns to in his India novel. The sub-tropical place is different to the English countryside: 'There is nothing there of the ordered progress of the English spring, with its slow extension from wood anemones through primroses into the buttercups of June. The flowers come all of a rush' (240). But here is a quarry which is worked by modern machinery, and even though in the 'quiet persistence of the earth ... the vegetation still flowers', such solitary places will go the way of the cities – that is succumb to the process of modernity, which will be 'the triumph of civilisation' (242). Clearly Forster is using the Alexandria book to work out his critique of modernity as a loss to civilization; indeed lost civilizations are re-imagined through a journey into the past, and the cultural golden age they represent is meant to act as a bulwark against the depredations of the machine age. Some version of this anti-modernity position can be seen in all the writers in this study. Travel to archaeological sites has the purpose of confirming this attitude of mind in Forster.

Forster's India

In 1912 Forster travelled to India to research his 'Indian novel'. He had made no progress, and had been in a writing crisis since the success of *Howards End* in 1910. He would visit India again in 1921 to try and finish the novel. Both trips, however, resulted in travel writing. In 'Salute to the Orient!' (1921), Forster writes about the 'prejudices and ideals' of western travellers to the East (*Abinger Harvest*, 245–59). He acknowledges that the Orient of the Arabian Nights is important to tourism, but it leads to confusion between the 'real East' and the 'faked East'. He notes that the European ladies who go to see the Harem have 'heavy faces' because they read the place as immoral and unhygienic. As a counterweight Forster reviews contemporary literature that has dealt with the Orient showing that some enlightened writers have been more open to getting closer to the 'real East'. But it is the term itself – the 'Orient' – which is the problem, because as Edward Said would also argue in *Orientalism* (1978), the countries of the so-called Orient should be carefully differentiated; in Forster's words: 'What is the use of generalizing? Syria isn't Egypt nor Turkey Arabia' (259) – a proto-post-colonialist attitude that is also found in *A Passage to India* (1924).[15]

In 'Adrift in India' (1914) Forster begins by describing the difference between India and England, its land and landscape, the impressions of muddle and chaos for the English visitor.[16] What is unusual about Jodhpur, however, is that the English community love the place and the local people, and thus the usual 'racial question' appears to have been solved (301). It may be the influence of the spirit of the place that has brought about this situation, with its 'sense of space', romance and heroism, and its long history and mythic ways; although like Alexandria, it may 'never survive archaeology' (304). Is this then the 'real India'? In an opening paragraph omitted in the published version Forster wrote: 'This particular city ... lies outside the tourist track ... It is still without facilities or hotels. Its sights, which are amazing, have never been classified, and its palace-fortress, perhaps the most wonderful in the world, remains the spiritual possession of the men who built it.'[17] The real India, like the real Italy, exists outside the tourist experience,

---

[15]   'All through 1922, as he worked on his novel, the British empire and its misdeeds were much on Forster's mind.' Furbank, vol. 2, 111. While in Alexandria Forster was incensed by the British treatment of Egyptians writing 'an impassioned letter to the *Manchester Guardian*' objecting to 'disgraceful' and 'brutal' British policies (Moffat, 178–9). Edward Said wrote that 'the phenomenon of Orientalism as I study it here deals principally, not with a correspondence between Orientalism and Orient, but with the internal consistency of Orientalism and its ideas about the Orient (the East as career) despite or beyond any correspondence, or lack thereof, with a "real" Orient'. *Orientalism*, 5.

[16]   The short pieces in 'Adrift in India' are reprinted in *Abinger Harvest*, 295ff.

[17]   Reprinted in 'Textual Notes', 440.

for the time being. The India of Forster's day was still divided between the 'Indian native State' and 'British India'. He was fortunate to have had the opportunity to experience both, which would pay off in his Indian novel. His two visits to India were recorded in *The Hill of Devi* (1953), and it is to this text of essays and letters that I now turn before moving on to Forster's fiction.

The letters he wrote from India in 1912 reveal his state of mind both as traveller and as writer and these together with letters from a second trip to India in 1921 are collected in *The Hill of Devi* (1953). But despite the author's experience of living there amongst Indians and witnessing and participating in daily life, customs and rituals, and of course reading thoroughly about the religious culture, the novel he is trying to write does not emerge easily. In a 'Note on *A Passage to India*' Forster writes:

> I began this novel before my 1921 visit, and took out the opening chapters with me, with the intention of continuing them. But as soon as they were confronted with the country they purported to describe, they seemed to wilt and go dead and I could do nothing with them ... The gap between India remembered and India experienced was too wide. When I got back to England the gap narrowed, and I was able to resume. (*The Hill of Devi*, 238)[18]

Forster goes there to experience the real India, taking the unfinished manuscript with him on the 1921 trip; and, like Conrad writing *Heart of Darkness*, he only manages to finish the novel later back home where the creative process of reflection and fictional reconstruction is possible. To turn travel into fiction Forster requires critical distance, the familiarity of home, and the better understanding of the gap between the cultures. It is an experience that Conrad also understood; as I argued in the previous chapter travel is turned into fiction after the fact enabling the play of invention. First impressions of the traveller are sometimes driven by instinctive reactions, which reveal ingrained attitudes. Forster's letters reprinted in *The Hill of Devi* reveal similar problems of attitude under the pressures of the English addressee, as I shall explain in what follows.

Forster is a restless traveller – itself a common trope in travel writing and literature. Like Thomas Mann's closet homosexual, Gustav von Aschenbach in *Death in Venice* (1912), this impulse to travel fulfils a passionate need for an exotic landscape: 'It was simply a desire to travel; but it had presented itself as nothing less than a seizure ... His imagination ... shaped for itself a paradigm of all the wonders and terrors of the manifold earth, of all that it was now suddenly trying to envisage' (Mann, 'Death in Venice', 199–200). Here, and in Forster's text too, homo-erotic desire is expressed figuratively as a Dionysian landscape. Forster writes in a letter from 1921 (italics in original[19]):

> *Our little sacred hill, generally so brown and sulky, is painted pale green now, and yesterday was a lovely sight, for there was a great popular festivity – people*

---

[18] Subsequent page references abbreviated as *THD* in text.

[19] All the letters are printed in italics.

in bright dresses going up and down the winding paths all day. At the foot of the hill men wrestled, resembling Greek statues in so far as they wore no clothes. Most were rather ugly, but one or two beautifully formed, and their savage cries, and the sunlit hill above them, and the scarlet groups of women on its slopes, and the temple on the summit thronged with worshippers, and the elephants with freshly painted faces – well, it was all very nice. (THD, 147)

In this extract, Forster's India is a carnivalesque celebration of an un-English state of being, but finally recuperated for the English addressee – brought back under control so to speak – by the more restrained expression, 'it was all very nice'. The text of *The Hill of Devi* is prefaced with some photos one of which is 'His Highness's Private Secretary', Forster, cross-dressed with some combination of western and Indian costume. Ashish Roy, quoting James Morris, is less flattering about this get-up, seeing the image as evidence of Forster's 'half-insider status': 'once preposterously photographed, wearing a long-skirted spotted gown and a sort of oriental tam-o'-shanter, in very English laced-up shoes against a painted background of flowers and mullioned windows' ('Framing the Other', 265). Forster appears to be on a vacation from Englishness, including those restrictions back home placed on masculinity and sexuality.

Forster's stay in India enables a play at being other; writing letters home mark the limit of the game. There is what Roy calls a 'uniquely fractured address' in *The Hill of Devi*, and it represents Forster's ambivalence towards the colonial other. But it is also 'fractured' in the textual sense too: with its letters from 1912–1913, and then from 1921, interspersed with other texts: photos, essays on politics ('The State and its Ruler'), explanations of the context and situation of the letters, a Note on *A Passage to India*, the final section 'Catastrophe' about the Maharajah's downfall through scandal and intrigue and the Preface from 1953. As Roy suggests, the collage of styles of writing has a disorienting effect on the colonialist archive; and as the first readers of the complete text under the umbrella title, *The Hill of Devi*, are situated in the immediate post-independence context (the book is published six years after Indian independence), they belong to the emergent post-colonialist mindset.

Forster registers the best moments of his guest status, 'garlanded with jasmine and roses', and carrying in his left hand 'a scarf of orange-coloured silk with gold ends' (*THD*, 31–2). He spends an evening with his hosts '*full of splendour yet free of formality*', eating without cutlery, sitting on the ground (not always comfortable and the source of some irony), contrasting to the lunch in the presence of the Agent to the Governor General, '*very stiff and straight*', where even the Rajah is '*quite another person*' (37). Forster is privileged to have seen '*so much of the side of life that is hidden from most English people*' (37–8). It is a life observed as well-meaning, colourful and emotional, yet chaotic and inefficient – a criticism that is reiterated more and more in the letters from the 1921 visit when he is Secretary to the Maharajah. The contradictions he notices lead to his own ambivalence towards India: '*It's so typical of the Oriental, who makes a howling mess over one thing and does another with perfect success and grace*' (51). And I think we can see that, although he, like Malcolm Darling, appears free of 'the feeling of racial superiority which was usual among Englishmen at the time' (64), he is not immune to the common Orientalism. Roy writes of the 'Orientalist impressionism' in descriptive passages of *The Hill of Devi* and *A Passage to India* which uses 'fascination and enchantment' as 'organizing categories' (Roy, 269) – whether the 'dark cave' in the Devi hill (*THD*, 76) or the Marabar Caves in the novel. The mercurial Maharajah is the unstable Oriental despot, moody and inconsistent. The western gaze, even when ostensibly framed by liberal humanism, as in Forster's case, is warmly affected at first sight, but on reflection is unable to separate the other from his otherness.[20] Forster himself also reaches this conclusion: '*and though I am dressed as a Hindu I shall never become one*' (161).[21] The other is impressive to the western eye in ritual, gaily coloured garments and carnivalesque behaviour – a counterweight to English 'civilized', restrained public codes: the Maharajah is even described as governing 'in gestures of carnivalesque excess' (Roy, 282). Forster confirms the entrenched beliefs of his English reader in 1921: '*To check the idleness, incompetence and extravagance is quite beyond me. I knew I should find them, but they are far worse than I imagined.*' These are no longer merely irritating impressions, because now in 1921 in an administrative position Forster struggles to do his job well; and, since his 1912 visit and all that has happened in the meantime, he sees the problem in a wider context: '*adding for your private ear that my extra worry is the relationship of so slackly administered a state to the general problem of Indian unrest*' (99). As the letters are English-addressed they are constrained by expectations – the prejudices of the English back home – even when Forster was no Anglo-Indian.[22]

The key signifier here and in *A Passage to India* is 'muddle', and it extends from poor administration to the culture itself. In the letters from 1921 he resorts at times to purely western class categories to describe certain behaviour as '*to some extent faults of taste*' (*THD*, 131). The Gokul Ashtami Festival celebrating the birth of Krishna – and the model for the Hindu last part of *A Passage to India* – is completely unromanticized, even comically portrayed, and sometimes seen as one long annoyance: '*The noise is so appalling ... fatuous and in bad taste ... no dignity, no taste, no form ... The whole of what one understands by music seems lost forever*' (*THD*, 158–63); other times as '*a pleasant mixture of ritual and informality*' (246); however, 'the situation soon degenerated into a wretched muddle' (247). Forster has become less tolerant of the otherness of the other.

Another form of muddle is the hybrid identity of the educated Indian, where the mixture of the two cultures, English and Indian, are not as acceptable to Forster

---

20 See Roy, 273.

21 A sentiment echoed later by D.H. Lawrence, who insisted that understanding otherness in the shape of the Native American Indian required the extinction of self. I discuss Lawrence's understanding of otherness in the next chapter.

22 'But he was anything but Anglo-Indian, only a life-long college man translated briefly into the Indian environment, and in a thoughtful, melancholy way, half-enchanted by it' (James Morris, cit. in Roy, 265).

as they might be to us today. On his first visit in 1912 Forster's room '*has pictures of Krishna on the walls, interspersed with the Archbishop of Canterbury crowning the King and Queen in Westminster Abbey*' (*THD*, 44). At a traditional princely Hindu wedding the band plays 'Oft in danger, oft in woe' (69). The Indian rulers themselves are often English-educated, like Forster's friend Masood, later Sir Syed Ross Masood ('my greatest Indian friend', 100) whom he first met in Weybridge in 1906, and who is portrayed in a letter of 1921 as the archetypal 'mimic man' adopting the upper-class speech style of the English gentleman: '"My dear chap, I ask you!" said Masood' (102). Forster though is not in favour of bilingualism even when trying to establish an English Literary Society, predicting 'the death of the Society if once it contracted Bilingualitis' (*THD*, 108).[23]

Nevertheless, in all the ambivalence about India some lessons are learnt which inform the critique of his own culture. First, the Hindu practices, chaotic as they appear to him, demonstrate 'a gap in Christianity' in its lack of laughter or play – Hinduism seems to him a gay religion (181–2).[24] Second, he insists on the injunction to 'follow the heart' and, he is told 'his mind will see everything clear' (177), which he will not accept if emotion is reduced to ritual expression. What he already formulated in the novel *Howards End* (1910) as the injunction to 'only connect' will become a complex process in his Indian novel amongst the English visitors searching for the real India, and between the cultures – English, Anglo-Indian, Hindu and Moslem. But will Forster be able to get beyond the constraining irony and distance that reads other cultures as it does its own – a specifically class-informed English reading practice? Reading Matthew Arnold might not help: '*Since my last letter I have been reading aloud (M. Arnold's essays mostly), which has made me feel more useful*' (107) – unless, of course, Forster believes that culture (meaning western literary culture) is the only answer to Indian anarchy.

The Hill of Devi, then, reveals the author struggling with a divided consciousness: he sees for himself what is going wrong in India, and this is often expressed in the terms of a cultural superiority – an Empire mentality (and one he will satirize in *A Passage to India*). Yet, there is also a celebration of difference which enables a play at being un-English and supported by the textual expression of sublimated desire for that difference, a desire displaced onto the otherness of the Indian other. And this informs the connections between travel, fiction, and the search for the space for the expression of an otherwise repressed sexuality – the links between *The Hill of Devi*, *Maurice* and *A Passage to India*. Indeed, the

---

[23]   Mimicry is a colonial discourse that expresses a hybrid identity, ambivalent and essentially inauthentic. As Homi K. Bhabha puts it, '*almost the same but not quite ... almost the same but not white*' (*The Location of Culture*, 89, italics in original). And as the infamous photograph of Forster cross-dressed in a mixture of oriental and English dress referred to above shows, he was also only able at times to indulge in the appearance of a hybrid identity.

[24]   Umberto Eco playfully reaches a similar conclusion about the absence of humour in the Church in *The Name of the Rose* (1980).

hidden reason for going in the first place was Syed Ross Masood. As Quentin Bailey explains, Forster 'had made several declarations of love to him in 1910 and 1911'; and he had returned to India, 'and Forster longed to see him again. There was, thus, a certain sexual charge to Forster's trip' (340).

Forster's travel writing expresses a desire to get away from the limits of his Englishness. But this turns out to be easier in Italy than the British colonial places – Egypt and India, even when he does consciously attempt to understand the parts of the native culture available to him either through his reading and research or his situation (as Secretary to the Maharajah, for example). If travel holds out a transgressive promise – a common underlying desire – Forster hopes to escape the class and sexual limitations back home.[25]

Fictions of Travel and Englishness

The traveller is supposed to come home changed; the ability to do so is an index of character, and used by Forster to critique the class and cultural limitations of English men and women abroad. Forster brings his fictional characters home 'to test the full extent of the touch of Italy upon their dutiful English hearts', as Wendy Moffat puts it (68). The weary and jaded traveller is a motif in Forster's fiction – Mr Lucas in 'The Road from Colonus', or Lucy Honeychurch in *A Room with a View* and Mrs Moore and Adela Quested in *A Passage to India* are examples of characters who, weary from the journey, find it hard to enjoy being abroad, especially as they first meet the other English tourists or expatriate residents; it seems to them worse there than suburban England. In each case, then, the plot of these travel stories revolves around the extent to which the protagonist is eventually able to respond to the place and the landscape, and discover the real – the real Italy or the real India.[26] Moreover, when the response comes, Italy or India will be England's other. But to find the real appears to be a problem, and one compounded by tourism itself. That is to say, the 'tourist gaze' may not see the real as the object is always already described in the discourse of the tour guide, even when it is *Baedeker* or the *Guide Bleu*. From the early short stories, through the 'Italian' novels – *Where Angels Fear to Tread* (1905), *A Room with a View* (1908) – to his 'Indian' novel, *A Passage to India* (1924), English middle-class characters are taken on a journey which promises experiential challenge, and to which only a few manage

---

25   Moffat's biography is a valuable source of information about Forster's sexuality – that 'great unrecorded history' of gay sexuality in the early twentieth century: 'Morgan was overwhelmed by powerful waves of lust. The beauty of men on the street "tormented" him' (Moffat, 103). It is now much clearer that getting away from England was at least partly sexually motivated. Moffat draws on the gay stories and diaries that Forster suppressed during his lifetime. For a fictional representation of Forster's gay life, and the creative process that culminates in *A Passage to India* see Damon Galgut, *Arctic Summer* (London: Atlantic Books, 2014).

26   The motif of 'the jaded traveller' is mentioned by Furbank, vol. 1, 103.

to respond positively. In the introduction to *Where Angels Fear to Tread*, Ruth Padel explains that: 'the other country [is] a place where people are different ... where feeling can become dangerously real and English values are jolted out of their complacency' (xi).

In this section of the chapter I will look at the importance of travel to questions of cultural and sexual identity in Forster's fiction, questions that reflect on the state of Englishness, on national cultural identity. Travel is given a greater metaphorical significance in the class and sexual identity problems of his protagonists, as they attempt to move out of the narrow boundaries at home into a freer expression of their erstwhile repressed or displaced desire. In his fiction Forster express the difficulties of achieving happiness when restricted by the narrow moral and class imperatives of the day, and especially by the heterosexual norm that prevented him from writing in other than displaced ways about transgressive desire. In Forster's stories of travel the subversive potential of an object of desire is used as a catalyst to expose the reaction of an individual or collective hysteria by the English abroad or at home – whether it be Harriet's tragic action to 'rescue' the child from its Italian father, Gino, in *Where Angels Fear to Tread*, or the expatriates or the 'better class of tourist' in Florence to the behaviour of Lucy Honeychurch in *A Room with a View* or the Anglo-Indians to the Adela Quested incident in the Marabar Caves in *A Passage to India*.

Travel also has a metaphorical and heuristic value in the fiction and stories set in England, where the journey is from town to country as in *Howards End* (1910), or is a trope for life's journey as in *The Longest Journey* (1907). And it is in these English settings that place takes on the full significance of Forster's ambivalent attitude to Englishness, either in the form of an archetypal landscape (southern England) as a refuge from modernity (represented in the London of *Howards End*), or the house, in the town or country, that belongs to a tradition of the English novel from Jane Austen – Pemberley or Mansfield Park in Austen; Windy Corner or Howards End in Forster – where the state of the national culture is reflected in the quality of life of those who live there or in the state of the property itself – like the dilapidated condition of Penge in *Maurice*. The house, however, is sometimes important more for the view through its windows: of the lawn and the roses of the neat garden at Windy Corner which, as its name suggests, is threatened by the wind; but also by the intrusion of George Emerson who stirs up the settled marriage arrangements in *A Room with a View*. I shall return to the recurrent signifiers of rooms with views in that novel later.

The house or home sometimes has an uncanny presence, evoked by ancestry or the ghostly presence of previous owners, like the first Mrs Wilcox for Margaret Schlegel once she finally settles in Howards End. But the landscape may also evoke the uncanny. The ancient parts of Wiltshire in *The Longest Journey* appear as a fitting end to Rickie Elliot's life, a journey from the cloistered intellectual brotherhood of Cambridge through an unsuccessful writing career and failed marriage, and finally to the disruptive influence of his subversive step-brother – a displaced queer relationship. Like Stonehenge, or the 'Cadbury Rings' in the novel,[27] sites of ancient Britain are a last refuge from modernity; but not for long as roads for the new motor car or housing developments are spreading suburbia into the countryside; or as small farms are in decline because of mass farming changing the shape of landscape.[28]

Forster has influenced our reading of place in his fiction by explaining in the 'Terminal Note' (dated September 1960) to *Maurice* that it was once possible to get lost in the English Greenwood; a place where one could be left alone, where – to put it in a different language – one's sexuality was not subject to the hetero-normative gaze. Forster's ideal of the Greenwood demonstrates the importance of place, especially natural or elemental places, for his fictions of travel: places of transgression where identity is transformed by the freer expression of an otherwise hidden sexuality.

In what follows, I shall begin with the early short stories, which experiment with the transgressive theme and the heuristic value of travel, and then discuss the 'Italian' novels, *Where Angels Fear to Tread* and *A Room with a View*, followed by the theme of the English journey in *The Longest Journey*, *Howards End* and *Maurice*, and finally the critique of British imperial attitudes in *A Passage to India*. In each case, characters are judged by the extent to which they can travel – and whether life's journey has been fulfilling – and whether they are open to otherness and other cultures.

Stories of Symbolic Spaces and Sexual Transgression

Forster's first published story, 'The Story of a Panic' (1904),[29] reveals the importance of travel and symbolic topography for his fiction. It is the story of a group of middle-class English tourists in Italy. Eustace, a 14-year-old boy comes into contact with Gennaro, the prototype Italian young man, who encourages the release of the repressed free spirit in the English boy. Eustace becomes 'Eustazio', as he is released from his English identity and under the influence of the wild wind turns into the pan-like satyr, a queer identity that defies all propriety when the boy leaps into Gennaro's arms (12). The story takes the form of a parable where the small confining space of the boy's bedroom is challenged by the woods, a space representing 'the great forces and manifestations of Nature ... in which all things can be hidden' (16–17). The woodland is the location of sexual transgression – a queer space like Forster's 'Greenwood'. For Gennaro it is the place for the free-roaming spirit; the narrator re-coding it as absurd, 'diabolical' and 'madness' (17).

---

[27]   As mentioned at the start of this chapter the place is based on Figsbury Rings in Wiltshire visited by Forster in 1904. See 'Author's Introduction', *The Longest Journey*, xxii.

[28]   In *Howards End* Henry Wilcox has a far from idealist view of farming and the 'back to the land' pundits: 'Mismanagement did it – besides, the days for small farms are over. It doesn't pay – except with intensive cultivation. Smallholdings, back to the land – ah! Philanthropic bunkum' (175).

[29]   'The Story of a Panic' in *Selected Stories*. Page numbers in text refer to the Penguin Classics edition.

The narrator represents the snobbish and racist English view of foreigners, which will play an important role in Forster's novels – a modernist strategy of contrasting perspectives, and a narrator whose views are not shared by the author.

Sexual panic is a theme throughout Forster's writing. But in this his first story, whose is the story of a panic? It is the middle-class English who panic at what they see as the corruption of the boy. Their overreaction leads to attempts to incarcerate him in a cage, and to the accidental death of Gennaro in helping the boy escape, a moment described as his escaping from the light 'looking like a great white moth' (23). Despite the resounding 'shouts and laughter of the escaping boy' (23) at the end of the story, the narrator reads the events within his limited cultural understanding, so that Gennaro is 'an affront to us all' (13) as he is too familiar in his address (breaking the speech rules), rarely showing 'deference' (20), having an 'ignorant animal nature', all of which the English need to combat from 'the most obvious dictates of logic and reason' (22); and when Gennaro dies the narrator comments: 'those miserable Italians have no stamina' (23) – drawing on the contemporary discourse of degeneracy to assert the superiority of the English race – critiques of which also appear in Conrad and Lawrence.

The story appears to undermine the values promoted by the narrator, which also assists the working of the uncanny, as the narrator attempts to recuperate the unfamiliar or strange elements of the story into a familiar discourse, re-coding the estranging actions of the boy and Gennaro's explanation into Christian or moral terms which seem to lack sufficient explanatory power; indeed, which appear the result of a panic reaction. The narrator's authority is undermined by the opposition between the development of a free spirit with its implicit sexual connotations, and 'the pettiness of the everyday' (Head, 87). While Gennaro argues that to have been in the woods is to have achieved an understanding of things, and that satyr-boys cannot be cooped up indoors or they will die, the narrator dismisses his words as typical of 'the working of the Southern mind' (21). Uncanniness is also achieved by Forster's use of incompatible genre conventions, which strain the expectations and credulity of the reader. Fantasy and intimations of the supernatural do not sit easily with realism.[30] Forster will have to find another way of telling this story of the transgressive potential of travel, and the encounter with the other which could release otherwise repressed desires. The journey beyond Englishness is invariably a kind of sexual epiphany.[31]

----

[30] Forster called the stories 'fantasies', and despite the violence and sexual implications, he felt the 12 stories selected could be published. The more explicitly homosexual stories were, like the novel *Maurice*, only published posthumously, as *The Life to Come and Other Stories* (1972). See David Leavitt and Mark Mitchell's introduction to *Selected Stories*, vii.

[31] Dominic Head comments that Forster's short stories have affinities with the modernist stories of James Joyce and Katherine Mansfield, 'who cultivate an ironic and opaque use of the revelation or epiphany to condense a rich sense of contingency in a very few words' (Head, 81). Head is referring to 'The Eternal Moment', but epiphanies are seen in other stories too. We might extend Forster's modernist credentials by accounting for his use of mythology.

'The Other Side of the Hedge' (1904) is also a parable of walking out of restrictive existence on a journey which has an 'unknown goal', but with a final vision of brotherhood (29). In 'The Celestial Omnibus' (1908) a boy defies his father to escape from the pedantry of the older generation and ride out of suburbia into a heavenly place of music and poetry; 'Other Kingdom' (1909) again has woodland as the place of transgressive play, despite the resistance of the landed gentry – here though it is a woman who 'danced away from our society and our life' (68) into the pagan wood of gods and satyrs. In each of these stories perspective is achieved by the limited understanding of other characters or narrators as the life of middle-class English society (indoors, in the drawing room) is opposed by the wild outdoors of the greenwood (but not of course the garden with its associations of neo-classical order).

In his short stories Forster is working out a paradigmatic story about modern identity, and one summed up by Cecil Vyse in *A Room with a View*: 'It makes a difference, doesn't it whether we fence ourselves in, or whether we are fenced out by the barriers of others' (116). The spatial trope is significant for our understanding of Cecil; but as we see in many of the stories, protagonists break through the fences that are within before they challenge those constructed by society. In 'The Road from Colonus' (1904), the Englishman abroad is transformed by his experience: 'Greece ... had made him discontented, and there are stirrings of life in discontent ... a strange desire had possessed him to die fighting' (80); he does not want to return to England. These travel stories sometimes also tell of lost opportunities to act on desire, a theme that is embodied in the fussy maiden aunt like Miss Bartlett in *A Room with a View* who comically portrays the old limited morality, which the younger generation must overcome.

In the early stories, Forster is experimenting with themes and imagery that he will develop in the novels: life as a journey, travel as transgression, symbolic topography and the limits of established English attitudes to sexuality and the other. In the next section of this chapter we will see how Forster's two 'Italian' novels develop such themes. Here, as in 'The Story of a Siren' (1920) Mediterranean travel tests 'all the commonplaces that are called reality' (154), as protagonists try to find a place in nature where they can be left alone to be themselves – beyond the interpellating gaze.

Italy and Back

With the exception of *Maurice*, as Ruth Padel points out, Forster's novel titles 'conjure a place, a way of looking, or a "journey" or "passage" towards it' (xi). In this section I shall concentrate on the journey to Italy as a testing ground for the limits of English class and cultural identity, for the critique of entrenched attitudes to foreigners – what Paul Peppis has called 'the pathologies of Englishness' – within the conventions of the marriage plot in the English middle-class novel (in Bradshaw, 49).[32] Forster is keen to show which characters are able to be changed

---

[32]   In *Where Angels Fear to Tread* Harriet represents that pathology, saying 'Foreigners are a filthy nation' (30), in *A Room* the Miss Alans 'regarded travel as a species of warfare,

by the experience of Italy, and which not. And here he breaks with the educational tradition of the Grand Tour, where travel to Italy would be a kind of finishing school for classical learning. As with 'The Story of a Panic' discussed above, Italy is meant to awaken the life of the senses – more of a 'sentimental education'. Ann Ardis sums up the Forsterian Italian journey:

> Forster's version of the Grand Tour functions not, as Samuel Johnson had argued, as an occasion for seeing 'what is expected a man should see', but instead as an opportunity for exposure to entirely unanticipated dimensions and categories of experience ... Italy functions as an occasion for getting beyond 'the muddle' of English social convention and traditional cultural values. (in Bradshaw, 71)

Travel abroad is a heuristic device for the exposure of desires; and also a story paradigm for the play of Forster's irony as he challenges his readers' own 'complacencies and rigidities' (Peppis, 51). But what that experience also seems to require is a clear distinction to be made from the start between tourism and travel; it is one that circulates throughout Forster's work, and in the works of the other writers studied in this book – indeed, as I argued in the general Introduction, the quarrel with tourism is central to the critique of modernity. However, the distinction between travel and tourism is not so clear cut.

Where Angels Fear to Tread begins with a departure and a warning: 'And don't, let me beg you, go with that awful tourist idea that Italy's only a museum and antiquities and art. Love and understand the Italians' (3). Philip Herriton's warning to his widowed sister-in-law, Lilia, in Charing Cross Station will be tested when she falls in love with and marries Gino; understanding him and his ways will be the problem not just for his English wife, but later after her death in childbirth for the other English characters who decide to 'rescue' the child in order to ensure him an English upbringing (and one whose advantages are less clear by the end of the novel). The ironies in the novel are located in the disjunction between Philip's Italophilia – and one shared by the author – and the entrenched snobbery and anti-foreign attitudes of Philip's sister, Harriet. For Philip, 'Italy really purifies and ennobles all who visit her. She is the school as well as the playground of the world'. And if the Goths can be 'transfigured' by Italy, so can Lilia, who is 'a philistine, appallingly ignorant', and whose taste in art is 'false' (6). The key word is 'transfigured', a process brought about by being in Italy, although presumably not as a common tourist – despite the requirement for a taste in art, which we have been told is an 'awful tourist idea' (that Italy is only its museums, antiquities and art) (3). Already the distinction between travel and tourism is being blurred. And if the invading barbarians can be changed by Italy, Harriet's hysterical and fatal action at the end of the novel in abducting the child makes her the real villain.[33]

---

only to be undertaken by those who have been fully armed at the Haymarket stores ... Quinine ... paper soap' (211).

[33]   Philip Herriton's Italophilia reminds us of Forster's own youthful love of the place, the sensuality of the place and the people, the ecstasy of the art. See Moffat, 58–60.

To be transformed by being in Italy implies an encounter beyond tourism. But, despite Forster's witty parody of guide-book discourse (12–13) – a parody which we will see again in the description of 'Chandrapore' at the beginning of *A Passage to India* – it seems to be difficult to get beyond Baedeker Italy, which, as James Buzard explains, 'regulates contact between touristic and Italian life' ('Forster's Trespasses' in Tambling, 22). Even Philip's declared belief in knowing the real Italy beneath the tourist description is constrained by an idealized version of Baedeker. The educated tourist appears throughout Forster's writing; but a contradiction emerges between the idealized place and its high cultural artefacts, on the one hand, and the material culture, the way of life, on the other.[34] The conclusion we can draw is that, in Buzard's words: 'Forster's characters repeatedly enact a failed encounter with the "real" which they believe themselves to have met' (26); the 'real' always eluding such appointments, as Lacan explained (*The Four Fundamental Concepts*, 53). It is this failed encounter that recurs in his travel fiction with particular consequences in the two 'Italian' novels, and also in the 'Indian' novel as Mrs Moore and Adela Quested want to see 'the real India'. As I argued in the general Introduction to this book, finding the real apart from perception of the object is a problem; the real is distorted by the traveller's desire, and is thus always already a form of misrecognition.[35] This problem of the gaze recurs in all the writers studied, and is a defining feature of their modernism.

Forster understood from his own tours of Italy, Egypt and India that the visitor needs to be informed and therefore there is no avoiding the process of prior textualization of the real. Moreover, he makes ironic capital out of this process by drawing attention to the gap between Baedeker Italy and the real Italy ('Italian Italy'[36]), as well as between desires and their realization in the field of the other – albeit the Italian other or the encoded restrictions of the English abroad (prefigured in Charlotte Bartlett, the chaperone in *A Room with a View*). However, Forster manages to create what Althusser called an 'internal distance'[37] to the ideology of tourism even while doubting that a traveller could get beyond its limits completely. In the novels, at best there are different classes of tourists: in *Where Angels Fear to Tread* if Lilia is the 'philistine', then Paul Herriton is 'the cultivated tourist' (73) who would be one of 'the better class of tourist', as the narrator defines it in *A Room with a View* (with due irony), to be distinguished from the type easily recognized by Miss Bartlett as 'the ill-bred people whom one does meet abroad' (24), like Harriet in *Where Angels Fear to Tread* (75). Miss Lavish in *A Room with a View* is keen to 'emancipate' Lucy Honeychurch from Baedeker, because 'he does but touch the surface of things. As to the true Italy – he does not even dream of it. The true Italy is to be found by patient observation' (36–7), a Ruskinian truth that

---

[34] In Raymond Williams's sense first defined in *Culture and Society* (1958). For a useful discussion of Williams and the cultural materialists see Eagleton, *The Idea of Culture*, 112–31.

[35] See Lacan, *The Seminar Book 1*, 167.

[36] See Furbank, vol. 1, 94.

[37] An idea suggested by Buzard, 14–15.

comes from the character who writes popular romance novels, one of which will be derived from her observing Lucy in Florence and rewriting it for her escapist readers! But all these observers of art and architecture, the informed sightseers, are put into perspective by Mr Emerson's view that they should not be spending time in old churches and museums, but should get out 'into the sunshine' (41). Lucy seems to heed the advice because 'the pernicious charm of Italy worked on her, and instead of acquiring information, she began to be happy' (41). It is, though, the British expatriates, who as 'the residential colony' are experts on Italy ('people who never walked about with Baedekers'[38]) and the best of the Italian life (71), but are portrayed by Forster as a sort of outpost of civilization with the English chaplain as their moral leader, as we see in the outing they take into the hills. The irony does its work well. Occasionally, though, it is supported by the view of the other ('the thoughts of the Italian cab-driver'): 'these English. They gain knowledge slowly, and perhaps too late' (91). In *Where Angels Fear to Tread*, Gino makes his position quite clear: 'I do not see why an English wife should be treated differently. This is Italy' (41).

Lilia's ignorance about Italian ways has led her to see only romance – her story paradigm. But she feels trapped in a place without 'real English tea-parties' (33). While at first she treats Gino like a little boy (34), it soon becomes clear that he does not fit the constructions she, as representative English woman abroad, attempts to impose on him. The common English reading of the uncompromising difference between the 'Latin man' and the 'northern woman' (49) is partly confirmed by the narrator (24), and by Lilia's observations (35). Gino's small-town provincial life is not ready for an independent woman, 'who answered to other laws ... for strange rumours were always blowing over the Alps of lands where men and women had the same amusements and interests, and he had often met that privileged maniac, the lady tourist, on her solitary walks'. He must save Lilia from herself, 'for after all she was a woman', and he is 'at all events a man' and knows 'what is right' (35–6).[39]

The romance of Italy either leads characters astray – Lilia's expatriation in search of romance, or Lucy Honeychurch discovering desire in Tuscany which upsets her chaperoned existence; or it confirms the romance paradigm despite evidence to the contrary, as in the novel published by Miss Lavish, which gives Lucy and George (and Miss Bartlett) away.

Whereas Lilia and Harriet in *Where Angels Fear to Tread*, or Miss Bartlett in *A Room with a View*, in their different ways learn nothing new from Italy, there are two female characters who do return home from Italy changed by

---

[38] 'We residents sometimes pity you poor tourists not a little – handed about like a parcel of goods from Venice to Florence, from Florence to Rome, living herded together in pensions or hotels, quite unconscious of anything that is outside Baedeker, their one anxiety to get "done" or "through" and go on somewhere else. The result is, they mix up towns, rivers, palaces in one inextricable whirl.' Mr Eager, *A Room with a View*, 81.

[39] For further comments of the different ways of seeing each other see *Where Angels Fear to Tread*, 37–41.

their experiences. Significantly, both are misread by male characters whose desires for them are awakened by the women's Italian influence. In *Where Angels Fear to Tread* Caroline Abbott is now in love; not with Philip as he thinks, but with Gino – indeed, they are both in love with him (133)! In *A Room with a View* Lucy Honeychurch's changes are noticed by others. Cecil Vyse recalls their meeting in Rome: 'That day she had seemed a typical tourist – shrill, crude, and gaunt with travel. But Italy worked some marvel on her. It gave her light, and – which he held more precious – it gave her shadow. Soon he detected in her a wonderful reticence. She was like a woman of Leonardo da Vinci's, whom we love not so much for herself as for the things that she will not tell us' (107). Cecil will have to learn not to read women as works of art. And as Lucy, slowly and hesitantly, comes to realize and finally acknowledge her desire for George Emerson, that newly born desire becomes visible to Cecil Vyse: 'But to Cecil, now that he was about to lose her, she seemed each moment more desirable … From a Leonardo she had become a living woman, with mysteries and forces of her own' (191). Mr Beebe is another keen observer of Lucy. He notices that where her speech allows her to hide behind the words of others[40] her piano playing gives her away: 'If Miss Honeychurch ever takes to live as she plays, it will be very exciting – both for us and for her' (52).[41] In a world where words are restricted by class codes that make them signs of already pre-structured relationships, music is a freer expression. In this sense, music functions expressively where words function phatically. Mr Beebe once again assists the reader in thinking about the significance of Lucy's piano playing: 'she must see beauty in life, or she could not play the piano as she did' (196). Are we not being encouraged to read Lucy's unconscious desire in her playing? The Beethoven or Schumann sonata is chosen for the expression of passion; the Mozart for the order of an attentive pursuit to distract her from the turmoil of her life (symptomatically reflected in the disorder of the wind in the garden) (198–200). The alternative to her music is to go away, to escape the talk and scandal she fears as the consequence of her broken engagement; and facing up to her real desire: 'I simply *must* go away. I have to' (202, italics in original). Her newly emerging desire is sublimated into her piano playing. What she needs to learn at the end is that there is suffering and passion too in a man, and that 'even men might suffer from unexplained desires, and need help' (172); but she 'could not see that Mr Emerson was profoundly religious, and differed from Mr Beebe chiefly by his acknowledgement of passion' (220).

Italy has taught the English women, Lucy and Caroline, about the life of the body where others have continued to prioritize the life of the mind, even when the lesson does not always emerge into consciousness immediately. The opposition between the life of the mind and the life of the body runs right through

---

[40] '"My dear," said the old man [Mr Emerson] gently, "I think that you are repeating what you have heard older people say"' (43).

[41] Music as a leitmotif is important in Forster's writing, thematically and structurally. I shall return to the discussion of the leitmotif and music later in this chapter.

Forster's writing[42] – as it does Lawrence's writing. If travelling abroad begins as a culturally enriching venture, it sometimes ends in the discovery of otherwise repressed desires.

Repressed desires are expressed in other ways too in Forster's writing. Description, when not parodying tourist guide-book discourse, is used as displacement for otherwise unutterable feelings – as we saw in *The Hill of Devi*. In *A Room with a View* Lucy has her first experience of the beauty of Italian art. At the point where she 'became discontented herself', she sees Italy: 'For one ravishing moment Italy appeared. She stood in the Square of the Annunziata and saw in the living terracotta those divine babes whom no cheap production can ever stale ... Lucy thought she had never seen anything more beautiful' (39). The souvenir world of the tourist is transcended for a moment, and the aura of art is revealed to her; indeed, she experiences a revelation that takes her beyond herself, beyond her discontentment. What we see here is *jouissance* that temporarily but profoundly fills the void of desire – a desire in Lucy that is still in need of an object; an experience close to religious ecstasy, as Lacan has shown in his discussion of Bernini's statue of *St Theresa*.[43] Then alone in the Piazza, 'the dust blew in her eyes, and she remembered that a young girl ought not to loiter in public places' (40) – the moment has passed and the symbolic order has re-established its authority by, in Charles Shepherdson's words, setting 'a limit to *jouissance* ... This limit is what Lacan calls the paternal metaphor' (*Vital Signs*, 71–2).

Another transgressive moment is the bathing scene in the 'sacred lake' in Part Two of *A Room with a View* and it allows Forster to express 'the forces of youth' outside the restrictions of decorum. The naked male bodies at play are located in the gaze of Mr Beebe ('Mr Beebe watched them'), until the intrusion of others brings the transgression back into the limitations of the symbolic order. Here we are in the Forsterian greenwood, where the male body is on display like 'the nymphs in the *Götterdämmerung*' (149); and the principal focus is on the body of George Emerson, 'Michelangelesque'. Mr Beebe cannot finally resist joining in the fun. Forster concludes the episode with a message (in what could also be Mr Beebe's thoughts) that has been implicit throughout: 'It had been a call to the blood and to the relaxed will, a passing benediction whose influence did not pass, a holiness, a spell, a momentary chalice for youth' (153). As Judith Scherer Herz has claimed, the scene of the bathing 'carries a sexual charge in its language, in the space it opens up in the narrative for other longings, other

---

[42]   Philip and Cecil prioritize the life of the mind, Gino and George the life of the body. Caroline Abbott tells Philip at the end of *Where Angels Fear to Tread*: 'you're without passion; you look on life as a spectacle; you don't enter it; you only find it funny or beautiful' (133).

[43]   'You only have to go and look at Bernini's statue in Rome to understand immediately that she's coming, there is no doubt about it. And what is her *jouissance*, her *coming* from? It is clear that the essential testimony of the mystics is that they are experiencing it but know nothing about it' (Mitchell and Rose, 147). For the original see Jacques Lacan, *Le Seminaire Livre XX: Encore* (Paris: Editions du Seuil, 1975), 70.

resolutions'. Forster constructs 'a richly queer text' through processes of disguise and displacement. The landscape of woodland and lake are 'given a sexual potency' in a scheme of queering that will become clearer in retrospect, after the publication of *Maurice* (in Bradshaw, 142–4). However, I would argue that the ground for a queer reading is already established in the earlier novel *Where Angels Fear to Tread* in the character of Philip Herriton who has developed a sense of the beauty of things: 'It caused him at the age of twenty to wear parti-coloured ties and a squashy hat, to be late for dinner on account of the sunset, and to catch art from Burne-Jones to Praxiteles' (51).

Philip's sensitive responsiveness clearly allows him to speak for travel to Italy in idealizing terms: it 'purifies and ennobles' and transfigures the visitor (6). But, as we have seen, only those who are susceptible to its influence will be so affected. At first Lilia appreciates the 'smaller towns … off the beaten track', that Philip has recommended (8). It is only after her marriage settles into the restrictive small-town Italian life that she realizes she is too English to fit in. Caroline Abbott is affected by the Italian night sky and 'the warm sweet air', and this puts a strain on her reason for being there: 'to champion morality and purity, and the holy life of an English home' (91), terms that have already been deconstructed by the limitations of Sawston, and the attractions of Monteriano – indeed, such clear-cut distinctions will be left ambivalent by the end of the novel. And views, as landscapes, vistas or sites in the field of the gaze, and also as opinions – the English views of the Italian man, for example – are a recurrent motif, not least in the novel, *A Room with a View*. I shall end this section with some comments on rooms and views in the novel, because it is through these recurrent signifiers that Forster insists on the spatial location of perspective, and thus the modernist emphasis on the shifting and subjective nature of perception.

'I connect you with a view – a certain type of view. Why shouldn't you connect me with a room?' Lucy associates Cecil with 'a drawing room … with no view' (125). He objects, hoping she would connect him with 'the open air', which becomes more implausible when we think of his dress code, manner and ascetic nature. We connect the open air rather with George Emerson, especially after the woodland bathing scene and the tennis. The signifier of 'a room with a view' is of course associated with tourism, a detail from hotel reservation; and around which the play of relations between the English characters in the Florence Pensione is disseminated. Indeed, like the *opera buffa* the theme or motif of 'rooms and views' circulates through the text, recurring in different variations of the theme, and thus enabling comedy when, for example, Miss Bartlett turns up at Windy Corner, once again trying not to make a nuisance but does as she begs 'to be given an inferior spare room – something with no view, anything' (161). Lucy's mother talks of 'our dear view' of the English garden and landscape of the Weald (214). Looking out of windows at the view appears to be the English thing to do. In the last chapter, George is with Lucy on their honeymoon back at the Pensione in Florence: 'he strolled to the window, opened it (as the English will), and leant out. There was the parapet, there the river, there to the left the beginnings of the hills' (227). The precise deixis of this view confirms its familiarity, both because they have been there before and because it is pre-textualized as a tourist view.[44] The window literally and metaphorically frames the view, a view that is always already framed in the sense of the set up necessary for the ideology of tourism – the Baedeker Italy. 'I have a view' declares Mr Emerson at the start (24), and the view becomes at once an object of exchange as the view of Florence is commodified. Its exchange also draws attention to the petty, fussy manners of the English represented by the maiden aunt, and Emerson's stubborn iconoclasm (always challenging received opinion), a device to upset those from 'the narrow world at Tunbridge Wells' (30). Lucy has to learn to see things through her own eyes, have her own views in her own words. She only manages to see the view independently at moments of epiphany when she forgets herself and gives way to unconscious desire. Just before George kisses her we read: 'from her feet the ground sloped sharply into view, and violets ran down in rivulets and streams and cataracts' (89), as if this is a spontaneous view mediated by the *jouissance* of the woman, that temporarily fills the void of desire before, for Lucy, the object itself appears. But, once again, it is the symbolic order's prohibition that immediately puts an end to the expression of love as Miss Bartlett calls Lucy back into being: 'The silence of life had been broken by Miss Bartlett, who had stood brown against the view' (89) – a view that had radiated symptomatically with nature's colours is once again turned dull.

Forster locates the view in a gaze from a particular point. Mr Eager, the English chaplain in Florence, is an art expert:

> 'The view thence [from the hills outside Florence] is most beautiful – far better than the hackneyed view from Fiesole [implying a common tourist sight in postcards]. It is the view that Alessio Baldovinetti is fond of introducing into his pictures. That man had a decided feeling for landscape. Decidedly. But who looks at it today? Ah, the world is too much with us.' (70–71)

For Mr Eager the view of the landscape is seen better through the artist's eyes; and as we have seen Cecil sees Lucy as a work of art, learning only when it is already too late to see her as a woman of flesh and blood. Sometimes there are subjects caught in the field of the gaze, and the object is not always under censure as when Charlotte Bartlett sees George embrace Lucy. Indeed, when George sets eyes on Lucy he sees 'radiant joy in her face' before he kisses her (89). And, as already mentioned, the gay scene of men bathing in the pond in the woods appears to be focalized through the gaze of Mr Beebe (149ff.).

These are all examples of the way the gaze of interpellation fixes the subject in ideology or desire, calls it into being – a play on point of view or focalization seen in the other writers too, and developed to a level of complexity by Henry James. It is used in many ways by Forster to show hidden desires or character limitations, or even the view of the other about the English. Views need places to look out from, or places as the object of the gaze. And it is not just in Forster's 'Italian' novels

---

[44]   In the first chapter it is Lucy who looks out of the window at the view of Florence seeing: 'the lights dancing on the Arno, and the cypresses of San Miniato, and the foothills of the Apennines, black against the rising moon' (34).

that perspective is associated with place. In the next section of this chapter the focus will be on the novels set in England, *The Longest Journey*, *Howards End* and *Maurice*. For it is in these English settings that place takes on the full significance of the national cultural problematic, as the countryside and its ancient landscape is used as a perspective from which to critique modernity.

In and around England

In Forster's novels set in England the country house once again is called upon to reflect the state of the national culture; the landscape to reflect a more ancient history like the 'Cadbury Rings' in Wiltshire in *The Longest Journey*, or the proverbial 'Greenwood' in *Maurice* which become places to return to at the end of a life of repressed or displaced desires, spaces in the English landscape apart from the interpellating gaze. In these condition-of-England novels life's journey is a search for the place that will become home.

In Forster's writing the country takes precedence over the town.[45] The second part of *A Room with a View* returns the story to the Edwardian England first described in *The Longest Journey*, and later the scene of *Howards End*, as well as *Maurice*. Here Forster works through his own returns from abroad when he had to find reasons for living in England[46] – or at least those parts of England still spared the depredations of modernity. In the discussion of Forster's travel writing, we saw his tendency to prefer the past to the present – the Golden Age of Alexandria for example. Similarly, Forster wants to recreate an ancient greenwood England for posterity just at the moment of its disappearance – as Peter J. Hutchings puts it, 'a particular place which embodies the past, as a retreat from the present' (in Tambling, 217).[47]

In these novels class is an important focus. Forster's novel registers the growing awareness in the early twentieth century of the gulf between the haves

---

[45]   Fictions of place, which belong to a tradition of the English novel as described by Raymond Williams in *The English Novel from Dickens to Lawrence* and *The Country and the City*.

[46]   Furbank tells us that Forster's return from India in 1922 'proved a difficult homecoming for him ... the sight of England depressed him' and he felt 'no enthusiasm at seeing the cliffs of England again'. Vol. 2, 105.

[47]   The process of nostalgia in reimaging the past as an ideal world lost to modernity is mirrored in the reception of Forster's work when it is reproduced by the culture industry of the 1980s in the film adaptations as a collective desire for a lost Edwardian world, 'a near-idyllic past for present pleasure' (Hutchings, 217). Hutchings quotes Salman Rushdie: 'the rise of Raj revisionism ... is the artistic counterpart of the rise of conservative ideologies in modern Britain'. In achieving their ideological goal, however, the films tend to reduce the ambivalences and ironies of the novels, and especially their queer implications. For example, as Hutchings argues, David Lean's adaptation of *A Passage to India* focuses more on the Adela Quested story and less on the Aziz/Fielding relationship, a move that appears to 'straighten' the plot (Hutchings, 218). For further discussion see Ian Baucom's *Out of Place: Englishness, Empire, and the Locations of Identity*.

and the have-nots, for many of the middle, and upper-middle classes: "'Money pads the edges of things," said Miss Schlegel. "God help those who have none"' (51). Forster's teaching at the Working Men's College from 1902 already made him conscious of the parasitic status of a rentier existence; and the life in the arts and the liberal mindset of the Schlegels in the novel are made possible by their relative financial independence. Leonard Bast is the poorly paid, white-collar worker trying to share the cultural and intellectual capital of the leisured classes while continually being threatened by the abyss of poverty.[48] Through his resentment and failure, he is a reminder of class and wealth difference in a novel that focuses on the two opposed families, the liberal-cultured Schlegels and the arch-capitalist Wilcoxes. The latter it is who reveal the overseas sources of wealth in British Imperialism, a displaced production through cheap labour and the natural resources of the colonies. Henry Wilcox's business is aptly called, 'the Imperial and West African Rubber Company' with its offices in London; and there is talk of 'Tariff Reform' as a 'last hope' because increasing globalization threatens Britain's monopoly status, and therefore the income of the rich. The Rubber Company is, of course, responding to the demands of modernity especially the new motor car. As Paul Delany puts it, 'an essential part of his [Forster's] case against the Wilcoxes, that Imperial family, is that they can enjoy their traditional comforts by doing their dirty work overseas and out of sight' (in Tambling, 74). They own several houses in England including Howards End, but are more interested in the financial value of the property than its cultural value. It is Margaret Schlegel who encourages the view of houses as places of heritage, becoming a guardian of ancestral rites. However, the final vision of a retreat from modernity into a pastoral idyll can only be a temporary solution, and hardly the resolution for the condition of England that the novel has been revealing.[49]

Forster's critique is influenced by C.F.G. Masterman's *The Condition of England* published in 1909; and in many respects *Howards End* is the fictional treatment of its argument. As I explained in the general Introduction, Masterman belongs to the long liberal tradition of questioning the effects of industrialism and modernity on the national culture, and one that is also taken up by D.H. Lawrence, which I discuss in the next chapter. The dehumanizing effects of modern capitalism have led to the 'monstrous inequalities of fortune', and made worse by the conspicuous display of wealth without 'social obligation' (Masterman, 25–8).[50] Masterman, like Forster,

---

[48]   Frank Kermode has raised doubts about Forster's ability to imagine the poorer classes in other than sexual terms (as we see in the character of Alec in *Maurice*). See Kermode, *Concerning E.M. Forster*, 97–103.

[49]   Delany argues that, 'Forster remained a perpetual Edwardian, even though he lived until 1970. That period was the golden age of rentier culture in England – which is why it figures so prominently in England's nostalgia industry today. Everyone wants 'a room with a view'; but England is peculiar in its insistence that the view should be one of the eternally sunlit meadows of the past' (78).

[50]   Masterman was on the editorial committee of the liberal monthly *Independent Review* launched in 1903, and Forster was asked to contribute; see Furbank, vol. 1, 107–9.

idealizes the rural past of country-house England, and deplores the development of suburbanization (35; 64–5). He yearns for the vanished 'yeoman class', as do Forster and Lawrence; a healthy and manly class because of the 'life in the fields' (77), as opposed to the mechanized urban existence which is making the nation unhealthy – at its worst in the industrial north.[51]

Now this antiquarianism is present in one form or another in all the writers discussed in this study, as a reaction to modernity; views which continue to circulate throughout the early twentieth century in popular books like H.V. Morton, *In Search of England* (1927) expressing nostalgia for an old village Englishness. Masterman's apocalyptic conclusions about the decline of civilization and the coming of the war achieves its most reactionary form in Oswald Spengler's *Decline of the West* (1918) – beliefs that are reiterated by Lawrence.

Masterman, like Forster, insists that the demands and inhibitions of class in society further constrain authentic being and genuine friendship. Moreover, the travelling new wealthy middle classes are sometimes the worst: 'when the Englishman goes abroad, the customs of the country, the opinions of the people amongst whom he lives, count for nothing' (Masterman, 48). This is 'the imperial citizen' who, in the belief in the superiority of the British Empire, 'despises the foreigner' (Masterman, 66). It is a character in all the travel fiction studied in this book, extending to the American abroad in James and Wharton.

'Once there was life in rural England' (Masterman, 150). This iconic statement by Masterman represents a widespread attitude of mind; it is one shared by Forster and Lawrence. It assumes that it was once possible to be close to nature by having an 'intimacy with the land' (148). Masterman is referring to the 'agricultural labourer'; but also assumes the responsibility of the landed gentry – a race of Englishmen that are disappearing. But there are traces of something ancient in the land – off the beaten track in Forster's England. He wrote in his Diary (12 September 1904): 'I walked out again to Figsbury Rings ... a haunting, magical place.' He comments further that he 'caught fire up on the Rings' in the Wiltshire downlands; and that 'a similar experience had already befallen me in Italy and had produced my first short story [he is referring to 'The Story of a Panic'] ... and for many years the Wiltshire landscape remained haunted by my fictional ghosts'.[52]

Forster locates his characters precisely. In *The Longest Journey* there are three iconic places that represent different aspects of Englishness (his Englishness). The eponymous 'journey' is meant to be a progress through each place as a stage in a development: from the fraternity of Cambridge ('the abode of peace', 55) with its aloof intellectual view of the world, to the repressive Public School and the small country town (and Rickie Elliot's failed marriage after Agnes had promised to help him live in the real world and keep Cambridge 'in its proper place', 66), and finally

---

Examples of his early travel sketches from the *Review* are reprinted in *Abinger Harvest* 163ff. Masterman encouraged discussion of the condition of England in the *Review*.

[51]   Masterman, 81ff. See 70 for his eugenic solution.

[52]   Quoted in Forster's 'Author's Introduction' to the 1960 Oxford World Classics reissue of *The Longest Journey*; now reprinted in the Penguin Classics edition 2006, xxii.

to the Wiltshire countryside (and the discovery of his brother) as quintessentially pre-modernity England. But it is a place of nostalgia for an England that has already succumbed to modernity, as Forster later commented:

> There was a freshness and an out-of-door wildness in those days which the present generation cannot imagine. I am glad to have known our countryside before its roads were too dangerous to walk on and its rivers too dirty to bathe in, before its butterflies and wild flowers were decimated by arsenical spray, before Shakespeare's Avon frothed with detergents and the fish floated belly-up in the Cam. ('Author's Introduction', xxiv–xxv)

The novel tries to capture the *genius loci* of the ancient Wiltshire landscape, which Forster was convinced was 'charged with an emotion, permanent as its origins were transitory'.[53]

It is interesting that a novel that begins with the epistemological question about the existence of objects apart from the observer[54] ends with the idea of the uncanny, a more intuitive kind of knowledge that goes beyond both rationalism and empiricism. Nicholas Royle reminds us that the experience of the uncanny is

> a peculiar commingling of the familiar and unfamiliar. It can take the form of ... the revelation of something unhomely at the heart of hearth and home ... At some level the feeling of the uncanny may be bound up with the most extreme nostalgia or 'homesickness', in other words a compulsion to return to an inorganic state, a desire (perhaps unconscious) to die, a death drive. (*The Uncanny*, 1–2)

I suggest, then, that at one level Rickie Elliot's English journey represents the culture's need to return to the ancient landscape in a bid to reject modernity – and to return to the place where he will die. But it also seems, unconsciously, to point to the death drive of the culture. While it represents the conventional descriptive value of English pastoralism, the Wiltshire landscape has a deeper symbolic value. In its 'evocation of the earth', according to Kermode, it represents a 'spiritual geography' (*Concerning E.M. Forster*, 167). It is 'a haunting and magical place', where you 'feel very primeval' (111), and one where the observing subject merges with it (as opposed to maintaining the distance of scientific objectivity) in the experience of the uncanny.[55]

There is deep feeling of heritage too in the topography: 'Here is the heart of our island: the Chilterns, the North Downs, the South Downs radiate hence.

---

[53]   'My Books and I', reprinted as appendix B in the Penguin Classics edition (2006) of *The Longest Journey*, 366.

[54]   'They were discussing the existence of objects. Do they exist only if there is someone to look at them? Or have they a real existence of their own?' (3). For the influence of Cambridge philosophy (G.E. Moore) on Bloomsbury modernism see Ann Banfield's *The Phantom Table: Woolf, Fry, Russell and the Epistemology of Modernism*.

[55]   D.H. Lawrence, as we will see in the next chapter, also wrote about 'the spirit of place', but his magical places were not just in England, but in any remote site not yet adopted by the tourist industry.

The fibres of England unite in Wiltshire ... here we should erect our national shrine' (126).[56] Rickie's half-brother Stephan Wonham prefers being outside in the open countryside at night where he can feel 'alive' (241) – like other free-roaming spirits in Forster's short stories. And the novel ends in a kind of georgic vision of Stephan as the English yeoman farmer, the keeper of the land and 'the future of our race, and that century after century, his thoughts and his passions would triumph in England' (289). As Gilbert Adair has suggested, the repressive class-bound England is thus offset by Forster's 'atmospheric evocation of mysteriously pristine English countryside (an evocation which reads like a literary paraphrase of the visionary landscapes of Stanley Spencer, Samuel Palmer and the Pre-Raphaelites)' (Introduction, xvi). But as a resolution to the contradictory forces in the novel – cloistered intellectualism versus living in the world or travel, the narrow view of Englishness promoted in the Public School versus the longer historical view of the yeoman culture with its class implications, and modernity versus pastoralism – the ending, as I already suggested, like the ending of *Howards End*, is utopian as it prioritizes the mythic undercurrents that have been circulating through the text. We could conclude in Paul Peppis's words that 'the mythical ending of *The Longest Journey* confirms that Forster's works participate in the period idealisation of the rural south ... [locating] an authentic England and an ideal Englishness there. Forster's England overtly criticises the relentless spread of urban modernity' (in Bradshaw, 53).[57] And as I have argued, Forster reiterates Masterman's critique of the condition of English modernity.

The landscape is not the only evocation of the uncanny. The house or home sometimes has an uncanny presence, evoked by ancestry or the ghostly presence of its previous owner, like the first Mrs Wilcox for Margaret Schlegel once she finally settles in Howards End. It is the place to end up in; an end house (at the end of a cul-de-sac), a quiet corner in the country away from the developments of modernity (at least until the next housing development encroaches on their patch); and the desire for the house to become a home drives (in the Freudian sense) Margaret Schlegel to make compromises in marrying Henry Wilcox. Derrida has commented that, '*Heimlichkeit* is also the German name of what we have in mind here as the "economic law of the proper" or of the "house", of domesticity, along with its genealogy of the properly familial, of its "patronage" and its "parentage"'.[58] Through the contingencies of the narrative, the unfamiliar is made familiar by domesticating it, making it familial. But we cannot shake off the traces of family secrets underlying the harmony and resolution: the semantics

---

[56] A similar English countryside – 'Clearbury Rings' – is described at the start of chapter XIX in *Howards End* as the England 'to show a foreigner' (142).

[57] Although we should note, as Carola M. Kaplan does, that Stephan is a modern farmer 'making improvements to alleviate the worst abuses he sees around him'; but also as a good businessman making a 'deal for the posthumous publication of Rickie's stories'. Both the art and the land are in good hands (in Tambling, 62). I suggest, however, that Forster wants both readings: the utopian yeoman farmer and the good businessman.

[58] Jacques Derrida, quoted by Nicholas Royle, *The Uncanny*, 94.

of the *heimlich* (signifying homely and secretive) haunt the ending of the novel: 'I feel that you and I and Henry are only fragments of that woman's mind. She knows everything. She is everything. She is the house, and the tree that leans over it' (268). Margaret's final realization is that life itself 'was a house' (281); and that 'a place as well as a person may catch the glow. Don't you see that all this leads to comfort in the end?' (288). She has made Howards End homely (289), a house that 'is the future as well as the past' – a place of memories as well as one to end the modern 'craze for motion' with a new civilization 'that won't be in movement, because it will rest on the earth' (290).[59] And when finally Henry Wilcox has decided to leave Howards End to his second wife, Margaret Schlegel, she feels 'there was something uncanny in her triumph' over the Wilcoxes (291); it is of course the fulfilment of a ghostly wish kept secret by the Wilcoxes as the first Mrs Wilcox had wanted to leave the house to her (292).

Reflecting the author's desire for a house of his own, in *The Longest Journey* and *Howards End* the narrative is a quest for a place that Rae H. Stoll has called a substitute for the lost home, which is the drive for the lost object of the mother's body. However: 'Desire for the real – that is, desire to recapture the object which bestows wholeness and gives significance to all other objects – cannot be satisfied; nevertheless, it remains a driving force' (in Tambling, 35). Objects which appear to have the attributes to satisfy desire – Cambridge and then Sawston for Rickie, for example – are so many misrecognized metonymies. In the end, the imaginary resolution to the problem of desire acts as closure – both novels end with paradisal images of home in the English countryside: a sorority of mothers in *Howards End*; Stephan the yeoman farmer in *The Longest Journey* who, 'bent down reverently and saluted the child: to whom he had given the name of his mother' (289). The end is to return to the lost object of the name of the Mother, in the safe womb of the English land – a mythic-utopian vision that will return as a political ideology after 1914.[60]

In these novels, then, there has been a journey in and around England. But it is one that appears to have been a return to the past in a reaction against the promise of modernity. Significantly, travel abroad has been refused.[61] Travel, as we have seen in the 'Italian' novels and some of the stories, can bring about change or desublimation of repressed desires. Rickie needs to travel to be able to write; travel abroad should give him a greater experience of the wider world. As we read early in *The Longest Journey*: 'At all events it was the beginning of life pastoral, behind which imagination cannot travel' (85). And later, despite plans: 'They did not get

---

[59] She is disturbed by speed when in a car, losing 'all sense of space' (170). Travelling down from London by car she feels that 'the landscape resumed its motion' and the 'whole journey ... had been unreal' (183). Another description of the new speed is the train journey Leonard Bast takes (275).

[60] Masterman wrote of 'the crumbling and decay of English rural life, and the vanishing of that "yeoman" class' (67).

[61] In *Howards End* characters go abroad to escape scandal (Helen), or to keep out of trouble (Paul Wilcox) or for work in the colonies.

to Italy at Easter' (173). After their marriage and a settled life in Sawston, Agnes 'was content with the daily round', and Rickie feels they will not want of money because they 'don't even spend any on travelling' (190). If they go anywhere, it is not to Italy or Greece, but 'a few visits together in England' (194). Friends suggest Rickie's lack of travel has damaged his writing: '"What happened to your short stories? ... Why have you stopped writing? Why haven't you been to Italy? You *must* write. You *must* go" ... This question he avoided. Italy must wait' (276–7). Is the alternative of travelling around England to see its ancient sites, which Stephan Wonham insists on, a satisfying substitute for foreign travel? If the answer is no, then the ending cannot be satisfactory either, because Rickie's failures (marriage, writing) are attributed to his lack of travel; and Stephan's back to the land idyll may be construed as retrogressive. It appears again in Forster's writing, as we see in the next section of this chapter in that quintessential Forsterian English space, the 'Greenwood' as the focus for a queering of Englishness in *Maurice*. But despite Forster's fascination with English places, the rural landscapes of the south, the ancient sites, as flights from modernity, the writer will not develop without foreign travel; and the sought-for English home in the countryside will not be spared the encroachments of the modern housing estate.

It is in these novels that Forster develops a symbolism and a mythic structure that moves the residual realism towards a modernist aesthetic, and one that will achieve is highest expression in *A Passage to India*. In *Maurice*, though, he adds to this developing aesthetic the question of sexuality as another condition of Englishness.

Maurice and the Queer Space of the Greenwood

Like the earlier novel, *The Longest Journey, Maurice* tells the story of the education of the English middle classes from prep school, to public school, and Cambridge – an education that was supposed to lead to physical health and the right values for the maintenance of patriarchy, but where the boys nevertheless remained 'backward, to receive upon the undefended flesh the first blows of the world' (15). Sex education was designed for a normative masculinity: 'He [Mr Ducie] spoke of the ideal man – chaste with asceticism. He sketched the glory of women ... To love a noble woman, to protect and serve her ... Male and Female!' (19) – the injunction to protect boys against same-sex desire that was rife in single-sex public schools.

Foucault has drawn our attention to the ways in which regimes of discipline have been designed to exercise power over the body. The institution of the school understood as an apparatus of the State has an immediate hold over the body. Such power relations, 'invest it, mark it, train it, torture it, force it to carry out tasks, to perform ceremonies, to emit signs' (Foucault, *Discipline and Punish*, 25). To prepare them for citizenship in the disciplinary society, pupils are supervised, constrained and punished – a coercive regime that is meant to be replicated and reinforced by the family. These mechanics of power should produce docile bodies useful to the economy and obedient to the political State (*Discipline and Punish*, 138). Discipline 'presupposes a mechanism that coerces by means of observation' (*Discipline and Punish*, 170). In Forster's novel, surveillance is ubiquitous: Maurice and Clive's idyllic day out in the countryside does not go unnoticed; it results in Maurice being sent down. In this sense we might talk of the universal pedagogic gaze, which Foucault defines as a 'gaze without an agent', not individual but instrumental, so that 'one and the same gaze watches for disorder, anticipates the danger of crime, penalising every deviation' ('Questions on Geography', 72).[62] Disciplinary practice is at the same time spatial practice because the use of space is regulated – so that, as Forster would say, the gay man needs somewhere to escape to, somewhere out of sight. Yet in *Maurice*, in order for the boys to grow up like their 'dear father in every way' (22), sexuality is surveilled and controlled by parents, the teachers (27), the police and the law. When Maurice confesses his homosexual inclination to Dr Barry, he is admonished: 'Man that is born of woman must go with woman if the human race is to continue' (30) – a reiteration of the heterosexual imperative.

If classical education based on the civilizing influence of the study of the literature and philosophy of Ancient Greece is central to becoming a gentleman, then to be successful it must deny or omit the unspoken in this cultural heritage, the 'unspeakable vice of the Greeks' (50). Clive Durham tries to teach Maurice Platonic love between men through his reading of Plato's *Symposium*, so that homosexual desire can be sublimated into homosocial bonding and thus 'never become carnal' (67). The intense homo-erotic bonding at school and at university is meant to give way to hetero-patriarchy in the adult. Same-sex desire is conventionally understood as a phase or stage in male development and Clive's story belongs to this hetero-normative plot, which achieves closure with his marriage. With Maurice, however, Forster transvaluates this conventional development plot by ending with the union of Maurice and Alec.

In the late nineteenth and the early twentieth century, homosexuality was pathologized and criminalized. In late Victorian evolutionary psychology it was understood to be a primitive stage of arrested development – a phylogenetic stage; and a perversion that if widespread would lead to the degeneration of the race. Forster challenges this homophobic and racist tradition by transvaluating hetero-normativity. He does this in two ways: first, through inverting the hetero-marriage plot, and instead proposing a return to the greenwood – a mythic place like the Sherwood Forest of the Robin Hood legend, where outlawed men can live in innocence and freedom. Maurice's drive is to replace the loss of his first object of desire, George the garden boy in his childhood past, and find a place of simple and uninhibited being; second, Forster insists that middle-class hetero-normativity is a sham – and this is fundamental to his critique of Englishness. Mature civilized being is predicated on control of the passions, and the right kind of desire, which will entail a fixing of the object of the man's desire in woman. It is no surprise that

---

[62]   The argument could be extended to the collective middle-class gaze keeping an eye of the English abroad so they do not misbehave. Versions of this controlling gaze occur in all the writers studied in this book. Henry James, *The Ambassadors* is the classic analysis of the moral gaze trying to discipline the American abroad, and I will return to it in Chapter 4.

hetero-marriage is the closing device of novels from Jane Austen and throughout the nineteenth century. It is the foundation of the laws of gender and sexuality.[63]

Forster's gay ending for *Maurice* was indeed too daring for his day. We can now understand it in terms of its challenge to the heterosexual imperative of the English novel: 'Successfully transforming the conventions of marriage fiction, Forster moves his Austen-like protagonist toward wisdom through courtship and concludes with a marriage that seals his moral growth. It was Carpenter who confirmed Forster in his sense of the 'new' homosexual and who proposed the terms for Forster's dual perspective on homosexual love' (Robert K. Martin in Tambling, 111). As Howard Booth argues, to challenge the platonic ideal of Clive's homosexual love, Forster 'wanted a more active central figure' who could represent a 'manly homosexuality' to counter the more passive victim of the literature at the time (in Bradshaw, 174; 183). Thematically and structurally, Forster challenges the limits of closure in the English novel, that long tradition of realism that tied up all the loose ends in the heterosexual marriage – following Jane Austen's proposition that a single man of good fortune is in want of a wife.[64] However, the fact that Forster delayed publication of *Maurice* until after his death means that he could only continue to tell his story about male 'friendship' in displaced form, disguising the homoeroticism – a reading available now to us today.

Place and topography play an important role in Forster's homosexual fiction. Here once again he proposed a back to nature philosophy to live a simple life and cultivate the inner feelings denied by life in middle-class, bourgeois society. The urge to return to the English countryside, as utopian refuge, provides the utopian closure of *The Longest Journey* and *Howards End*. However, by returning to the mythic space of the ancient English wood, the gay men in *Maurice* hope to be able to lead an authentic and uninhibited existence. Such ideal longing is given a sense of urgency in a novel set at a time when homosexual men contravened the laws of society if they did not conceal their true selves behind the mask of respectability. When he wrote the novel before the Great War Forster was inspired by a visit to Edward Carpenter, the campaigner for more tolerant attitudes to same-sex relationships.[65] Forster believed the greenwood was then still imaginable as a happy ending for Maurice and Alec, 'an untamed son of the woods' (192) – a mythical place outside the reach of the controlling gaze where the men could transcend class differences: 'They must live outside class, without relations or money; they must work and stick to each other till death.' Forster wants to insist

---

[63]   See Freud's ambivalence towards repression as the basis of civilization in *Civilization and its Discontents* (1930). In his diary entry for 27 February 1905 Forster wrote: 'artists now realise that marriage, the old full stop, is not an end at all' (cit. in Furbank, vol. 1, 132). And in his diary for 15 December 1910, in Furbank's words, he 'sketched out a scheme, or rather a "desire", for a new novel, one in which he might get away from the conventional marriage plot' (vol. 1, 192).

[64]   See the opening statement of *Pride and Prejudice* (1813).

[65]   Kermode reminds us that Carpenter's *Love's Coming of Age* was widely read and 'made him the most prominent challenger of conventional morality'. *Concerning E.M. Forster*, 150.

that 'England belonged to them' (208–9). The novel appears to be a suppressed wish fulfilment (because published only belatedly), a romance of the greenwood. But as Forster argues in 1960 in the 'Terminal Note', the greenwood had been destroyed by modernity:

> The book ... belongs to an England where it was still possible to get lost. It belongs to the last moment of the greenwood ... Our greenwood ended catastrophically and inevitably. Two great wars demanded and bequeathed regimentation which the public services adopted and extended, science lent her aid, and the wildness of our island, never extensive, was stamped upon and built over and patrolled in no time. There is no forest or fell to escape to today, no cave in which to curl up, no deserted valley for those who wish neither to reform nor corrupt society but to be left alone. (221)[66]

Being left alone surrounded by friends is an ideal situation that recurs throughout Forster's life. Whether in the mythic space of the greenwood, the cloistered haven of Cambridge, or Bloomsbury, however, desire is sublimated into the aesthetic. In *Maurice*, same-sex desire is given a higher value by Clive in its Platonic version: 'the precise influence of Desire upon our aesthetic judgements' (86) – thus displacing the object from the body to art.[67] But the aesthetic goes beyond the refinement of desire to the very form of the novel.

Aestheticism belongs to a debate well-known to Forster and his Bloomsbury friends;[68] and *Maurice* prioritizes aesthetic values. One form of the new aesthetic central to early modernism is symbolism, which through repetition and variation enables a structure of motifs in the text. There is a pattern of images with symbolic resonances around light and dark – a symbolism that also carries a lot of weight in Conrad's writing, as we saw in the previous chapter. In *Maurice*, sometimes the implication is that the light within us needs to be allowed to shine; sometimes darkness symbolizes sexual ignorance or unawakened sexuality. The public school is ironically called 'Sunnington', ironic because it is where the boys are kept in the dark. A key passage in this symbolism is when Maurice visits his dying grandfather who has constructed an elaborate cosmology where God is in the sun and the black sunspots 'reveal God to men' (122). Clive first helps Maurice out of the darkness – 'The light grew radiant' (74) – then sends him back into it. Forster transvaluates the darkness of 'abomination' – a signifier associated with the 'sin' of homosexual love and with disgust and inhumanity. The scene of

---

[66] For an example of Clive and Maurice having a blissful day together in an idyllic English countryside see 73–4. Of course, Forster did not live to see the decriminalizing of homosexuality.

[67] A ploy used famously in that other homo-erotic story of the early twentieth century, Thomas Mann's *Death in Venice* (1912).

[68] As we saw in the discussion of Hellenism as a foil to modernity in *Alexandria*, Forster sometimes idealized a version of classical 'aesthetic' life. The dangers of aestheticism, however, are incorporated in the character of Cecil Vyse in *A Room with a View*. I discuss the 'ideology of the aesthetic' in chapters 4 and 5.

hypnosis-therapy is in a dark room with a single light shining on the picture of a woman; but Maurice misrecognizes it for a man, his instinctive object of desire (158–9). Lasker Jones, the therapist diagnoses 'congenital homosexuality', and 'cannot promise a cure' (158) – a daring suggestion at the time that it is not just a phase but that Maurice is by nature attracted to other men, and thus rejecting the evolutionary psychology practiced in the novel by Dr Barry.

The gay content is also expressed through repetition and variation of key signifiers in the text. For example, through ellipses and euphemisms, there is a play of 'queer' and its commonly associated signifiers: 'sodomy', being 'unmanly' (32); Risley is called 'this queer fish' (36); love between men is 'criminal morbidity' (57) or just being 'that way' (68), indulging in 'the unspeakable vice of the Greeks' (84). Maurice is divided by 'illicit' desire: 'There was now a complete break between his public and private actions' (148). Clive turns against 'queerness' (152), while Maurice remains an 'invert' (187). When sex between men occurs there is an ellipsis in the break between chapters. However, when desire is spoken 'in the middle of the sunlit court a breath of liberty touched him' (50). Indeed, it is an idealized image of nature – the natural space for the expression of an otherwise repressed or suppressed desire. This expression of desire in displaced form circulates throughout Forster's fiction.

There is a significant, recurrent spatial symbolism in the novel focussing around the interior and the exterior. The closed space of the drawing room of polite middle-class society stands against the plenitude of nature, the house against the greenwood. A key scene is where Maurice and Clive go into the countryside for a swim (72–4), a place where they can breathe more freely – 'the air they breathed was pure' (72). Here they become uninhibited: 'They laid their cheeks together and began laughing' (73). By contrast: 'Indoors was his place and there he'd moulder, a respectable pillar of society who has never had a chance to misbehave' (163–4). In the offices of Messrs Hill and Hall, Maurice can see that middle-class clientele 'had never known real joy. Society had catered for them too completely' (190). The symbolism of darkness and the interior are brought together in this critique: 'The clientele … whose highest desire seemed shelter – continuous shelter – not a lair in the darkness to be reached against fear, but shelter everywhere and always, until the existence of earth and sky is forgotten' (190). As in *Howards End*, the house itself has a transcendent significance. Indeed, in *Maurice* the gentrified house, Penge, is falling to pieces, the roof leaks and it is described as 'in bad repair' (83), or dilapidated (145, 149, 209) – quite a contrast to the well-kept estate of Pemberley in Jane Austen's *Pride and Prejudice*: in the tradition of country-house fiction, such places are symptomatic of the state of England.

Thus *Maurice* is also a condition-of-England novel: 'Maurice was stepping into the niche that England had prepared for him' (53). The novel focuses on the formation of class snobbery through 'public-schoolishness' (54); Clive and Maurice are young 'misogynists' (92), and Maurice is described as 'a promising suburban tyrant' (93) who looks like 'a solid young citizen … quiet, honourable, prosperous without vulgarity. On such does England rely' (135). Moreover, Maurice 'disliked playing [cricket] with his social inferiors' (175). Lower-class resentment is present in the figure of Alec Scudder, the gamekeeper who declares, 'I'm as good as you' (196).[69] And it is class difference that is the problem between lovers ('he had gone outside his class' with Alec) because of the threat of blackmail (180–82). Finally, Alec and Maurice 'must live outside class' (208–9). In Forster's story, class is supposed to be transcended by gay love. It recurs as male 'friendship' in Forster's *A Passage to India*.

What I think *Maurice* does, however, is to radicalize gender and sexuality by addressing the question of same-sex desire directly – too directly for publication in his day. Moreover, the novel also advances Forster's writing more towards modernist symbolism and motif-structure. It is in his masterpiece, *A Passage to India* that the modernist writing reaches its greatest achievement; but also where the identity problematic takes on the full implication of a critique of Englishness and British imperialism.

A Passage to India: The Location of the Other

After returning from the first visit to India in 1912 to research his new novel, it is not *A Passage to India* that Forster writes but *Maurice*. In a rush of creativity the novel about love between men is written.[70] Then the suppressed story of the love between Maurice and Alec is sublimated into the friendship between the two men, Fielding and Aziz. What begins as an attempt to break both sexual and class taboos in *Maurice*, ends up attempting to break down racial barriers in *A Passage to India*. Forster, like other writers of his generation, accused English class society of constraining authentic being and genuine friendship. Whereas in *The Hill of Devi* India is 'a site of friendship' (Baucom, 120), in *A Passage to India* any such attempt at friendship is disabled not least by the arrogant and hysterical behaviour of the Anglo-India ruling class – the 'Turtons and Burtons'.

Having just read *A Passage to India* D.H. Lawrence wrote to E.M. Forster in July 1924 that 'The day of our white dominance is over, and no new day can come till this of ours has passed into night' (Boulton, 281). And in October 1924, writing from New Mexico to the English critic John Middleton Murry, Lawrence says:

> All races have one root, once one gets there. Many stems from one root: the stems never to commingle or 'understand' one another. I agree Forster doesn't 'understand' his Hindu. And India to him is just negative: because he doesn't go down to the root to meet it. But the *Passage to India* interested me very much. At least the repudiation of our white bunk is genuine, sincere, and pretty thorough, it seems to me. (Boulton, 285–6)

Lawrence, Forster and Conrad before them established the terms for a critique of British imperialism which enable a re-reading of these writers

---

[69]   Scudder is an inverted version of Mellors in Lawrence's *Lady Chatterley's Lover*.

[70]   Clearly there is a connection between the two novels that emerges out of Forster visiting India. What was ostensibly, publicly, a cultural journey for purposes of research, turns out to be sexually important for Forster – as Quentin Bailey has claimed 'Forster ... had returned to India' to see Syed Ross Masood again (340).

as proto-post-colonialist. Lawrence clearly speaks for the liberal-minded reader in 1924 who understood and appreciated the novel, *A Passage to India*, because it was a novel of its time, a time when the superiority of the western model of civilization was being questioned even more, a critique fundamental to anti-modernity modernism: 'a questioning of attitudes to the "other" and to colonialism ... modernism, and its philosophical underpinning, had ... found ways of producing texts that allowed for multiple voices and respectful relations to alterity and difference' (Booth and Rigby, 2–5). Indeed, as we have seen elsewhere in Forster's writing, questions are being posed about Englishness itself; and the problem of national cultural identity becomes more acute as the rule of empire starts to break down.

The title, like the rest of the novel, does not settle on a single meaning. Amongst its meanings, 'a passage' signifies travel (by boat), the ticket itself, and a right to be conveyed; the act of moving through or passed something; access through a corridor or door to another part of the building; a noteworthy portion of a written text; a phrase or short section of a musical composition; and the action or process of passing from one place or condition to another.[71] In the passage to the other, cultural diversity seems a muddle. However, for those who want to impose the unity of a single cultural reality, cultural relativity appears to offer no consolation, only disillusion. Thus the title of the novel may be read as ironic. The meanings that religion and politics insist on are put into perspective in the novel by the mysterious presence of nature symbolized in the caves, an absent centre or empty space where the only response to human wishes is an empty and haunting echo – a refusal of response, and one that rejects cultural constructions that have read human identity into nature as in the mirror of the soul, the proof of God's creative powers, the awe of the sublime or simply the consolations of the picturesque. This symbolic negation appears to be a rejection of the consoling closures of Forster's earlier fiction, like *The Longest Journey* and *Howards End*. In this it is a rejection of the romanticism in so much travel narrative, undermining the desire for the exotic.[72] Nature's refusal to respond to man's constructions is Mrs Moore's discovery, and it haunts her to death. She and Adela Quested want to see 'the real India', but they need to remove their English tourist spectacles first. This proves difficult – as it has in Forster's previous travel stories, and even his own travel writing – as the real of place appears to consist of illusions, misunderstandings, rigid social and religious codes, insurmountable differences, and deep-seated prejudices, which in *A Passage to India* collectively contribute to the misrecognition of India. The Indian landscape is not after all the English Lake District, and significantly the latter is the place where Adela meets Ronny Heaslop, 'among the grand scenery of the English Lakes' (*A Passage to India*, 77)[73], a landscape that seems conducive to

---

[71] Definitions taken from the *New Penguin Dictionary* (2000).

[72] See Goodyear in Tambling, 163–7, for further discussion of the empty symbolism of the Indian landscape and the caves.

[73] Further page references abbreviated as *PI* in text.

harmonious relationships, at least within the single culture. Compared to the Indian landscape Grasmere and its topography it is 'Romantic yet manageable' (150).

In the opening pages, landscape is described in tourist guide discourse (reminding us of the Baedeker parodies in *A Room with a View*): 'Except for the Marabar Caves – and they are twenty miles off – the city of Chandrapore presents nothing extraordinary ...' (*PI*, 5). However, the inadequacy of the description to touch more than the surface of the place is important, because, on the one level it shows how place, like the other, is subject to perception conditioned by individual and collective constructions; and on another level, symbolism and recurrent motifs construct an aesthetic level of implication beyond realism (and the tourist guidebook) – a style of writing that Forster had been developing, as I have been arguing in this chapter. For example, right from the start the signifier 'extraordinary' is already associated with the Marabar Caves, just as the Indian landscape is characterized by the symbolism of a dark hostile nature that is resistant to idealization. It is the combined effect of conflicting perceptions of the real and the deconstruction of prejudices and idealizations that enable the author's irony. The clash of worldviews required for the larger ideological problematic in this novel – and the one central to Forster's critique of British imperialism – begins more explicitly in chapter 2 as a conversation amongst local Moslem friends raises the key question – and one also addressed in *The Hill of Devi* – as to whether 'it is possible to be friends with an Englishman' (*PI*, 8). This question will be dealt with on several levels in the text.

In *A Passage to India* topography symbolizes cultural difference as a matter of deep unconscious being. 'The overarching sky', like literature, can both encompass and transcend the gulf between East and West, and between Hindu and Moslem. The problem of locating the real is seen already in the opening description of the novel: the tourist guide discourse is as inadequate as any other discourse for representing place. The Indian city both is and is not what it seems: 'a totally different place'; 'a city of gardens'; 'no city, but a forest sparsely scattered with huts'; 'a tropical pleasance, washed by a noble river' – depending on whether it is viewed from the ground above at the Civil Station or close up when the newcomer from the west will 'acquire disillusion'. Mrs Moore and Adela Quested will take longer to become disillusioned in their search for the '*real* India' (21, italics in original); destined to fail because after having 'made such a romantic voyage across the Mediterranean and through the sands of Egypt to the harbour of Bombay' they have found only 'the dullness' of the Anglo-Indian life. Like Philip Herriton who advises Lilia in *Where Angels Fear to Tread* to 'love and understand the Italians, for the people are more marvellous than the land' (3), Fielding encourages the visitors to 'try seeing Indians' (*PI*, 23). But such encounters will be fraught with misunderstandings derived from misconceptions, because seeing is not necessarily understanding. However, Mrs Moore, who represents the tourist gaze, will not give up easily:

> Mrs Moore, whom the Club had stupefied, woke up outside. She watched the moon, whose radiance stained with primrose the purple of the surrounding sky. In England the moon had seemed dead and alien; here she was caught in the

shawl of night together with the earth and all the other stars. A sudden sense of unity, of kinship with the heavenly bodies, passed into the old woman and out, like water through a tank, leaving a strange freshness behind. (26)

But here she makes a category mistake by reading the surrounding sky as a sign of a greater cosmic significance that will enable human understanding between the cultures, races and religions. Nature is a tempting illusion. It is not just the danger of romanticizing the Indian landscape, but also the effect of place on cultural identity. Fielding is different because he has travelled widely, and with an open mind it seems. Travelling on a train for the first time in India, 'The journey remained in his mind as significant' as there are two other Englishmen in the compartment, one young and new to the East the other 'a seasoned Anglo-Indian of his own age. A gulf divided him from either: he had seen too many cities and men to be the first or to become the second' (*PI*, 56). He had no trouble having friends back home in England, 'so why was it not the same out here?' (57) Ronny Heaslop is the focus for this other English identity in India. His fiancée, Adela confirms Fielding's view that it is India itself that is to blame: 'It was as if irritation exuded from the very soil. Could one have been so petty on a Scotch moor or an Italian alp? Fielding wondered afterward. There seemed no reserve of tranquillity to draw upon in India' (71). Despite his openness to other cultures, Fielding realizes he is more at home in the cradle of European, or even the ancient Egyptian civilization, because 'the Mediterranean is the human norm':

> The buildings of Venice, like the mountains of Crete and the fields of Egypt, stood in the right place, whereas in poor India everything was placed wrong. He had forgotten the beauty of form among idol temples and lumpy hills; indeed, without form, how can there be beauty? ... The harmony between the works of man and the earth that upholds them, the civilization that has escaped muddle, the spirit in a reasonable form, with flesh and blood subsisting. (*PI*, 265)

Leaving the Mediterranean in an easterly direction, the traveller approaches 'the monstrous and extraordinary', leading to 'the strangest experience of all' (266). The associations of the signifier 'extraordinary' have already been established in the novel (in the beginning of the first chapter and the start of part 2); and like 'harmony' we do by now understand these are not universal concepts but Eurocentric ones that Fielding, as representative liberal post-Enlightenment man, realizes define the limits of his understanding and acceptance of India – as indeed Forster himself records in *The Hill of Devi*. It is not Aziz's (Moslem), or Godbole's (Hindu) notion of harmony – and Forster demonstrates the profound differences that stand in the way of a unified view of India, as best he could as an English writer and traveller. As we have seen, he himself insists his time spent in India qualified him for the complex task, but only once he was back in England and had the necessary critical distance to his subject. The representation of India is located in that gap between memory of place and the experience of it, between psychology and geography. And if the Marabar Caves symbolize the centre of that experience in his novel then the void there only echoes the wishes projected onto it, or, in another trope Forster uses, the darkness as a mirror to reflect back what the traveller thinks she has found there – as in the case of Mrs Moore. In Adela Quested's case the result is a reflection of her own hysteria, and one that will be exposed as the collective pathology of the English imperialists.

Patrick Brantlinger gives us a broader historical narrative for this hysterical attitude to the native other: it belongs to 'an imperialist heritage of division and mutual hate' after the Indian Mutiny of 1857, which 'lies at the centre of E.M. Forster's *A Passage to India* … The Mutiny atmosphere makes all of the British characters, with the exception of Fielding, behave hysterically' (*Rule of Darkness*, 222–3).[74] This collective reaction is sparked off by one woman's 'hysterical English imagination' which, even though she admits her delusion, is symptomatic of the impossibility of friendship between Fielding and Aziz – symptomatic, indeed, of 'the entire history of British imperialism in India' (Brantlinger, 223) – 'the universal brotherhood he sometimes dreamt of, but as soon as it was put into prose it became untrue' (*PI*, 135).

Expectations that condition the tourist gaze waiting for a 'magnificent' sunrise are not fulfilled: 'As she spoke, the sky to the left turned angry orange. Colour throbbed and mounted behind a pattern of trees … They awaited the miracle. But at the supreme moment … nothing occurred' (128). The landscape being unreliable and unresponsive displaces Adela's disappointment; and once again, the English Lake District is recalled collectively as substitution gratification: 'Romantic yet manageable, it sprang from a kindlier planet. Here an untidy plain stretched to the knees of the Marabar' (129). The English landscape belongs to Fielding's harmonious order. If the Hills of Marabar are a place of 'spiritual silence', it is also where no 'thoughts develop' and everything 'seemed … infected with illusion' (131); and in this place where 'nothing was explained, and yet there was no romance' (131), the protagonists are left to their own resources. Mrs Moore finds the caves a 'horrid, stuffy place really' (132), and then she is shocked by 'a terrifying echo' (137) which 'began in some indescribable way to undermine her hold on life' because it seemed to tell her that 'Everything exists, nothing has value' (139) – the Marabar is beyond romanticizing, and her experience of the void reminds us of Kurtz's dying revelation of 'the horror' in *Heart of Darkness*. What is indescribable is, of course, unknowable; and we have seen the Indian landscape and the caves are not amenable to western categories of description – like the uncanny or the exotic; and even when what may have happened there is called rape, this turns out to be another false naming.[75]

Adela Quested enters the caves with her guide Aziz deep in thought about 'Ronny's limitations' (*PI*, 141) and Aziz's physical presence in comparison –

---

[74]   Kermode adds that although the novel makes no direct reference to the Amritsar massacre of 1919 Forster knew about it, and that it is 'virtually certain' these events 'influenced *A Passage to India*', especially in his portrayal of the Club 'with its arbitrary and hysterical reactions' (*Concerning E.M. Forster*, 126–7).

[75]   For an incisive discussion of the western limits of representing India in the novel see Benita Parry, 'The Politics of Representation in *A Passage to India*' in Tambling, 133–50.

'beauty, thick hair, a fine skin' (143) – metonymies marking her desire, even when she keeps unconscious desire at bay through her social conscience. But she is also affected by being alone in the cave, with first deep and empty silence, then an echo which remains inside her until the moment later when she admits that she was not assaulted – although, by implication, Aziz's presence contributed to her confused state of mind. When she asks Mrs Moore what the echo is she is told that only she can know intuitively (188); and Adela's hysteria is blamed on her being neurotic, and thus hallucinating the incident in the caves (225).

Confronting such recalcitrant difference in a visible place the western subject is stripped of all illusions and is left to realize that her own cultural real is a construct without universal value. This personal revelation, first of Mrs Moore, then Adela Quested, of inner emptiness acts as a strategy in the novel to undermine the greater political question of British imperial rule in India. The gulf between East and West may not even be as great, the novel claims, as 'the fissures in the Indian soil are infinite: Hinduism, so solid from a distance, is riven into sects and clans, which radiate and join, and change their names according to the aspect from which they are approached' (278).[76] For, whether the Marabar hills or the English countryside, the distance between the eye and the object of the gaze enables the subject to see what it needs to see. Once out of the void of the caves signification returns with a vengeance, as Anglo-Indian paranoia always already knows that something will have happened in the caves when a white woman is left alone with a native man.[77]

A further consideration in the representational problematic in *A Passage to India* is that when Forster establishes the relationship between place and culture in terms of the western tradition of aesthetics, a landscape reflecting the truth of a culture, its sense of harmony between man and nature, this notion of harmony is itself a western concept – as the last section of the novel insists. Here, Forster presents Godbole's Hindu world as ritual carnival and spiritual communion with nature, achieving a balance in the end between a western enlightened irony, a detachment that turns what he describes into comedy, and a respect for the joy of celebration for the birth of Krishna – a space between cultures negotiated by art.

Forster's art is modernist because, like Conrad's, or D.H. Lawrence's – as we shall see in the next chapter – it not only strives to unfix limited perspectives and worn-out values but also to work with other ways of expressing truths, like symbolism, repetition, and recurrent motifs. The recurrent leitmotif creates a rhythm of symbolic associations across the text, as it does in musical composition –

---

[76] Such internal divisions undermine the totalizing gestures of Orientalism by definition. As Said put it, 'we immediately note that "the Arab" or "Arabs" have an aura of apartness, definiteness and collective self-consistency such as to wipe out any traces of individual Arabs with narratable life histories'. *Orientalism*, 229. As I argued earlier in this chapter, Forster was sensitive to such totalizing misreading of the Orient. See *Abinger Harvest*, 259. It is a sensitivity we also see in Conrad, as discussed in the previous chapter.

[77] For an excellent paper on misrecognition see Timothy Christensen's 'Bearing the White Man's Burden: Misrecognition and Cultural Difference in E.M. Forster's *A Passage to India*'.

reminding us of Walter Pater's dictum that underpins modernism: 'All art constantly aspires to the condition of music' (Pater, 124).[78] One example of the recurrent leitmotif is the wasp that Mrs Moore sees on a peg (30) and later, after her death, Godbole recalls 'One old English-woman and one little, little wasp ... It does not seem much, still, it is more than I am myself' (276). This association illustrates a principle of simple love for the lowliest creature that takes men and women out of their destructive self-absorption. More generally, the places – Mosque, Caves and Temple – establish recurrent patterns of cultural and natural spaces with symbolic resonances, like symphonic tones and movements. These locations also correspond to the motifs of arch, echo and sky. In the latter the sky overarches man's petty differences, and it is suggested at the outset as a key principle that the distances between the cultures are not as great as those between the stars: 'the distance between the earth and them [the stars] is nothing to the distance behind them' (6). Whereas the Mosque and the Temple represent cultural and religious realities, the caves are like a vortex (a modernist trope) where reality is tested and found wanting, and all values are relative.

What Forster achieves in *A Passage to India* is coherence through the formal structure of the novel that the different cultural realities lack. It seems it is only in the constructed order of art, like in myth, that the real can be located. For Forster, the work of art is 'the only material object in the universe which may possess internal harmony' (*Two Cheers for Democracy*, 90). It is an idea of order that Kermode has called Forster's 'aesthetic imperative' (*Concerning E.M. Forster*, 134). It helps make sense of the estranging experience of otherness. And we can see that Fielding speaks for the author in his belief in the aesthetic harmony of classic European Culture; but also in the philosophical underpinning of the novel: 'we exist not in ourselves, but in terms of each other's minds' (234) – and it is this proposition that undermines the essentialism that the Anglo-Indians reproduce in their relationship to the space of the other.

Conclusion

As a vitalist like D.H. Lawrence, opposed to the effects of the machine age, Forster tried to recover some sense of the spiritual even when looking to other cultures and religions to counter the materialism of western modernity. He wanted to stress spontaneity in personal and sexual relations; and in this connection prioritized, as we have seen, the natural over the social worlds in his fiction. Forster's protagonists are seeking the location of happiness, but it is difficult to find in the condition of England or its Empire places. *A Passage to India* ends with the suggestion that friendship across racial difference is not possible, not yet, and not in British India. *Maurice* and *The Longest Journey* suggest that happiness is only to be found in a

---

[78]   For further discussion of music in Forster's novels and the influence of classical composition (musical rhythm) on his sense of structure, especially the work of Beethoven and Wagner see chapter 2 in Frank Kermode, *Concerning E.M. Forster* (28–52). Forster also discusses the importance of pattern and rhythm in *Aspects of the Novel* (1927).

mythic place, an imaginary, idealized farm or woodland – although such places are already on the verge of extinction because of the inexorable march of modernity. Even the quiet homeliness of Howards End is threatened by the ubiquitous housing development. In *A Passage to India* Forster implies that, in David Adams's words, 'Home is no longer a particular household, England, the Mediterranean world, or the British empire, but a metaphor for universal unity and harmony' (*Colonial Odysseys*, 37) – as Forster discovered one can feel at home wherever friendship is offered. In any case, travel has not been the solution either to the discontents of home seen in *The Longest Journey*, part two of *A Room with a View*, *Howards End* and especially *Maurice*. *A Passage to India* projects the discontents of home onto India, exposing the pathology that undermines the apparent stability of English identity, taking the intolerance towards sexual difference in *Maurice* into racial difference in a critique of British imperial psychology where the other is always a sexual degenerate, and all white women are in danger of rape.

It is Adela Quested who has the responsibility, finally, to incorporate a truth about travel that goes further than the lessons of Forster's Italian stories: travel and colonial travel are different journeys because feeling at home with the Anglo-Indians will preclude, by definition, seeing the real India. Even when a typical English tourist in Italy will only at best see Baedeker Italy, travel to India is different from travel to Italy because, as Fielding (speaking for Forster) insists the Mediterranean is the spiritual home for western subjects. India can only be, even for the English tourist, an occupied land, a place of resentment and conflict. *A Passage to India* appears to be an object lesson in Freud's analysis of culture and repression in *Civilization and Its Discontents*, because what we see from the governing Anglo-Indian community is a sublimated cultural unconscious, so that a repressed sexuality is displaced onto the Indian other with all the force of a collective paranoia. The homophobia in England in *Maurice* has become the racism in India in *A Passage to India*, and the English version of civilization that underpins British imperialism has been discredited. What Adela Quested discovers is that there are limits to the transgressive and transformative potential of travel; limits constrained not only by collective prejudices but by the inability of individuals to change or at least have an open mind towards difference. To reiterate Forster's central claim: 'it is this undeveloped heart that is largely responsible for the difficulties of Englishmen abroad'; they are 'afraid to feel' ('Notes on the English Character' in *Abinger Harvest*, 5)[79] – sexual panic can end in hysteria.

Moreover, it is the same fear that, expressed in forms of public censorship and collective reaction, restricts creative freedom, as Forster (and Lawrence) knew only too well. In 1935 Forster complained that for writers in England 'more than elsewhere, their creative work is hampered because they can't write freely about sex' ('Liberty in England' in *Abinger Harvest*, 64) – and here he has in mind the suppression of Lawrence's *The Rainbow* (1915) and Radclyffe Hall's *The Well of*

---

[79]   Patrick Parrinder claimed in *Nation and Novel*: 'If any novelist of the time was dedicated to investigating the English character it was E.M. Forster' (291).

Loneliness (1928).[80] Yet, he does his creative work in any case, because the need to write about sexual identity in indirect ways leads him to experiment beyond realism. Indeed, under the pressure of representing truths that go beyond Victorian and Edwardian cultural and sexual values a new and less stable writing emerges – to undermine single, unified perspectives for the sake of a 'gay' modernism; and one that only since Forster's posthumous publications (and the Furbank and Moffat biographies) we are able to appreciate.

As this chapter has argued, travel has a heuristic value because it offers the chance for the broadening of cultural – and sexual – horizons. And this, Forster's working proposition, was tested out on himself and on his fictional characters. When being abroad lead to joy and happiness, homecoming was difficult – to a grey and depressing England. But England – rural southern England – could work its magic: the woodland or landscape would then be the place to evade the tribulations of repression, class and modernity. Some of Forster's critique of England and Englishness, class and sexuality, will resurface in D.H. Lawrence – as we will see in the next chapter. It was Lawrence who called Forster 'the last Englishman'. From Baden Baden in 1924, Lawrence wrote these words to Forster: 'To me you are the last Englishman. And I am the one after that' (cit. in Furbank, vol. 2, 163).

---

[80]   Forster lent his support to the defence at the *Lady Chatterley* trial.

Chapter 3
D.H. Lawrence:
Travel, Otherness and the Sense of Place

Introduction

Beginning with Lawrence's travel writing, and then addressing his narrative fiction which reflects on travel and displacement, I will chart successive stages of Lawrence's journey first away from home, then from England – to Germany, Switzerland and Italy; and then out of Europe to Australia, New Mexico and Mexico, before finally returning to England and Europe. It is a journey offering new and challenging encounters with the other, and raising important questions about Englishness, imperialism, cultural difference and modernity – questions also raised by Conrad and Forster, as addressed in the two previous chapters. A large part of the discussion here in this chapter too will concern the encounter with culture difference and the notion of otherness. In Lawrence's words, 'Now we must learn to think in terms of difference and otherness' (*The Symbolic Meaning*, 17). Driven by restlessness, Lawrence pursues a ceaseless quest for a place to live, and one that more and more resembles that lost place of his youth, Haggs Farm, as he tries a series of farmsteads in England and abroad – the most important being Kiowa Ranch near Taos, New Mexico. It is as if the whole of Lawrence's travelling life was in fact a search for a home; once 'expelled' from England, and in self-exile, and despite three failed attempts to return home, he reluctantly accepted a nomadic existence abroad. This began in earnest after the Great War when, starting in Germany and Italy, he actually travelled round the world. And when ill health rendered the harsher climates he preferred impossible, he returned to southern Europe. Expatriation or self-exile, as we see in other chapters of this study, is a condition of the modernist artist. As Caren Kaplan suggests, 'exile becomes a vocational imperative' for modernist writers who are thus 'prototypes of "deracination", examples of the "artist as displaced person"' (*Questions of Travel*, 38–9). In Lawrence, there is a tension between the nomadic and sedentary – a tension we see in the other writers in this study, like Forster's desire to travel, to get away from the limits of home, while always searching for a place to call home; or Conrad writing from a series of English houses about the life of travel to exotic places he experienced as mariner. Expatriation as a need and a perspective is central to the work of Henry James and Edith Wharton, as the following two chapters will elaborate.

Lawrence was a persistently autobiographical writer, using the places and the people he knew to work through the moments of crisis in his life in fictional narratives, to understand himself and his relationships better. He often wrote about where he was at the moment of writing, giving his work a sense of immediacy, and, most importantly for this chapter, a sense of place, which makes him a topographical writer. Indeed, I want to insist on the importance of the effect of place on the fictional characters, an effect rehearsed by the author in his own travel writing.[1]

In what follows, there will be a focus on Lawrence's landscapes – from pastoral England to the 'savage' landscapes of the antipodes and the New World. However, it is important to keep in mind his own reiterated insistence on the land too as the location of cultural memory and as cultivation – like the generations of Brangwen farmers in the opening pages of *The Rainbow*, and the Bavarian peasants in the fields before the Alps in the travel essay 'The Crucifix across the Mountains' (1913).[2] The land is a sacred place to Native Americans: they dance the land, as we see in the travel sketch, 'The Dance of the Sprouting Corn' (1924). Farming and dancing the land – spatial practices – are instances of the organic connection between man and nature that refuse the idealization of the pastoral tradition and the alienations of the machine age. I will have more to say about the relationship between landscape and land in Lawrence's writing, because it is here that he establishes the importance of the topography of lived experience.

Paul Fussell (1980) already insisted on the importance of place in Lawrence's writing. Not only are questions of identity – senses of being – tied up with responses to place in his fiction, and the place where he writes part of what he writes; but crucially there is an implicit assumption that the reader is, in Fussell's words, 'willing to imagine everything spatially, everything in a place' (143). Lawrence's sense of place becomes insistent. His topographies range from the garden, the woodland, the farmland, to the barren landscape or Alpine vista and the island – the places of nature; and they are usually opposed to the poky suffocating domestic interiors, or the alienating city – the places of society and class. The tight spaces indoors are always repressive, while the outdoors is the space of freedom and the expression of passion. For example, the school in *The Rainbow* becomes a prison for the idealistic Ursula, and both this novel and its 'sequel', *Women in Love*, work through the idea of 'a progressive enlargement of spatial horizons' (Michelucci, 86)[3] – even when in *Women in Love* the location

---

[1]   As David Ellis puts it in *D.H. Lawrence: Dying Game 1922–1930*, Lawrence 'was someone who could usually write anywhere', and that much of the writings in the 1920s 'were begun and finished in the same place' – *Kangaroo* in Australia and *The Plumed Serpent* in Mexico, for example (395). Lawrence also appears to have a vivid recollection of journeys made and places visited, as we know from *Sea and Sardinia* written up just after the trip. And Lawrence's preferred place of writing was the garden or woodland: 'sitting in the open against an olive tree in order to write, retreating into the neighbouring woods' (Ellis, 300).

[2]   In a review (1930) of essays by English artist Eric Gill Lawrence wrote: 'Only in the country, among peasants, where the old ritual of the seasons lives on in its beauty, is there still some living, instinctive "faith" in the God of Life' (cit. in Ellis, 529).

[3]   Michelucci's study is exemplary in taking further Fussell's suggestions about place in Lawrence.

shift abroad to Switzerland at the end has tragic consequences. Enlarging spatial horizons is a cultural process where difference becomes paramount, for Lawrence and his fictional characters.

The journey is a trope in Lawrence's writing for the life of the culture as well as the individual. Travelling away from home is like going back to primitive origins, not though to regress to a state of primitivism, but in the hope of discovering a pre-Christian religious sense lost to materialism. The journey has significance for Lawrence even in contemplating death, as we see in his late poem, 'The Ship of Death' (1929): 'Now it is autumn and the falling fruit / And the long journey towards oblivion ... / Build then the ship of death, for you must take / The longest journey, to oblivion' (*Complete Poems*, 716–20). The idea that one should prepare for the journey of death he learnt from his study of Etruscan culture, where death was understood as a continuance of life or as Lawrence put it: 'the mystery of the journey out of life, and into death' (*Sketches of Etruscan Places* in *D.H.Lawrence and Italy*, 378).[4]

Lawrence's Travel Writing[5]

The Desire to Travel

In words familiar to readers of western travel writing – indeed expressing sentiments Forster would have shared – Lawrence wrote:

> How wonderful it must have been to Ulysses to venture into this Mediterranean and open his eyes on all the loveliness of the tall coasts. How marvellous to steal with his ship into these magic harbours. There is something eternally morning-glamorous about these lands as they rise from the sea. And it is always the Odyssey which comes back to one as one looks at them. (*Sea and Sardinia* [1921] in *D.H. Lawrence and Italy*, 318)

The location is magical and classical; it is the cultural origins of the western idea of travel.

In the opening words of his travel book *Sea and Sardinia* Lawrence is clear about what motivates his travel: 'Comes over one an absolute necessity to move. And what is more, to move in some particular direction' (141). And the direction of travel is 'west or south' he declares in *Twilight in Italy* (*DHLI*, 117). Going west in England takes you to Cornwall and Ireland, the location of Celtic civilization; going south in Europe takes you to Italy and the remaining mountain peasant villages still unaffected by modernity. In his further travels, Lawrence insisted on approaching America from the west, via Ceylon, Australia, New Zealand and

---

4 Subsequent page references abbreviated as *DHLI* in text.

5 An earlier version of this section was published as 'Home Thoughts from Abroad: Cultural Difference and the Critique of Modernity in D.H. Lawrence's *Twilight in Italy* (1916) and Other Travel Writing' in *Landscape and Englishness*, 137–61.

Tahiti to San Francisco, thus avoiding New York;[6] and then once in Taos, New Mexico going on further south into Mexico which he believed to be the 'real America'. Indeed, in 1920 he wrote that America 'must turn again to catch the spirit of her dark, aboriginal continent' and get back to pre-Columbian native cultures, and the time before the Pilgrim Fathers ('America, Listen to your Own', rept. in *Phoenix*, 90). It is not that he is insisting on a complete return to primitivism;[7] but for Lawrence as for many other artists and writers in the period of modernism the attraction to pre-modern civilizations becomes both the goal of travel and a device for a critique of modernity.[8]

Travel has a more general aim and one usually expressed in the ideal form of the quest for paradise. In a review published in 1926 of H.M. Tomlinson's *Gifts of Fortune: Some Hints to Those about to Travel*, Lawrence wrote: 'We travel, perhaps, with a secret and absurd hope of setting foot on the Hesperides, of running our boat up a little creek and landing in the Garden of Eden.' However, high hopes always lead to disappointment: 'There is no Garden of Eden, and the Hesperides never were. Yet in our very search for them, we touch the coasts of illusion, and come into contact with other worlds' (*Phoenix*, 343). It remains to be seen in the following discussion the extent to which Lawrence does manage to 'come into contact with other worlds'.

If the desire to travel derives from restlessness at home, then it has something oedipal about it. Freud wrote in 'A Disturbance of Memory on the Acropolis' (1936) that travel repeats a childhood wish 'to run away from home' (Standard Edition, vol. 22, 247). Even as early as 1908, in a letter to May Holbrook (2 December) Lawrence is complaining that 'one does seem buried in Eastwood' (his hometown) (*Selected Letters*, 17). Once in Italy he writes from Villa di Gargnano to Arthur McLeod of the 'hopelessness ... grubbiness and despair' of England (4 October 1912, *Selected Letters*, 47). By 1913 Lawrence does not want to live in England anymore, as he feels he has become a different person since his first travels in Italy (1912) because '[t]his is all so different from anything I have known before' (letter to Helen Corke, 29 May 1913, *Selected Letters*, 59). After the war, Lawrence embarks on a personal quest for a different way of life to the perceived mechanizing effects of modernity, and travel becomes the dominant narrative trope in his fiction. At first, however – and expressed in *Twilight in Italy*, as in *Sea and Sardinia* – he still believes in old Europe. Once disillusioned, though, he will search further afield in the New World for cultural and religious alternatives. I think we can see that being abroad can focus the English traveller's dissatisfaction with home.

Lawrence's mood on leaving England is expressed in the largely autobiographical novel, *Kangaroo* (1923) in the thoughts of his alter ego, Somers: 'As he looked

---

6   'I would really like to miss New York.' See letter to Mabel Dodge Sterne, 5 November 1921 in *The Selected Letters of D.H. Lawrence*, 226.

7   'But there is no going back' (*Phoenix*, 99).

8   Examples range from Picasso's use of the African mask in his painting, to Gauguin's exoticism, to T.S. Eliot's mythography in *The Waste Land* influenced by Frazer's *The Golden Bough* (2 vols 1890, 12 vols 1911–1915) and Weston's *From Ritual to Romance* (1920).

back from the boat, when they had left Folkestone behind and only England was there, England looked like a grey, dreary-grey coffin sinking in the sea behind, with her dead grey cliffs, and the white, worn-out cloth of snow above' (258).[9] Similar words occur in *The Lost Girl* (1920), as Alvina and Ciccio leave England for Italy on the ferry from Folkestone: 'For there behind, behind all the sunshine, was England ... England, like a long, ash-grey coffin slowly submerging' (347).[10] What is important to notice here is that the leaving of England is thus remembered in a symbolic topography – a dead landscape. Much later, after living in New Mexico, Lawrence returns home and describes the view from a train: 'Outside, a tight little landscape goes by ... with sunshine like thin water'; 'Here you get an island no bigger than a back garden, chock-full of people who never realise there is anything outside their native back garden, pretending to direct the destinies of the world' ('On Coming Home' in *Reflections on the Death of a Porcupine and Other Essays*, 179; 183).

In another largely autobiographical novel, *Mr Noon*, Lawrence recalls waking up for the first time abroad. On a spring morning in 1912 in Bavaria, Gilbert Noon is intoxicated by a new sense of space: the 'vast patchwork of Europe', its landscape, rivers and mountains opening up 'infinite multiplicity of connections'. He became 'unEnglished', and sees England from the outside as 'tiny ... and tight, and so partial', and English culture whose 'truths and standards and ideals were just local, not universal' (107).[11] Gilbert Noon, like the author, had to 'grow out of ... his English insularity', as Kinkead-Weekes puts it (*D.H. Lawrence: Triumph to Exile*, 619), and broaden his horizons.[12] The desire to travel is tied up with the necessity to get away from the perceived limits of England prefigured in the morbid tropes of being buried at home, or the grey-dreary coffin. In this frame of mind Lawrence is bound to idealize the colourful ways of life and the plenitude of landscapes in Italy and elsewhere – at least at first sight. As topography symbolizes the essence of the culture, so cultural differences enable a critical perspective on home – as we see in much of the topographical writing throughout this study.

Locations of the Real and the Depredations of Modernity

In his travel writings Lawrence describes places where the old ways of the traditional life are threatened by modernity. In *Twilight in Italy* rural Italy is suffering the same fate as rural England; and this is visible in the landscape of the degenerating lemon groves in the Lake Garda region and the threat to traditional masculine

---

9   Subsequent page references abbreviated as *K* in text.

10   Subsequent page references abbreviated as *TLG* in text.

11   Subsequent page references abbreviated as *MN* in text.

12   But how un-English was Lawrence himself to become? In the summer of 1926 on his third and, as it turned out, final visit to England, he realized that after the years of travel, in David Ellis's words, 'had made him feel how "English" he was in many of his attitudes ... it had not noticeably and consistently increased his fondness for England itself' (*D.H. Lawrence: Dying Game*, 320).

identity in its village communities. The condition of England is projected onto the Italian landscape and its people, as are the representational codes of western landscape. Lawrence appropriates the places he visits to illustrate his concerns about the depredations of modernity, and to do so he draws on discourses common at the time – those of cultural decline and degeneration; and the romanticized description of place.

Neil Roberts has suggested Lawrence's representation of place is an example of Bakhtin's idea of the 'chronotope' (*D.H. Lawrence, Travel and Cultural Difference*). Landscape is a chronotope when there is an interrelation of the spatial and the temporal in an image or a trope, enabling a historical dimension to have a precise location. In Bakhtin's words: 'Time, as it were, thickens, takes on flesh, becomes artistically visible; likewise, space becomes charged and responsive to the movements of time, plot and history' (*The Dialogic Imagination*, 84). Two types of chronotopic perspective in travel narrative which we see particularly in Lawrence's writing are 'adventure-time' and 'quest-time'. The former is characterized by the contingencies of the journey to different places where the traveller observes cultural diversity without in any way being affected by cultural difference.[13] 'Adventure-time' is the paradigm of the imperialist traveller – important especially to Conrad's travel stories. 'Quest-time', however, is characterized by a predetermined goal that will change the traveller as he or she searches for cultural difference. For Roberts, *Sea and Sardinia* is an example of 'adventure-time', while *Mornings in Mexico* and *Etruscan Places* are examples of 'quest-time'.[14] However, I would suggest that when Lawrence reiterates his desire to see and experience 'the real landscape' (*DHLI*, 117) and otherness, the representation of place is somewhere between the actual topography and what Andrew Thacker calls 'the space of the psyche' (*Moving Through Modernity*, 3).[15] Like Forster and his fictional characters who demand to see the real Italy or the real India, Lawrence's driving force to see the real is also the desire for the encounter with the other in its own homeland. But to what extent does the desire to see the real lead to misrecognition? As discussed in the general introduction, for Lacan misrecognition 'represents a certain organisation of affirmations and negations, to which the subject is attached.' And, he concludes, 'there must surely be, behind his misrecognition, a kind of knowledge of what there is to misrecognise' (Lacan, *The Seminar Book I*, 167). In other words, Lawrence has in mind an ideal other – the unselfconscious peasant in Italy, or the Native American close to nature – as the object of his quest; and, by extension that object or other, in the Lacanian schema, is always a metonymy,

---

[13]   Where 'cultural diversity' implies the liberal acknowledgment of multiculturalism, 'cultural difference' – in Homi K. Bhabha's words – 'focuses on the problem of the ambivalence of cultural authority: the attempt to dominate in the name of a cultural supremacy' (*The Location of Culture*, 34).

[14]   For further discussion see Roberts, 121–4.

[15]   The idea of 'mental space' as distinct from 'social space' was proposed by Henri Lefebvre in *The Production of Space*. He even suggested a 'psychoanalysis of space' that might investigate spatial pathologies – see Lefebvre, 99.

the figure of speech for desire itself (Lacan, *Ecrits*, 175). For Lawrence that desire is to witness primitivism before it is lost to modernity, the topos of native culture before its time runs out. The encounter with the other is, therefore, always at least partially a failed encounter because of the difference between the real (a projection of desire) and reality. Lawrence becomes aware of that unbridgeable otherness especially in Mexico: 'The Indian way of consciousness is different from ... our way of consciousness' ('Indians and Entertainment' in *Mornings in Mexico*, 61).[16]

In his travel and travel writing cultural difference and otherness are important to Lawrence, no matter how difficult they are to encounter. And, as with the other writers studied, there is, in consequence of the quest for cultural otherness, a reiterated critique of British and later American imperialist attitudes and practices. However, he occupies a contradictory position as sometime critic of dominant western values, but one who would at times resort to the racist and patriarchal discourses in circulation.

Home Thoughts from Abroad

In a letter to E.M. Forster, Lawrence complained that 'England herself seems like a ship adrift, entirely without course or anchorage' (30 May 1916 in *Selected Letters*, 129). It is in this frame of mind that he takes up a critical position in his travel writing. The 'foreign reality' is sometimes observed as a general impression from the outside; at other times he attempts to understand the locals in more intimate portraits of particular individuals. In *Twilight in Italy* there is, for example, a woodcutter from the mountains who is admired for his dancing; and Lawrence focuses on the body: 'he is inconceivably vigorous in body, and his dancing is almost perfect ... He is like a god, a strange natural phenomenon, most intimate, compelling' (*DHLI*, 83–4); Southern sensuousness is contrasted to 'the vague Northern reserve' of the English women present (85). Lawrence is not always able to get beyond the popular romanticizing of the Italian: the local men, Il Duro and John, are described as instinctual and primitive. But John 'had suffered very much in America'. He had been jeered at and called abusive names; he had become a foreigner. Modernity had taken away his innocence, his 'pure elemental flame' had been 'shaken out of his gentle, sensitive nature'; but he had made money (98–9). This is not Lawrence's idea of travel – unsettled migrating people seeking a better life elsewhere for purely materialist purposes. Instead, the aim of travel is to get away from the effects of modernity by searching for places where an older, traditional masculinity still exists.

In *Twilight in Italy* Lawrence sees cultural difference in the light of his critique of England: the changes in the region of Lake Garda to the countryside and the indigenous people are the same as those that have already happened back home around Eastwood, Lawrence's home region, as he describes it in the late essay, 'Nottingham and the Mining Countryside' (1929). In this, as in much of his writing,

---

[16] Subsequent page references to this collection of *Mornings in Mexico* abbreviated as *MM* in text.

landscape is given a greater symbolic force as the essence of the culture. Lawrence belongs to the ruralist tradition where the agricultural past is idealized as a time when English life was apparently organically unified; and, by contrast, the present life of industrial England has become mechanical. In this version of English history, old rural England has gone forever with its organic, village communities. Modern industrial Britain has spoilt the country and the life of the people. The organic has given way to the mechanistic, instinct to self-consciousness.[17] In the Garda region of Italy, the traditional lemon farming is in ruins, the men emigrating to find work. Lawrence blames modernity and the machine age (and implicitly globalized capitalism) ('The Lemon Gardens' in *DHLI*, 51–3). The people are losing their instinctive relationship to the land and nature. It is an instinctive existence that has already disappeared from England where once the men of Lawrence's father's generation brought with them from the coal mines a 'curious dark intimacy ... a lustrous sort of inner darkness' ('Nottingham and the Mining Countryside', rept. in *Phoenix*, 136). The old England of Lawrence's youth where 'Robin Hood and his merry men were not very far away' (133) is the 'old agricultural England of Shakespeare and Milton and Fielding and George Eliot' (135). The conclusion to this reminiscence is that: 'The real tragedy of England, as I see it, is the tragedy of ugliness. The country is so lovely: the man-made world is so vile' (137).

What we see in this late essay is that Lawrence's attitudes to modernity were more or less consistent throughout his writing life. It is not just a matter of romanticizing the countryside and the old ways as such. The problem comes down to a question of gender: the women 'nagged about material things', spoiling the men as men. The mothers encouraged the sons to 'get on': 'In my father's generation, with the old wild England behind them, and the lack of education, the man was not beaten down' (*Phoenix*, 137). With the addition of the gender gloss, this critique is a familiar one. Raymond Williams argued back in 1958 that Lawrence adopted a nineteenth-century critique of industrial capitalism that derived from Carlyle's Romantic humanism[18] and from William Morris's socialism. In Lawrence, this critique consistently takes the form of dramatizing the loss of the instinctual, spontaneous self, and one which he located deep in the place of his origin, a place and a way of life from which he had escaped. Williams points to the key words in the Lawrence lexicon: 'mechanical', 'disintegrated' and 'amorphous', to describe the effect of industrial capitalism on the individual and society (*Culture and Society*, 119).

---

[17] Lawrence says all this in the novel he had just written, *Lady Chatterley's Lover*. Later in this chapter we look at Connie's thoughts as she travels in her chauffeur-driven car around Tevershall: 'England my England! But which is my England?' (*Lady Chatterley's Lover*, 156). Subsequent page references abbreviated as *LCL* in text.

[18] In 1906 (aged 21) Lawrence is reading Carlyle obsessively, as John Worthen explains: 'What had bitten him were almost certainly Carlyle's energetic denunciations of Mammon and self-consciousness, and his assertions of Soul, Aristocracy and Individual'. Of course, 'Lawrence took from Carlyle what he needed – and then transformed it into his own way of understanding and feeling.' (*D.H. Lawrence: The Early Years 1885–1912*, 122).

In *Twilight in Italy* we see an early example in Lawrence of travel as a quest for other ways of life where the old organic relationships still obtain. But time is running out. For as he put it in that other Italian travel book, *Sea and Sardinia* in old Europe 'the race of men is almost extinct' – like the old coal miners of his father's generation (*DHLI*, 197). Moreover, even when he travels further afield to the New World in search of regenerative cultural paradigms, man's instinctive ways of being will continue to be based on a fundamentalist masculinity, as the ideal other. In a letter to his publisher, Thomas Seltzer (9 January 1922), Lawrence said that travelling to America he hoped for 'some kind of emotional impetus from the aboriginal Indian and from the aboriginal air and land, that will carry one over this crisis of the world's soul depression, into a new epoch' (cit. in Neil Roberts, 49).

Twilight of Civilization

Lawrence and Frieda stayed for about seven months, from 18 September 1912 to 3 April 1913, in Villa di Gargnano, on the western side of Lake Garda in Northern Italy, with a view of the lake. In the introduction to the essays collected in *Twilight in Italy and Other Essays*, the Italian Lawrence scholar Stefania Michelucci describes the place:

> For hundreds of years, the hills around Gargnano were transformed into a paradise of lemon orchards ... Although the large-scale cultivations of lemons died out at the beginning of the twentieth century, the structures of the lemon houses have left an unmistakable mark on the landscape ... The lemon industry, which had originally brought wealth and stability to the region, had already undergone an initial decline at the beginning of the twentieth century ... (xv–xvi)[19]

Michelucci goes on to explain that inland, in the hills, there are remote villages where time seems to have stood still. Some of the villages retain their simple way of living off the land, and Lawrence was attracted to this aspect. Here is his description of San Gaudenzio in 1912, just before the war:

> In the autumn the little rosy cyclamens blossom in the shade of this west side of the lake. They are very cold and fragrant, and their scent seems to belong to Greece, to the Bacchae. They are real flowers of the past. They seem to be blossoming in the landscape of Phaedra and Helen. They bend down, they brood like little chill fires. They are little living myths that I cannot understand ... It is so still and transcendent, the cypress trees poise like flames of forgotten darkness, that should have been blown out at the end of the summer ... The dawns come white and translucent, the lake is a moonstone in the dark hills, then across the lake there stretches a vein of fire, then a whole, orange, flashing track over the whiteness. (*DHLI*, 68–9)

Michelucci's lemon orchards are a place with a geography, history and economy. The description is factual, in the recognizable discourse of the travel guide.

---

[19]   See also Michelucci, *Space and Place in the Works of D.H. Lawrence*.

Lawrence's description of the landscape is constructed out of the codes of western art and classical myth. The last part of the description appears to have been painted by Turner![20] The mythic-Romantic real of the Lawrentian landscape is an imaginary counter-weight to the real world of a modernizing and industrializing Europe – as it is in the tradition of Italophilic travel writing seen also in the other writers in this study. And as Neil Roberts claims, 'Lawrence never did "purely descriptive" writing ... Interpretation is inwoven with description in an artful way' (89).

But despite this idealized first encounter with the Italian landscape, Lawrence's Italian journey will end in disillusion. The 'European Twilight' is a leitmotif on the eve of war as old Europe is heading towards destruction. The later essays in *Twilight in Italy* and the final revision for publication (in 1916) confirmed the premonitions felt in the early essays.[21] The loss of stable regional communities belongs to a common restlessness, as local economies collapse and the men leave to seek their fortune in America. In Europe too there are migrant workers crossing borders, becoming despised foreign workers, as greater pan-European virtues celebrated by Lawrence elsewhere in his text collapse into petty parochial tensions. These tensions were soon to be expressed on the larger stage of the Great War. *Twilight in Italy* records a period of crisis in the region of Lake Garda with the collapse of the lemon industry, but also the greater crisis of modernity and of the coming of the war, symbolized in the spread of the industrial machine: 'And England was conquering the world with her machines and her horrible destruction of natural life ... teeming swarms of disintegrated human beings seething and perishing rapidly away ...' (*DHLI*, 46). As well as it being the start of Lawrence's own restless migrations in search of a new cultural space, *Twilight in Italy* could be read as belonging to the contemporary discourse of cultural decline through the force of modernity in the work of Nietzsche, Nordau and Spengler.

Lawrence's cultural analysis is expressed in the discourse of 'decomposition' and 'disintegration' common in the analysis of the crisis in western culture in the late nineteenth and early twentieth century – and one we saw in Conrad too. In Lawrence we read: 'It is as if the whole social form were breaking down, and the human element swarmed within the disintegration, like maggots in cheese' (133). He takes up again what began with the description of the decaying lemon gardens of San Gaudenzio – the twilight of a peasant culture and then the coming of war: 'It is passing away from Italy as it has passed from England. The peasant is passing away, the workman is taking his place. The stability is gone ... it is all passing away. Giovanni is in America, unless he has come back to the war' (79).

The landscape itself is degenerate, sterile: 'And there they stand, the pillars and walls erect, but a dead emptiness prevailing' (79). Jopi Nyman comments: 'it portrays degeneration through explicitly gendered language. While the pillars

---

[20] Lawrence's landscape description illustrates Daniels and Cosgrove's idea that landscape is a 'cultural image' with symbolic value. Landscape is thus encoded text. See their introduction to *The Iconography of Landscape: Essays on the Symbolic Representation, Design and Use of Past Environments*.

[21] As Michelucci explains in her introduction to the 1997 edition, xvii.

stand erect, in modern Italy these metaphors of masculinity have become sterile. There is no place for true masculinity which as a redemptive force would save western civilization' (110). Once Lawrence moves away from Europe, however, and even while he wants a new masculinity to lead the way out of the crisis, he will sometimes prefer the landscape without an agent. Indeed, as we will see later in this chapter, the 'savage' landscapes of Australia, New Mexico and Mexico will have a value beyond agency.

Towards the end of *Twilight in Italy* the coming war fuels a critique of militarism and industrialism in the same breath: 'At the bottom was a little town with a factory or quarry or foundry, some place with long, smoking chimneys; which made me feel quite at home among the mountains.' He continues: 'It is the hideous rawness of the world of men, the horrible, desolating harshness of the advance of the industrial world upon the world of nature that is so painful. It looks as though the industrial spread of mankind were a sort of dry disintegration advancing and advancing, a process of dry disintegration ...' (124–5). This portrait of the cultural crisis focuses on the common social organism as a disintegrating body (133). There are still pockets of isolated life where 'one felt the old organism still living' (134). But Milan, although full of vivid life, was final proof in this Italian journey of 'the perfect mechanising of human life' (136).

Lawrence's analysis of the cultural crisis has much in common with the popular historian Oswald Spengler. He also described the decline of the west as a displacement of an organic by a mechanical state of being (*The Decline of the West*, 4, 20–21).[22] The discourse of decline is modelled on that of the decline of the Roman empire, that is classical culture which represents a history of what Spengler calls a 'higher mankind' (12). The twilight of a culture for Spengler is when it becomes a civilization. '*Pure* Civilisation, as a historical process, consists in a progressive exhaustion of forms that have become inorganic or dead' (25, emphasis in original). And as we have seen, for Lawrence this is the process of modernity, prefigured in the loss of the organic connection between man and the land, between essential cultural tradition and the Americanization of the Italian peasant. It is also an atrophy of the instinctual life by modern self-consciousness and materialism, seen in the migrant worker leaving for America (98–100).

Spengler also laments the development in the early twentieth century where a people 'born of and grown on the soil' become a 'new sort of nomad, cohering unstably in fluid masses, the parasitical city dweller, traditionless, utter matter-of-fact ... not a folk but a mob' (Spengler, 25). A culture 'blooms on the soil of an exactly definable landscape, to which plant-wise it remains bound' (73). In this sense, a culture is an organism. Once the living culture is uprooted from the native soil it disintegrates.[23] Lawrence argues the same point in his travel writing where

---

[22] Michelucci also draws attention to Lawrence's 'Spengler-like reflections on the destiny of Europe and western civilisation'. See her *Space and Place in the Works of D.H. Lawrence*, 89.

[23] 'This metaphysics of a collective soul which develops and dies like a plant puts Spengler in the company of vitalist philosophers such as Nietzsche, Simmel, and particularly Bergson ...' (Theodor W. Adorno, *Prisms*, 67).

place has vital, organic connection with indigenous culture.[24] Modernity is the end of the 'creative life-force' (34) of the culture, in both Spengler's and Lawrence's cultural history.[25] Freud's version of the crisis does not insist on the distinction between culture and civilization in the Spenglerian manner. *Kultur* for Freud is civilization in its distinction from primitivism but at the price of repression and neurosis. Sublimation is all that remains for the modern, civilized subject, which for Lawrence is a mental activity and thus not instinctive enough.[26]

What this comparison of Spengler and Lawrence proves, I think, is that Lawrence belongs to the growing tradition of European *Kulturkritik* that became a defining feature of modernism – which insisted on the disparity between human need and the Culture at large. Modernity, as I defined the concept in the general introduction, was marked by the instrumentalization of life, seen especially in the commodification of culture; and in my study that process is visible in the growth of mass tourism where places become so many sights for easy consumption. All the writers in this book take up a position on tourism. *Kulturkritik* lead to a widespread pessimism, which in its extreme forms expressed the loss of value and the decline of civilization in apocalyptic terms. Lawrence tended in this direction.[27]

In thinking the decline of the culture, Lawrence and his contemporaries assumed the connection of culture and race. For Spengler: 'A race has its roots. Race and landscape belong together ... the landscape exercises a secret force' (254). 'Rootedness' is a key concept in Lawrence's organicism. And as Anne Fernihough explains, rootedness is characterized by 'the overriding feeling' of 'alienation or rootlessness: humanities kinship with the soil had been forgotten' (*D.H. Lawrence: Aesthetics and Ideology*, 22). Fernihough continues – and I quote at length because I think she has captured well the Spenglerian critique in Lawrence:

> This alienation was seen to have been caused by the tyranny of rationalism and the intellect in modern society, and a concomitant outwardness, an expansive materialism; 'interiority', it was felt, must be brought back. The term 'disintegration' (*Zersetzung*) was used to evoke the weakening, in an industrial society, of the 'natural' bonds between people, and the erosion, through intellectual critique, of the traditional foundations of social cohesion. Descriptions of city-dwellers as 'soulless automatons', as mere 'statistics' or 'ciphers' in regard to their position in what was now perceived to be the social

---

[24]   Spengler also writes that 'the Culture is born out of its mother-landscape' (93). The organic theory of culture was soon to take on more sinister forms in European fascism.

[25]   For Lawrence, as we have already seen, industrialization is 'a process of dry disintegration' (124).

[26]   See Sigmund Freud, *Civilization and its Discontents*, and D.H. Lawrence, *Psychoanalysis and the Unconscious*.

[27]   Significantly his last book was *Apocalypse* (1931). For further discussion of Lawrence's apocalyptic theory of history and culture see Peter Fjagesund's *The Apocalyptic World of D.H. Lawrence*.

'machine' (suggesting a severance of organic links) pervaded the *völkisch* writing of the period. (22–3)[28]

Lawrence found his wished-for native culture in the great expansive landscapes of New Mexico and Mexico, where he could experience 'a surviving religious culture' (Worthen, *D.H. Lawrence: The Early Years*, 273) and its deep connections with a 'savage nature' – places he reaches via Ceylon and Australia after finding Europe 'weary and wearying' (cit. in *D.H. Lawrence: The Early Years*, 304), and wanting a place that was 'freer, less constricted, less industrial, less civilised' (240). New Mexico would become 'the place Lawrence had been looking for all his life' (273), away from the degenerating effects of modernity in England and old Europe, and where Lawrence would try to get beyond the restrictions of his Englishness by coming into contacts with these 'other worlds'.

Lawrence's quest for places where peasant cultures and primitivism still existed shares common currency with the other writers in this study in the sense of utopian compensation for the reifications of modernity – Conrad's adventure of the sea, Forster's queer space of the English 'Greenwood'; and, as I shall argue in the following chapters, James's and Wharton's gentrified England or old Europe as compensations for the 'vulgarity' of American modernity.[29]

Landscape, the Spirit of Place and the Other

Having established, then, that in travel writing landscape is an object of cultural knowledge, and foreign places are described by the traveller through the codes of landscape representation, it should also be clear that this tends to have the effect of collapsing difference, even while desiring contact with the other, of appropriating the other into the same. Thus a picturesque sunset will be recognized as a work of western art, or the less elevated form of the picture postcard; and art paradigms – the art-gaze – give the English traveller in Italy a ready-made perspective and a descriptive language; and the tourist a ready-made landscape-for-the-gaze – as Forster's Italian novels demonstrate. For Lawrence, however, a landscape in New Mexico is an anti-picturesque construction, a 'savage' landscape. The savage and the sublime belong to the Romantic vision; the picturesque is its more 'civilized' counterpart. It is the difference between the Romantic and the Neo-Classical conception of landscape. You only need think of the difference between Shelley's wild Alpine landscape and the values of the Pemberley estate in Jane Austen's *Pride and Prejudice*.[30]

---

[28] Völkisch ideologies, as Fernihough reminds us, were 'prevalent in Germany in the 1910s and 1920s' (21) and were fundamental to the emergence of fascist thought: 'Blut und Boden' ('Blood and Soil'). As Adorno bluntly put it: 'Spengler predicted Goebbels' (*Prisms*, 57).

[29] To reiterate Jameson, modernism can be read as 'a Utopian compensation for everything reification brings with it' (*The Political Unconscious*, 236).

[30] 'In the wild woods, among the mountains lone, / Where waterfalls around it leap for ever, / Where woods and winds contend, and a vast river / Over its rocks ceaselessly

In *Twilight in Italy* the traveller witnesses and records cultural diversity but laments the collapse of real difference, blaming it on the process of sameness caused by modernity. The foreign culture is an inferior version of England, because it is destined to make all the same mistakes. Lawrence travels to find a place where he can live a more instinctive life apart from modernity, and where he can be himself. Once disappointed, he will travel to the next hopeful destination. It is not that Lawrence does not attempt to understand difference from his perspective as visitor, outsider, even intruder. He defines the contact zone as that place 'where the life of strange creatures and beings flickers on us and makes it take strange new developments.'[31] Estrangement is a key term here, because otherness is always recognized and acknowledged but never really known: 'When I stand with another man, who is himself, and when I am truly myself, then I am only aware of a presence, and of the strange reality of Otherness. There is me, and there is *another being* ... There is only this strange recognition of *present otherness*.' Identity is here defined in terms of difference. When in *Twilight in Italy* Lawrence observes an old woman spinning, what attracts him is that she takes no notice of his presence while she works unselfconsciously, and from this he draws the conclusion that 'there is something which is unknown to me and which nevertheless exists ... that world is not my world. I can only know there is that which is not me. I am the microcosm, but the macrocosm is that which is not me' (21).

Otherness is a positive term when first expressed in the novel *Women in Love*: 'For she was to him what he was to her, the immemorial magnificence of mystic, palpable, real otherness' ('Democracy' in *Reflections on the Death of a Porcupine and Other Essays*, 80, emphasis in the original). However, later on a boat from Ceylon to Australia, he writes to Lady Cynthia Asquith, 30 April 1922, insisting: 'But you don't catch me going back on my whiteness and Englishness and myself' (*Selected Letters*, 239). Here the other is a less positive term as Lawrence reiterates the colonialist fear of 'going native'; and the encounter with the indigenous other is not a transformative experience at all. Once Lawrence has been to Australia and Mexico, the other has become a threat. The Australian bush is itself an evil force: 'He felt it was watching, and waiting' (*K*, 14); and the native Mexican, in Neil Roberts's words, 'an unbridgeable difference' (19).[32] In Lawrence's essay on Fenimore Cooper the Native American landscape has 'a powerful disintegrating influence upon the white psyche', as there is 'too much menace in the landscape' (*Studies in Classic American Literature*, 56). The American landscape 'has never

---

bursts and raves' from Percy Bysshe Shelley, 'Mont Blanc' (1816) reprinted in *The Norton Anthology of Poetry*, 616. 'The park was very large, and contained great variety of ground. They ... drove for some time through a beautiful wood stretching over a wide extent ... and the eye was instantly caught by Pemberley House ... She had never seen a place for which nature had done more, or where natural beauty had been so little counteracted by an awkward taste' (Austen, *Pride and Prejudice*, 228).

[31]   Review of Tomlinson, *Gifts of Fortune* in *Phoenix*, 239.

[32]   This discussion of otherness draws on some of the ideas in Roberts's study.

been at one with the white man ... the very landscape, in its very beauty, seems a bit devilish and grinning, opposed to us' (*Studies in Classic American Literature*, 61). Landscape empty of people has become its own agency. When human agents are present, the other is not only observed but is watching you. The subject position of the traveller is being redefined as an object of curiosity for the native gaze:

> His eyes immediately rested on two figures approaching from the direction of the conservatorium, across the grass lawn ... They looked different from other people ...
> A smile flitted over the face of the man in the overalls – or rather a grin. Seeing the strange, foreign-looking little man with the beard and the absent air of self-possession walking unheeding over the grass, the workman instinctively grinned. A comical-looking bloke! Perhaps a Bolshy.
> The foreign-looking stranger turned his eyes and caught the workman grinning. Half-sheepishly, the mechanic had eased round to nudge his mate to look also at the comical looking bloke. And the bloke caught them both. They wiped the grin off their faces. Because the little bloke looked at them quite straight, so observant, and so indifferent. (*K*, 7)

Here Lawrence captures the moment of the traveller being seen as other by the local inhabitants. Pretending indifference is a strategy to defend an inviolable sense of identity against the critical gaze of the other. Returning the gaze is a gesture of defiance. It is also a conflict among men in a chauvinistic battle of wills in the classic colonial encounter. This feeling of being jeered at by the natives recurs throughout Lawrence's travel writing and fiction. It follows, as Neil Roberts argues, that 'when difference (for example sexual or cultural) is experienced as Otherness, any genuine engagement is foreclosed, but the encounter will be of intense if unacknowledged unconscious significance' (24).[33] In these terms the encounter in the contact zone can only be one of misrecognition.

Lawrence does, though, appear to be aware of the problem of misrecognition. By the end of *Twilight in Italy*, on 'The Return Journey', he describes the prospect from the top of a hill overlooking Lake Zurich, and wonders whether the reality of what he sees is the real: 'I could not bear to look at it ... I had a feeling as if it were false, a large relief-map that I was looking down upon, and which I wanted to smash. It seemed to intervene between me and some reality. I could not believe that that was the real world. It was a figment, a fabrication, like a dull landscape painted on a wall, to hide the real landscape' (*DHLI*, 117). But what is 'the real landscape'? When the real does not coincide with reality it is an effect of the imaginary. In Lacan's words: 'The place of the real ... stretches from the trauma to the phantasy – in so far as the phantasy is never anything more than the screen that conceals something quite primary, something determinant in the function of repetition' (*Ecrits*, 60). Continually driven by the desire for the sight of a pre-industrialized landscape, and the encounter with the primitive other, Lawrence

---

[33] As Lacan argued, 'the unconscious is the discourse of the Other' (*Ecrits*, 193).

reveals a quite conscious wish-fulfilment, but one that is often disappointed. Thus the real reveals itself in the failed encounter with the reality of the other (Lacan, *Ecrits*, 53).

There are moments in Lawrence, however, when he does get beyond misrecognition and come into direct contact with 'other worlds' – when he experiences 'the spirit of place': 'Every continent has its own great spirit of place. Every people is polarised in some particular locality, which is home, the homeland. Different places on the face of the earth have different vital effluence, different vibration, different chemical exhalation, different polarity with different stars: call it what you like. But the spirit of place is a great reality' (*Studies in Classic American Literature*, 12). The spirit of place is aboriginal, and in its traces Lawrence finds his solace from the instrumentalities of modernity.[34] How can you know the spirit of place? Presumably by intuition: you can sense it by simply being there. In his sketch of Taos, New Mexico (1922) Lawrence writes:

> You cannot come upon the ruins of the great old monasteries of England, beside their waters, in some lovely valley, now remote, without feeling that here is one of the choice spots of the earth, where the spirit dwelt ... Taos Pueblo affects me rather like one of the old monasteries. When you get there you feel something final. There is an arrival. The nodality still holds good ... like a dark ganglion spinning invisible threads of consciousness. A sense of dryness, almost of weariness, about the pueblo. And a sense of the inalterable. It brings a sick sort of feeling over me, always, to get into the Indian vibration. Like breathing chlorine. ('Taos' in *MM*, 125–6)

The spirit of place is experienced as something dynamic, as movement or kinetic energy, even 'ritual movement'. In his description of the native Indian dance ritual kinesics enable communion between man and the earth, as the Native Americans dance the land 'with the throbbing, pulsing, clapping rhythm that comes from the dark, creative blood in man, to stimulate the tremulous, pulsating protoplasm in the seed germ' ('Indians and Entertainment' in *MM*, 63).[35]

Some claims have been made for Lawrence's success in getting close to the reality of other cultures in the New World, and thus acknowledging difference. Mark Kinkead-Weekes, for instance, has claimed that Lawrence's writing on Native American culture during his life at Kiowa Ranch in New Mexico was 'an extraordinary imaginative effort to get inside Indian culture, seen now in many ways superior to his own' ('Decolonising Imagination', 73). Lawrence himself wrote of the difficulties involved in getting close to such a different culture to his own: 'But I stand on the far edge of their firelight and am neither denied nor accepted' ('Indians and an Englishman' [1922] in *MM*, 120). He was instantly aware of something different in the New World: 'But the moment I saw the brilliant, proud morning shine high up over the deserts of Santa Fe, something

---

[34] As I argued in *Radicalizing Lawrence*, 273.

[35] For further discussion see Jack Stewart, 'Movement, Space, and Rhetoric in Lawrence's Travel Writing' in Cushman and Ingersoll's *D.H. Lawrence: New Worlds*, 157–8.

stood still in my soul, and I started to attend' ('New Mexico' [1928] in *MM*, 176).[36]
In his new clarity he sees the danger of misreading the Native American through
the representation of the 'Red Indian' in Fenimore Cooper's 'leather stocking
novels', in 'the wild and woolly west'.[37] He recognizes a people who live close to
nature, and dance the land:

> They lean from left to right, two seed-like shakes of the rattle each time, and the
> heavy, rhythmic stamp of the foot, and the low, sombre, secretive chant-call each
> time. It is a strange low sound, such as we never hear, and it reveals how deep,
> how deep the men are in the mystery they are practicing, how sunk deep below
> our world, to the world ... where are the roots of corn, and where the little rivers
> of unchanneled, uncreated life-passion run like dark, trickling lightning, to the
> roots of the corn and to the feet and loins of men, from the earth's innermost dark
> sun. ('The Hopi Snake dance' [1924], rept. in *MM*, 86)[38]

When, later, back in Italy he visits the site of the extinct Etruscan civilization he
sees final proof that a people can live in harmony with their environment. In David
Ellis's words: 'After all his travels, Lawrence felt that he had finally discovered
in the Etruscans the traces of a people with the right attitude to life ... a people
who had sought to live in harmony with their natural environment rather than
exploiting or dominating it' (251).

If the reality of the other culture is spatial and spiritual at the same time, it
is hardly surprising that Lawrence locates native individuals in their cultural
Ur-space, a space haunted by a sort of tribal spirit. The Mexican landscape is
a 'psychic condition' in *The Plumed Serpent*;[39] the bush in Australia is 'biding
its time with a terrible ageless watchfulness, waiting for a far-off end, watching
the myriad intruding white men' (*K*, 15) – reminding us of the African jungle
watching that other fantastic invasion in Conrad's *Heart of Darkness*. In the travel
sketch, 'The Crucifixes across the Mountains' which opens the collection *Twilight
in Italy*, Lawrence describes the crucifixes he sees by the roadside in the Bavarian
Alps on his way south: 'The crucifixes are there, not mere attributes of the road,
yet still having something to do with it. The imperial processions, blessed by the
Pope and accompanied by the great bishops, must have planted the holy idol like
a new plant among the mountains, there where it multiplied and grew according to
the soil, and the race that received it' (5). In Lawrence's travel writing and fiction,
as Michael Bell has argued, there is 'continuity between the landscape and a given

---

[36] It reads like the moment in Forster when he 'started to attend' to Italy.

[37] As he explains in 'Indians and an Englishman': 'And in my heart, born in England
and kindled with Fenimore Cooper, it wasn't the wild and woolly west it was the nomad
nations ...' (*MM*, 115). See Ellis, 62–7 for further discussion.

[38] The ritual movement reminds us of the Brangwen farmers at the beginning of
The Rainbow or the Bavarian peasant farmers working the land in the travel sketch, 'The
Crucifix across the Mountains'.

[39] A point made by Michael Bell in *D.H. Lawrence: Language and Being*, 170 and
discussed by Neil Roberts, 123.

psychic quality. In both modes he combines literal geographical observation with psychic symbolism' (171). Moreover, it is the remote place beyond modernity that has this 'psychic quality' for Lawrence; and it is the object of his journey, as we see in the following passage from *Sea and Sardinia*:

> This is what is so attractive about the remote places, the Abruzzi, for example. Life is so primitive, so pagan, so strangely heathen and half-savage. And yet it is human life. And the wildest country is half humanised ... Wherever one is in Italy, either one is conscious of the present, or of the mediaeval influences, or of the far mysterious gods of the early Mediterranean. Wherever one is, the place has its conscious genius. Man has lived there and brought forth his consciousness there and in some way brought that place to consciousness, given it its expression, and, really, finished it ... So that for us to go to Italy ... Strange and wonderful chords awake in us. (*DHLI*, 250–51)

This fascination with remote places Lawrence shares with Forster. Here the Mediterranean Ur-landscape has a 'savage' aura; it is a primal and primeval place, like the remote places of ancient Britain as we see in Lawrence's description of the Cornish coast: 'The shore is absolutely primeval: those heavy, black rocks, like solid darkness, and the heavy water like a sort of first twilight breaking against them, and not changing them. It is really like the first craggy breaking of dawn in the world, a sense of the primeval darkness just behind, before the Creation' (letter to J.D. Beresford, February 1916 in *Selected Letters*, 117). If this Ur-landscape is central to Lawrence's quest, we also have to understand that to know the agent in the landscape as otherness requires the extinction of self: 'The Indian way of consciousness is different from and fatal to our way of consciousness. Our way of consciousness is different from and fatal to the Indian ... And we can understand the consciousness of the Indian only in terms of the death of our own consciousness' ('Indians and Entertainment' in *MM*, 61).[40] It is certainly in such moments of clarity that Lawrence gets beyond pure misrecognition. But does he also get beyond the 'imperial imaginary' that dominated the western gaze?

Mary Louise Pratt traces the 'imperial imaginary' in the signifying practices of travel writing, where 'transculturation' is required in the zone of contact between cultures. Transculturation is the process of improvising communication between cultures while avoiding the assertion of power (*Imperial Eyes*, 6). Can any western traveller in the age of Empire – no matter how liberal-minded – get beyond the imperial gaze? And, of course, this is an issue for all the travelling authors studied in this book. How much transculturation is there in Lawrence's travel writing when he claims he wants 'to come into contact with other worlds'? To what extent does he sometimes represent cultural difference as superiority, as in the conventions of British writing of the period?

To answer these questions, we should return to Lawrence's twin concern with race and gender in his quest for a new masculinity and a revived potency. Jonathan Dollimore calls this 'aesthetics of energy' whereby 'human desire is

---

40   For a further discussion of this example see Neil Roberts, 32.

revitalized and rescued from a social decadence'. He suggests that 'Lawrence, like other modernists, was attracted by potency in proportion to his conviction that the energies of the modern world were failing' (259). It is a masculine quest that appears as phallic desire in *Sea and Sardinia*: 'So that for us to go to Italy and to *penetrate* into Italy, is like a most fascinating act of self-discovery – back, back down the old ways of time. Strange and wonderful chords awake in us, and vibrate again after many hundreds of years of complete forgetfulness' (*DHLI*, 251). As I argued above, Lawrence's quest for an authentic masculinity beyond modernity and western feminism is directed towards the ideal object. Examples range from the idealized mountain peasant of the early travel writing to the morally questionable native other in the novel, *The Plumed Serpent*, where Lawrence's 'white psyche' plays its part in the gaze of the other.[41]

In *Twilight in Italy* the object of the traveller's gaze is the male body. John Worthen writes about Lawrence's 'specific attraction to a man's body' throughout his writing (*D.H. Lawrence: The Life of an Outsider*, 172–3).[42] The figure in the landscape, 'remote, out of contact' with modern civilization (5), has a purely physical, unselfconscious blood relationship with the land. He is exemplary of an ancient unchanging way of life, seen again in the Brangwen farmers working the land in the opening pages of the novel, *The Rainbow*. Indeed, the paratactic style serves to enact the oneness of the peasant farmer with the soil – like the Native American Indian dancing the land – enforcing a 'blood and soil' racial ideology:

> The body bent forwards towards the earth, closing round on itself: the arms clasped full of hay, clasped round the hay that presses soft and close to the breast and the body, that pricks heat into the arms, and the skin of the breast, and fills the lungs with the sleepy scent of dried herbs … It is this, this endless heat and rousedness of physical sensation which keeps the body full and potent, and flushed the mind with a blood heat, a blood sleep … It is the life and the fulfilment of the peasant, this flow of sensuous experience. (*Twilight in Italy*, *DHLI*, 6–7)[43]

Lawrence soon realizes, however, that the exclusive 'preoccupation with the physical was just as limiting as the northern gratification of the mind' (Tracy, 14). But the purely physical sense of being acts as a foil to the modern, self-conscious,

---

[41] However, Lawrence appears to ignore the machismo of pre-modern societies. Perhaps I could suggest he only recognizes this at the point when he rejects it for male tenderness in *Lady Chatterley's Lover*.

[42] Worthen insists that 'attraction was not the same as desire' (173). Lacan writes: 'The image of the other's form is assumed by the subject. Thanks to this surface, situated within the subject, what is introduced into human psychology is this relation between the outside and the inside whereby the subject knows himself, gets acquainted with himself as a body … It is within this see-saw movement, the movement of exchange with the other, that man becomes aware of himself as body, as the empty form of the body.' *Seminar Book I*, 170.

[43] See for comparison *The Rainbow*, 10, where the Brangwen men farmers work the land and feel 'the pulse and the body of the soil', and so on.

cynical being, where the life of the mind denies the life of the body. The 'carved Christs' on the crucifixes in the mountains are the first images of the male body, tormented (*DHLI*, 11–12). In San Gaudenzio, Lawrence observes the local men dancing with each other, focusing on the 'vigorous' masculine body (83) – a pan-like masculinity, as Lawrence embellishes the gender essentialism with the mythologizing of the man (91). But once again the conclusion is, 'there was nothing between us except our complete difference' (92).

Lawrence's own sympathy for the traveller uprooting and going abroad to an uncertain future carries with it more than a sense of changing places. In the case of the migrant worker, his sense of identity undergoes a process of disintegration because he is attracted to the materialism of capitalist America, as we see in Il Duro's diminished masculinity. What is waiting for the pre-modern peasant is exemplified in the Englishman Lawrence meets at an inn in the Alps on 'The Return Journey'. He represents the 'machine principle': 'I could feel so well the machine that had him in its grip. He slaved for a year, mechanically, in London, riding in the tube, working in the office. Then for a fortnight he was let free. So he rushed to Switzerland, with a tour planned out' (*DHLI*, 121). The man is, of course, the ever-despised tourist on his packaged holiday. Moreover, in his travel writing as well as in his fiction Lawrence returns time and again to the condition of England which stands as the paradigm of all that is wrong with modernity. It is the future of Italy, a future whose first stages are already visible in the landscape and the people.[44] However, sometimes modernity is more commonly understood as Americanization, as Italian migrant workers return from the US with a new set of material values; other times, it is the commodification of Native American life itself as it becomes a tourist attraction for white Americans.[45]

What this section of the chapter has shown, I think, is that Lawrence's travel writing addresses the contexts of modernity as a crisis manifested in a loss of cultural identity. But in doing so he often reveals a deep-seated sense of Englishness which, despite his rage against the limits of home and the global influence of capitalism, he takes with him on his journey around the world – 'I am English, and my Englishness is my vision' he asserted in 1915.[46] Yet, once in Italy again after the war, he comments from Capri (1921): 'Oh, my dear countrymen, how I detest you wherever I find you!' (cit. in Worthen, *D.H. Lawrence: The Life of an Outsider*, 226) – an attitude to fellow countrymen abroad often shared by the other writers in this study. This characterizes the contradictions we find in

---

[44]   See Nyman, 86–116, for further discussion of Lawrence's construction of Italy.

[45]   There is a poster from around the time of Lawrence's stay in New Mexico advertising motor tours to camp 'with the original Americans' (sic), reprinted in Marta Weigle and Kyle Fiore's *Santa Fe and Taos: The Writer's Era 1916–1941*, 150. This book also reprints Lawrence's piece on Taos. Lawrence refers to the Hopi snake dance as a tourist attraction: 'and where already hundreds of motor cars are herded in an official camping ground …' (*MM*, 80).

[46]   Letter to Lady Cynthia Asquith, October 1915. Cit. in Kinkead-Weekes, *D.H. Lawrence: Triumph to Exile*, 277.

his travel writing and letters from abroad, because there are indeed occasional pro-English and pro-colonialist comments tinged with racism, even when there is predominantly a more thoroughgoing questioning of western values. For example, between 1917 and 1925 Lawrence's attempts to engage with other cultures and their people in the hope of regenerating old Europe do not always seem to get beyond the prevailing colonialist discourses. Then he did believe that new landscapes could provide alternative ways of living, even when he is still unhappy with the superiority of western civilization and its belief in progress. And yet, in the *Memoir to Maurice Magnus* (1922) he wrote: 'One felt the splendour of the British Empire, let the world say what it likes', lamenting its decline, and this 'view that the British Empire is weakening' is blamed on its decline in masculinity (qtd in Howard Booth, 'Lawrence in Doubt: A Theory of the "Other" and its Collapse', 209). He disliked Ceylon (today's Sri Lanka) where he calls the natives 'silly dark people' – which reads like the reactionary comments of a 'beleaguered British imperialist', as Howard Booth put it ('Lawrence in Doubt', 210). At other times in his travels Lawrence continues to reinforce his conviction that it is necessary to engage with the other, even the non-European other, to attempt to reverse the process of dissolution and decay, and get beyond his Englishness. But the conclusion seems unavoidable that it was impossible, as Booth has argued, always 'to think and write in the modernist period wholly outside colonial and racist discourses' ('Lawrence in Doubt', 219). In this sense, Lawrence was not always able to come into contact with new worlds, even when he would soon make that 'extraordinary imaginative effort to get inside Indian culture', in the New and Old Mexico, as Kinkead-Weekes put it ('Decolonising Imagination', 73).[47] I am reminded of Forster's 'fractured address' in *The Hill of Devi,* discussed in the previous chapter – sometimes less tolerant of other cultures, and sometimes sympathetic. It remains to be seen in what follows in the rest of this chapter whether D.H. Lawrence manages to get beyond this contradiction in his travel fiction, like Forster did in his.

Landscape and Being: Lawrence's Fictional Travel Stories

The Journey as Storytelling Paradigm

Travel is central to many of Lawrence's short stories. For example, 'The Borderline' (1924, in *Selected Short Stories*) is located in a war-torn European landscape, as Lawrence imagines a spiritual journey back to the cultural origins of western civilization with emphasis on degradation and disintegration, Spenglerian terms for the cultural crisis we also see in other texts. There is the search for solutions in the past or mythology, here Germanic myth implying a feudal order with its

---

[47] However, we should acknowledge the extent to which being in New Mexico 'challenged and eventually utterly changed' such racist reactions. Worthen, *D.H. Lawrence: The Life of an Outsider*, 265.

aristocratic and patriarchal leadership. Landscape and cityscape give the story its topographical substance. The protagonist, Katherine is given the perspective from the window of the train (a modern perspective) of the ruined landscape of the former battlefields in the description of the 'Marne country' (375–6).[48] And then the city (Strasbourg) is a 'city of the dead' (377).[49] Symbolic spaces, like 'old Father Rhine' (380–81) evoke the spirit of place and its cultural origins as 'racial memory' at the time of the 'waning civilization' (382). In 'The Woman Who Rode Away' (1925, rept. in *Selected Short Stories*) the location is the 'savage' landscape of New Mexico which is used strategically as a contrast to the 'deadness within deadness' (391) of the more 'civilized' places. The unnamed woman goes on a psychic journey as if enacting a deep wish-fulfilment, a death drive, which ends in her brutal and phallic death. Once in the hands of the Chilchuis she loses her sense of identity, so the sex object in modern Western culture becomes a 'mystic' object in native primitive culture. In both cultures her identity is sacrificed to a form of patriarchy. Here, Lawrence seems to have gone a long way from his Englishness and the parochial concerns with class towards an implicit critique of the Imperialist mindset of the day – along the lines of Conrad's *Heart of Darkness* – even when this story is set in America. In this short story, as in much of Lawrence's fiction, the trope of the journey is given added significance by the symbolic resonances of places. For example, 'The Man Who Loved Islands' (1927) appears to be a final reckoning with Lawrence's ideal of '*Rananim*' – his 'imagined community' – of finding a remote island to retreat to with a few chosen friends.[50] The story is a philosophical allegory of a man who wants to leave the modern materialistic world and live alone; but it ends up illustrating the thesis that 'no man is an island'.

Travel and topography have a significant presence in Lawrence's novels too from the start. There are literal and figurative journeys as protagonists try to move out of the narrow boundaries of their social or domestic existence, either within England, as in the early fiction, or abroad in the work from *Women in Love*. In his travel fiction, protagonists will go on a sort of existential journey, which, like the author's, will begin in dissatisfaction with home and then a broadening of horizons, or, to use another Lawrentian trope, a widening circle. But when all else fails it seems that the future has to be abroad because the limits of England have been made manifest. If the solution to the problems of living a satisfying life in England will be to go abroad – and as we have seen it will be Lawrence's own future – then Canada will be a possibility in the early fiction, like it is in the short story, 'The Daughters of the Vicar' (1914) where marriage between one of the

---

[48] Lawrence wrote about the same journey in 'Letter from Germany' (1924), reprinted in *MM*, 149ff.

[49] '... through the half-deserted town' – recalling the description of London in T.S. Eliot's 'The Love Song of J. Alfred Prufrock' (1917): 'Let us go, through certain half-deserted streets, / The muttering retreats / Of restless nights in one-night cheap hotels' (*Collected Poems*, 13).

[50] 'In my island, I wanted people to come without class ... a real community ... of many fulfilled individualities ... But, I can't find anybody.' Letter to E.M. Forster, 28 January 1915, *Selected Letters*, 86.

daughters and a young coal miner is unthinkable in class-bound England, leaving them little choice but to emigrate to Canada (*Selected Short Stories*, 151).

English Places: The Trespasser *and* The Rainbow

In *The Trespasser* (1912), Siegmund travels down to the Isle of Wight to spend time with his 'lover' Helena, and to get away from a stultifying, conventional family life, into a new relationship with a woman that will enable him to express his full passionate being. But the woman in question is a 'dreaming woman', that New Woman 'with whom passion exhausts itself at the mouth', while to 'the real man she was very cruel' (*The Trespasser*, 64). After returning from his failed affair, and rejected by his wife and children, Siegmund's story ends tragically. This apparently mundane story of deception and betrayal has a mythic-romance framework that gives the journey a greater significance. The expectations of adventure are high: 'he was elated as a young man setting forth to travel', an elation that transcends the day: 'It was no time, it was Romance, going back to Tristan' (55). The Wagnerian epic-tragic form of *Tristan and Isolde* gives desire a powerful force beyond the mundane, echoing the aesthetic in Nietzsche as transgressive of moral imperatives.[51] But the Wagnerian passionate man will not have a place in the modern world.

In all of Lawrence's writing set in England, the greatest value is always invested in the landscape. Moreover, it is a perspective located in a particular character's seeing – 'The rippling sunlight on the sea was the Rhine Maidens spreading their bright hair in the sun. That was her [Helena's] favourite way of thinking' (75); or Siegmund's view from the train of the passing southern countryside: 'the great downs were naked like a breast leaning kindly to him. The earth is always kind: it loves us and would foster us like a nurse. The downs were big and tender and simple. Siegmund looked at the farm, folded in a hollow, and wondered what fortunate folk were there, nourished and quiet, hearing the vague roar of the train that was carrying him home' (164). Here we see what will become key issues in all Lawrence's work, like the distinction between the landscape and the land, the simple rural life and modernity (prefigured in the roar of the train, and later in London the modern metropolis); but also the libidinized landscape (in the more or less clichéd trope of Mother Earth, now kinder to the man than the woman on the island). Once the protagonist feels the rejection of his family he contemplates 'a fresh life … farming in Canada' (181).

The ideal of a farm was a recurrent one in Lawrence as we saw in the previous section of this chapter. In the opening pages of *The Rainbow* (1915) Lawrence describes life on the farm in mythic-historic terms. Indeed, here we find a classic instance of the myth of origin in the form of the genealogy of the Brangwens; and framed in a discourse which is a complex redeployment of the Old Testament Genesis story and a Georgic pastoral poem to represent Lawrence's ideal of a pre-industrial Golden Age when man was apparently at one with the natural world:

---

[51]   For further discussion of Lawrence's appropriation of the Nietzschean-Wagnerian 'tragic aesthetic' see George Hyde, *D.H. Lawrence*, 25–9.

'They knew the intercourse between heaven and earth, sunshine drawn into the breast and bowels, the rain sucked up in the daytime, nakedness that comes under the wind in autumn ... Their life and inter-relations were such; feeling the pulse and the body of the soil, that opened to their furrow for the grain, and became smooth and supple after their ploughing ...' (*The Rainbow*, 9–10).[52] As Frank Kermode noticed, Lawrence's writing here has a 'genuine archaic and ritualistic force' (*Lawrence*, 45). George Hyde described it as 'saturated in scripture' (42). The paratactic style captures the rhythm of the seasons, the work of the men on the land and the succession of the generations, reinforcing a truth that will reappear at key moments in the novel, either thematically or figuratively.[53] The recurrent patterns of nature and the succession of generations present a cyclical history whose conservative force is used to counter a modern linear history with its progressive teleology in the novel. However, the two histories will be linked causally by a third history, and one derived from the Old Testament discourse in these opening pages, namely: apocalyptic history.[54] Once the traditional life is destroyed by industrialization, old values and simple faiths are thrown into doubt, a spiritual degeneration sets in, and the fallen world will be visited by the flood before the rainbow can stand again on the cleansed earth.

It is the women who begin this process as they question the settled life of this pastoral idyll: 'But the women wanted another form of life than this' (11). A gendered opposition will take on the force of an archetypal structure: the women will look for change, the men will resist. In the beginning of the novel the women already face outwards to the world beyond their narrow confines. But it is a magic land shaped by literature and focussed on the squire's lady who is characterized as the living epic that 'inspired their lives ... they had their own Odyssey' (12).[55] In a neat reversal of the history of classical literature, Lawrence has the women preparing to go on the spiritual journey while the men stay at home (the female Odyssey opposes the male Georgic). As the modern world encroaches progressively more on the lives of the Brangwens, this gambit of giving the women the role of keepers of the soul of mankind will take on paradigmatic status.[56]

---

[52] Subsequent page references abbreviated as *R* in text.

[53] And as we see in the travel writing, the Bavarian peasants in the mountains are described in similar terms: 'The body bent forwards towards the earth, closing round on itself: the arms clasped full of hay ...' (*Twilight in Italy*, *DHLI*, 6–7); as are the Native Americans dancing the land: 'dancing the dance-step naked and fine, prancing through the lines, up and down the lines ... the hands flutter softly down, and draw up the water, draw up the earth-quickening, earth to sky, sky to earth, influences above to influences below, to meet in the germ-quick of corn, where life is' ('The Dance of the Sprouting Corn', in *MM*, 75).

[54] See Peter Fjagesund, *The Apocalyptic World of D.H. Lawrence*.

[55] Travelling and the ambivalent relation of the traveller to his or her roots are crucial to Lawrence, as the biographies and letters confirm.

[56] After the war Lawrence will change his mind about the role of women, largely preferring instead male leadership.

The organic, pastoral life is contrasted sharply with 'the nightmare' of Wiggiston colliery around 1880. It is a dualistic perspective that will continue to dominate Lawrence's thinking about history. It is still there at the end of his life when he writes the essay 'Nottingham and the Mining Countryside', where, as I discussed above, Lawrence reduces history and social relations to the opposition between an ideal organic past and a mechanistic present.[57] The ugliness of industrialism (history) is contrasted with the loveliness of an ideal past (literature). But like the essay, 'Nottingham and the Mining Countryside', Lawrence's 'historical' perspective in the novel, although amply referenced to real changes in the lives of the people and the topology of the land, is closer to mythology and parable. Lawrence's history of England will be nothing more or less than ideological, a chronicle of the three generations of Brangwens that will enable him to illustrate his case against industrialism.

The terms of the opposition between nature and society are consistent throughout Lawrence's work. Nature is the plenitude where the 'organic self' may develop, and where sex usually takes place. Tight, poky, interiors usually have a negative resonance in Lawrence. The classic version of this opposition between the inside and the outside, the oppressive domestic space and the garden or landscape is in *Sons and Lovers* (1913), when the mother is thrown out of the house after a violent assault by the drunken father and recovers in the moonlit, fragrant garden (32–4).[58] In *The Rainbow* simple, colourful and expansive nature is used to express states of mind: 'She [Ursula] came to school in the morning seeing the hawthorn flowers wet, the little rosy grains swimming in a bowl of dew. The larks quivered their song into the new sunshine, and the country was so glad. It was a violation to plunge into the dust and greyness of the town' (*R*, 379). Sexually violent states are dramatized expressionistically – itself an indication of Lawrence's modernist experiment in style – as when Ursula responds to the phallic desire of the man as waves or vibrations emanating out of *her* sexual response to him (like the van Gogh field of sunflowers in the hot wind):

> Coming out of the lane along the darkness, with the dark space spreading down to the wind … So lingering along, they came to a great oak-tree by the path. In all its budding mass it roared to the wind, and its trunk vibrated in every fibre, powerful, indomitable … And in the roaring circle under the tree … The man, what was he? – a dark, powerful vibration that encompassed her. (*R*, 417–18)

Earlier in the novel we read: 'He went out into the wind … And all the sky was teeming and tearing along, a vast disorder of flying shapes' (48). When Ursula and

---

[57]   Graham Holderness insisted that the mining communities were both organic and mechanical, and that Lawrence's idealist totalities are symptoms of his aestheticizing of history where old England is the rural places of English literature, a place where apparently life was instinctive and unselfconscious (*D.H. Lawrence: History, Ideology and Fiction*, 38).

[58]   But here there is an interesting ambivalence on the woman's part, as the garden represents an object of her unconscious solace, yet appears to her consciousness as 'mysterious' once she has recovered her composure, and 'she began to burn to be indoors' (35). For a Lacanian reading see my *Radicalizing Lawrence*, 81–3.

Skrebensky spend the night out on the Sussex Downs – he only on sufferance, she communing naked with nature and the prehistoric earth-works – the sunrise is one of Lawrence's great van Gogh descriptions: 'The rose hovered and quivered, burned, fused to flame, to a transient red, whilst the yellow urged out in great waves, thrown from the ever-increasing fountain, great waves of yellow flinging into the sky, scattering its spray over the darkness, which became bluer and bluer, paler, till soon it would itself be a radiance, which had been darkness' (431). Here, as in Lawrence's other travel fiction, landscape is both a projection of states of mind and the land itself as trace of something ancient; and sometimes the landscape itself is a 'psychic condition'.[59]

The new dawn is for Ursula Brangwen one where 'everything was newly washed into being, in a flood of new, golden creation' (431). The motif of the new dawn of being returns at the end of the novel: 'She was the naked, clear kernel thrusting forth the clear, powerful shoot ... striving to take new root ... She was gradually absorbed into growth' (456). It is symbolism with ontological implications. Moreover, in a series of fictional narratives there is clearly – to reiterate Michelucci's words – 'a progressive enlargement of spatial horizons' (*Space and Place in the Works of D.H.Lawrence*, 86) which allows for a critique of the limitations of life in England that is, as we have seen, always present in the travel writing and essays, and will henceforth be more prominent in the fiction. In *Women in Love* Gudrun Brangwen's spatial horizons are enlarged in the end by going abroad. Once she is out of England, her words have a paradigmatic ring to them: 'One could never feel like this in England, for the simple reason that the damper is *never* lifted off one, there. It is quite impossible to really let go, in England, of that I am assured' (*Women in Love*, 394, emphasis in original). And these are sentiments that also resound in E.M. Forster's writing, as we saw in the last chapter.

Leaving England becomes a more reiterated narrative device in Lawrence's fiction, mirroring his own expatriation after the war. The thought of a better life elsewhere is translated into actual travel abroad in the novels written in the early 1920s: *The Lost Girl*, *Mr Noon* and *Aaron's Rod*. In each case, the story begins in England, and ends abroad in Italy or Germany; and the fictional narrative paradigm is travel writing – all three novels are indeed travel stories with different degrees of autobiographical reference; and it is to these novels that we now turn.

From England to Europe: Fictional Journeys in The Lost Girl *and* Mr Noon

Written in self-imposed exile in Sicily, *The Lost Girl* is the story of a young woman's revolt in provincial Woodhouse (a fictional Eastwood) who runs away to Italy. Lawrence sets the first half of the novel in the provincial Midlands of his own early life, and ends it in Italy where he was now living. The early parts

---

[59]   The 'psychic condition' of the Australian Bush in *Kangaroo* or the Mexico of *The Plumed Serpent* is mentioned by Neil Roberts, 123. For further discussion of Lawrence's Expressionism see Jack F. Stewart's article 'Expressionism in *The Rainbow*', 298–315.

are written in the style of Dickensian comic realism, with Alvina breaking out of grey, repressive Victorianism by getting to know a troupe of travelling play-actors and their Red Indian fantasy world. His critique of England and Englishness spills over into the second part of novel, which draws on Lawrence's travelogues. However, the story of the woman who emancipates herself is now given a new twist, and one that records the change in his attitude towards women: her struggle for independence ends in her willing submission to the phallic man; and – like in Forster's *Where Angels Fear to Tread* – the female protagonist's Englishness will be a hindrance once in a remote Italian mountain village.[60] In Lawrence's novel, the need to get beyond the stifling constraints of conformity on a number of levels required, it seems, extreme measures – and one of them was simply to get away from England at whatever cost for Alvina. This makes the narrative a travel story, and more specifically a quest narrative.

Like Lawrence's travel writing in *Twilight in Italy*, the last pages of the novel describe what Hilary Simpson called 'the primitive but breathtakingly beautiful landscape' (100) in the Abruzzi Mountains where Ciccio takes Alvina, and where she literally fulfils her destiny as the lost girl. It is here in a remote region of Italy that Ciccio expects Alvina, now his wife, to live. But like the beautiful yet 'savage' landscape around Taos in New Mexico for Lawrence, this Italian landscape proves too barren and the place too remote for Alvina; places 'which resist us, which have the power to overthrow our psychic being. It seems as if every country has its potent negative centres, localities which savagely and triumphantly refuse our living culture. And Alvina had struck one of these, here on the edge of the Abruzzi' (*TLG*, 370–71, cit. in Bahlke, 65). However, Ciccio is not the idealized Italian peasant of Lawrence's Italian travel writing, because he is not 'sensitive to the values of civilization' but rather 'the "alien other", the man and *daemon*, who appears beautiful and terrifying to Alvina', as Bahlke puts it (64).[61] It seems that the landscape will not be consolation enough for the disappointment with the Italian lover.

Mr Noon – unfinished and unpublished in Lawrence's lifetime – is also divided into two parts, the first part in the English Midlands and the second abroad. This time, though, Lawrence takes his characters first to Germany – the Germany of his own visit, and 'elopement', and walking tour south over the Alps in 1912. The second part of the novel, especially, is autobiographical fiction, sending us back to Lawrence's pre-war letters and travel sketches, but written in the register of *Sea and Sardinia*, that is in the lively, cynical and satirical mode of the author

---

[60]   For such a comparison see George Bahlke's '"See Naples and Die": Two Heroines' Italian Journeys', where we read that in both novels 'an English woman tries to find, in a radically different culture, freedom from British constraint and repression' (55). A major difference though is the parodist and intertextual play in Lawrence's text. For a discussion of the literary parodies and the play of voices in this novel see my paper 'Parody, Stylization, and Dialogics: A Bakhtinian Reading of *The Lost Girl*'.

[61]   Forster's Gino in *Where Angels Fear to Tread* comes off better as a sensitive man and thus a foil to the prejudices and hysterics of the English abroad.

who would not forgive England for rejecting his major work, *The Rainbow* and *Women in Love.*[62] As travel broadens horizons, Gilbert Noon, like Alvina, gains perspective on his own limited origins: 'For the first time he saw England from the outside: tiny she seemed, and tight, and so partial ... her all-in-allness was a delusion of her natives. Her marvellous truths and standards and ideals were just local, not universal.' Looking down from the mountains into the 'great Isar valley' and surrounded by snow-capped peaks, Bavarian gentians, and thinking of the Danube with its 'enormous meanderings', Gilbert Noon 'became unEnglished' (*MN*, 107–8).

Mr Noon and *The Lost Girl* are classic examples of the fictional travel narrative. However, they are not only used as home thoughts from abroad. In *The Lost Girl* Alvina soon develops a critical attitude to life in provincial Italy; Gilbert Noon is not just fascinated by the natural beauty and hospitality of Upper Bavaria, the Isar valley and the Alpine regions, but is also critical of German officialdom and militarism (the time is just before the Great War) and 'the North German with his inhuman cold-blooded theorizing and mechanizing' (*MN*, 272) that has spoilt that 'fresh, northern forest-leaved soul' (283).[63] Once Gilbert and Johanna leave Germany on their walking tour, the relief is palpable. Arriving in southern Tyrol, 'one knew one had passed the mysterious dividing line' (281). This was a different world. Yet, once again, initial enthusiasm for the 'UnGerman' south is dampened by the evident lack of efficiency, and the appallingly unhygienic conditions in which they now have to live. And this pattern of excitement for the new place swiftly followed by moments of disillusion, structures the fictional travel narrative – as it often does in Lawrence's travel writing. It is a pattern that reveals a restless quest for the right place, that earthly paradise where Lawrence will be able to realize his utopian vision. If it cannot be England then it must be abroad; first in southern Europe, then Australia, and then New Mexico, so that an almost nomadic existence recorded in letters and travel sketches is also now the paradigm for fictional narratives – every successive novel being a fiction of the place visited by the author.

An example of the fluctuation in attitudes is seen in the portrayal of the Bavarian mountain peasant farmers. At first they represent the simple, unspoilt, pre-modern life where man is at one with his natural environment – like the farmer observed in the travel sketch 'The Crucifixes across the Mountains' in *Twilight in Italy* and the generations of Brangwen farmers working the land in the novel *The Rainbow* (*R*, 9–10). However, we are soon made aware of the narrow, fearful existence dominated as it is by 'a strange, medieval Catholicism' symbolized in 'these terrible crucifixes' by the roadside. It is the strange mix of paganism and Christianity that Gilbert Noon and Lawrence notice which the ancient Romans

---

[62]   'I shall never forgive England *The Rainbow*.' Cit. in Kinkead-Weekes, *D.H. Lawrence: Triumph to Exile*, 520.

[63]   Wagnerian German myth has always attracted Lawrence, as we saw in the early novel, *The Trespasser*, and we also see in *Women in Love*. It is used in *Mr Noon* as an alternative to the realities of modern Prussia, as Lawrence saw it.

already knew: 'the ancient Roman terror of the northern tree-dark gods', lurking in the primeval woods (*MN*, 249). This ambivalence is characteristic of Lawrence's writing in the 1920s: an attraction to pagan rites and its manifestation in the spirit of place while not wishing a regression to the primitive, and yet a reiteration of an older male desire: 'But the peasant's was the other kind of desire: the male desire for possession of the female, not the spiritual man offering himself up sexually. She would get no worship from the mountaineer: only lusty mating and possession' (250).

The gender tension between an unselfconscious passionate relationship between men and women and modern subjects free from the repressions of convention emerges in *Mr Noon*, as it registers a marriage crisis with the new wife's easy infidelity on their honeymoon. Lawrence appears to be working through a personal problem emerging from Frieda's attitudes, which were influenced by the sexual liberationist theories and practice of Otto Gross. Indeed, *Mr Noon* records the challenge of Gross to Lawrence's own sexual theory of consummate marriage, and the new direction which he was to take after *Mr Noon* may well have been a reaction: Gross's matriarchal sexual role for women, showing the way to change society through sexual freedom by giving themselves freely to the needs of men without moral scruple, was thus to be displaced by Lawrence's call for male leadership and woman's utter submission.[64]

Mr Noon as fictional autobiography is, in many ways, a continuation of the style and structure of *The Lost Girl*, with its first part in England, and its second part in Europe; with its extended metaphor of the journey of self-discovery. Both novels are a kind of rite of passage to Italy; and satire, comedy and parody are common to both novels. *Mr Noon* is a carnival of parodies and self-parodies, of intertextualities and the stylization of speech genres – a modernist experiment by definition.[65]

---

[64]   Gross was a disaffiliated Freudian who believed that the sexual liberation of the individual would lead to more fundamental social change. Lawrence would have not objected to this. But Gross insisted that women should be taught to lead the way by giving themselves freely especially to artistic young men. As Worthen explains, 'Nietzschean, Freudian, vitalist', Gross's ideas promoted 'the saving sexual relationship outside the bonds of society: they stressed how a sexually liberated woman could escape the trammels of the ordinary and be an inspiration for intellectual and striving men … In many ways, they offered Lawrence the themes for his next eight years of writing; and (above all) they offered a way of thinking about Frieda' (*D.H. Lawrence: The Early Years*, 443–4). But the Lawrence writing his fictional autobiography in *Mr Noon* was now on the side of male leadership as he first expressed it in a letter to Katherine Mansfield in 1918: 'I do think a woman must yield some sort of precedence to a man … the women must follow as it were unquestioning … I believe this. Frieda doesn't. Hence our fight' (*Selected Letters*, 163).

[65]   Mark Kinkead-Weekes describes the comedy in *Mr Noon* as follows: 'Lawrence experiments with Fielding's comic epic, which creates not only the distancing of comedy but also a teasing relation between showman-author and "gentle reader". All the comic-epic devices are present: perverse anti-climax, inflated apostrophe, "heroic" sports, battles with monsters or villains and the learned survey of a tract of knowledge (i.e. "spooning") …

The Quest for a New Masculinity: Aaron's Rod, Kangaroo *and* The Plumed Serpent

With *Aaron's Rod* the journey abroad as geographical and spiritual displacement focuses on masculinity. Men must be reborn into an instinctive masculinity, which as Lawrence's writing of the 1920s insists is a very old instinct that has been forgotten. Henceforth there will be a return to the hierarchical order of patriarchy, and one based on ancient models close to the Old Testament Church Fathers, or a pre-Columbian 'natural aristocracy', as Lawrence understood it. In his essay, 'On Being a Man' (1923) Lawrence reiterates a feeling common at the time that the war had ruined manhood: 'These are the heroes of the Great War. They went and fought like heroes, truly, to prove their manhood' (rept. in *Reflections on the Death of a Porcupine and Other Essays*, 219). But they did this from a wrong idea of manhood. Like 'heroic automata', they understood themselves within the given masculine codes of heroism, unquestioningly believing they were making the world safe for democracy. It was a missed opportunity ('On Being a Man', 221). Lawrence will take his fictional protagonists abroad in search of alternative cultural models of man, and try out in the fiction notions of political and spiritual leadership. The process of a cultural regeneration through spiritual revivalism is dramatized in *The Plumed Serpent*.[66] However, we should acknowledge that these fictions are stories men invent and tell each other. They are stories of quest, travel, adventure and leadership – almost Conradian stories. They allow men to imagine a superior place for themselves at a time of crisis in masculinity. And they are ancient, traditional masculine narratives. Indeed, as Ben Knights has argued in *Writing Masculinities*, masculinity is itself a way of telling stories; and Lawrence's narratives are gendered as men tell one story, women tell another. Moreover, now in Lawrence's fiction women are given a debunking role in a world of idealist men, or are positioned as focalizers with mixed feelings about male supremacy. Indeed, Lawrence, like Conrad, deconstructs such male narratives by questioning their plausibility in a cynical world, even while lamenting their loss.

For the story of Aaron Sissons abandoning his wife and children on Christmas Eve in the provincial Midlands for an itinerant life as a musician Lawrence employs what George Hyde has called 'the contingencies of the travelogue' (92). Once in Italy, the action hovers on the edge of the *opera buffa* with its plot of the adulterous wife, the younger music teacher and the cuckolded husband; and, as Hyde points out, 'punctuated by comic opera fantasies' (95). The rejection of the love of the family is a prelude to Lawrence's turn against the new, self-aware,

---

Something of the irritation of 1920, as well as the alienation from England, gets into the tone even of the first part, much more in the second, and the irony is increasingly subversive, moving towards contempt.' *D.H. Lawrence: Triumph to Exile*, 615. For further discussion see my *Radicalizing Lawrence*, 192–202.

[66] For the sources of Lawrence's political ideas, see Rick Rylance, 'Lawrence's Politics', in Keith Brown, ed., *Rethinking Lawrence*; Peter Fjagesund, *The Apocalyptic World of D.H. Lawrence*; and Anne Fernihough, *D.H. Lawrence: Aesthetics and Ideology*.

domineering woman. But this male version of the story of motherly, female love is countered at another level by the picaresque and the quest – male narratives, which although characterized by the structure of the journey derive from quite different literary traditions: the first comic-satirical, the second a modern version of a psychological exploration into the self. Both share the structure of travelling to the unknown and of chance encounters. The picaro, however, is often a victim of circumstances in his quasi-aimless wanderings; the quester has a clearly defined goal, and has to prove his manliness by achieving that goal. The picaresque originated as an anti-Chivalric genre debunking the codes of heroism and honour. Adopting the spirit of the letter, Lawrence reworks these contradictory sub-genres in pastiche form. There are passages of travel-writing; there is the popular novel of adultery and its comic opera variety, with the implication that it appeals to women, like its romance variety of the handsome young stranger who rejuvenates the older woman. There is the melodrama and sensation of popular political drama with its scenes of violent confrontation and an anarchist's bomb exploding in a café; there are other male stories of war, now in their modern variety of horror instead of heroism, and told obsessively to the other men by the veteran, war-affected Captain Herbertson. Moreover, the modernist destabilizing of forms spills over into the question of gender: these men are the new hysterics who have lost their manliness through the war and taken on all the symptoms of women first analyzed by Breuer and Freud.[67]

Aaron Sissons, though, remains the idealist, dreaming a vision of the future. At first it is of an England, part Midlands part Cornwall, with an organized communal existence. Then in a lake-city in Mexico, which he journeys to in a boat he sees the vision of an idol. Aaron refuses to interpret his dream; but, enigmatic as it is, we can detect the idea of the future as a journey towards a new social formation which is also a return to older ritual. However, it is not clear whether this is a utopia or a dystopia; it does look forward to the travel to other continents that Aaron plans. But the future looks suspiciously like a fascist state, which answers the question Lilly poses to Aaron: 'Is it that you want to love, or to be obeyed?' (*Aaron's Rod*, 293). The era of love is over. A new male leadership will teach men to acknowledge their inner instinctual power as the source of life and creativity. Aaron should not give up just because his flute has been broken. But he is not so certain anymore about Rawdon Lilly's new masculinity. It is an uncertainty the reader shares, and one encouraged by the recurrence of critical voices from the female characters challenging the male frenzy of misogyny and idealist solutions – a characteristic of Lawrence's modernism of the 1920s to allow critical voices which will even question ideas of his (Lawrence) expressed in his essays. Indeed, he called this strategy 'thought-adventure', as if it is his thoughts on masculinity

---

[67] Joseph Breuer and Sigmund Freud, *Studies in Hysteria* (1895). Freud's own experiences in the Great War confirmed his belief – first proposed against the established view in an 1886 lecture in Vienna – that hysteria is not restricted to women. See Peter Gay, *Freud: A Life for our Time*, 53–4.

that he takes on a journey, an adventure, to test them out. And in *Aaron's Rod* – and in *Kangaroo* – these thoughts are found wanting.[68]

It seems that travel is the only remedy offered for the crisis of masculinity. The next destination is Australia in the novel *Kangaroo* – the next stage in a fictional journey away from English and European modernity. This travelogue-novel exposes the limits of male leadership; for if Australian men are not the force for change to a new culture of male leadership – as the novel suggests – then it seems that the aboriginal Ur-culture represented in the bush will be the focus for a cosmic force and that will symbolically dwarf the grand narratives of the new masculinity, once Somers comes to terms with it. This rhetoric extends to the coastline which takes on an increasingly therapeutic function for Somers, as the machinations of political groups and the characters on whose charisma they rely for their success begin to collapse into bar-room brawls. The Australian land and seascapes have to carry the full utopian weight, while Harriett has a debunking voice for the men's ideals. She belongs to the old 'aristocratic principle of Europe' (*K*, 21) – as *alter ego* for Frieda[69] – which disqualifies her from the general democratizing tendency of the new country at the social level, while making her ancestry the ideal model for the leaders of the new political class. So, even when at times Australia appears to be a relief from the old European tension, and at the same time a terrifying freedom for Somers, because the 'great sense of vacant spaces' is absent of 'any inner meaning', the local people have 'no inner life, no high command, no interest in anything, finally' (27).

Harriett's greatest tirade comes near the centre of the book and casts a greater shadow over the men's idealism:

> What is all their revolution bosh to me! There have been revolutions enough, in my opinion, and each one more foolish than the last. And this will be the most foolish of the lot. – And what have *you* got to do with revolutions, you petty and conceited creature? You and revolutions! You're not big enough, not grateful enough to do anything real. I give you my energy and my life, and you want to put me aside as if I was a charwoman. (162)

Harriett is determined to keep the 'vital connection' with Somers. She represents Lawrence's pre-war theory of consummate marriage (a union of equal partners, a oneness that respects difference), combined with the newer insistence on the difference between 'a vitally active man' and 'that worst of male vices, the vice of abstraction and mechanisation' (*K*, 164), which she is given to think is typical of conceited men. This, of course, is Lawrence speaking: going it alone without any vital organic connection through 'the root of marriage ... with God, with wife, with mankind'; insisting on exclusively male activity, Somers 'had ruptured the root flow' (164). Male bonding through political ideals is already being condemned as

---

[68]   The idea of the novel as 'thought-adventure' is proposed in a blatant authorial intrusion in the text in *Kangaroo*, 279.

[69]   Harriett is referred to here as the 'Q.B.', recalling Lawrence's nickname for Frieda in *Sea and Sardinia*.

willed and mechanical, not natural and instinctual; and the old grand narratives of man's invention and the forms of their expression are discredited.

The grand narrative of the Nation State, though, is also discredited in the long, autobiographical chapter, 'The Nightmare'. Here a memory triggered off by the violence threatened by the novel's eponymous protagonist Kangaroo works through the events during the war, which changed Somers forever. The story is that of Lawrence and Frieda, harassed by the authorities, expelled from Cornwall on suspicion of spying, and culminating in his suffering physical humiliation at the hands of Army medics in the recruitment centre in Derby. The chapter in the novel – with Somers more transparently playing Lawrence's part – illustrates the idea of bullying (thus being continuous with the Kangaroo episode), and extends to a trenchant critique of the state of English democracy which the war has changed into rule by mass hysteria, itself reflected in the popular press.[70] We are given a clear idea of the extent to which newspapers would go to 'break the independent soul in any man who would not hunt with the criminal mob', as Somers puts it in *Kangaroo* (212). Now that the writing of the new, dominant mass media has destroyed the soul of the culture, England has become 'expressionless' (212). Leaving on the boat from Harwich he sees 'snow on the downs like a shroud' so that England appears 'like a grey, dreary-grey coffin sinking in the sea behind' (258) – a reminder of the other leave-takings in Lawrence's fiction. Somers may feel 'broken off from the England he belonged to' (259), but he will still be tied to it by literature.

After the disappointment of male bonding in Australia, the only possibility left, it seems, lies with nature in the form of the 'ancient land ... The dark world before conscious responsibility was born' (178). For Somers, the Australian landscape overwhelms any attempt 'to be an alert conscious man'. He can only 'drift into a sort of obscurity', as the ancient spirit of the land forces him into a kind of 'torpor' of semi-consciousness and indifference – a return to the Lawrentian ideal organic state of the Brangwen men at the start of *The Rainbow*, where men, as he puts it in *Kangaroo*, 'didn't have emotions and personal consciousness, but were shadowy like trees, and on the whole silent, with numb brains and slow limbs and a great indifference' (*K*, 179) – clearly a recurrent concern in Lawrence. However, in context, Somers has an ambivalent attitude to the forceful presence of the ancient land. The land is at times solace, at other times threat. Somers at times sounds like Lawrence preaching a return to a kind of primitive state where man was at one with the cosmos. At other times, nature reminds him that he does not belong in Australia, reinforcing his sense of isolation, so that he cannot wait to leave. But will he ever find what he wants even assuming he knows what he wants? Towards the

---

[70] Tony Pinkney has drawn attention to the way Lawrence illustrates with unprecedented accuracy Gramsci's concept of hegemony, 'grasping how deeply a dominant ideology seeps into the fibres of lived experience' (*D.H. Lawrence*, 117). In the novel, the ideology is 'Bottomleyism', named after the owner of the jingoistic popular newspaper *John Bull*. Forster also complained of the new regimentation of life in 'Terminal Note' (1960), reprinted in *Maurice*, 221.

end of the novel, Jaz says what others have said about Lawrence: 'seems to me you just go round the world looking for things you're not going to give in to' (348). Harriett sees the problem in personal terms, and is cynical to the end about his metaphysical pretensions. 'Metaphysical! ... You'd think to hear him he was nothing but a tea-pot brewing metaphysical tea ... He's always breaking his heart over something – anything except me. To me he's a nether millstone' (*K*, 349). The male-leadership project is not rejected yet *per se*, but rather Australia is not the location for the ideal community that will lead the culture out of decadence. Lawrence will have to look elsewhere; in fact he will have one last attempt – in the Mexico of *The Plumed Serpent*.

Somers's solution – and the only one Lawrence proposes – for the cultural and political crisis, is that man must learn to listen to his own soul, to 'turn to the old dark gods' (265). It is not possible to do this in Australia, nor in *Kangaroo*. But it signals the point where the novel ends its 'thought-adventure', and demands the next leave-taking, in the continuing quest for a location where the new man can be in touch with his dark god, and imagine a way of leading the culture out of its crisis of modernity. This will be the 'thought-adventure' of *The Plumed Serpent*. For, as Catherine Carswell was the first to insist, Lawrence's 'savage pilgrimage' culminated in *The Plumed Serpent* where he tries to imagine a revival of pre-Christian, pre-white culture.[71] After this, he will return, finally, to the scene of his early writing – a return to 'Bestwood' – with *Lady Chatterley's Lover*.

But before moving on I think it might be helpful just to sum up what makes the Australian novel a modernist novel. For besides the thematic modernism represented by the questions of modernity and male leadership and the self-conscious manner of 'thought-adventure', there is also a formal textual experiment. Despite the justified criticism that the novel is often too openly autobiographical and doctrinal, when it is difficult to distinguish Somers from Lawrence or Harriett from Frieda; and that its experimental features are 'only superficially' modernist in the Joycean spirit (Ellis, 40–42), reading the novel after the belated publication of *Mr Noon*, we might suspect that Lawrence is challenging the reader of the conventional realist novel. Thus I suggest that *Kangaroo* is comic and serious by turns; experimental in ways that rhyme with the representational crisis of modernism – as I have been describing it in this study. Moreover, I think the sardonic tone, authorial intrusions, and formal fragmentariness are correlatives for Somers' experience of cultural dislocation and alienation – a modernist representation of the lived experience of modernity.[72] The 'thought-adventure' is also an adventure of writing.

One example of the formal experiment is the shift in genre in chapter 9, 'Harriett and Lovatt at Sea in Marriage', where their crisis is reinscribed in the parody of an eighteenth century comic discourse on marriage (similar to the discourse on

---

[71] '... a pinnacle ... is reached in *The Plumed Serpent* ... For this tale Lawrence needed ... all his savage pilgrimage' (Carswell, 183).

[72] For further support of the modernism of the novel see Pinkney, 114–15. In the introduction to *Kangaroo*, Macdonald Daly also argues for the deconstructive effects of the text.

'Spooning' in *Mr Noon*). Here the writing indulges in the semantic associations of 'all at sea' and 'adrift', in a proto-deconstructive play on the figure of marriage as a bark with the woman now as the captain, 'in her grand capacity of motherhood and attendant wifehood' (170).[73] The register is highly literary, the tone cynical, and the style drifts from Fieldingesque moralizing discourse and instruction manual for young couples, to Sternean burlesque and biblical parable. Furthermore, the writing is a textual mirror of the story, and a highly stylized comic summary. Another example of genre shift is chapter 14, 'Bits', because with its quotations of local trivia and gossip from the Sydney *Bulletin*, it is symptomatic of a greater fragmentation of the codes, registers and unities of the old English novel. The metonymies of realism are further dispersed into their synechdochies, as textual bits break loose from the unifying whole and become part-objects of the real whose meaningful connections are left to the reader, as in collage. Thus the textual process carries a level of meaning, semiotically, about the way we make sense by imposing coherence on what are essentially fragments of perception. The formal experiment comments on the 'thought-adventure' as the men attempt to impose order and meaning through their new grand narrative of male leadership. Thus – as I have been arguing throughout this section of the chapter – the unbinding of conventional textual cohesion deconstructs the male bonding it represents.

Lawrence goes even further, however. The narrator intrudes at a meta-narrative level, addressing the reader directly, in the spirit of *Mr Noon*, and with Joyce's *Ulysses* in mind: 'Now a novel is supposed to be ...' 'We insist that a novel is ... a thought-adventure, if it is to be anything at all complete' (279). Yet, if the new genre of 'thought-adventure' is supposed to give the novel its sense of completeness, its cohesion and unity, then the text's own deconstructive strategies indicate that this is an impossible demand. Somers speaks the author's truth when he is given to think: 'The bulk of mankind haven't got any central selves ... They're all bits' (*K*, 280). This 'gramophone of a novel' replays in such passages the thoughts of the author. In other passages, the narrator's address to the reader is more aggressive: 'I hope, dear reader, you like plenty of conversation in the novel' (282). And later, more cynical as well: 'Chapter follows chapter, and nothing doing ... If you don't like the novel, don't read it' (284). Cynicism easily elides into jokey word-play when the expression 'queen bee' becomes: 'Beatitudes, beatitudes. Bee attitudes or any other attitudes' (283), in the Joycean spirit where the mood of a self-cynical, world-weary writer (continuous with the attitudes communicated at the meta-narrative level in the abandoned *Mr Noon*) undermines the assertions of the new masculinity.[74] Lawrence will make one last 'thought-experiment' in the new location of Mexico in the novel *The Plumed Serpent*.

---

[73] The metaphor of travel should also be noted; after all, the trip to Australia is supposed to be regenerative but does not fulfil its goal – except as ever in Lawrence with the discovery of another wild and primitive landscape.

[74] It is in the early 1920s that Lawrence was writing about the state of novel in essays like 'Morality and the Novel' (1925) where he insisted that a 'really new novel' would always provoke 'resistance' (*Phoenix*, 531). For further discussion see Worthen, *D.H. Lawrence and the Idea of the Novel*.

Just as *Aaron's Rod* is Lawrence's Italian novel, and *Kangaroo* his Australian novel, *The Plumed Serpent* is his American novel.[75] The America of *The Plumed Serpent* is the pre-Columbian civilizations, the Aztec, Maya and Incas. The Indians of New Mexico and Mexico are their descendants. To reiterate what Lawrence wrote in 'America, Listen to Your Own': 'America must turn again to catch the spirit of her dark aboriginal continent.' Americans must 'catch the pulse' of the 'life-mysteries' of the time before the Pilgrim Fathers and before Cortés and Columbus. 'It means a surpassing of the old European life-form ... a departure from the old European morality, ethic ... even a departure from the old range of emotions and sensibilities' (*Phoenix*, 90–91). In his American novel, Lawrence sends Kate Leslie on the journey into the heart of Mexico – the location of the 'solar plexus of North America'. It will be an exasperating experience, as modern Mexico is a 'paleface overlay' of North American materialist values and the Spanish church, while the remnants of the great pyramids and temples threaten with a blind malevolence, a reminder that the 'white superimposition' is temporary, and the old-gods in the form of 'snake-blooded birds' always have their fangs ready to bite ('Au Revoir, U.S.A.' [1923], rept. in *Phoenix*, 105–6).

The western experience of Mexico will turn out to be a complex process of decoding for Kate Leslie, as representative white European, but also as a woman. Through her we get an anti-colonialist reading; yet she will need all her resources of common sense to resist the invitation to stay as she becomes involved in the cult of *Quetzalcoatl* (the plumed serpent). She will have to undergo the force of a reconstructing from wilful woman into a submissive wife, justified through a mythology of the male 'dark mysteries', and supported by a combination of Frazerian anthropology and indigenous revivalism. But how far is the assertion of the 'ancient phallic mysteries' endorsed and sustained as the basis of the new masculinity and the abolition of the modern woman? Are the recurrent critical perspectives, the protesting voice of the woman and the instabilities of the writing (its literary modernism) – common to Lawrence's writing in the 1920s as I have been arguing in the preceding discussions – sufficient to deconstruct the persistent masculinist fiction in *The Plumed Serpent*?

Lawrence uses the opportunities afforded by the social gatherings in this novel for his anti-American invective: North America represents an advanced stage in the cultural degeneration, hegemonically spreading its materialist values throughout Mexico. Americanization – as it was for the Italian men in *Twilight in Italy* – is the greatest danger for Mexico, breaking the blood-tie with the pre-Columbian culture. It is the second wave of colonialization after Cortés. The signs of both 'invasions' are in the Spanish Church and the American factory, respectively (*TPS*, 113). Once bound to the machine, which is to say, the modern spirit itself, the native Indian soul is lost. It is a spirit symbolized by the car, the 'real insanity of America' (146–50). And modern Mexico seems incapable of doing anything about it, Kate coming to the conclusion that the Mexicans 'are a people without

---

[75]   Further page references abbreviated as *TPS* in text.

the energy of *getting on*', and could not fail 'to be hopelessly exploited', as indeed they have for centuries (*TPS*, 183).[76]

Kate expresses a theory of racial superiority. The white races have dominated the dark races; but the white man, for all his words, is 'hollow with misgiving about his own supremacy.' Once he shows any signs of weakness, 'the dark races will at once attack him, to pull him down into the old gulfs' (182). Yet the 'backward races' (183) will have their indigenous culture returned to them, a culture which the text values from the outset as superior to the dominant Eurocentric ideology – and which of course expresses Lawrence's own strongly felt views on such indigenous cultures in his essays and travel writing. However, racial difference is conflated with sexuality: 'these dark-faced silent men ... were columns of dark blood.' The white Americans were 'bloodless, acidulous ... with their nasty whiteness ...!' (79). The signifier 'blood', like the signifier 'dark' disseminates ambivalently through the text. Connotations of sexual potency and virility, but also violence (when the blood is roused to hatred, blood will be shed), racial purity, and class or caste as social and tribal superiority percolate through the text. Kate comes from the European aristocracy and has Irish-Celtic blood. The 'dark eyes' are traces of the proud and potent aboriginal blood of the native Indian. Ramón and Cipriano are western educated, but of native Mexican origin. 'Dark eyes' are associated with instinctual passion and violence. Yet these connotations have specific contexts in the psychology of Kate's changing moods. She has to get beyond her Christian fears of an atavistic hell to make her divided self whole again through the last great mystery left, and the one degraded most in the modern world, namely sex (yet later she will deny that sex has any importance at all). Once settled in her house in the country, the water of the lake is 'sperm-like' (127), and the 'jarring, exasperating reality had melted away, a soft world of potency stood in its place, the velvety dark flux from the earth' (143). Here, potency is associated with the signifier 'dark' as a natural cosmic process. Her moods will still fluctuate, but through Ramón she will understand the force of the 'dark sun' (157), and the potential for rebirth.

The problem with the association of the 'dark races' with sexual potency is that it gets close to the orientalist stereotype of the profligate and virile black man, the 'noble savage', or the Sheik with his Harem, and the sexual fantasy of the aristocratic white woman being seduced by the black man. Kate is given to such stereotyping herself: 'Kate watched his [Cipriano's] deep, strong Indian chest ... How dark he was, and how primitively physical, beautiful' (*TPS*, 239). She is not unaware of these associations in the western mentality. She sees Teresa as 'the Harem type', and Ramón as her 'Sultan' (433) revelling in his 'pasha satisfaction' (435). In her feminist mood, however, Kate is damning of the 'male conceit and haughtiness swelling his blood and making him feel endless' (436); but equally damning of the 'ancient female power, which consists in glorifying

---

[76] Interestingly, Lawrence emphasizes the very expression his mother would have used, as if to recall the best authority he knew on how to 'get on' in life. See Worthen, *D.H. Lawrence: The Early Years*, 326, and 500–501.

the blood-male'. She wonders whether it was not 'degrading' (435); and is no longer certain. Here, Lawrence is drawing on the clichés of popular literature, just as he will in *Lady Chatterley's Lover* with the common story of the Lady and the Gamekeeper.

Like the Australian bush, the Mexican land has deep topographical significance. The recurrent signifier 'volcano' whose 'lava rock' beneath the earth's crust is the deepest trace of history (64); the volcanic threatens the stability of the earth, acting as metaphor for an ancient vibration, underground and beyond the control of modern man and his science, and a reminder of impending seismographic explosion. It becomes a symbol of Lawrence's deep wish to blow up the world and start again, as Ramón is given to say: 'Oh! If only the world would blow up like a bomb' (307). Kate is 'swept away in some silent tide, to the old, antediluvian silence' (324), which by association refers to the clean-sweep made in the proverbial flood, and also implicates the cultural crisis in renewal through destruction. As in all mythology, a prelapsarian paradise (as in the lost city of Atlantis) is a powerful image. As motif of cosmic vibration, the volcano, by extension, encapsulates the theory of a new authority, and a new self-discipline as the people learn the natural vibration with the earth through perfecting 'animistic dancing', which Cipriano prefers to imposing 'machine discipline' on his men. The old Indians danced 'to gain power ... over the *living* forces or potencies of the earth' (400).[77] The volcano represents the earth's potency. Its vibration is felt by the people (*TPS*, 87). It is a sign of death, a threat of imminent catastrophe, which influences the fatalistic attitude of the people. Kate senses this volcanic menace in the spirit of the place. After witnessing the ritual dancing and the incantatory chanting of the hymns, she feels that 'here and here alone ... life burned with a deep new fire' (156). When she first loses her will to resist Cipriano, we read: 'her will, her very self gone, leaving her lying in molten life' (356). The core of the novel is the rebirth of Cipriano as Pan, assisted by Kate in the role of the newly reconstructed woman. However, in the end – like the female characters in Lawrence's previous novels – she remains critical of the new masculinity. When Kate thinks: 'How wonderful sex can be, when men keep it powerful and sacred, and it fills the world! Like sunshine through and through one', the next sentence is: 'But I'm not going to submit, even there. Why should one give in, to anything!' (473). In the end, her critical stance towards macho men, and submissive women like Teresa, places a strain on the plausibility of her giving in to the exclusively male sexual pleasure, to a phallic priority.

The structure of recurrent leitmotifs establishes a play of connotations around the key signifiers: 'blood', 'dark', 'serpent' and 'volcano'. An extra, implicit level of meaning is inscribed through this 'aesthetic structure'. Meanings are unfixed as any one signifier slides between several possible connotations, so that cultural understanding becomes an interplay of constructions, Christian and

---

[77] In 'Indians and Entertainment' (1924) Lawrence describes the dance: 'the men tread the rhythm into the centre of the earth ... the strange falling back of the dark blood into the downward rhythm, the rhythm of pure forgetting and pure renewal' (*MM*, 63–4).

anthropological, literary or philosophical. Thus at the semiotic and narrative levels the text keeps in play a series of connotations which work against single, transparent meaning – a modernist strategy by definition. That Lawrence tries to abolish dissemination, difference and irony through the increasing dominance of myth and ritual is a generic and ideological assertion that is only partly held in check by Kate's continued resistance, the undecidability of the ending and the truth emerging throughout the text that myth and ritual, above all, are constructions. The textual play of meaning thus works against the ideology of male leadership and phallic priority as the basis of the new masculinity – a deconstructive effect of the form against its own content.[78]

The Return to English Places: Lady Chatterley's Lover

Once the 'savage pilgrimage' is abandoned, Lawrence returns to familiar territory with *Lady Chatterley's Lover*: the industrial Midlands of *Sons and Lovers*, *The Rainbow*, *Women in Love*, the first part of *The Lost Girl* and *Mr Noon*. In August and September 1926 Lawrence had revisited 'the country of [his] heart' (Lawrence cit. in Ellis, *D.H. Lawrence: Dying Game*, 316), the Derbyshire and Nottinghamshire countryside; yet he also became sensitive to the radicalization of class resentment amongst the mining communities brought about by the General Strike. Lawrence's impressions were recorded in the essay, 'Return to Bestwood' (1926) written once he was back in Italy. Now Lawrence sees the world of his childhood gone forever; and 'the women seem to have changed the most in this, that they have no respect for anything' (*Phoenix II*, 258). The great houses of the landed gentry have spawned ugly mining settlements, and the industry that gives them their wealth has ruined the countryside and the health of the people, with the coal dust that settles everywhere and the sulphurous smell on the wind. The miners themselves, once 'men from the underworld' when the author was a boy, have lost that 'strange power of life', their vitality, and have become the ghosts of themselves since the war (263). It seems that England is 'on the brink of class war' (265), and this is reflected in his last novel.

Lady Chatterley's Lover – a condition-of-England novel – is a critique of the English ruling class, the aristocracy, represented by Sir Clifford and his cronies. Mellors is seen to be the 'natural aristocrat', a superior being above social-class distinctions, because he is 'most alive' in his relation to the universe, and not subject to the degeneration of the modern machine – a consistent Lawrentian principle and reiterated in the essay, 'Aristocracy' (1925, in *Reflections on the Death of a Porcupine and Other Essays*, 367–76), where he envisages a 'new aristocracy', going beyond national and class boundaries, of such men who will

---

[78] '... some works which are highly "phallocentric" in their semantics, their intended meaning, even their theses, can produce paradoxical effects, paradoxically antiphallocentric through the audacity of a writing which in fact disturbs the order or the logic of phallocentrism or touches on limits where things are reversed: in that case the fragility, the precariousness, even the ruin of order is more apparent' (Derrida, 50).

rule the world in a kind of pagan utopia. But Lawrence's displacement of class politics by a pastoral mythology and utopian fantasy – a tendency already evident in *The Rainbow* – is contradicted in the novel by the detailed description and representation of political and class realities as Sir Clifford's class still has the power at the end of the novel, despite Lawrence's attempts to displace class by sex, albeit in its new form: explicitly phallic yet combined with tenderness between the man and the woman. A new 'phallic consciousness' to displace the phallocentric masculinity of the previous novels emerges out of Lawrence's Etruscan experience – so that once again travel inspires the literary imaginary.

In February 1927 Lawrence went on his last tour to the 'Etruscan places'.[79] His imaginary recreation of the ancient Italian civilization from the archaeological sites became a paradigm for the values Lawrence promotes in his late doctrine: to add to his continued belief in vitality, fullness of life, spontaneity and harmony with the natural world, he now wants a delicate sensitivity, and above all, 'the natural beauty of proportion of the phallic consciousness' ('Etruscan Places' in *DHLI*, 339).[80] The Etruscans are everything the Romans are not (and this has a contemporary agenda too, as Mussolini's Italian fascists promoted everything Roman) (23). The tombs are symbolically gendered, as the phallus or the ark or arx (i.e. womb) are still visible by the doors of tombs, male or female respectively. Lawrence opposes these symbols to the dominant Roman values of empire, dominion, riches, social gain: 'You cannot dance gaily to the double flute and at the same time conquer nations or rake in large sums of money' (342). It should not be surprising, then, that in *Lady Chatterley's Lover* Sir Clifford represents the Roman Emperor wanting to impose his will on the mines and turn the workers into his slaves. Clifford's political views are encapsulated thus: 'The masses are always the same, and will always be the same. Nero's slaves were extremely little different from our colliers or the Ford motor-car workmen' (*LCL*, 182). Rylance describes how Clifford's politics reflect the solutions entertained by the authoritarian Right in England in the late 1920s after the General Strike, 'based on firm perceptions of class role, national – and racial – purpose, and the need for a Caesarist leader for England' (177). The Etruscan civilization, as Lawrence understood it, gave him a model for a utopian alternative to the growing fascism in Europe. Tenderness is now quite explicitly opposed to all forms of masculinist will and power. Mellors, the newly characterized gamekeeper, will represent this new mode of being a man.

For Lawrence, then, the Etruscans are the antipathy of the people of Tevershall and Wragby Hall in the novel. They were 'a vivid, life-accepting people, who must have lived with real fullness ... dancing in their coloured wraps ... dancing and fluting along through the little olive trees, out in the fresh day' (*LCL*, 365–6). It is an image projected onto Mellors's utopia which ends the novel. It seems that the Etruscans believed in the power of nature, the cosmic forces of the earth – derived

---

[79] For an account of the trip see Ellis, *D.H. Lawrence: Dying Game*, 348–63.

[80] Re-imagining ancient civilizations we also see in Forster's Alexandria, as discussed in the previous chapter.

from their lived experiences of volcanoes, earthquakes, and the power of the sea, the roots of plants, and the life of trees. Knowledge is derived from the experience of living naturally, and not by scientific formula or the abstractions of aesthetics – familiar Lawrence doctrine, which, in the case of Etruscan civilization, could not be easily countered for there was little actual archaeological evidence.

In a novel that, like much of Lawrence's fiction, gives priority to the life of the body, the location of the story is symptomatic: there is an important and quite conventionally paradigmatic opposition between the Hall and the Woods, the social and the natural environment for the story of the Lady and the Gamekeeper. Lawrence's English woodland reminds us of E.M. Forster's 'greenwood' where, as Forster put it, once 'it was possible to get lost' (Forster, 'Terminal Note' to *Maurice*, 221).[81] Indeed, in correspondence with Rolf Gardiner,[82] especially the letter of the 3 December 1926, Lawrence encourages the establishing of an alternative community, perhaps on a farm, with a different lifestyle based on colourful clothing, dance and mass music. It is a development of '*Rananim*' tried out by Ramón in *The Plumed Serpent*. Also in the letter to Gardiner, 7 January 1928, Lawrence praises his involvement with the German *Bünde*, the Youth Movement that promoted outdoor activities, farm-work and the '*Freikörperkultur*'.[83] Connie Chatterley has already experienced the German Youth Movement, the '*Wandervogel*', when she was younger (described in the beginning of the novel); and Mellors has explained his utopia to her: as a leader he would tell his men to take their clothes off and look at themselves, come alive, wear more colourful clothes, clean up the countryside, rebuild Tevershall and restrict birth as the world is already overcrowded (*LCL*, 219–20). Lawrence, like Forster, therefore tries to imagine an alternative to the repressions of English culture – and like Forster there is an imaginary 'queering' of England at stake.

It is in the scene of the car-ride through Tevershall that Lawrence once again returns to the rural English landscape, but seen through Connie's perspective – both a class-specific view and a pastoral idealizing one seen elsewhere in Lawrence. It is a fictional version of the late essay 'Nottingham and the Mining Countryside' and a reworking of the topographical symbolism in the short story 'England, my England' (1921). At first she sees only the worst sights of the miners' dwellings: 'the long squalid straggle of Tevershall, the blackened brick dwellings ... black with coal-dust ... dismalness ... The utter negation of natural beauty ... the utter death of the human intuitive faculty was appalling ... The England of today ... was producing a new race of mankind, over-conscious in the money and social and political side, on the spontaneous intuitive side dead' (152–3). But once out in the countryside, there are 'the tattered remnants of the old coaching and

---

[81]   See discussion in the previous chapter.

[82]   For further discussion see Ellis, *D.H. Lawrence: Dying Game*, 308.

[83]   Lawrence was, however, cautious of the Bünde's 'drift into nationalistic, and ultimately, fighting bodies'. He felt that German militarism was not a model for the English. See *Selected Letters*, 376–7. Gardiner himself later sympathized with the Nazis.

cottage England, even the England of Robin Hood'. And speaking for Lawrence, Connie asks: 'England my England! But which is *my* England?' The England of the past, represented in its best old halls and literature ('from the days of Good Queen Ann and Tom Jones'), and now the England of modern industrialism: 'The industrial England blots out the agricultural England ... The new England blots out the old England. And the continuity is not organic, but mechanical' (156). In the short story 'England, My England' the ending is apocalyptic as Egbert's disillusion drives him to choose death in the war in France.[84] In *Lady Chatterley's Lover* Mellors in the end encourages Connie to come away with him and live on a farm – a reiterated utopian solution in Lawrence's fiction.

There are three versions of the *Lady Chatterley* novel in print, and the above reading is of the third and final version.[85] The principal difference between the third version and the other two is the attention to writing as Lawrence returns to the self-conscious modernism of the other 1920s fiction. For example, when he wants to insist that the modern woman is divided by her social self and her inner desires, Connie's sexual experience with Mellors is captured in a '*jouissance-text*', itself a kind of writing that was radical in its day. Here Lawrence invents a poetic writing, part biblical, part psychoanalytic. All the other talk about sex in his writing is put into perspective by his representation of the female *jouissance*: '[T]here awoke in her new strange thrills rippling inside her ... like a flapping overlapping of soft flames, soft as feathers, running to points of brilliance, exquisite, exquisite, and melting her all molten inside ... She lay unconscious of the wild little cries she uttered at last ...' (133–4). Like his use of German Expressionism earlier in his writing life to capture unconscious thoughts and feelings – in *Sons and Lovers* and *The Rainbow*, for example – Lawrence is prepared to demonstrate the limits of realism to represent desire or sexuality in such daring and quite deliberate explicitness.

What is also most noticeably different in the third version is the often cynical tone, made all the more effective by the use of a narrator. Here, he reintroduces the cynical narrator more typical of his post-*Mr Noon* writing. This device makes the third version more consistent with the tone of Lawrence's fiction in the 1920s. In fact, he employs both devices: the narrator being more prominent in the satirical passages, for instance. Interjections like: 'Heaven knows why' (8), and cynical comments like: 'Both sisters ... mixed with the young Cambridge group, the group that stood for "freedom" and flannel trousers, and soft shirts open at the neck, and

---

[84]   The story's ironic title refers to the patriotic poem by W.E. Henley (1900): 'What have I done for you, / England, my England? / What is there I would not do, / England, my own?' Lawrence begins the story with an evocation of the spirit of place, a residue of English history and tradition, and remnant of old 'savage England'. It is English country-house fiction, with an estate and gardens whose oak trees are quintessential symbols of Englishness. See *England, my England and Other Stories*, edited by Bruce Steele. The title story is the 1921 version.

[85]   For a reading of the differences between the three versions, see chapter 6 in my *Radicalizing Lawrence*.

a well-bred sort of emotional anarchy' (9); or the familiarizing direct address to the reader about the choice of words: 'or perhaps rebel is too strong a word; far too strong' (10). Additionally, there are those direct addresses to the reader more common in popular fiction: 'Poor Connie! As the year drew on, it was the fear of nothingness in her life that affected her' (50). Then there is the often-quoted meta-fictional comment on the theory of the novel: the novel is important because it can 'inform and lead into new places the flow of our sympathetic consciousness ... can reveal the most ... passional secret places of life' (101). Moreover, it is here that the narrator and the author are indistinguishable, as Lawrence reiterates his principal thesis on why the novel matters. *Lady Chatterley's Lover* is inclusive enough to contain Mrs Bolton's gossip-text, Clifford's politics, Mellors's utopian thought, and Connie's '*jouissance-text*'. In the car-ride through Tevershall, Connie's focalization is sometimes interrupted by the narrator, showing the limits of her view: 'But if you looked'; and: 'But as a matter of fact, though even Connie did not know it ...' (154). Authorial comment sometimes breaks the flow of her consciousness during sex, for the sake of a doctrinal point: '... Cold and derisive her queer female mind stood apart' (172); or it sometimes interjects general statements of truth (as in the convention of the nineteenth-century novel): 'And that is how we are. By the strength of will we cut off our inner intuitive knowledge from our admitted consciousness' (288). The comic Sternean narrator from *Mr Noon* reappears in the farcical scene when Clifford loses control of the wheel-chair, and thus undermines his confident claim that he is riding upon 'the achievements of the mind of man' (179). Burlesque through literary parody (as in the eighteenth-century convention of the mock-heroic) is familiar to readers of *Mr Noon*: 'Oh last of all ships, through the hyacinthine shallows! oh pinnace on the last wild waters, sailing in the last voyage of our civilization! ... Oh captain, my Captain, our splendid trip is done! (185).[86] Here the persona of the narrator emerges as literate and humorously critical. His sense of comedy unsettles any attempt to take the novel seriously at times, like the minor incident when Mellors seems about to say something momentous to Connie, then sneezes and forgets what he was going to say. The narrator comments: 'And it was one of the disappointments of her life, that he never finished' (*LCL*, 228). We can see then that Lawrence manages a fine balancing act between the comic-satiric writing where the narrator plays a key role, and the more explicit authorial doctrine, and the poetry of the woman's '*jouissance*'. Lydia Blanchard sums up the achievement as follows: 'By the time Lawrence comes to write *Lady Chatterley's Lover*, he is able to perform the extraordinarily difficult artistic feat of simultaneously parodying his own canon and reaffirming his belief in life and growth, trusting the reader to understand the complex play that underlines his final novel' (103).[87]

---

[86] The last words are recognizably adapted from Walt Whitman. For a detailed discussion of the literary allusions see Dennis Jackson's 'Lawrence's Allusive Art in *Lady Chatterley's Lover*'.

[87] I would add that the balance between the serious and the comic in modernism is exemplified in T.S. Eliot's 'The Waste Land'.

Conclusion

States of being, fully acknowledged as, at best, instinctively and spontaneously sexual, are fundamental to the identity problematic in Lawrence's writing. He shares with Forster the belief in the lack in the English way of life of his day, which always comes down to an inability to be oneself. Questions of the state of the culture are an integral part of Lawrence's writing life, whether as home thoughts from abroad in the travel writing and travel fiction, or in the fiction set in England to which he returns at the end. What is consistent throughout his work is the importance of topography: place always takes on an actual and a transcendent significance – as setting or location, as landscape with historical-cultural trace or deeper spiritual resonance, and as object of projection or reaction for the protagonist in the fiction or the author in the travel writing. The ideal place for Lawrence was always somewhere with an ancient and persistent aura – a place to walk.[88] Topography and ontology, a sense of place is deeply associated with a sense of being. And the itinerate modernist is a rootless protagonist in the narrative of modernity – Lawrence's writing life is a life of travel in search of the ideal place to live after he left England; at best '*Rananim*', that 'imagined community' to retreat to with a few chosen friends, and one that might have appealed to Forster.[89]

In all the travel writing and the travel fiction Lawrence imagines the pressures of otherness on the identity of the traveller. At best he acknowledges cultural difference as a barrier between the subject and the other; in the fiction located in England that barrier is class. At the same time he reiterates an ideal other as the object of his quest for a renewed masculinity – the English yeoman farmer, Bavarian or Italian mountain peasant, Sardinian traditional man, Native American Indian or the 'new aristocrat' as a leader of men at a time of cultural crisis. Finally, the Etruscan man returns him to the paradigm of the gaily clad dancing man. However, the search for older forms of masculinity to set against the instrumentalities of modernity does not result in his identifying with the other. Difference may be desired, but different 'ways of consciousness' are the sign of 'complete difference'. The location of the object includes an imaginary process, and one we have seen in Lawrence's representation of landscape as well as the native other. Lawrence insists that the other is another subject, but importantly in the case of his ideal other a subject without self-consciousness – that is one that lives an instinctive life close to nature. However, Lawrence tests out his ideal in the fiction through what he called 'thought-adventure'. Thus it is that his fictional protagonists take his journeys and fail to complete their quests because there is

---

[88] Lawrence recommended in a letter to Rolf Gardiner: 'You should do a hike ... keep on the high ground from Crich and go round Tansley Moor round to Matlock Bridge ... But it's the real England – the hard pith of England.' December 1926, *Selected Letters*, 330. Lawrence was a hiker all his life, when health permitted it. He did several accompanied Alpine tours, and much else besides wherever he was living.

[89] See letter to E.M. Forster, 28 January 1915, *Selected Letters*, 86.

always a non-correspondence between the ideal object and the real other – which is cultural difference *per se*.

Furthermore, as I hope to have shown in this chapter, Lawrence's 'thought-adventure' is at the same time an adventure of writing. He draws on different paradigms of modernism to suit his purpose: expressionist in the representation of key moments of the self in crisis, and the subject-in-desire in *Sons and Lovers* and *The Rainbow*, but more self-consciously satirical in the fiction from *Women in Love* onwards.[90] The intricacies of the organic form of *The Rainbow* with its prose rhythms and repetitions, its recurrent leitmotifs establish a Lawrentian style that stretches the limits of realism towards new senses of coherence at a time of greater instabilities of identity. These are complex processes of textualization that define Lawrence's modernism, and they share some similarities with Forster's uses of the recurrent leitmotif especially in *A Passage to India*, as I described it in the previous chapter. What Lawrence called the 'modified repetition' is fundamental to his idea of organic form – a theory of writing cognate with his organic theory of culture.[91]

Lawrence's critique of modernity is in tune with the modernist responses of his contemporaries – Conrad, Forster and Eliot; and in particular, Kracauer's dominant idea that the human subject under the pressures of modernity has become 'a cog in a powerful soulless machine' (Frisby, 113). Kracauer's description is reminiscent of Mark Gertler's 1916 painting, 'The Merry-Go-Round', which impressed Lawrence as the best articulation of the mechanization and spiritual emptiness of modern existence.[92] Fictional versions of this critique appear throughout Lawrence's work, as this chapter has sought to demonstrate.

Lawrence's aesthetic and his tendency to turn to mythic solutions for the cultural crisis seem to be a compensation for fragmentation in life which, as Jameson maintained, was a defining feature of modernism: 'a Utopian compensation for everything reification brings with it' (*The Political Unconscious*, 236). At such moments Lawrence's response is apocalyptic, and one that may be characterized as neo-Romantic with his valorization of peasant cultures as the last hope of mankind. However, what I hope to have shown is that Lawrence's writing sometimes has deconstructive effects on his myth-making, his essentialist notions of the self and his sexual ideologies.

Lawrence's position on modernity was ambivalent. He celebrated the loss of the old stable ego on which to base his characters, because he saw it as an illusion grounded in false notions of identity, and thus opened up his textualizations to

---

[90]   For further discussion of Lawrence's 'expressionist turn' see Hans Ulrich Seeber, 'D.H. Lawrence und der deutsche Expressionismus' in *Sprachkunst* 13 (1982), 151–72.

[91]   In the Foreword (1919) to *Women in Love*, Lawrence wrote: 'In point of style, fault is often found with the continual, slightly modified repetition. The only answer is that it is natural to the author: and that every natural crisis in emotion or passion or understanding comes from this pulsing, frictional to-and-fro, which works up to culmination.' Reprinted in *Women in Love* Appendix I, 486.

[92]   The painting is reproduced on the back cover of Mark Kinkead-Weekes's biography, *D.H. Lawrence: Triumph to Exile*.

the problematics of modern subjectivity.[93] Yet, he called for a revival of a more instinctual relationship in a consummate marriage whose paradigms were based on his reading of the ancient civilizations of Britain, Mexico and old Italy as pre-modern worlds that were for him the radical alternatives to the spiritual depredations of modernity. Mythic solutions and the attractions of primitivism were, of course, widespread in literary and artistic modernism. Lawrence's case is unusual because he wants to displace the stability of the traditional ego with a greater instinctuality, which, in the age of Freud, was bound to lead to greater degrees of instability – although ones that Lawrence believed would be regenerative. However, despite the doctrinaire assertions in his fictional and essayistic writing, Lawrence's attempts to represent new senses of the self in a sexual ontology result in a contradiction that emerges throughout his work. When representing the unconscious, the discourses of modern sexuality, the problematics of femininity and masculinity, the insincerity of social intercourse, the destruction of the countryside by the industrial machine or the end of old class certainties without the emergence of a new aristocracy to lead the culture into regeneration, Lawrence's writing experiments with different modernist paradigms. His works are sometimes examples of expressionism, symbolism, organic form, parody and collage, myth and impressionism (exemplified, for instance, in Connie Chatterley's drive through Tevershall), as Lawrence deconstructs the broader conventions of the English novel. Thus his narrative resolutions are utopic and inconclusive while his stylistic modernism is deconstructive.

What this chapter has shown, and what links Lawrence to the general *Zeitgeist* of the period in which he was writing, is that his '*Kulturpessimismus*' carries over into the writing itself as it undermines the old novelistic certainties through the play of style and structure. This modernist process begins in the disruptions of realism and narrative closure through open-endedness in *Sons and Lovers* and *The Rainbow*; and then with *Women in Love* turns into a more thoroughgoing destabilization of the organic text as the crisis of identity of the characters is reflected in the form of the novel itself. Even as *The Lost Girl* strives to become a traditional novel it resorts to parody of the genre, only finally to abandon the attempt altogether and become travel-writing as the central protagonists move to the barren Abruzzi mountains and an uncertain future. Indeed, much of the fiction of the 1920s draws on Lawrence's own travel writing as narrative paradigm: the second parts of *The Lost Girl* and *Mr Noon*, *Aaron's Rod*, *Kangaroo* and *The Plumed Serpent* are all characterized by travel and the detailed description of exotic places and symbolic landscapes, as if landscape itself – the spirit of place – remained the only sense of truth. Topography and travel, the journey as narrative

---

[93]   While working on *The Wedding Ring*, the earlier version of *The Rainbow*, Lawrence wrote to Edward Garnett (5 June 1914): 'You mustn't look in my novel for the old stable ego of the character. There is another ego, according to whose action the individual is unrecognisable ... the characters fall into the form of some other rhythmic form ...' *Selected Letters*, 77–9.

paradigm, the encounter with other cultures as a critique of modernity, as we also see in Conrad and Forster, belong to Lawrence's significant contribution to English literary modernism.

The following two chapters change the focus to the American scene, represented in the work of Henry James and Edith Wharton.

Chapter 4
Henry James:
Journeys of Expatriation

Introduction

Although Henry James's family home was in Cambridge, Massachusetts, he was encouraged from an early age to see old Europe as the location of culture and civilization and he spent much of his life in France or Italy, finally settling in England (but still travelling frequently to France or Italy). Like other ambitious modern writers – Joyce comes immediately to mind – he felt the need of expatriation, to be free from the constraints of home.[1] His education in French and French literature allowed him to feel at home in that culture if not at first in the place. However, he travelled more in Italy than anywhere else in Europe making 14 visits in 38 years. Ian Watt has suggested that 'James's imaginative geography of Italy was somewhat similar to E.M. Forster's'. They both chose Italy as the setting for novels, and as places that would 'stand for the polar opposites to their native ways of life' (foreword to Maves, *Sensuous Pessimism*, x). James, however, also chose France for the same effect, as we see in *The American* (1877) and *The Ambassadors* (1903), for example.

As a topographical writer, his early source of income came from travel sketches; and these he continued to write most of his life. They have been collected in *A Little Tour of France* (1900), *English Hours* (1905), *The American Scene* (1907) and *Italian Hours* (1909). But, as I will argue in this chapter, topographies have both aesthetic and epistemological values in a series of stories and novels set in Italy or France, where visiting or expatriate American characters undergo life-changing experiences that challenge both cultural and individual self-understanding. I look at the significance of travel and the encounter with the foreign culture, first in the travel writing, then the short story, 'Travelling Companions' (1870); and then two novels mostly set in Italy, *Daisy Miller* (1878) and *The Portrait of a Lady* (1881); and finally two novels set in France, *The American* (1877) and *The Ambassadors* (1903). The intention is to revisit what has been called 'the international theme' in James's writing, drawing on the travel writing as already the record of the 'story

---

[1]   '"Europe" after all was freedom: from the James family, from Cambridge provincialities, from American puritanical attitudes' (Brooks, *Henry James Goes to Paris*, 79). The idea of travel and living abroad belonged to James's imaginary from childhood, as Fred Kaplan explains in *Henry James: The Imagination of Genius – A Biography*: 'These summer migrations soon became subsumed with larger voyages, the insistent wrenching of travel, of residence abroad, that eventually encouraged him to think of himself and his siblings as hotel children, less tied than most others to some settled place, to some topographical loyalty' (18–19).

seeker's journey' (James's own term) where place evokes narrative (*lieu-récit*); that is the location of stories (history, legend, anecdote).[2] Place has also comparative cultural value: his work, the fiction and the travel writing, set Europe against America, the Old World against the New, traditional high culture and classical antiquity against modernity, travel or 'sensitive tourism' (James's term) against mass tourism (the American tourist).[3] These oppositions are worked through in his travel writing, reaching a set of conclusions when he returns to America after a long absence and writes *The American Scene*; and they are an integral part of the thematic structure of the stories and novels about the American abroad, which address the question of national and cultural identity.

Henry James's Travel Writing

The European Journey – The 'Conscientious Tourist' and 'The Sentimental Traveller'

In James's life and work there appears from the start to be an overwhelming desire to leave home and travel in Europe, to find an expatriate home more congenial to his artistic development. Italy is the idealized place where difference is in the streets and buildings, the architecture and the art, a place with history and life that a young provincial American might dream about. In *Italian Hours*, such a figure is described, and one which is the prototype of a character that will recur in James's novels and stories, and which may also stand for the author himself in his youthful longing to leave home:

> Meanwhile it occurs to me that by a remote New England fireside an unsophisticated young person of either sex is reading in an old volume of travels or an old romantic tale some account of these anniversaries and appointed revels as old Catholic lands offer them to view. Across the page swims a vision of sculptured palace-fronts draped in crimson and gold and shining in a southern sun; of a motley train of maskers sweeping on in voluptuous confusion and pelting each other with nosegays and love-letters. Into the quiet room, quenching the rhythm of the Connecticut clock, floats an uproar of delighted voices, a medley of foreign sounds, an echo of far-heard music of a strangely alien cadence. But the dusk is falling, and the unsophisticated young person closes the book wearily and wanders to the window. The dusk is falling on the beaten snow. Down the road is a white wooden meeting-house, looking very grey among the drifts. The young person surveys the prospect a while, and then wanders back and stares at the fire. The Carnival of Venice, of Florence, of Rome; colour and costume, romance and rapture! The young person gazes in the firelight at the flickering

---

[2]   In *English Hours* we read, 'There are places whose very aspect is a story or a song.' *Collected Travel Writing: Great Britain and America*, 91. Henceforth abbreviated as *EH* in text.

[3]   Henry James 'was one of the first novelists to grasp the social significance of tourism'. David Lodge, Introduction to *Daisy Miller*, xvi.

chiaroscuro of the future, discerns at last the glowing phantasm of opportunity, and determines with a wild heart-beat to go and see it all – twenty years hence! (James, 'Florentine Notes' in *Italian Hours*, 249)[4]

Italy is represented as the polar opposite of America: abroad is an ideal place full of colour, sound and life; home is monochrome, white and grey, quiet and empty of life. Indeed, real life is elsewhere, a romantic and 'voluptuous confusion' to challenge the regulated simple life in Connecticut. Significantly it is a vision of the future inspired by reading about far-off places, and the texts could be either travel writing or fiction; the style though is romantic and escapist in the idealization of the other places. We could go further and suggest that James remembers his own desire to travel as a carnivalization (in Bakhtin's sense) of provincial life at home; and we can find examples of his early impressions of Italy that are as rapturous as the wish-fulfilling fantasy described above. In a letter to his brother William from Italy Henry James writes: 'From midday to dusk I have been roaming the streets … At last – for the first time – I live! It beats everything: it leaves the Rome of your fancy – your education – nowhere … I went reeling and moaning thro' the streets, in a fever of enjoyment' (Letter to William James, 1969, rept. in introduction to *Italian Hours*, ix). Place is enjoyed most when the real and art appear as one. Venice is itself an 'art-world' where 'the correspondence between the real aspects and the little polished canvases is so constant and exquisite, do art and life seem so interfused … All the splendour of light and colour, all the Venetian air and the Venetian history are on the walls and ceilings of the palaces … all the images and visions they have left upon the canvas, seem to tremble in the sunbeams and dance upon the waves' (*IH*, 21). It is as if the Catholic culture of Italy enables James to transcend the limits of the Protestant culture of America, with a licence to aesthetic enjoyment. He enjoyed Catholic Rome, as Fred Kaplan explains, 'as if it were theatre', and 'he saw how Catholicism, in Rome particularly, might have the advantage of providing a sensual door into a spiritual house' (112–13).[5] Indeed, to experience place as *jouissance* brings together the sublime and the aesthetic; however, the latter (the aesthetic) will take precedence over the former (the sublime) in the later travel writing as youthful exuberance will be tempered by measured appreciation in a new stylistic complexity, and one seen also in the fiction. For example, in 1872 James writes about Rome: 'The aesthetic is so intense that you feel you should live on the taste of it, should extract the nutritive essence of the atmosphere. For positively it's *such* an atmosphere!' (*IH*, 177, italics in original). By comparison, in 1909 James writes:

---

[4]   *Italian Hours* henceforth abbreviated as *IH* in text. In *The American Scene*, James recalls his belief in the superiority of Europe as a 'yearning' of a 'romantically affected' young American (268–9). Once in Venice, James plunges immediately 'into an aesthetic-touristic frenzy of palaces and paintings', especially the paintings of the Renaissance (Fred Kaplan, 106–8). This youthful longing to travel reminds us of Conrad's childhood map-reading.

[5]   However, James still preferred above all the Rome of Marcus Aurelius.

> we passed through prodigious perched and huddled, adorably scattered and animated and even crowded Tivoli, from the universal happy spray of the drumming Anio waterfalls, all set in their permanent rainbows and Sibylline temples and classic allusions and Byronic quotations; a wondrous romantic jumble of such things ... and plunging constantly deeper into splendid solitary gravities, supreme romantic solemnities, of landscape ... (*IH*, 197–8)

Here the late style creates a distance, in its syntactic complexity, to the scene described where the early writing has a more immediate relation to the object. Admittedly, the early example derives from the traveller's note-books and not the more usual essay written after the fact.[6] The object, art or landscape, becomes more and more what is both visible and what is seen – just as character point of view becomes James's principal technique of narration in the fiction, as we shall see later on in this chapter.

By the 1890s James is experimenting with new, modernist ways of representation in travel writing. Buildings in Venice are read as part of a compositional whole, a classical work of art; but it is the impression of the place reflected by the light on the water that informs perception: 'with their vague sea-stained pinks and drabs, into that strange gaiety of light and colour which is made up of the reflection of superannuated things ... in that universal privilege of Venetian objects which consists of being both the picture and the point of view' (*IH*, 34–5). The object and its perception is the basis of characterization and narrative in the fiction too: refusing omniscient narration, James famously dramatized the limits of characters' self-understanding and their readings of the other – the other subjected to misreading or misguided schemes (especially in the marriage plots). I discuss James's narrative experiment in his fiction in some detail later. Perception of the object as projection is already rehearsed in the travel writing. As early as 1873 James writes: 'One sees after all, however, even among the most palpable realities, very much what the play of one's imagination projects there' (*IH*, 133).

The general squalor of modern urban Italy, and the restoration and modernization of its historic buildings are criticized as James affirms throughout the travel essays on Italy the classical and renaissance art and architecture as the archive of civilization itself. Clearly, as John Auchard puts it in the introduction to *Italian Hours*, 'James was providing more than a pleasant travelogue. He was posing questions about the durability of civilization itself' (xxiv). In a wholesale rejection of modernity – and one that returns again and again in his work, and which I discuss in more detail later in this chapter – James's focus is on the Italian past and how it should continue to influence the present: 'more than ever yet, the present appeared to become really classic, to sigh with strange elusive sounds

---

[6]   Pure exaltation – the position of the aestheticism of Walter Pater – is rejected for morally responsible observation: James's figure of the 'sentimental tourist' is responsible as the keeper of the treasures of civilization, just as art is not for its own sake but has a moral purpose that transcends history and cultural origins. For a recent discussion of James's quarrel with Paterian aestheticism see Steven Salmoni's '"The Very Air we Breathe": The Aesthetics of Experience in Henry James's "From Chambéry to Milan"'.

of Virgil and Theocritus … we yield to these visions as we must' (*IH*, 316). The aesthetic is not just a personal experience of uplift, but 'the subtlest daughter of History' (*IH*, 316). Modern Italy, like New York (critiqued in *The American Scene*), is hated for its 'vulgar' developments and 'extreme bad taste'; for the Italy of 'three hundred years ago had the best taste in the world', and 'all this modern crudity runs riot over the relics of the great period' (*IH*, 102). History is the force James sets against modernity. As Steven Salmoni agues: 'The many lamentations that James makes against what he believes to be the disruptions wrought upon Italy by the process of modernisation are a testament to the force of this almost metaphysical "sense of the past"'. And as James believes these changes to the landscape, towns and buildings are 'irreversible', he speaks more and more for 'the weight of the past', immersing himself in history (Salmoni, 224).[7]

The aesthetic archive is, though, being assaulted by mass tourism. The 'herd of fellow gazers' are the new 'barbarians' turning Venice into 'a battered peep show and bazaar', a 'curiosity shop' (*IH*, 10–15). Of course, James is keen to differentiate his own travels from the typical tourist. An excursion to Lake Como, 'though brief, lasted long enough to suggest to me that I too was a hero of romance with leisure for a love-affair, and not a hurrying tourist with a Bradshaw [a current tourist guidebook] in his pocket'. The 'hurrying tourist' is 'the unsophisticated tourist, the American at least' (*IH*, 86–7). There are more observations about mass tourism in a notebook from 1873: Switzerland is full of 'Cook's tourists' who 'vulgarise' the places they visit, even when for James Switzerland is the perfect tourist haven, a 'show country' (*IH*, 89). He reiterates the classic opposition between mass tourism and individual travel, between the sightseeing with its 'superficial' observations of the packaged tour and the informed visitor, or 'conscientious tourist' (*A Little Tour in France* in *Collected Travel Writings: The Continent*, 86)[8] who returns again and again with 'the sense of an acquired passion for the place and of an incalculable number of gathered impressions' (*IH*, 193). James, educated and informed, refuses the mass 'tourist gaze'. There are many examples in James's travel writing where, after a leisurely stroll through the streets, he seeks out the quiet spot away from the throng of tourists for some contemplation, a square or church where he 'can linger and remain and return' (*IH*, 10); 'I was glad to retire to a comparatively uninvaded corner of the abbey and divert myself with the view', before returning to 'the clamorous little piazza' (*IH*, 164). In his tour of England, recorded in *English Hours*, James seeks out a tranquil place, either in a park or the picturesque countryside like Eaton Hall near Chester where there is 'stillness and space – grassy oak-studded space' (*EH*, 60); or 'a walk to Haddon Hall, along a meadow-path by the Wye' (*EH*, 73). The spirit of place conjures up 'the old life, the old manners' (*EH*, 74). But it is precisely here that James blurs the distinction between the connoisseur traveller as 'sentimental tourist'[9] and the despised, uneducated

---

7 James shares the over-evaluation of the High Culture's past with Forster and Wharton.

8 Subsequent page references abbreviated as *LTF* in text.

9 A term reiterated. See *EH*, 52, 66, 67, 142 and 175.

American tourist. For James also goes to Stratford – 'The American tourist usually comes straight to this quarter of England' (*EH*, 174) – delights in the sights of 'old English houses' (*EH*, 176, 179), even hoping to see the ubiquitous ghost 'a gray friar who is seen in the dusky hours at the end of passages' (*EH*, 190), an expectation shared with Isabel Archer in *The Portrait of a Lady* when she arrives at Gardencourt, a romantic old English country house which the American visitor expects to be haunted (*The Portrait of a Lady*, 100). The tourist imaginary is meant here to signal a limitation, a naivety in the young protagonist. But, like his fictional character, Henry James indulges in literary tourism[10]: Shakespeare country (*EH*, 78), Browning in Westminster Abbey (*EH*, 47ff.), the statue of Dr Johnson in Lichfield (*EH*, 67), Dickens country (Rochester, Medway, Gadshill) (*EH*, 122ff.), Jane Austen country (*EH*, 195). Even the locals are read as literary types: Hodge and Gaffer, or the heroine at the ball (*EH*, 260–62). In Suffolk James writes of 'the birthplace of a Copperfield' (*EH*, 253–4); at the Epsom Derby everyone 'prepared for "larks"' (*EH*, 151), an echo of Dickens; and the world of the factory and the workhouse is read through *Oliver Twist* (*EH*, 273). In France James visits Balzac's birthplace, Tours (*LTF*, 19ff.), and the Touraine region generally which is 'essentially France', because it is 'the land of Rabelais, of Descartes, of Balzac, of good books and good company, as well as good dinners' (*LTF*, 20). References are made to George Sand (*LTF*, 58, 184), Rousseau (68), Victor Hugo (161), Alphonse Daudet (176, 204, 225), John Locke's stay in Montpellier (182); Stendhal's *Mémoires d'un touriste* is recommended for 'every traveller in France' (183–4, 203, 212); Matthew Arnold is quoted (181, 244, 261). James follows in the footsteps of Alphonse de Lamartine at Macon (258–9), and stays at the 'Hôtel de Pétrarque et de Laure' after visiting the famous gorge at Vaucluse (244–9). Locals are once again read as characters who might have stepped out of a novel (e.g., *LTF*, 249); signs of typical Frenchness in places and buildings are read through literature or art (21, 30, 68, 80, 141–2), although they do not always live up to their literary representation (30, 76, 91). Fiction and history are equal sources of information as James does the tour of the great houses and castles, and the ancient classical ruins – all sights of the Grand Tour and now part of the tourist itinerary.[11]

As we can see, then, Henry James is concerned with the way places of interest are being commodified by mass tourism; and yet he sometimes manages to blur the distinction between travel and tourism, despite the best efforts of his own practice. As well as literary tourism, he admits to 'the pleasure of cathedral-hunting' (*EH*, 82), always has a travel-itinerary of the great houses and castles in England, doing the same in his tour of France as he follows the Loire valley.

---

[10]   Chapter 3 in Nicola J. Watson's *The Literary Tourist* contains a discussion of the role of haunted houses in literary tourism.

[11]   In *Italian Hours* we find references to other writers who visited Italy: Byron (46, 109); Shelley and Keats (110, 172); Browning (72); Goethe (210), and many others, some of whom died in Venice or are buried in the Protestant cemetery in Rome – and where James has his character Daisy Miller buried.

In all cases, James is looking for the signs of Englishness or Frenchness, even when he so often reproduces those signs from literature (Dickens's Medway, Balzac's Touraine) – as a classic literary tourist. The iconic English village green or peaceful cathedral close; in France the 'soft agglomeration of gardens, vineyards, scattered villas, gables and turrets of slated-roofed château, terraced with grey balustrades' (*LTF*, 25) characterizing the Frenchness of Tours; and most obviously the Venice of its canals, gondoliers, the Rialto bridge (*IH*, 47) as signs of what James himself calls the 'Venetian "effect"' (*IH*, 52) – all these signs which have been reproduced in countless photos and decorated postcards belong to the burgeoning tourist industry already in James's day. They are the objects of the collective tourist gaze, a gaze that is constructed through visible signs. As Jonathan Culler has argued: 'the tourist is interested in everything as a sign of itself ... All over the world the unsung armies of semioticians, the tourists, are fanning out in search of the signs of Frenchness, typical Italian behaviour, exemplary Oriental scenes, typical American thruways, traditional English pubs' (cit. in John Urry, *The Tourist Gaze*, 3). The tourist is pre-conditioned to read the signs of the typical. However, the guide-books that emerged during the era of the Grand Tour – Baedeker, Murray – promoted a more differentiated, passionate romantic way of seeing, a 'scenic tourism' for individual development (Urry, 4).[12] Henry James insists that he belongs to the classic, individualist tour. Yet we can see a tension in his travel writing between the desire for the typical available at first sight, and the deeper aesthetics of place attained by quiet contemplation.

In all his travel writing, James is always a compulsive seeker of the picturesque scene. Here we should distinguish between the sublime and the picturesque – a distinction originally made in the eighteenth century. Kendall Johnson explains that 'whereas the picturesque signalled a break from the regiment of beauty, it also offered a foothold for recovering perspective on the vast whole, folding consciousness back from sublimity's aporia and into the delight of orchestrating a visual gestalt' (*Henry James and the Visual*, 8). Consistent with his critique of Pater, James – as we have seen – prefers a controlling distance between observation and the object instead of a complete immersion in it. The picturesque as an aesthetic concept, however, had become overused by the late nineteenth century; indeed, it had been commodified by tourism – now belonging to the 'banal grammar of the sightseeing bourgeoisie' (Johnson, 9). As an 'ideological legacy of eighteenth-century visual aesthetics' (Johnson, 11) it suits James's nostalgia for the taste and manners of the past.

There are, though, two further points to consider in appreciating James's insistence on the picturesque. First, as Johnson argues, 'in the United States it had a much more vigorous legacy, fuelled in the first half of the nineteenth century by Emerson and Hawthorne' and others, as well as being revived by Ruskin as a way of training 'the visual sympathy' (Johnson, 31), and therefore James can reinforce his credentials as an American cultural critic by employing the picturesque as an aesthetic code for reading landscapes at home and abroad. Second, James appears

---

[12] Forster thought of guide books as a literary genre, as we saw in Chapter 2.

to use the picturesque in his work to signal the limitations of narrators (and therefore characters) to face up to 'the threatening consequences of modernity' (Johnson, 9). The question is does James as narrator of the travel writing also use the term ironically? To answer this question we should distinguish once again between the early and the late James of the travel writing.

As argued above, there are instances in the Italian travel writing where we are privileged to compare the early and the late perspectives and styles. As we saw, the early texts indulge in a more direct response to the object; the late style enables a greater distance, a more reflective intellectual response. James himself reflects (in the third person, even) on the difference: 'compare the musing *mature* visitor's "feeling about Rome" with that of the extremely agitated, even though extremely inexpert, consciousness reflected in the previous pages ... The city of his first unpremeditated rapture shines to memory ... on the occasion of my first visit to Rome, thirty-eight years before' (*IH*, 194–5, emphasis in original). The criticism of his earlier self appears to be a question of style; the mature traveller is able to control his reaction better. However, the aesthetic qualities of the ancient city are still there to be appreciated. What he says about the picturesque in 1873 still holds in 1909: 'I made a note after my first stroll at Albano to the effect that I had been talking of the "picturesque" all my life, but that now for a change I beheld it' (*IH*, 152). Moreover, the pleasure gained from the contemplation of art, architecture, or nature is prevented 'from becoming vulgar' by knowledge, 'the intellectual background of all enjoyment in Rome' (*IH*, 149) – which for landscape means to read it through art, or as artistic composition, instead of simply through the untutored, hurried tourist gaze. Travelling from Rome to Florence the scenery is like 'background by an Umbrian master as it ideally should have been' (*IH*, 205); in Perugia 'almost everything in fact lends itself to the historic, the romantic, the aesthetic fallacy' (*IH*, 212). James admits to his 'almost systematised aesthetic use of place' (*IH*, 231), where natural scenery is admired for its 'compositional beauty'; for the way a place like Siena appears to have a satisfying 'combination of elements' (*IH*, 232). Thus, clearly the term, picturesque, is used in all seriousness throughout James's travel writing; although always qualified as an informed and educated view to be distinguished from the superficial gaze of the common tourist.

The most consistent object of admiration, and the most romanticized place, is the ruin. The ruin is always preferred to restoration – a preference Henry James shares with Edith Wharton: 'The deeply interesting little cathedral of the eighth century, which stood there on the edge of the sea, as touching in its ruin, with its grassy threshold and primitive mosaics, as the bleached bones of a human skeleton washed ashore by the tide, has now been restored and made cheerful, and the charm of the place, its strange and suggestive desolation, has well-nigh departed' (*IH*, 30). In France he complains about the restoration of the Château de Blois: 'The work of restoration has been as ingenious as it is profuse, but it rather chills the imagination' (*LTF*, 42). Ruins are preferred because they are 'more romantic' (*LTF*, 170), more 'alive' (*LTF*, 194), especially in 'the light of a magnificent moon' (*LTF*, 216). Ruins enable a play of the imagination, a feeling of touching the distant past. They are haunted places, attractive therefore to the 'story-seeker' as *lieu-récit* – even when often commodified into tourist sites. And the contemplative value of the ruin is symptomatic for James's attitude to the places he visits: archives of classical or renaissance Italy, as examples of the 'aesthetic culture' (*IH*, 250), which the tourist cannot appreciate in the brief time of the packaged tour.

Indeed, time is an important aspect of real travel, because for James the quality of the experience is measured by the time taken. I have already noted his preference for the quiet contemplation in a secluded place away from the bustle of the crowds, like the 'deeper stillness' (*EH*, 84) or 'sweet seclusion' (*EH*, 165) of an English park or cathedral close, or the 'little three-sided cloister, attached to the cathedral' at Chichester where 'you may sit upon a gravestone' and 'listen to the cawing of the rooks and the twittering of the swallows' and 'hear a slow footstep echoing in the cloisters' (*EH*, 210). Such travel, with its 'old idleness' (*IH*, 272), is the privilege of the leisured classes, strolling the Italian city in 'slow contemplative perambulation' – the ideal form of Jamesian 'enjoyment' (*IH*, 281), which is already being replaced by not just the rushing tourist groups but the speed and technology of the new transport, the railway, and (by the later travel writing) the motor car and the 'cloud of motor-dust' hanging over the streets (*IH*, 285–6). However, he seems to enjoy the greater convenience of being driven around the countryside in a car and observing autumnal New England: 'the wonder-working motor-car ... spreading its wings to the magnificence of movement' (39). Using the railways, James prefers 'the slowest of Sunday trains, pottering up to London' (*EH*, 15), or the 'little friendly, familiar dawdling train' in provincial France where he has time to look at the scenery through the carriage window (*LTF*, 192) – although he soon complains about 'the insufferable delays over one's luggage, the porterless platform, the overcrowded and illiberal train' (*LTF*, 256); and does end his little tour of France by taking the express train from Dijon to Paris.

For James, as for others who have the means and the leisure, travel is an aesthetic experience. Appreciation and contemplation require slow travel and quiet places – values that are becoming increasingly rare in the noise and bustle of mass tourism, and the speed of transport in the era of modernity. The places he wants to see are of course those already suffering the process of commodification as the locations for sightseeing. I think though we can see that James, more than any of the other writers in his study, was aware that he was also a tourist, but a 'conscientious' literary and art tourist, sensitized by his reading and aesthetic education.

The American Scene – *Modernity and Nostalgia*

James's most sustained discussion of modernity and modern travel can be found in *The American Scene* (1907), a record of his tour of the US after a 20-year absence. The modern metropolis is New York, with its skyscrapers, elevators, vast highways, speeding cars and Pullman trains. However, as Colm Tóibín explains, James preferred the New York of 1848 to 1855, which he remembers with the nostalgia of his lost childhood as a homogeneous simple community (*Gemeinschaft*) analogous to village life (*All a Novelist Needs*, 54).[13] One should perhaps read *The American Scene* alongside the story he wrote at about the same time, 'The Jolly Corner' (1908), which imagines a similar homecoming where the protagonist is haunted by the selves he might have been had he stayed in New York. The American expatriate Spencer Brydon returns after more than 30 years in Europe to take care of the property he has inherited, the family house. But there he experiences a haunting by his alter ego, an encounter as mirror image of a self-confronting rather than a real ghost – even when James is clever enough to allow the narrative to hover between the uncanny and the projection of consciousness as he did so effectively in 'The Turn of the Screw' (1898). Whereas Brydon is impressed by the changes he sees in New York, wondering whether he might have made his fortune had he stayed (becoming 'a billionaire!'), James confirms his decision to leave for a life in Europe and England ('The Jolly Corner' in James, *Collected Stories* vol. 2, 955).[14]

In the New York of 1905 he saw 'the terrible novelty of modernity' (Tóibín, 66–7). His return 'home' confirms his expatriate status, as he now has what Ross Posnock has called a 'decentred relation to America'; home as 'a stable point of origin' is deconstructed (50). America is now synonymous with modern capitalism.[15] Speed, that most challenging aspect of modernity, has changed perception; the countryside seen from the train window has a new relationship to the observer than the one got from the 'old informal earthy coach road' (*The American Scene*, 24).[16] From the window of the Pullman there was 'little in the prospect' to enjoy, and everything 'was monotonized' (226). He writes about 'the great moving proscenium of the Pullman' (319) and asks, 'Where was the charm of boundless immensity as over-looked from a car-window? – with the general pretension to charm, the general conquest of nature and space, affirmed, immediately around you, by the general pretension of the Pullman' (340); and

---

[13]   A counterweight to travel is the quiet place to write which James needs more and more as his writing life dominates. Whether a London flat where 'he kept his own "land's centre" – his desk – most of the time' (Fred Kaplan, 229), or 'some green corner of Britain' (James, cit. in Fred Kaplan, 418), Lamb House in Rye, James desired 'sedentary domesticity' (Fred Kaplan, 437) for his writing.

[14]   The difference between James and his protagonist is contained in Brydon's reflection on his travel and homecoming: 'He had come back, yes – come back from further away than any man but himself had ever travelled; but it was strange how with this sense what he had come back *to* seemed really the great thing, and as if his prodigious journey had been all for the sake of it' ('The Jolly Corner', 975, italics in original).

[15]   James was also critical of the new American imperialism. From the late 1890s it had acquired territories in Central and South America, and in 1908 invaded the Philippines to bring 'civilization' to the natives. James wrote to his brother William: 'I agree with you no end – we have ceased to be, among the big nations, the one great thing that made up for our so many crudities and made us above all superior and unique – the only one with clean hands and no record of across-the-seas murder and theft ...' (cit. in Fred Kaplan, 433).

[16]   Further references in text.

being 'seated by the great square of plate-glass through which the missionary Pullman appeared to invite me to admire the achievements it proclaimed. It was in this respect the great symbolic agent' (342).[17]

Throughout his work, but especially explicit in *The American Scene*, which may be taken as a *summa* of his persistent critique of modernity, James structures his argument through the opposition between the mechanical and the organic, where the modernized metropolis like New York is like the 'infernal machine' (209) while Philadelphia still represents 'organic social relations' (206) built on family ties in the spirit of William Penn (207). The 'fury' of the New York pavements is opposed to the historic and 'spacious' streets of Philadelphia (207–8). New York appears as a dystopic vision of the modern metropolis – and one later captured in Fritz Lang's film, *Metropolis* (1926). It is contrasted to the New England arcadia in autumn and 'the figure of the rich old Harvard organism brooding' (46) where he could briefly 'walk in the idyll' (47). New York in contrast is all energy, power, where everything 'rushed and shrieked … some colossal set of clockworks, some steel-souled machine-room … horizontal pistons working at high pressure' (59). In a city dominated by the ethos of Wall Street, the price of the future is the end of history. Reconstruction as modernization of the city is captured in the trope of the skyscraper blotting out the little old church (42–3, 142) which is interpreted as 'a repudiation of the past, so far as there had been a past to repudiate' (43). The past, like tradition, is organic, the present mechanical – an opposition we see in Lawrence too; its most popular version being found in Spengler, *The Decline of the West*, as I explained in the previous chapter.

Once out of the city, the old America is a solace, the 'small original Hawthornesque world keeping the other, the smoky modernism, at a distance' (*The American Scene*, 200). Baltimore is a peaceful historic place (229) with a 'potentially harmonizing' quality, and 'romantic parks and woodlands that were all suburban yet all Arcadian' (234). Of course there are places in New York too that retain the old charm, like the Waldorf-Astoria, Tiffany's or Central Park. But it is the new money-making that dominates the modern world. It is not simply that the country is preferred to the city, however, as we see clearly in James's critique of the American South. From Richmond in his journey south place is the 'haunted scene' of the Civil War (272ff.); the Confederacy a 'fallacy', the South 'a vast Slave State' (274), resulting from the worship of 'false gods' (290). In the 'humiliation of defeat' the South continues to live in the past but is 'shabby and sordid' (292). Yet there are traces of a better time of European influence in the grand style still visible in the old hotels, 'the ghost of a rococo tradition' (298–9), and old towns in the Spanish style (336–8) – a loss of identity that James laments (in Charleston) in gender terms: 'whereas the ancient order was masculine, fierce and moustachioed, the present is at the most a sort of sick lioness who has so

---

[17]   Sara Blair explains that by 1905, when James was touring around America, 'Pullman had become a watchword for progressive efficiency … [it] had successfully begun to remake American travel', to make it fashionable and stylish (*Henry James and the Writing of Race and Nation*, 193–4).

visibly parted with her teeth and claws that we may patronisingly walk all round her' (307). If masculinity has lost its vigour so has the white race in general. In the South there is a new post-war black presence, in some places in greater numbers than whites – seen from the vantage point of a seat in the Pullman; and the whites are 'of aspect so forlorn and depressed for the most part as to deprecate, though not cynically, only quite tragically, any imputation of value' (293). The 'negroes' were morally inferior even when 'the lustier race' (293), a race with a 'deep-seated ineptitude' even as servants (312). And the Pullman trains, like the palace hotels and country clubs, became the very symbol of wealth and luxury enjoyed by the new exclusive managerial classes with its black servant class on board. Indeed, as Blair reminds us, 'Aboard the train, Pullman revived the social relations of white supremacy' (202).

Speed, gender and race: these are the coordinates of a perceived crisis in modern American identity; a crisis that is worked out in detail in *The American Scene*, and worked through in the fiction in the international theme of Americans abroad. The national identity problematic for James – himself an expatriate who left because America was not European enough and now back home complains that America is not American enough – is most visible on Ellis Island, the port of entry for immigrants. Here he notes with some concern, 'the ceaseless process of the recruiting of our race ... the introduction of fresh ... foreign matter into our heterogeneous system' (*The American Scene*, 50). It is his witnessing 'the terrible little Ellis Island' that gets him to pose the question of what it means to be American, 'to share the sanctity of his American consciousness, the intimacy of his American patriotism, with the inconceivable alien' (66). The new multi-racial character of America is a shock to James, who has enough trouble thinking outside his close-knit family and class identity.[18] The worries he expresses about the future of the race – white, Anglo-Saxon – are common anxieties of the late nineteenth and early twentieth centuries.

From about the 1870s – the period of Henry James's writing – there was a serious concern about the fate of whiteness exacerbated by a new and widespread encounter with other cultures through travel, exploration and ethnographies. A new taxonomy of race documented the foreign face and primitive practices to reassure the colonial west of its superiority and its continued survival as the fittest race. But racial supremacy was not as secure as it seemed. Fears of 'contaminating' the blood through miscegenation grew, and eugenics societies were formed to discourage mixed race marriages. As Blair explains: 'In the post-Darwinian moment, the very terms of human identity – categories of race, nation, and species – had become arbitrary' (22). Henry James, like the other writers discussed in this study, belongs to this period mindset. In all his travel writing and fiction he charts difference, even when predominantly from the perspective of residual post-enlightenment cultural ideology – the ideology of the aesthetic where the unity and integrity of the work of art is the highest value. But in *The American Scene* there is a

---

[18]   Indeed, he sees immigration as a threat to the culture and language of 'the Anglo-American alliance' (Fred Kaplan, 496).

greater concern with difference as a matter of race, and one that belongs to a widespread urge at the time 'to quantify difference – blackness, the primitive, the alien', which 'encodes increasing anxiety about the meaning of whiteness itself'. Clearly 'whiteness' is becoming unstable as a racial signifier (Blair, 26).[19] And we could read James's whole effort at recording the great works of European art and architecture in his travel writing as affirming a cultural superiority. It is as if the aesthetic can compensate for the forms of degeneration blamed on modernity itself. However, the aesthetic is in short supply in the America of James's 1904 visit. The only forms of compensation are personal memories, literary landscapes and places, pastoral idylls, and the few remaining older buildings in the cities. The result of his observations of the influx of Eastern European Jews, Italians (speaking 'a rude form of Italian', *The American Scene*, 172) and other ethnic groups, and the establishment of 'vast foreign quarters of the city [New York]' (94–5), coupled with the growth of the new type of American businessman, is that James feels he is a foreigner in his own country; or at least he vindicates his choice of expatriation, preferring a cosmopolitan existence – itself a privilege of his class, education and independence. Moreover, his anxieties about American identity and difference are racist at worst, indulging in the common observations of facial features as indexes of racial inferiority, as we see on a visit to the theatre: 'as I took in on one side the hue of the Galician cheek, the light of the Moldavian eye, the whole pervasive facial mystery, swaying at the best, for the moment, over the gulf, on the vertiginous bridge of American confectionery – and took in on the other the perfect "Yankee" quality of the challenge which stared back at them as in the white light of its hereditary thinness' (149). Thus it is that difference provokes tensions as James's ideal homogenous America – class differences notwithstanding – is threatened by what he calls 'the dreadful chill of change' (172).

As we saw above in James's critique of the American South, a loss of cultural integrity is also a loss of masculinity. The new man of modernity is the businessman, whose inferiority of character according to James may be read on his face. Modern American women, by contrast, 'appear to be of markedly finer texture than the men, and that one of the liveliest signs of this difference is precisely in their less narrowly specialized, their less commercialized, distinctly more generalized, physiognomic character' (*The American Scene*, 51). Interestingly, James reads character through appearance – in the manner of Balzac. The American woman is 'two-thirds of the apparent life – which means that she is absolutely all of the social' (255). In Charleston, 'the gardens were a matter for the women' (305). However, although the modern American woman has all the advantages in the house of 'mechanical appliances' (256), she does not share the European woman's sophistications. Indeed, American women 'in particular failed in an extraordinary degree to engage the imagination' (335). Edith Wharton, as we will see in the next chapter, engages more thoroughly in a comparison between modern French and American women, and finds the latter wanting in a number of ways. James is

---

[19] For a different reading of the race question see the discussion in chapter 2 of Kalpana Seshadri-Crooks, *Desiring Whiteness: A Lacanian Analysis of Race*.

more concerned that American man participates less actively in society than his European counterpart (255) – we should, of course, understand 'society' in its narrow sense of 'polite society', a sense consistent in the whole of James's work.

How does James translate the critique of modernity in the travel writing into the fiction? The discussion in the rest of this chapter turns to a selection of James's fiction with European settings – symbolic and symptomatic uses of Italy, France and England as topographies first described in the travel writing – for the dramas of encounter of the Americans abroad, raising larger questions about the Old World (Europe) and the New World (America). We will see which of the displaced Americans are able to free themselves from the constraints of the homeland, and which ones are prevented from change by bringing their narrow perspectives with them – a use of travel we saw in Forster's fiction for investigating questions of Englishness.

Additionally, I trace James's attempts to write the American Balzac novel as a conscious rejection of French modernism – the Flaubertian novel – with reference to Peter Brooks's excellent study, *Henry James Goes to Paris* (2007). It is a central argument in this chapter, as it is in Brooks, that James's attitudes to realism and modernism change as his style does, from the early to the late writing – in the travel writing, and in the fiction as we shall see now.

Fictions of Travel

Henry James's travel and travel writing gave him a narrative paradigm for his stories and novels. One of the earliest examples is 'Travelling Companions' (1870) where an American expatriate travels down from Germany where he has been living to Italy, and there he encounters a rich young female American, falls in love with her, and although not accepted at first eventually marries her. Going to Italy is the fulfilment of a dream: 'From my earliest manhood, beneath a German sky, I had dreamed of this Italian Pilgrimage'. Where Germany is associated with the 'Northern Senses', Italy is 'the wholesome cup of pleasure' ('Travelling Companions', 602).[20] The South is the location of desire and pleasure. It is neither Germany nor 'New Jersey' (605) for the American traveller. And here already we have an opposition which we saw in James's travel writing between the old world and the new, between northern rationalism (Protestant culture) and southern sensualism (Catholic culture) – an essentialist opposition important to the other writers in this study. Indeed, there are long passages of this story that appear to be transcribed from the travel writing collected in *Italian Hours*. In the story the narrator describes the 'fierce blinding efflorescence of fantastic forms of marble ... the marble shines forever ...' (603); in 'From a Roman Note-Book' (1872) we read: 'One has come to Italy to know marbles and love them ... Colour has in no other form so cool and unfading a purity and lustre' (*IH*, 179). The narrator in the story recounts being in Venice where from the lagoon at sunset he sees 'the

---

rosy flush on the marble palaces' (TC, 687). Carl Maves sees this early effort to write the story of Americans abroad as 'a comparatively primitive effort ... more a travelogue than a work of fiction'. The plot may be fiction, but the detail of place is 'pure autobiography' (Maves, 10). James will develop his international theme in his writing. In 'Travelling Companions' the Italian setting for the love story is itself archetypal. The aesthetic contemplation and appreciation of the great art works and architecture establishes a way of seeing the object that is then also the mode of seeing the female other as object of desire.

It is her 'frankness and freedom' as American woman that first attracts him (TC, 603) appearing in symbiosis with what he perceives to be the more carefree world of Italy where they 'must forget all [their] cares and duties and sorrows. We must go in for the beautiful' (605). The priority of the aesthetic in the travel writing – including attacks on the 'vulgarity' of tourism (see TC, 611) – is transposed into the story to such an extent that it tends to overwhelm the romance plot, and leaves little space for anything other than stereotype character sketches, which then reduces the story to allegory. In Maves's words: 'The American woman is the new Madonna, the Old World is wasting away and the New World must restore it; Italy offers Americans art, while America can offer Italy only gold' (17). James will use Italy for more subtle purposes in subsequent fiction, getting a better balance between the foreign setting and the encounters of the Americans abroad, so that the sensuous and the aesthetic will affect the 'critical faculties' (Maves, 18) and the moral certainties of protagonists in more ambivalent and interesting ways. But in each case, as we will see, it is the Italy as seen by the foreigner, and less the views of Italians; indeed, when Italian characters appear they are stereotypes like the Vicenza family in the story, 'Travelling Companions' getting the American narrator to buy from them a 'pretended Correggio' (609ff.); or like the 'wondrous physical glory of the Italian race' understood as 'subjects for Titian and Paul Veronese' (612). The American father, Mr Evans, is also a representative type: 'Without taste, without culture or polish, he nevertheless produced an impression of substance in character' with 'good-humoured tolerance and easy morality' (613).

Miss Evans becomes Brooke's travelling companion: 'we had learned to know Venice together, and the knowledge had helped us to know each other' (TC, 684) – Italian travel enables an intimacy that would have been less possible back home in America. The 'atmosphere of romance' (685) is transferred from the place to the 'companion'. But the intelligent modern American woman sees through the man's desire: 'it's not with me that you're in love, but with that painted picture. All this Italian beauty and delight has thrown you into a romantic state of mind' (686). It turns out that she has lost her fiancé in the American Civil War, which evokes in him more dignified thoughts about her (691). They continue their Italian tour together, and get closer through their shared appreciation of Italy's art and landscape. But Brooke is better at aesthetic appreciation than expressing his sexual feelings ('perhaps I was incapable of passion', 692) – a truly Jamesian man, and one who will return in much more developed and subtle form in Lambert Strether in *The Ambassadors* (1903). His marriage proposal is not accepted at first; but after a year's gap (TC, 694) during which he continues to travel around the cities of Italy, becoming 'a wiser man' for having explored 'ruins' and studied 'classical topography' with 'an old German archaeologist', his ersatz travelling companion (a classic case of sublimation) (695), Miss Evans re-emerges mourning the death of her father, and Brooke becomes the helpless woman's new protector – an ending poorly worked but fitting the rather stereotyped story. However, this early attempt already introduces us in rudimentary form to the themes of the Americans abroad, the heiress or rich businessman in search of a husband or wife, and the uses of travel and foreign setting as narrative strategies for dramas of encounter and identity. James does more with this material in *Daisy Miller*.[21]

Daisy Miller

In this early novella, James begins to explore the themes of the newly rich American abroad, the older codes of behaviour and the younger independent modern woman who appears to flout convention. Winterbourne, the European-educated American expatriate protagonist, is like his predecessor in 'Travelling Companions' now 'dishabituated to the American tone' and 'too innocent' of American ways to know whether Daisy Miller is being defiant of conventions or simply naïve in her public conduct (*Daisy Miller*, 12).[22] Compared to Miss Evans in the earlier story, Daisy Miller is 'completely uncultivated' even when 'wonderfully pretty' – and these are observations from the point of view of her male admirers. It is Winterbourne's aunt who insists that Daisy is 'very common' in her direct and flirtatious manner, and snubs her (17); and we do have to read the story in the tradition of the novel of manners even as we see James's ironic portrayal of the rich expatriate Americans who reinforce such conventional gender and moral values. Winterbourne understands enough to realize that as a young man he 'was not at liberty to speak to a young unmarried lady except under certain rarely occurring conditions' (7). And Mrs Miller is criticized for not 'protecting' her daughter, as she is obliged to (24). We are not sure whether to expect a certain openness and defiance of stuffy drawing-room convention from the new American woman, or whether she is corrupted by being in the more sensuous Italy.

In 'Travelling Companions', Brooke was attracted to Miss Evans because she represented the 'frankness and freedom' of American women (TC, 603). In *Daisy Miller* this view is given a new twist; and it is as if the eponymous heroine is being used to challenge fixed codes of behaviour, but also – and crucial

---

[21]   Another early attempt to tell the story of the American abroad is 'The Passionate Pilgrim' (1871). Here, the American protagonist returns to the Old World – England in this case – to make a claim on a share of an inherited property. The descriptive passages are straight out of travel writing, full of American wonder at the picturesque English countryside and the Country House, and at times resorting to a Wordsworthian lyricism: 'and yet there broods upon this charming hamlet an old-time quietude and privacy' (James, *Collected Stories vol. 1*, 92). James will learn to integrate better topography and narrative. Significantly, though, there is an ironic disjunction between the idealized place and its unscrupulous inhabitants.

[22]   Subsequent page references abbreviated as *DM* in text.

to James's developing narrative technique – as the object of conflicting points of view (in the senses of both opinions and focalizers). James is beginning to master the technique of storytelling without omniscience, which will allow more implicit ironies and ambiguities. However, first readers were not always prepared to accept the ambiguity surrounding Daisy Miller's conduct. Eliza Linton, a contemporary writer concerned with the 'Woman Question', wrote to the author seeking clarification about whether the reader is meant to see Daisy Miller as a modern woman defiant of gender convention or naïve and innocent. In his reply James insists on her innocence and how this works to cause a 'social rumpus' which neither Daisy nor her mother appreciate.[23] Yet he has Winterbourne worry about 'the ambiguity of Daisy's behaviour' (*DM*, 59), and finally decide that she was very devious and cunning (60). His reading of her character has by then in the story changed, and is never innocent of motive. However, even after her death he 'often thought of … her mystifying manners' (63).

In James's writing it is not as important what the author thinks of his character as what the characters think of each other and how that affects what happens. The interplay of inhibited or unreliable perspectives becomes a complex form of storytelling. Moreover, it is this social conflict between the American characters in Italy that takes precedence over the setting itself (a marked improvement over the excess of travelogue in 'Travelling Companions'). However, it is important to notice that the attitudes to iconic places are used as a value to judge the characters – an implicit authorial judgment. Thus Daisy's limitations are being exposed by her lack of historical awareness or reverence for St Peter's or the Coliseum.[24] Her mother wanted her to see Europe 'for herself' (*DM*, 34), but we know that her ability to see is limited when we think what Henry James expects of the informed tourist. In any case Mrs Miller is disappointed with Rome, preferring Zurich (35) – an implicit judgment of her in the Jamesian opposition between vulgar and sentimental tourists, and one expressed in his travel writing.

The opposition between the American and the Italian is sometimes an opposition of gazes. Winterbourne is a voyeur; he 'had a great relish for feminine beauty; he was addicted to observing and analysing it' (*DM*, 8). Giovanelli belongs to 'the slow-moving, idle-gazing Roman crowd' who 'bestowed much attention upon the extremely pretty young foreign lady' (38). She sees him leaning against a tree 'staring at the women in the carriages' (39). The Italian man is morally dangerous for Winterbourne and the other Americans in Rome – an attitude exposed by Forster in his Italian novels and stories. Daisy Miller is letting herself be treated as the object of his 'lawless passion', a view shared by Mrs Walker (41). Whereas the obvious autobiographic elements in 'Travelling Companions' allowed us to accuse the young writer of reproducing cultural stereotypes, here in *Daisy Miller* the use of unreliable narrative perspectives locates such views in characters through character thoughts or free indirect discourse, and serves to underline their limitations. Instead of catching the count (*DM*, 54) as the rich American heiress should, she falls for the

---

[23] See Appendix 1 in *Daisy Miller* 67ff. for the reproduced correspondence.

[24] As Maves argues (60).

'gigolo' and is condemned by the Americans and in the eyes of the 'cynical streets of Rome' – thus managing to cause offence on both sides.

Winterbourne, like Brooke in 'Travelling Companions', and like the author, is a 'lover of the picturesque' (*DM*, 59), but an inhibited lover. It is not implausible that Daisy prefers the more urbane Italian. Moreover the inhibitions of the aptly named Winterbourne are congruent with the strict behavioural codes of society represented by his aunt and the unforgiving Mrs Walker. While art and landscape can be enjoyed as pure aesthetic pleasure, Daisy's pleasure is condemned as 'abnormal'. However, her image, like the vistas of Rome, may be secretly enjoyed: 'He stood looking off at the enchanted harmony of line and colour that remotely encircles the city, inhaling the softly humid odours and feeling the freshness of the year and the antiquity of the place reaffirm themselves in mysterious interfusion. It seemed to him also that Daisy had never looked so pretty' (56). There is here a clash between the aesthetic, a solitary pleasure of contemplation, and the dominant morality publically enforced. He can admire her appearance but despise her social standing: 'She was a young lady whom a gentleman need no longer be at pains to respect' (59–60).

Daisy Miller dies of ignorance, not listening to advice about the 'Roman fever' (malaria). James refuses any overall judgment, but leaves open the possibility for us to see some sort of divine punishment for her transgression. Yet there is no sentimental deathbed scene (a popular expectation amongst Victorian readers).[25] It is, though, more plausible to read her death as a result of ignorance coupled with impetuous behaviour; ignorance, that is, of place, climate, culture; and also the extent to which the other Americans treat her as a problem. Winterbourne himself is aware that he misread the situation, not in his case because of his ignorance of Italy but because he had 'lived too long in foreign parts' (*DM*, 64) and therefore no longer understood American women; as if you lose your understanding of your home culture as an expatriate – a worry expressed by James too on his return to America in *The American Scene*.

Is *Daisy Miller*, then, no more than a test case, as it is after all subtitled, 'A Study'? But a test case of what? The dangers of being abroad without knowledge of the climate, customs and manners? The rich American tourists in Italy – a favourite target in James's travel writing? The problems of interracial relationships, reflecting contemporary fears of miscegenation? A study in misreading? As David Lodge says in the introduction to *Daisy Miller*, the story 'is as much about Winterbourne as it is about Daisy Miller' (xvi) in its focus on characters as narrators with limited or restrictive views; but also first readers who still expect authorial clarity and single meaning, and fail to appreciate free indirect discourse. We should also notice that the story is made up of observations from angles and perspectives of scenes and encounters, and therefore the subtitle implies a visual study as in portrait painting, a trope that recurs in James's writing: in the travel

---

[25] Fredric Jameson famously claimed that the 'sentimental and the melodramatic' were the two paradigmatic narrative strategies for moralizing in nineteenth-century fiction. See *The Political Unconscious*, 186.

writing where landscapes and town vistas are described as if they are composed as works of art or even recall famous paintings in the Renaissance or Romantic traditions; and in the fiction, most famously in *The Portrait of a Lady*, to which we now turn.

The Portrait of a Lady

The European settings for dramatic encounters reach a high point with this novel which James began writing in Florence in 1880 and finished in Venice the following year, and which begins and ends in the pastoral England described in *English Hours*, and where most of the story is played out in Rome amongst American expatriates. However, James uses place as setting in an integrated and symptomatic manner that manages to avoid the pitfalls of reducing story to travelogue, while still insisting on the thematic significance of travel and foreign setting. As Maves explains: '*The Portrait of a Lady* thus marks a thorough assimilation of Italian themes into the concerns of Jamesian fiction as a whole. There are no native characters, there is little scenic description, there is scant use of the Italian emotion; nevertheless the moral as well as physical territory surveyed is one James persistently associated with Italy.' What James attempts to demonstrate is the 'the corruption engendered by cultural hybridization'. Gilbert Osmond's problems of character appear to arise because he is an American brought up in Italy (Maves, 72–3). His lack of moral integrity is seen in 'the chasm between his aesthetic ideals and ignoble actions' (Maves, 74). However, I would add that here James is consistent in his belief that the aesthetic educates the character but carries with it a moral responsibility. Italy for James and for his expatriate American characters is the place for indulging in the aesthetic – as we have seen. But Gilbert Osmond shows us what can go wrong. To make the point clearer James uses Osmond's sister, the Countess Gemini, as an example of how absurd the affectation of sophistication can get without the brother's more 'refined' taste – she is an expatriate who behaves like a tourist.[26] It is Madame Merle, the other Italianate American, who is instrumental in the machinations of the marriage plot, who admits to Isabel Archer: 'If we are not good Americans we are certainly poor Europeans; we have no natural place here. We are mere parasites, crawling over the surface; we haven't our feet in the soil' (*The Portrait of a Lady*, cit. in Maves, 76)[27] – implying an organic sense of culture, and one Lawrence also promoted in his work as we saw in the previous chapter.

Questions of identity are tied up with place. James begins and ends *The Portrait of a Lady* in the iconic grounds of the English country house: 'upon the lawn of an old English country-house … It stood upon a low hill, above the river' (59); 'she strolled again under the great oaks whose shadows were long upon the acres of turf' (630). When Isabel Archer first arrives at Gardencourt, the English country house with the name of the Edenic pastoral world so admired by

---

[26] Robert Weisbuch even claims that Osmond's aestheticism makes 'the skin crawl' (114).

[27] Subsequent page references abbreviated as *PL* in text.

James in *English Hours*, she sees it through her literary imaginary: 'Oh, I hoped there would be a lord; it's just like a novel!' (*PL*, 70); and she expects a haunting too, 'isn't there a ghost?' (100). The story of the rich American woman abroad in search of a suitable husband becomes, in Robert Weisbuch's words, 'an encounter with the real' ('James and the Idea of Evil', 113) by degrees of disillusion, first in England then Italy. It seems it will take a lot though to shake her self-confidence and positive energy; yet she is no Daisy Miller. Her aunt, Mrs Touchett, a seasoned traveller in Europe, encourages her to go and live in Florence as part of her education. Her late father 'wished his daughters ... to see as much of the world as possible', and had whet their appetite with three transatlantic trips when they were children. Isabel has therefore an educated curiosity to see more of Europe (*PL*, 88). The death of the Father – to put this in a different language – appears to set her adrift from the law of the Father. The restlessness that drives her travel will also compel her postponement of marriage (despite suitable proposals) until she makes the wrong decision. Unlike other female characters in marriage plots, like Elizabeth Bennet and Dorothea Brooke (in *Pride and Prejudice* and *Middlemarch*, respectively), Isabel will have to deal with Gilbert Osmond and Madame Merle – the personifications of calculated wickedness and evil,[28] coming out of the tradition of romance in the American novel, and also Laclos's *Les Liaisons Dangereuses* (1782) where ex-lovers plot the seduction and ruin of a naïve young woman. But it is not as if James's protagonist has not been warned: 'you're drifting to some great mistake' her friend and companion Henrietta Stackpole tells her – 'like the heroine of an immoral novel' (*PL*, 219) (which was code then for a French novel!).

Drifting is a dominant trope – and one that recurs in Wharton's fiction too. It pits the nomadic against the sedentary, travel against settling down. But once married to Osmond, sedentary life in the traditional domestic form becomes a sort of imprisonment. Osmond himself, although patriarchal, cannot prevent the drift of identity: expatriate life in Italy leaves them 'without responsibilities ... with nothing to hold us together'. Here we return to the idea that the American abroad runs the risk of a loss of identity living 'among things and people not our own ... marrying foreigners, forming artificial tastes' (*PL*, 311). But will marrying your own kind make any difference? If the example of Osmond and Isabel is instructive, then happiness is only possible in a nomadic existence not a sedentary one.

Travel – to see Europe – is portrayed as adventurous, educational and healthy. Travel gives the young woman 'liberty' (*PL*, 74) from the narrow life at home, fulfilling 'a desire to leave the past behind ... begin afresh' (86); in her imagination it starts by taking the form of adventure: 'A swift carriage, of a dark night, rattling with four horses over roads that one can't see – that's my idea of happiness', she tells Henrietta (219). She takes a while to get beyond her romantic view of travel: 'happy things don't repeat themselves [she reflects], and her adventure wore already the changed, seaward face of some romantic island from which, after feasting on purple grapes, she was putting off while the breeze rose' (359). But eventually she is aware that she has changed, grown up: 'She had ranged,

---

[28]   A point stressed by Weisbuch.

she would have said, through space, and surveyed much of mankind, and was therefore now, in her own eyes, a very different person from the frivolous young woman from Albany who had begun to take the measure of Europe on the lawn at Gardencourt a couple of year before' (*PL*, 370). James is careful to tell us that this is how she sees herself ('Isabel had developed less, however, than Lily [her sister]', 372); and we are left to judge for ourselves the extent to which travel has changed Isabel Archer.

She still travels – this time in the company of Madame Merle, as the latter notices, 'rapidly and recklessly; she was like a thirsty person draining cup after cup' (*PL*, 374). It is tempting to read her travel here symptomatically: Isabel is putting off, postponing her thoughts about Osmond, where 'restless' and 'reckless' are signifiers of unconscious disturbance. Travel is now an exercise in displacement: 'the girl had in these days a thousand uses for her sense of the romantic, which was more active than it had ever been', taking her as far away as the Pyramids of Egypt and the Acropolis (376). But even once back in Italy her restlessness knows no bounds, as if to keep moving is to repress other thoughts. However, once together with Osmond, at first, place is a stimulant for happiness: 'It was in Italy that they had met, Italy had been a party to their first impressions of each other, and Italy should be a party to their happiness. Osmond had the attachment of old acquaintance and Isabel the stimulus of new, which seemed to assure her a future at a higher level of consciousness of the beautiful' (403). Of course, James adds a note of doubt in that 'seemed'. Her happiness will be a short-lived illusion.

Restlessness as a state of mind is expressed in the trope of drifting in other characters too: 'Ralph … drifted about the house like a rudderless vessel in a rocky stream' (*PL*, 390). But it is he who gives us the best description of Isabel's character through the trope of travel: 'You seemed to me to be soaring far up in the blue – to be sailing in the bright light, over the heads of men. Suddenly someone tosses you a faded rosebud – a missile that should never have reached you – and straight you drop to the ground' (395).

The Portrait of a Lady is a novel in which characters travel. The aunt, Mrs Touchett mostly lives in Florence apart from her wealthy husband when not simply travelling; and she encourages Isabel to travel. Ralph Touchett spends 'a couple of years in travelling' after Oxford, and 'wintered abroad' for his health (93–4). Madame Merle is at first seen as wise because she has the self-confidence of the travelled (228): 'she had been a dweller in many lands and had social ties in a dozen different countries' (245) – the ideal cosmopolitan identity that is finally undermined by the plot. Lord Warburton is a seasoned traveller, and uses travel to get over being rejected by Isabel. Casper Goodwood, Isabel's persistent American suitor 'had the air of a man who had travelled hard' (377) going away only to return sporadically with renewed hope that she will finally accept him. Henrietta Stackpole's reasons for travel change. She begins in curiosity to see the Old World and to gather experience for her writing, but later travels for Isabel's sake: 'She had crossed the stormy ocean in midwinter because she had guessed that Isabel was sad' (535). As Isabel travels back to England to be with the dying Ralph her mood is displaced onto the dreary winter landscape. The euphoria of travel is replaced in these last scenes of the novel by the journey as a trope for the depressive position. Her desire is now to return to 'her starting-point' and 'cease utterly' in the 'sanctuary' of Gardencourt – a death drive replacing travel with immobility as the end of being. The lowest point of her depressive state is 'the grey curtain of indifference' (607). However, she feels too young to 'live only to suffer' (607), and back in London the 'genial' Mr Bantling (608) and the ever determined Henrietta wait to sort Isabel out; yet we assume she will return to her disastrous marriage despite everything.

If in the end winter in England represented the perfect symbiosis for Isabel's state of mind, earlier in the novel it was Rome: 'She had long before this taken old Rome into her confidence, for in a world of ruins the ruin of her happiness seemed a less unnatural catastrophe' (*PL*, 564). Mood and place are perfectly suited. We know from James's travel writing that ruins are a natural place for silent contemplation. However, this moment among the Roman ruins is significantly different from the superficial pleasure of the English country house at the start of the novel. Joel Porte explains:

> But Isabel has found amid the ruins of Rome not simply the double of her own despair but rather a solace and consolation – a way of rendering the subjective objective, of seeing herself from the outside. It was romantic and foolish of her to think of the European experience as no more than an opportunity for a Gothic frisson – a private thrill at seeing crumbling castles and predictable ghosts. (24)

What we have here among the ruins is a symptomatic use of place that goes far beyond place as merely an index of character – that Balzacian technique where we enter the garden then the house before we are introduced to the character that lives there. In *French Poets and Novelists* James describes Balzac's technique of starting a novel with a solid *mise-en-scène*: 'The place in which an event occurred was in his view of equal moment with the event itself; it was part of the action ... There is accordingly a very much greater amount of description ... mainly of towns, houses and rooms' (92).[29]

The description of Gardencourt at the start of James's novel is an example of such realism because it establishes a level of typicality, albeit more a reproduction of literary archetypes. However, the relationship between character and place towards the end of the novel is used more symptomatically as a way of indicating Isabel's greater awareness of the surrounding world as in sympathy with her expressive needs at moments of crisis. We see the expression of powerful feelings in the final confrontation with Casper Goodwood – 'the only person with an unsatisfied claim on her' (*PL*, 533); and it is sexuality itself that requires an indirect description,

---

[29]   A classic example is Balzac's novel, *Eugénie Grandet* (1834). In Part 1, which in the English translation is entitled, 'Grandet's Place', we are guided into a typical country town in Touraine, through the cobbled streets, and up to the front door, and into the house. The character of the place reveals the character of the person living there. Honoré de Balzac, *Eugénie Grandet* (Paris: Editions Gallimard, 1972), 19ff. English translation Henry Reed (New York: Signet Classics, 1964), 13ff.

one that relies wholly on metaphor and metonymy – the tropes of symptom and desire.[30] He makes a last desperate appeal to her to leave her heartless husband; but the appeal goes beyond words and becomes physical as he forces an embrace on her. His look she realizes is the gaze of male desire: 'there was something in his face that she wished not to see' (631); she feels 'a new sensation' that causes a 'feeling of danger' (632). He is now a physical presence, and even his words affect her deepest feelings: 'his words dropped deep into her soul. They produced a stillness in all her being' (632). She is both aroused and resistant. Her passion is expressed in spatial tropes: 'this was the hot wind in the desert' (634); 'she floated in fathomless waters … a rushing torrent … for a moment [wanting Casper] was a kind of rapture in which she felt herself sink and sink' (635). She begs him to leave her alone. But his kiss 'was like white lightening. A flash that spread, and spread again … his hard manhood … this act of possession'. She frees herself from his phallic embrace and runs away (635–6). Throughout the scene she appears passive, and is aware at a deeper level of a loss of control – 'she had an immense desire to appear to resist' (*PL*, 635), yet her unconscious desire to give in is expressed in the text through metaphor. This scene where there is a struggle between attraction and repulsion confirms our suspicions that Isabel is a deeply troubled woman.[31] Has she not been avoiding physical love throughout – the attractive men who she rejects or puts off (Warburton, Goodwood) – and does not James, with his attention to detail in this passage, want us to understand this new portrait of the lady which encourages us to see a more modern ambiguity in the female subject?

An enduring image is Isabel holding the dying Ralph in her arms: 'with you dying in my arms, I'm happier than I have been for a long time … Oh my brother!' (*PL*, 622–3). It is a '*Pietà*' reproduction which reinforces Victorian sentimental and melancholic codes, on the one level; and on another signifies the limits of her sexuality as the dying man, once a potential lover, is now made passive. At the beginning of the novel Isabel Archer is the attractive, self-confident 'tall girl in a black dress' (69), with the 'high spirit' (71) and wilfulness of the modern American woman; she is 'clever' and 'bookish' (88–9), and cultivates her image in her directness with the eligible English or American men she meets in England and then Italy. But in comparison to Henrietta Stackpole she is no feminist; instead she appears egoistical, even narcissistic, and lacking parental guidance – a residual Victorian orphan at sea in the sophisticated and duplicitous Old World; or to put it differently, without the law of the Father and with the liberty bestowed by a secret benefactor – she loses her way. What we discover in the end is that Isabel is only superficially open to the world, giving the impression of 'this spontaneous young woman from Albany' (115), an 'independent spirit' (205) and appearing to refuse marriage as her destiny. In fact, she is manipulated by Madame Merle and Osmond into marriage, reduced to the victim of a common plot where she pays dearly for refusing to heed the warnings of others. And Madame Merle has gained

---

[30] Lacan insisted, 'the symptom *is* a metaphor … as desire is a metonymy' (*Ecrits*, 175, emphasis in original).

[31] A point made by Porte, 8.

her confidence by being misrecognized as a role model, the sophisticated travelled woman, but also as a surrogate mother to fill the maternal absence in Isabel's life. The lack of the Mother appears to both shape Isabel's 'dream of self-fashioning' and serve as 'submerged organising principle of the text' – as Beth Sharon Ash argues in her insightful psychoanalytic reading (123). Isabel's aunt, Mrs Touchett is also a 'false mother' offering no emotional support. Henrietta Stackpole acts as a surrogate sister, but is not listened to, appearing as a comic figure that gradually takes on weight as the arbiter of the Woman Question which emerges thematically with the appearance of Osmond's daughter, Pansy, as the ultimate submissive girl fashioned by the patriarchal father, 'impregnated with the idea of submission ... a passive spectator of the operation of her fate' (*PL*, 286). As the novel ends, it is Henrietta who once again offers support to the depressed Isabel.

We could, though, expand the psychoanalytic reading to include a cultural implication. The greater freedom of the new American woman, in Isabel's case doubly released from financial worries (her father's inheritance, and her secret benefactor), and with a greater mobility to travel but also, in Ash's words, 'a new mobility in relations with others' (126) – transcending the class and gender restrictions of the Old World – results in an egocentrism that manifests itself as narcissistic illusion. As Ash argues, it is James's insight, cultural and psychological at once, that 'American "normalcy" tends towards narcissistic pathology' – Isabel believes she is classless and free and self-fashioning in the spirit of American democratic modernity (the American dream), but this turns out to be a delusion. Worse still, it looks as if the Puritan legacy of American cultural origins remains as a deep, cultural unconscious for Isabel Archer – it is her travelling companion and it will restrict her enjoyment of physical love; and it could help explain why such an apparently independent woman 'full of desire and desirable' ends up 'confined to a conjugal prison cell' (Ash, 127).[32]

The theme of the American abroad is, here in this novel as elsewhere in James's writing, a focus for cultural critique. Ralph's father, living now in England at Gardencourt as an expatriate, declares he has 'no intention of disamericanizing' (*PL*, 91), despite living the life of the English landed gentry, and being accepted as such by that class. The young American women who have been taught to express themselves openly at home in the New World, and to 'have emotions and opinions' (108), are seen in England and then Italy at first to have the advantage of not belonging to 'any class' (110) strictly speaking. It is through the parvenu American that James can both critique American ignorance and naivety, and the English obsession with class and breeding (111). In the words of the much-travelled Mrs Touchett, the American point-of-view is 'shockingly narrow' (114). Lord Warburton is no better in his view of Americans announcing that Americans in England 'would need to have a great many things explained to them' (124). Isabel Archer, of course, challenges the English prejudice: 'It's a pity you can't see my war-paint and feathers' (123) – and for the first readers there is an echo here of the

---

[32]   And one made worse by her being surrounded by the ghastly antiques that Osmond collects and treasures (James undermines his character through his poor taste).

popular view of America promoted by the travelling Wild West shows at the time. As Oscar Wilde provocatively announced in 1887, '[a] terrible danger is hanging over the Americans in London. Their future and their reputation this season depend entirely on the success of Buffalo Bill and Mrs. Brown-Potter. The former is certain to draw; for English people are far more interested in American barbarism than they are in American civilization.'[33] Henrietta Stackpole, though, has the 'smell of the Future', representing a determined 'free play of intelligence' (147–8) coming from a country of the 'free-born' (172–3) with the new democratic values and the American 'civic idea' which she sees as giving her country an advantage over an England which appears to have 'plenty of meaningless customs'. She does not approve of the privileges of class, and contrary to the deference and passivity expected of women in traditional circles, demands from Lord Warburton direct eye-contact (183). She is given an important role as travelling cultural critic, proving 'to be an indestructible sight-seer' (194), and through her profession (as travelling journalist) acquainting herself 'in the western world, with every form of caravansary' (149). She is no 'superficial' traveller simply sightseeing (499), but instead acts as an important commentator on Europe as a 'decaying civilization' (535), while her travelling companion Mr Bantling reproduces the stereotype expectations of the Englishman in America, as Henrietta notices: 'It seemed to be generally believed in England that we wore tomahawks and feathers' – the whole episode briefly serving to redress the balance by seeing the limits of England from the American viewpoint (539–40). Madame Merle offers a less flattering view of England to the dominant pastoral one: 'fog and beer and soot ... the national aroma' (241). More anti-tourist comments appear when Isabel Archer first tours Florence and can see from her aunt's old house there 'the familiar commodities of the age of advertisements' (297); and later in the novel we read of the dreaded American tourists who spend 'twenty-four hours in Florence' (387). For, despite her other failings, Isabel is an educated tourist spending time looking at the great works of art and discussing them with her cousin, Ralph (296–7), and generally tending towards the romantic view of old Italy, like the author.

Travel enables stories about cultural identity, predominantly the American abroad – the author and his principal characters – whose preconceptions are tested by encounters with cultural difference and other expatriates in a foreign setting. But as we have seen James was always concerned with the form such stories and encounters should take. For all its 'romantic realism' the ending of *The Portrait of a Lady* is inconclusive. The novel is driven by Isabel Archer's indecision and postponement; and this drive characterizes the ending too: will Casper wait for her? Will Isabel return to her husband at least for the sake of Pansy? There is potential for the story to continue, for further developments in the plot. Maurice Blanchot has drawn attention to 'the pure *indeterminacy*' of James's work 'without depriving it of all the possibilities it contains'. For Blanchot, 'the essence of James's art' is that it allows us 'to feel other forms, the infinite and weightless

---

[33] Oscar Wilde, 'The American Invasion', *Court and Society Review* (March 1887), cit. in Kendall Johnson, 1.

space of the narrative as it might have been' (Maurice Blanchot, cit. in Gabriel Josipovici, *Whatever Happened to Modernism?*, 89–90. Emphasis in original). Blanchot is writing about the late novels; but indeterminacy is here also in the inconclusiveness of *The Portrait of a Lady* that already signals dissatisfaction with the principle of closure in the classic nineteenth-century realist novel. *The Portrait of a Lady* is a novel consisting of different subgenres: beginning in the tradition of country-house fiction, there is the marriage plot, the orphan's story, the secret benefactor, the romance of Italy and the melodrama of deception, as James works his way through the possibilities of the novel at the time. Indeed, the novel he published just after leaving Paris, *The American*, rehearses the whole question of genre by a play of forms.[34]

The American

Henry James's newly won awareness of what it means to be an expatriate American in Paris – in Peter Brooks's words, 'as the fascinating seductress of Anglo-Americans', and the perfect backdrop, the 'gilded trap' for his fictional American protagonist; and the difficulties of entering French society are worked through in *The American* – which he began writing in Paris in 1875.[35] Christopher Newman – the new man from the New World, the modern capitalist who made his fortune in the post-Civil War boom – is in want of a wife. The story follows the course of the protagonist's uncomplicated desire: 'to see the world, to have a good time, to improve my mind, and, if the fancy takes me, to marry a wife' (*The American*, 51).[36] Needing to get away from the stress of money-making in Wall Street, he wants 'the biggest kind of entertainment a man can get. People, places, art, nature, everything!' (58). His capitalist mind thinks of a wife as another possession, as 'the best article in the market' (71), and he is 'fond of statistics; he liked to know how things were done' (86–7). Despite Newman being everything about the modern American James usually despises, the author allows the enthusiasm for travel and the naivety of the traveller to be presented sympathetically. It is a useful strategy, because Newman's open character will throw into greater relief the closed and impenetrable world of the French aristocracy into which he attempts to marry. And that world is symbolized early on by Newman's impressions of the facades of houses in the residential suburbs of Paris as presenting 'to the outer world a face as impassive and as suggestive of the concentration of privacy within as the blank walls of Eastern seraglios' (79) – representing an orientalist invitation for his desire. But this is only the first of Newman's misreadings. It is followed by

---

[34] James is already testing the limits – or antinomies – of realism, which Jameson has reminded us is, in any case, 'a hybrid concept' (*The Antinomies of Realism*, 5).

[35] Brooks continues: 'It is indeed Paris as a kind of icon of the American imagination – Paris as *la ville lumière* – that James wanted for the adventure of his American self-made man in search of something other, something more: a woman, and an alternative to American money-grubbing culture' (*Henry James Goes to Paris*, 50–51).

[36] Subsequent page references abbreviated as *TA* in text.

his mistaking the Marquis who comes to the door for the butler (81). Principally, he assumes that when a rich American proposes to a French countess, Madame de Cintré, he will be accepted. But the family, lead by the mother, the 'old feudal countess', will not agree to allow marriage between a common businessman and a countess: it is a matter of class and family name; as the mother says to him, he has no 'antecedents', and 'we really cannot reconcile ourselves to a commercial person' (318). It takes a long time though for the determined Newman to accept 'the folly of his errand', and that he would never be allowed to become a member of that 'tribe' (424) – strong words that surely reflect the author's feelings of being himself excluded from French society during his Paris sojourn; and ones more personally felt when we see Newman as not the American James himself was but the type read though French eyes and often seen in the tourist or expatriate living in Paris that James also criticized.

However, before the marriage plot begins, James takes his protagonist on a journey. It is the classic grand tour through Europe, taking in the Rhineland, Switzerland and Northern Italy (*TA*, 101–16); and later doing France – Paris to Poitiers, the picturesque Loire valley with its castles and ruins (344–7). French topography comes out of the travel sketches he was writing at the time – as James records it in *A Little Tour of France* – including descriptions of Paris. But Newman is not James's 'sentimental traveller' because for him Europe is 'a great bazaar, where one might stroll about and purchase handsome things' and see everything while enjoying the modern technology of travel (103–4). He has a travelling companion, Babcock, a young American who tries to convince Newman to abandon amusement and entertainment for the serious appreciation of art (110–11). But Babcock is also there to represent the narrow moral position of the American Christian, and one who puts Newman's easy-going tourism in a more favourable light. An important point is being made as James admired the moral seriousness of George Eliot's fiction, but not the all-too-American version he was living abroad to avoid.[37] Newman may be naïve at times, but he 'wanted to improve his mind' by travelling through Europe (103); and he does realize that 'the business of money-getting appeared extremely dry and sterile', which is easily said after 'you have filled your pockets' (an authorial comment; *TA*, 114).

After the tour of Europe the marriage plot begins in earnest. While it clearly enables the clash of cultures and class, it also produces a play of genres that destabilizes the text. Indeed, it as if with this novel James indicates his own uncertainty about the direction his fiction might take – which is perhaps a reflection of his own uncertainty about French culture as a paradigm for his art. For what begins in the realist mode of classic Balzac,[38] with some interludes of travel

---

[37]　A point made by Brooks, 70.

[38]　'On a brilliant day in May, in the year 1868, a gentleman was reclining at his ease on the great circular divan which at that period occupied the centre of the Salon Carré, in the Museum of the Louvre … His physiognomy would have sufficiently indicated that he was a shrewd and capable fellow … An observer, with anything of an eye for national types, would have no difficulty in determining the local origin of this undeveloped connoisseur … a powerful specimen of an American' (*TA*, 33–4).

narrative, slips into quest romance and gothic in the story of Newman's attempts to marry Madame de Cintré, the resistances of her family and the melodrama surrounding the family secret which Newman can use to get his revenge, and which in the end he refuses. It is an ending which William Spengemann describes as 'the moral triumph of American good nature over European treachery' (introduction to *The American*, 8) – and which complicates at least the opposition between the Old World and the New, as if cultural inferiority could be compensated for by moral superiority; the innocence of the New World (in the figure of Newman) triumphing over the scheming of the Old World (the Bellegarde family). Yet, the Gothic appears as the Old World's History haunting modernity; Europe as the site where the past refuses to go away – the site of Newman's desire because History is a lack in America.

The Gothic is topographically established with the description of the Bellegarde Paris residence, as Newman enters 'through a vestibule, vast, dim, and cold, up a broad stone staircase with an ancient iron balustrade' (*TA*, 123). The family country residence plays even more on the generic implications: 'He stood there awhile, looking through the bars of the large time-stained face of the edifice, and wondered to what crime it was that the dark old house … had given convenient occasion … it was an evil-looking place' (361). Moreover, as the gothic melodrama requires, the housekeeper Mrs Bread (conveniently of English origin) helps the protagonist discover the family secret in a letter from the father who died in suspicious circumstances – a secret that could destroy the honour of the thousand year old family. Newman is at first drawn in by the romance of legend, but soon insists on the rightness of American democratic ideals against old French autocracy, as the story reveals the truth of the dictum uttered by Valentin de Bellegarde that 'old trees have crooked branches … old races have old secrets' (163). It is this younger brother who befriends Newman who even fights a duel, which he acknowledges as 'a remnant of a high-tempered time' and which he wants to 'cling to' (309). The whole family seems to belong to the feudal past; instead of marrying Newman, Madame de Cintré prefers to commit herself to a Carmelite convent, to withdraw from the world 'in a cell – for life …' Newman finds the idea 'too dark and horrible for belief', a 'grotesque entombing' (354–5). And when he visits the old convent in Paris, its topography is described 'like a page torn out of a romance' which he finds difficult to understand (402). He has to get away from the horror of this masochistic medievalism. A change of scene takes him to London, and some walking in the parks, Windsor, Richmond, Hyde Park and the healing distraction of 'the great serious English trees' (431). After England he returns to America but remains restless. The final scenes of the novel see him back in Paris walking the streets in a kind of death-driven state of mind. But the area around the convent in which Madame de Cintré is 'entombed', has a 'barren stillness', and finally he comes to terms with the impossible situation and refuses to use the incriminating letter for revenge (446–9). In the end then Newman gives up his quest romance because the lady in the tower is unattainable; and what starts out as a conventional marriage plot in the traditions of the English and French realist novel has become a gothic romance fitting the residual ideology of the Bellegarde family's self-understanding. The novel has to end with the protagonist refusing to play their game any longer; and James to end the play of genres.

The critical reception has not been kind to *The American*. The abrupt change of form from realism to romance, as Brooks argues, 'its swerve toward the gothic, the sudden melodramatization of experience' (57–8), is seen as a weakness. In this reading, this evaluation, James's search for a direction ends in popular fiction. However, this judgement notwithstanding, it might be more useful to read the novel as a self-conscious attempt at trying out narrative possibilities; and ones that reflect the author's own struggle while in Paris to write the new American novel. In this light Brooks comments:

> Writing in Paris a novel about an American's experience of Paris, suspended between visits to Flaubert's group of 'realists' and the monthly instalments of George Eliot's *Daniel Deronda*, he is searching his way. That search is recorded also in the many essays James devoted to the novelists he sensed had the most to teach him: Balzac, Turgenev, Eliot, Flaubert, Zola. The year in Paris resulted not only in *The American* but also in the volume of essays published in 1878 under the title *French Poets and Novelists*. (58–9)

James would continue to argue that the English and American novel needed to learn the lessons of French literature to 'really come of age' (Brooks, 59).

Travel as we have seen is an occasion for cultural exchange; and while his American characters often see in Europe what is lacking at home, for James this lack is additionally a question of literature – the great European realists and modernists.[39] Modernist art in *The American*, however, is not liked. When Newman accompanies Valentin de Bellegarde to the Louvre James uses the scene to have a dig at the representational 'distortions' of the new art where a woman might be 'clothed in green tulle' with her feet 'out of focus' (*TA*, 194); or where a novice painter-copyist, Mademoiselle Noémie is observed in the act of painting through the critical eyes of the two men:

> And, dipping a brush into a clot of red paint, she drew a great horizontal daub across her unfinished picture.
> 'What is that?' asked Newman.
> Without answering, she drew another long crimson daub, in a vertical direction, down the middle of her canvas, and so, in a moment, completed the rough indication of a cross. 'It is a sign of the truth,' she said at last.

---

[39] Here we should not underestimate the place of that other American, Nathaniel Hawthorne, in James's writing. As Jonathan Freedman explains in his introduction to *The Cambridge Companion to Henry James*, Hawthorne's influence can be seen in the theme of 'the fate of the American art-lover abroad', or for example in 'that admixture of realistic plots and character descriptions with the machinery of sheer romance that defines Hawthorne' (13).

> The two men looked at each other, and Valentin indulged in another flash of
> physiognomical eloquence.
> 'You have spoiled your picture,' said Newman. (198–9)

Another female artist will later attempt a different kind of painting, but only when
left alone without uncomprehending eyes: Virginia Woolf's Lily Briscoe will
complete her painting despite being told, 'women can't write, women can't paint'
(*To the Lighthouse*, 213).[40] In James's text there is an implicit clash of discourses
between the Balzacian echo of 'physiognomical eloquence' and the daub of paint
on canvas, the surface signs that are transparently read clash with the attention to
a thicker surface – a difference in this passage between realism and modernism.
It will be in the final novel to be discussed in this chapter that the lessons of
modernism will emerge as central to James's writing – and significantly, it will be
in a reworking of the travel story of the American in Paris, and the clash between
the values of the Old and the New World through the complexities of the late style
and its implications for modernist epistemology.

The Ambassadors

In his Introduction to *The Ambassadors* Adrian Poole argues: 'As in James's earlier
fiction, Europe is a kind of theatre in which Americans find themselves exposed to
each others' views' (xxii).[41] But here in this late novel James is more confident of
his ground, schematically opposing places and characters in the Old and the New
World to represent values – Paris and 'Woollett'. Paris, Poole continues, is 'the city
of art and artifice, imagination and illusion, delight and delirium, to plain, literal,
powerful, moneyed Woollett' (xxv). However, this thematic schema which tempts
us with allegorical reading about the state of American culture is complicated by
a figurative play of signifiers: of travel, adventure, danger; of displaced desires;
of the aesthetic object as transcendental value; of the theatricality of the social
scene; of spatial practices – 'These first walks in Europe … a kind of finely lurid
intimation of what one might find at the end of the process' (*A*, 46); of enjoyment
in living life to the full and 'the failure to enjoy', as if the Puritan inheritance meets
its final challenge for James's protagonist Lambert Strether in France (30) – 'a final
impulse to burn his ships' (115), and a constant fear of 'missing the train' (176)
(with its sexual connotations); the recurrent motif of 'cold thoughts' from America
(324, 404, 406) against the enlivening effects of vibrant Paris, or the offer of Miss
Gostrey's 'fireside' (90); and finally the visual seduction of old Paris which would
linger in the memory on returning home to a more austere environment lacking

---

[40]   Towards the end of the novel we read: 'There it was – her picture. Yes, with all its
greens and blues, its lines running up and across … With a sudden intensity, as if she saw it
clear for a second, she drew a line there, in the centre. It was done; it was finished. Yes, she
thought, laying down her brush in extreme fatigue, I have had my vision' (225–6).

[41]   All references in text are to the 2008 Penguin Classics edition of the novel.
Subsequent references abbreviated as *A* in the text.

history: 'He should soon be going to where such things were not, and it would be a small mercy for memory, for fancy ... He knew in advance he should look back on the perception actually sharpest with him as on the view of something old, old, old, the oldest thing he had ever personally touched' – and memories of perceptions and place will remind Strether that he had the chance to be happy, 'to be natural and simple' (434).

However, in addition to the play of the figurative, there is a play of perception, which complicates the narrative – and I will look at these textual complexities in some detail in what follows.[42] James's late fiction takes problems of seeing and understanding already tried out in earlier fiction much further, where narrative point of view is given to a character who misreads the situations he tries to observe – realizing experiments he had first attempted in, for example, *What Maisie Knew* (1897) and *The Turn of the Screw* (1898). The three late novels – *The Wings of the Dove* (1902), *The Ambassadors* (1903) and *The Golden Bowl* (1904) – as Fred Kaplan claims, 'embody a culmination of his concern with the international theme. Now raised to a level of intense complication and subtlety, the theme is transformed from the satirical comedy of misperception into a drama of the search for self-knowledge' (467–8). Thus, *The Ambassadors* as our example of Henry James's late fiction depends, as Peter Brooks puts it, 'on the play of seeing and the unseen, of knowledge and ignorance' (2–3), to the extent that the formal and thematic issues are closely connected: the limitation of the central character, and the rigid views he is supposed to import from America as 'ambassador' are undermined on a number of levels. And here James inverts the positions of Americans and French aristocratic families from where they stood in *The American*. Now the home of Madame de Vionnet is a welcoming place, as clearly James himself has come to terms with French culture and is now much closer to the French modernism he rejected in the 1870s. James has no qualms anymore about including inferences of sexuality in the story, and this 'marks a "French" aspect of the novel ... tracking down the sexual nature of Chad's liaison with Madame de Vionnet'; but also the indirect or oblique presentation of the narrative James borrows from the French novel (Brooks, 200).

The journey of the American protagonist, Lambert Strether is metaphoric and actual. He is sent to France to report on the behaviour of Mrs Newsome's son, Chad, and persuade him to return home and be saved from what she believes to be the corrupting influence of Paris. But the journey has also existential implications for Strether as cultural and emotional displacement that will test the limits of his character. The difference between the New World of America and the Old World of Europe is presented in this novel in even starker terms than usual in James's writing. As he put it in *English Hours*: 'the American traveller arriving at this venerable town [Chester] finds himself transported, without a sensible gradation, from the edge of the New World to the very heart of the Old ... the first impressions of an observant American in England – of our old friend the sentimental tourist –

---

[42] Alexandra Peat rightly claims that the novel is 'about the limits of perception and the potential for pushing against or shifting those limits' (76).

stir up within him such a cloud of sensibility' (53). In the novel, Strether undergoes a culture shock after disembarking from his transatlantic crossing, but soon finds solace in old England: 'The ordered English garden, in the freshness of the day, was delightful to Strether' (*A*, 44). But he is not always at ease – not quite James's 'sentimental tourist' – and least at ease with his travelling companion, Maria Gostrey. His observations of the 'ordered English country' are 'deeply mixed' with 'certain images of his inward picture' (30). Miss Gostrey will be his keenest observer, warning him from the start about the 'failure to enjoy'; but he wants to insist that it is 'the failure of Woollett', that is to say his provincial American life, which prevents him from enjoying life to the full (30). Nevertheless she will be his 'general guide – to "Europe"', a 'sort of superior "courier-maid"' (31) – and more than it, she will tempt him with a relationship which he will not find easy to accept. James may draw on his travel sketches for picturesque description, but he uses travel and place for their effect on character; and this is established already with Strether's lack of enjoyment of England, and is continued with the assumption as Mrs Newsome's ambassador (representing her country's national interest) that Chad may have been affected by his 'milieu', may have in fact been 'brutalized' by being in Paris; a view which is challenged from the outset by Maria Gostrey who suggests that he could instead have been 'refined' by Paris (69).[43]

The effect of 'milieu' on character comes from James's acquaintance with French literature, from Balzac to Zola, and the influence on them of so-called scientific determinism – ideas that feed into the emergent organic theories of culture, which in turn underpinned racism. Thus, for example, Balzac's aim – taken further by Zola – in a whole series of novels was to study the human 'species' as a product of race, heredity (a form of evolutionary psychology) and environment with 'scientific' precision. It was a literature for a positivist era drawing on the work of Auguste Comte and Hippolyte Taine.[44] Now if the positivist view of the effect of milieu (Paris, for example) on character is associated with Mrs Newsome and expressed by her 'ambassador', Strether, then I think we can assume that its validity is being questioned, and by extension the whole positivist ideology of French realism (Balzac) and naturalism (Zola). It is through Strether's growing doubts about being qualified as ambassador – as promoting the Woollett worldview – that James's critique is implicitly expressed. What this means it that he is interested in the psychology of character as an effect of place and travel – in this case the way travel may have a corrupting effect, and how this is understood

---

[43]   In Peat's words: 'When Strether chooses Maria Gostrey as his "introduction to things" (*The Ambassadors*, 28), he takes the first step towards renouncing the Woollett view of Europe and adopting a more open attitude towards Europe … Under Maria's direction, he replaces the moralistic viewpoint of New England with an aesthetic idealisation of European art and culture' (75).

[44]   Auguste Comte, *Catéchisme positiviste* (1852). Hippolyte Taine, *Essais de critique et d'histoire* (1858). Henry James comments, 'Balzac's "Comédie Humaine" is on the imaginative line very much what Comte's "Positive Philosophy" is on the scientific' (*French Poets and Novelists*, 80).

by the characters in the novel – a moral anxiety expressed by the English abroad in Forster's fiction too. The identity problematic in James's late writing has become more complex, more modernist. He may remain faithful to the lessons of Balzac, the force of the broader social canvas, the detail of character and place; but he appears to have moved towards a more indeterminate presentation of character with a play of unconscious desires and motivated or chance encounters without explicit moral judgement. Most importantly his use of character point-of-view without authorial comment achieves a level of sophistication in *The Ambassadors*, enhanced by a density of style that serves to reflect the complexities of the thought-processes in the character-narrators. It is this late style that works against any simple, reductionist view of the psychology or cultural difference.

An indication of the new complexity is early in the text when we read that Strether is 'burdened ... with the oddity of a double consciousness. There was detachment in his zeal and curiosity in his indifference' (22). He is divided by the force that drives the social manners expected of his class, like detachment (the mode of the good critic) and the pose of indifference (creating a controlling distance at the level of feelings). Yet he also has zeal and curiosity; so that if he wants to pursue his instincts fully he will have to abandon detachment and indifference. But how easy will this be?

Henry James belongs to the tradition of the novel of manners and therefore he presents the thought and speech of characters that belong to a narrowly defined class of the wealthy and educated in a style suitable to polite society. There is always a pressure on speech to limit what may be disclosed, to rely on implicit communication where things can remain unsaid as the like-minded interlocutor is expected to understand inferences without the point needing to be spelled out – 'the disposition to talk as "society" talked' as James puts it in *The Ambassadors* (47); that is saying what is expected and nothing more: 'The only thing he was clear about was that, luckily, nothing indiscreet had in fact been said' (170). Speech can also be used to mark cultural difference in manners: the reticent Englishman compared to the young American heiress who speaks her mind perhaps too readily (*Daisy Miller*, *The Portrait of a Lady*); the polite but insincere address of the French aristocrat whose tone signals a superior attitude to the direct yet naïve American (*The American*). However, in the late writing (*The Ambassadors*) James takes the presentation of speech and thought much further into evasions and effusions, so that there is a gap between thought and speech, as there is between desire and action. At its worst, polite society creates paralysis as a social condition; in Strether's alarming words to Miss Gostrey, 'we're paralysed. We exchange a long scared look, we publicly tremble' (*A*, 49). The late style also has larger ethical and epistemological significance; and the problems of knowledge and ignorance go beyond point-of-view – that is the relative differences between observers – into what Tony Inglis called 'that vertiginous sense of abysses, disjunctions and voids, the impingement of the Other through the Look, inhibitions about language and interpretations, and plots turning on renunciation and disjunction [that] define a dimension of offended consciousness and existential terror in James's work' ('Reading late James', 93). Simply the fear of giving offence, of receiving a sharply rebuking stare and of being seen in what could be interpreted as a compromising situation which would lead to scandal – these are the parameters of the other's gaze, an example of which we saw in the way Daisy Miller is ostracized by the American expatriate community in Rome for her public display of flirting with a local Italian. In *The Ambassadors* Strether incorporates the self-conscious anxieties of polite society; it is reflected in his evasive speech and thought, and dramatizes his inhibited sense of being.[45] His limited way of seeing and being leads him to make assumptions about others which do not always turn out to be correct – his inability to see that Chad and Madame de Vionnet are lovers, and that Chad would nevertheless return home the better for it, and the shock of the revelation are carefully made plausible by James's detailed portrayal of Strether's character.

The complexities of style, the elaborate syntax of the Jamesian sentence make the reader work hard at understanding and appreciating the ontological problematic: the instabilities of identity are revealed at the level of language as 'the need to fabricate, project, interpret, conceal and renounce', as Inglis puts it (85).[46] Moreover, that complexity expresses the cultural difference between the Old World and the New, as Strether thinks of the difficulties of explaining the situation in Paris, as he understands it, to Chad's mother back in Woollett – and I quote at some length to capture a fuller sense of the complex thoughts expressed in a complex syntax:

> Again and again as the days passed he had a sense of the pertinence of communicating quickly with Woollett – communicating with a quickness with which telegraphy alone would rhyme; the fruit really of a fine fancy in him for keeping things straight, for the happy forestalment of error. No one could explain better when needful, nor put more conscience into an account or report; which burden of conscience is perhaps exactly the reason why his heart always sank when the clouds of explanation gathered. His highest ingenuity was in keeping the sky of life clear of them. Whether or no he had a grand idea of the lucid, he held that nothing ever was in fact – for any one else – explained. One went through the vain motions, but it was mostly a waste of life. A personal relation was a relation only so long as people either perfectly understood or, better still, didn't care if they didn't. For the moment they cared if they didn't it was living by the sweat of one's brow; and the sweat of one's brow was just what one might buy one's self off from by keeping the ground free of the wild weed of delusion. It easily grew too fast, and the Atlantic cable now alone could race with it. That agency would each day have testified for him to something that was not what Woollett had argued. He was not at this moment absolutely sure that the effect of

---

45   Even in the last scene of the novel as Maria Gostrey makes one last attempt to get Strether to tell her what he really thinks: 'Yes. No. That is I *have* no ideas. I'm afraid of them.' And when asked why, after all that has happened, he wanted to return to America (and not stay with her) he says: 'I don't know. There will always be something' (*A*, 469). He is evasive to the end.

46   For Colm Tóibín, James in the late novels needs a 'language of infinite suggestion and layered nuance to dramatize consciousness' (111). Tóibín's novel, *The Master* (London: Picador, 2004) captures the struggles of late Henry James with the subtleties of style.

the morrow's – or rather of the night's – appreciation of the crisis wouldn't be to
determine some brief missive. 'Have at last seen him, but oh dear!' … It hovered
somehow as preparing them all – yet preparing them for what? (*A*, 120–21)

Evidently, simple statements cannot account for the complexity of the situation,
or the different ways of reading it. Keeping things simple and clear is desirable,
but apparently not possible – neither for Strether, nor for Henry James. And the
difficulties in the language represent both the psychological and societal pressures
on the character.

There is a similar stylistic complexity emergent in the later travel writing. As
we saw earlier in this chapter in the Italian travel writing there is a difference
between the early and the late styles, and one that concerns the relationship to the
object: a more direct response to the object in the early travel note-books where
the late style enables a greater distance; a more reflective intellectual response.
In the late style of the travel writing and the fiction, the response to the real – the
other or cultural difference – is distanced from the subject perceiving the object.
Moreover, this process of distanciation spills over into the relationship with the
other, or the expression of feelings in the novel. What counts as critical distance to
the initial response to place in the travel writing becomes in the novel an evasive
epistemology; and it is an index of Strether's character, a style suited to his deep-
seated inhibitions. In this way language and psychology are cohesive – as the
passage quoted above illustrates.

If it is hard enough for characters to learn to read the signs, to decipher what
they are looking at, then it even more difficult for the reader. William James
famously complained to his brother about this difficulty: 'Why won't you, just
to please Brother, sit down and write a new book, with no twilight or mustiness
in the plot, with great vigor and decisiveness in the action. No fencing in the
dialogue, or psychological commentaries, and absolute straightness in style' (cit. in
Brooks, 179). However, some of the difficulty of such writing is mitigated by that
other level of language – the figurative – which adds a layer of meaning through
inference and recurrence so that a leitmotif is introduced. Travel is represented
thus literarily and figuratively.

Strether understands his journey as a moral mission to save Chad Newsome
from the corruption of Paris. He has come as the mother's ambassador, even
though he has 'a droll dread of her', feels he is 'literally running away from Mrs.
Newsome' (*A*, 41) and believes less and less in his ability to carry out his mission
successfully (206ff.) as he begins to discover pleasure – like the new enjoyment
gained by his first walks in Europe which open his eyes to the possibility, first
suggested by Miss Gostrey, that Madame de Vionnet has been good for Chad.
Indeed, he starts to notice Chad's new 'candour' (111) and 'easy talk' (138). Later
Strether is replaced as ambassador by Mrs Sarah Pocock who is much better
qualified to represent Mrs Newsome (274–5). Released from his moral duty,
Strether travels more impulsively, randomly in the Paris suburbs and surrounding
rural landscape, which of course has the benign effect of the picturesque described
in the travel writing. Train excursions allow for 'a modest adventure' which
reminds him of better times in a 'special-green vision' of home, an American

'shady woody horizon'; but cautiously only travelling no further than 'an hour's run' from Paris (410–11). In the pleasant countryside, with a 'book in his pocket' and a 'little rustic inn … with authentic wine' he can relax alone, at peace with a sense of 'the finer harmony of things' (412). But it is then in this mood that he will discover that Chad and Madame de Vionnet are lovers, as they appear on the scene unexpectedly.

Earlier, Strether becomes 'homesick and freshly restless; he could really for the time have fancied himself stranded with her [Mamie, Chad's sister] on a far shore, during an ominous calm, in a quaint community of shipwreck. Their little interview was like a picnic on a coral strand' (*A*, 338). Travel is here figuratively a desire to escape from himself and his situation. When Mrs Pocock 'wants some scenery' she leaves Paris for Switzerland, which as we know is code in James for the tourist destination used as a judgement of character – like Daisy Miller's mother preferring Zurich to Rome.

Mrs Newsome, of course, does not travel; she sends others abroad – her son to be educated, her ambassadors to keep an eye on him. She represents the limits of home. Trying to free up his conscience from her pernicious influence (she pursues him with letters that remind him of home), Strether walks the streets of Paris, and in the Luxembourg Gardens wonders why indeed he had 'such an extraordinary sense of escape' (*A*, 77). He feels 'washed up on the sunny strand by the waves of a single day', yet fears he is adrift without 'his compass and his helm' (78), his grasp on his mission, his need to 'pull himself together' (78). Already he is subject to another kind of opposed influence: Paris is teaching him to 'live all you can; it is a mistake not to'; he is in danger of 'missing the train' (176). He recalls happier times when his younger self, newlywed and a survivor of the Civil War, visited Paris (81); but that memory of youth is 'like some unmapped hinterland from a rough coast settlement' (82).

Tropes of place and travel recur throughout the novel. As Adrian Poole puts it 'James was drawn to metaphors of voyage and flood, of embarking and being launched and shipwrecked and cast ashore on a desert island, of floating and sinking and drowning, of being immersed and saturated.' Poole continues, such tropes represent 'images of risk, of potential self-loss and self surrender', and they have 'deep literary associations, not least promoted by Shakespeare, in *The Winter's Tale* and above all *The Tempest*, to which James was particularly drawn' (xxvii). Strether feels he is 'so often at sea' (*A*, 102); but at his best moments he is inspired to wander in the gardens or the countryside at peace with himself, fulfilling the desire: *Et in Arcadia Ego*.

Levels of inauthenticity are also intimated by constant references to society as theatre or play, a trope of staging. This motif begins in the London theatre before recurring throughout the text: 'It was an evening, it was a world of types, and this was a connection above all in which the figures and faces in the stalls were interchangeable with those on the stage' (*A*, 58) – insinuating, as Shakespeare did of course, that all the world is a stage. On entering Mrs Pocock's Paris salon Strether thinks: 'Madame de Vionnet was already on the field, and this gave the drama a quicker pace than he felt it as yet – though his suspense had increased – in the power of any act of his own to do' (293), where the figurative associations are given the double sense of 'play' as in stage play and game ('already on the field' of play), and therefore the spatial implications of the salon mark out a social drama of gazes, speech acts and power. Later in the same scene, Strether comments: 'It was indeed as if they were arranged, gathered for a performance, the performance of "Europe" by his confederate and himself' (304); and 'performance' or 'perform' appear four times on the one page to emphasize the point and Strether's state of mind. Then in another social situation we read that 'she [Miss Barrace] had quitted the other room ... dropped out of the play, abandoned, in a word, the stage itself, that she might stand a minute behind the scenes with Strether' (356).[47] 'Scene' is another recurrent signifier in James's writing, including the travel writing as *The American Scene* reminds us. A key passage where 'scene', 'play' and 'stage' come together with 'picture' and 'text' is the following:

> For this had been all day at bottom the spell of the picture – that it was essentially more than anything else a scene and a stage, that the very air of the play was in the rustle of the willows and the tone of the sky. The play and the characters had, without his knowing it till now, peopled all his spaces for him, and it seemed somehow quite happy that they should offer themselves, in the conditions so supplied, with a kind of inevitability ... Not a single one of his observations but somehow fell into a place in it; not a breath of the cooler evening that wasn't somehow a syllable of the text. The text was simply, when condensed, that in *these* places such things were, and that if it was in them one elected to move about one had to make one's account with what one lighted upon ... that the picture and the play seemed to melt together ... (416)

The scene is a social space of encounter and a clash of ways of seeing, broadly American and European. When scene becomes scenery it is important to notice who the observer is and the purpose of the observation. Here the real and the relationship to the object are artifice both in the play of characters and in the visual as picture. We know already from the travel writing that James's fondness for the picturesque together with his knowledge of art allowed him to see landscape as artwork or pastoral text. Now he can use the trope of writing the world as construct of the already represented to reproduce Strether's imaginative relation to the real which is more successful and satisfying for him than his relation to those that 'peopled all his spaces for him'. If Strether has an active, even poetic relation to nature, he has a passive one to the social world. What this illustrates about the novel is that James, as Poole argues, 'gives free rein to the figurative', so that there is 'an important contrast between metaphor and platitude' – the latter being the source of comedy around misunderstandings of key words like '"good", "free", "honest", "virtuous", "straight", "grand", "fine", "wonderful", "magnificent", "sublime". People hear in these words, very much as they see, just what they want or expect to.' Strether's growing divorce from Woollett values is thus indicated at the figurative as well as the literal levels. Indeed, his 'openness to the language of

---

47   Further references to the tropes of play or game in the novel: 359, 386, 387 and 390.

metaphor helps him get in touch with what he really thinks and feels and believes' (Poole, xxxiii).

Conclusion

Realism in the novel and tourism in travel writing share the drive for a semiotics of the typical. Scenery may be the sign of the typical in either the travel writing or the fiction – the American South, the English country house, Balzac's Touraine – and serve the realist description or the tourist gaze. But despite Henry James's insistence on the continued importance of Balzac to his idea of the novel, we seem to have stumbled upon a contradiction in his scheme of values. For just as the tourist gaze is an inferior mode of observation, so the literal and transparent representation is inferior to the figurative. James seems to acknowledge the latter implicitly in his late fiction, as we have seen in *The Ambassadors*. Travel to Europe has a benign effect on Lambert Strether, coming as he does under new influences that affect his way of seeing. As he becomes critical of home there is a greater gap between speech and thought, the social and the imaginative, his outer and inner life. James demonstrates this change through his increasing use of figurative language, allowing Strether at least an imaginative poetic resistance to the reductionist prosaic world of the Mrs Newsomes – and it is an effect of Europe on James himself, a release into poesis and *jouissance*.

In James's writing, travel for the American is the search for history – in the monuments, art and classical ruins; in the stones of Venice and Rome (the post-Ruskinian informed travel); history as lack for the New World. In *The Portrait of a Lady* Isabel Archer responds to 'the deep appeal of Rome ... as she trod the pavements of the Forum ... crossed the threshold of Saint Peter's ... She had always been fond of history, and here was history in the stones of the street and the atoms of the sunshine' (336). As we saw in James's travel writing, the Old World – the great houses and cathedrals of England, the castles and monuments and ancient ruins of France and Italy – satisfies the American traveller's desire for history and culture. What history there is in America is more recent, and is being replaced by modernity in the metropolitan developments, as James describes it in *The American Scene*.[48]

In his study of Hawthorne (1879) James claims that art can only flourish 'where the soil is deep' and that 'it takes a great deal of history to produce a little literature' (cit. in John F. Sears, introduction to *The American Scene*, xvii).[49] American modernity has no time for history; and for James it produces no

---

[48]   Kasia Boddy explains that American travellers 'wanted to drink from the fount of European culture ... In the American imagination Europe has traditionally functioned as a place of contrast; it was the place against which America defined itself, the place where Americans could conduct what Henry James termed the "virtual quarrel of ours with our own country"' (239–41).

[49]   James also writes in *The American Scene*: 'it takes an endless amount of history to make even a little tradition' (127).

literature of merit – which is of course an injustice to the work of the American writers of radical naturalism like Dreiser and Sinclair.[50] Instead, the literature of the Old World is for James, the unapologetic literary tourist, the source of history and cultural knowledge. But if America has not produced a significant body of literature because of its lack of history, how could James's own writing be any better? Clearly he would have to work within European traditions to succeed. Peter Brooks in *Henry James Goes to Paris* (2007) traces the influence of French literary culture on James's writing,[51] focusing on his attitudes to realism and modernism, and how his approach changes from the early to the late writing – in the fiction and the travel writing: 'James in 1912 was a modernist master, but one who clung to a notion of representation of the real that he saw as indispensable to the very project of the novel – a project that leads him over and over again to set against Flaubert's practice the more nourishing example of Balzac' (2).

Reading James's fiction chronologically reveals a growing sophistication in the use of narrative point of view whereby the story becomes a play 'of seeing and unseen, of knowledge and ignorance' (Brooks, 2–3). Thus, despite his initial resistance to French modernism in art and literature, James brings to the novel 'a kind of radical perspectivism' (Brooks, 2) analogous to the modernist aesthetic in art from impressionism to cubism, even while remaining faithful to the romantic plot and psychological realism. He refuses omniscience and moralizing authority (the hallmark of Balzac and George Eliot), to locate observation in character, and by multiplying the points of observations and the number of character-observers create ironies through conflicting viewpoints. Isabel Archer is an example of a developing story-telling technique: despite her initial self-confidence, her limitations are indicated in 'the discovery of the latent meanings of her disastrous marriage' (Brooks, 3). Bafflement leads to recognition. And this process is developed in James's writing in radical ways, as we saw in *The Ambassadors*.[52]

In his concern to portray the inner struggle of his protagonist James moved away from realism to modernism through the liberal use of free indirect discourse, the refusal of a moralizing omniscient authorial voice, an indirection of narrative, a greater syntactical complexity to match a destabilizing epistemology, and a freer play of metaphor than in his earlier writing. These are hallmarks of modernism and ones that emerged gradually in James's writing, as we see in the differences

---

[50]   For example: Theodor Dreiser, *Sister Carrie* (1900); Upton Sinclair, *The Jungle* (1906) and *The Metropolis* (1908).

[51]   'James felt himself at home in France and in French culture … It was probably Balzac's Paris that lured James abroad more than anything else' (Brooks, 8).

[52]   Part of the problem with James's early attitude to French art and literature may have been the difficulty he found as a foreigner in entering French society (Brooks, 15). His preferred reading at first is George Eliot's *Daniel Deronda*, just published, which convinced him at the time that English culture was superior to French in its 'richness of concern with the place of character and ethical choices' (Brooks, 25). It is in this frame of mind that he rejects Flaubert, Impressionism and then Zola (as 'indecent'). He misestimates the radical import of the new art and literature (Brooks, 30).

between *The American* and *The Ambassadors*. In the former, although he tries out different genres it 'appears to come straight out of Balzac', as Peter Brooks puts it (28). By the late fiction, James has himself become 'one of the chief modernist pioneers in fiction … after negotiating the lessons of Flaubert in original ways, and without ever wholly sacrificing the lessons of Balzac and George Eliot' (Brooks, 28).[53] It appears, however, that early James is concerned with aesthetics predominantly in the travel writing, and works out his understanding of art there, not in any analytic discourse but in his 'descriptive evocation of things' (Brooks, 28). Brooks concludes: 'James's misestimation of the new art of his time is striking. We think of James as an artistic innovator, an experimenter in techniques of seeing and telling, one whose own manner came in many ways to resemble that of an impressionist, even a *pointilliste*' (Brooks, 31, italics in original).

Yet, as I hope to have shown in this chapter, there are analogous developments in the travel writing and the fiction. In the travel writing the object, art or landscape, becomes more and more what is both visible and what is seen, just as character point of view becomes James's principal technique of narration in the fiction. The object and its perception is the basis of characterization and narrative in the fiction too: James, as we have seen in this chapter, famously dramatized the limits of characters' self-understanding and their readings of the other – the other subjected to misreading or misguided schemes (especially in the marriage plots).

There is in both fiction and travel texts a critique of modernity: James structures his argument through the opposition between the mechanical and the organic – an opposition shared with other writers in this study. Yet he is ambivalent about speed and technology of the new transport, the railway, and, at least by the later travel writing and fiction, the motor car.[54] There is also the classic opposition we see throughout this study between mass tourism and individual travel, between the sightseeing (with its superficial observations) of the packaged tour and the informed visitor. The tourist imaginary is meant here to signal a limitation, a naivety in the young protagonist in the fiction. The tourist is pre-conditioned to read the signs of the typical, looking for the signs of Englishness, Frenchness, Italianness or Americanness. James himself was always a compulsive seeker of the picturesque scene – the ideology of the aesthetic where the unity and integrity of the work of art is the highest value; as if the aesthetic can compensate for the forms of degeneration blamed on modernity itself. Thus in his entire work there is an aesthetic imperative – as there is in Forster and Wharton. The most consistent object of admiration, and the most romanticized place, is the ruin. The ruin is

---

[53]   Auerbach already in the 1940s explained that in Flaubert 'realism becomes impartial, impersonal, and objective'; character consciousness and ways of seeing are presented without authorial commentary. And 'he believes that the truth of the phenomenal world is also revealed in linguistic expression', at the level of style. Here we have, I suggest, the essential difference between Balzac's realism and Flaubert's modernism; and where Henry James writes in fact more and more like Flaubert (Auerbach, *Mimesis*, 482–90).

[54]   See Brooks, 'Epilogue: Chariots of Fire' (205ff.) for a brief discussion of James motoring with Edith Wharton in 1907 and his enthusiastic response to the new experience.

always preferred to restoration. The spirit of place conjures up 'the old life, the old manners' (*EH*, 74), and there are key moments in the novels where the spirit of such a place has a symbolic or symptomatic importance. Literary tourism recurs throughout the travel writing as it does the fiction. It gives all his writing an intertextual density indicating the value of literary culture and history. Finally, there is concern with gender and race in the travel writing and the fiction: there are comparisons between modern French and American women;[55] and American and Italian, French and English men (mostly of the same class); and especially in *The American Scene* we see an anxiety about the fate of the white races exacerbated by a new and widespread encounter with other cultures through immigration and travel. The force of cultural encounters then spills over into the novels where representative Americans abroad, male or female, negotiate otherness – the otherness of foreign cultures or that of the expatriate. As this chapter has argued, travel enables narratives – travel stories – as Henry James's own travel experience and the sketches he sent home – his topographical focus – influence the kind of novels he wrote; as travel itself becomes the principal trope of his writing.

---

[55] We could say of James what he says of Balzac, 'the greatest triumphs are the characters of the women' (*French Poets and Novelists*, 108).

Chapter 5
Edith Wharton:
The Aesthetic Value of Travel

Introduction

Best known for her novels and stories, Edith Wharton travelled abroad in Europe and North Africa, developed a taste for expatriate life from her childhood, and finally settled for the rest of her life in France from 1911. This chapter will first focus on Wharton's travel writing before discussing a selection of her fiction. It is in the travel writing that she works out the importance of being abroad in Europe for herself and the development of her writing. Moreover, writing about journeys became a paradigm for telling stories. Her descriptions of places, buildings, gardens and landscapes established a set of values that form the cornerstone of a cultural critique of modernity, and one she shared in many ways with the other writers discussed in this study, but especially with Henry James. Indeed, Wharton also works the international theme described in the last chapter, either setting the story abroad or taking her American characters to Europe for part of the story. Being abroad becomes an examination of cultural competence, of openness to otherness and difference. Taken together Henry James and Edith Wharton represent American culture at the point of its crisis, when new money and old money, the *nouveau riche* and the old aristocracy clash at the advent of modernity. The differences between Wharton and James will emerge in what follows.

As many Wharton scholars have said, it is their friendship which led early critics to see her in his shadow, as a kind of female copy of the 'master'; the early reception of her work being influenced by articles with titles like 'Henry James's Heiress: The Importance of Edith Wharton' by Q.D. Leavis, which 'reinforced the image of Wharton's overshadowing by James' as Pamela Knights explains (*The Cambridge Introduction to Edith Wharton*, 128). However, since R.W.B. Lewis's seminal biography (1975) there has been a much more varied approach to Wharton and her work, sometimes addressing the 'Woman Question', or the satire of her social critique and the details of cultural history in her writing. There has also been some interest in her uses of topography and travel – and I shall be engaging with this interest in some detail.[1] For those interested in the James-Wharton 'legend', chapter 8 in Hermione Lee's monumental biography has the last word. Lee suggests that the common view from the start of Wharton's writing career of her as 'a female Henry James' has prevented any consideration of the ways she might have influenced him. For example, her *Italian Backgrounds* might have

---

[1]   Knights points out that Wharton's travel writing has so far been given 'comparatively little attention'. *The Cambridge Introduction to Edith Wharton*, 136.

had 'an effect on *Italian Hours*'; and that 'Wharton's presence is certainly felt in *The American Scene*'s treatment of wealth' (214–15). She certainly encouraged James's appreciation of the romance of the motor car, despite his notorious rejection of most things modern, as I explained in the previous chapter. Wharton recalls (in 1920) their driving around in the hills of Western Massachusetts: 'We had motored so much together in Europe that allusions to Roman ruins and Gothic cathedrals furnished a great part of the pleasantries with which his mind played over what he has called "the thin empty lonely American beauty"' (Wegener, ed., *The Uncollected Critical Writings of Edith Wharton*, 141). By the time of the success of *The House of Mirth* (1905), Wharton had tired of the comparison with James, complaining of the 'continued cry that I am an echo of Mr James (whose books of the last ten years I can't read, much as I delight in the man)' (cit. in Lee, 215–16). We should not, though, underestimate the extent to which he encouraged her in her writing, in her travels to Europe and her expatriation.

James and Wharton clearly share themes and concerns in their writing which came from a shared American and European social and cultural background. As Janet Beer sums it up: 'They came from the same country and social class, they both expatriated themselves to Europe, they both treated the subject of the American abroad, they both wrote travel books, they both wrote novels, short stories, and criticism, they were friends, they had many friends in common' (57). Wharton's novella, *Madame de Treymes* (1907) and the travel book, *A Motor-Flight through France* (1908), 'owe a great deal to Henry James's novel, *The American* ... and his travel book, *A Little Tour of France*' (Beer, 58). And *The Reef* (1912) has been described as her most Jamesian novel (Lee, 218), with its use of two different characters' consciousness for shifting viewpoint, and the elliptic style, in a play of concealments and indecision; Beer even suggesting that in this novel Wharton 'loses her voice, finds Henry James's, and regains her own in time to write *The Custom of the Country*' (Beer, 57). I shall return to *Madame de Treymes* and *The Reef* later in this chapter to see where they differ from James, even when it is clear that Wharton shares with him many themes and concerns and styles of writing. What James and Wharton shared most was their travels in Europe and a profound educated interest in European high culture and its history, which established a set of values reflected in their lives and their writing. Wharton's passion for Europe is first seen in *The Cruise of the Vanadis*, an early travel text deriving from a dairy she kept of her tour of the Mediterranean in 1888 in some luxury, and one which confirms her belief in the origins of western culture.[2]

Suffice it to suggest at this point that she follows James's injunction to 'do' New York, after her first novel, *The Valley of Decision* was set back in Italian history (cit. in Knights, *Cambridge Introduction*, 57). However, even when her best writing – *The House of Mirth* (1905), *The Custom of the Country* (1913)

---

[2]   The cruise on a yacht as a form of luxury travel will appear in her novels. In *The House of Mirth* Lily Bart will be invited on a Mediterranean cruise on the 'Sabrina' but it will prove a social disaster; and Undine Spragg in *The Custom of the Country* will be invited to join Peter van Degen on his yacht, the 'Semantic' – the names of the yachts hinting at Wharton's satirical intentions.

and *The Age of Innocence* (1920) – is set in New York, these novels are also significantly about travel and journeys metaphorically and literally to one degree or another; and parts of their narrative are set abroad. This chapter, then, will focus on travel and place as narrative and setting, and as tropes for the cultural and individual problematic of the characters. For, even before what she called her 'motor-flights', the traveller's observations, like the plots of the novels and stories, enable the emergence of cultural differences from topography. However, as we will see in what follows, Wharton reproduces the orientalist discourse of the day, particularly in her last travel book *In Morocco* where she openly supports French colonialism. Yet, in a different frame of mind, her critical portrayal of the leisure class in the best novels draws on the Social Darwinism deriving from the work of Herbert Spencer and Thorstein Veblen.

Wharton's Travel Writing

The Mediterranean as the Location of the Origins of Culture

In her first travel writing Wharton reproduces the organic theory of culture where race and land, the people and the climate are essentially connected – a cultural theory she has in common with the other writers in this study. In particular, the romance of the south, the Mediterranean as the crucible of civilization, which Wharton shares with Forster and James, implies a conventional cultural essentialism, yet one legitimated by its derivation from literary sources. Indeed, Wharton – a literary and art tourist – travels in the knowledge of her predecessors, a tradition of travelling writers modelled on Goethe whose *Italian Journey* she had read, and whom she quotes at the start of *The Cruise of the Vanadis*. From *Faust* we read: 'Yea! If only the coat were mine, / To carry me to places strange, / Not for costly treasures would I exchange, / Not for a king's coat fine' (*The Cruise of the Vanadis*, 32).[3] The wanderlust Goethe expresses in his travel writing and literature, a northern longing for the south, its colour and light, is called upon by Wharton to underpin her travel and to give her a model for reading European culture through its history, art and literature. The aim of travel is to go to the land where the lemon-tree blossoms. It is a literary rite of passage, a journey of self-discovery. But, as Lee insists, 'her "travel-fever" [Wharton's own words] was not born of mere restlessness or indulgence. She dedicated herself to the study of European culture through twenty years of reading and travelling ... She was transforming herself from eager tourist to cultural expert' (Lee, 85–6). What she sees, in a predetermined itinerary of ancient or classical sites, is already textualized through her prior reading: Algiers harbour built by Christian slaves is read through 'Goethe's description' (*CV*, 36); in the Gulf of Tunis she sees 'a clump of mountains ethereal as Shelley's "peaked isles"' (39); in Sicily wondering whether 'Girgenti' was the site of the '"splendid-loving Acragas" of Pindar, the "topaz-bastioned city" of Symonds' (70). And even though she claims that 'this

---

[3]   Subsequent page references abbreviated as *CV* in text.

journal is written ... to note as exactly as possible the impression which I myself received' (67), impressions of landscape continue to be filtered through literature: 'in fact, no better description than Homer's could be given of the countryside about Corfu' (91). According to Lee, she had 'her marked-up copy of Andrew Lang's translation of the *Odyssey* on the cruise, as she would again in 1926' (Lee, 84). And as with both Forster and James, Wharton's reading produces high expectations: 'I had read so much of the beauties of Milo [harbour] that my first feeling was one of disappointment' (*CV*, 100) – the real and the object of the gaze do not always coincide. A glass of wine can remind her and her travelling companions of the '"sweet wine" so popular with the heroes of the *Odyssey*' (103). But though she admits to 'our ignorance of Eastern customs' (103), it seems that guidebooks are not always as 'reliable' as classical literature: '*The Mediterranean Hand Book* proved as untrustworthy as usual' (104); to avoid disenchantment Wharton prefers Gautier's poetic description of Syra as 'La Reine des Cyclades' (105). Her Mediterranean journey traces that of the Crusaders and the Knights of Malta recalling a history of conflict between Christendom and Ottoman Islam (121ff.); she visits the Monastery of St. John the Divine on the Greek island of Patmos (143) and notices the cultural hybridity in Smyrna still inhabited by 'savage-looking' Turks, Albanians 'side by side with fashionable-dressed Levantines and Europeans', which she reads as a curious 'mixture of Orientalism and European civilisation' (149). Her own odyssey, however, will not succeed in her seeing the exclusive male preserves of the Mt Athos Monasteries (174–5). But she will, like Henry James, note the contrast between the ancient ruins and the signs of modernity – 'the sea-shore is disfigured by several factories' (185); a harbour 'disfigured' (216) by modern housing – while celebrating 'the sunburnt ruins of the Parthenon' (189). Mythology is always read into the landscape: 'it is under these trees that Ulysses is supposed to have lain when the Phaeacians landed him on the shores of Ithaca'; (but the roads are good enough because they are 'an English legacy, of course'!) (194).[4] However, not everywhere in the region is significant for its cultural heritage. Montenegro is desolate, squalid and poverty-stricken (207), a non-place because of its apparent lack of 'culture' – a place to hurry away from when 'there was still a great deal to be seen' (216) – that is a highly selective itinerary for her tour based on high cultural value.

This, Wharton's first travelogue, based on a diary kept during a cruise in 1888 and worked on later into a denser informed text,[5] already establishes certain dominant values expressed as a set of key oppositions: civilization and barbarism, classical and modern, harmony and chaos, the past and the present, Europe and America (the tasteless Prince's Palace in Montenegro 'might pass for a particularly ugly New-England inn', *CV*, 207), the south and the north, light and dark. Notice the number of references, as in Goethe's *Italian Journey*, to the

---

[4]   The 'of course' indicating an attitude towards colonialism to which we will return later in this chapter.

[5]   A point suggested by Knights: 'A substantial chronicle, possibly edited some time after the journey.' *Cambridge Introduction*, 55.

bright sunlight and colourful flora and fauna of the Mediterranean region,[6] and to plenitude and closure, which will reverberate throughout her travel writing and fiction, especially as we see women confined to the domestic sphere in the Moroccan harem or the New York drawing-room. Underlying these oppositions is the belief that the Mediterranean is the location for the origin of culture – a claim shared with Fielding in Forster's *A Passage to India* for whom 'the Mediterranean is the human norm', because it is the place of classical 'harmony', as we saw in Chapter 2 (Forster, *A Passage to India*, 266).

In these key oppositions, and especially in her understanding of 'culture', Wharton belongs from the start to the classical tradition of Grand Tour travel. Moreover, one should not, of course, overlook her privileged position in the leisure classes who can travel in some style, and always use the yacht as a site of that privilege and as a safe place from where she and her travelling companions can make excursions to the sites of the classical world and return to eat and sleep on board in comfort. Wharton would write a lot about the leisure class, from her insider position, and we will return to the questions of class and privilege later in this chapter. Just as she begins travel writing, like Henry James, in the tradition of Goethe, she will begin her fiction writing in the great tradition of the realist novel of manners while developing a set of modernist themes and styles of presenting character consciousness. In both the travel writing and the fiction, as I hope to show, Wharton addresses modernity.

Orientalism and Cultural Imperialism

Another opposition that Wharton establishes right at the start of her writing life is that between travel and tourism – an opposition important to so many other travelling writers, including those discussed in this study. Like them Wharton notices the 'tourist gaze' was beginning to supersede 'those more intimate glimpses which help to compose the image of each city, to preserve its personality in the traveller's mind' (*Italian Backgrounds* in *Wharton Abroad*, 111).[7] The 'observant eye of the traveller' is rewarded with 'a treasure of quiet impression', while 'the hurried sight-seer may discover only dull streets and featureless house-fronts' (*Wharton Abroad*, 91).[8] Sight-seeing is not real seeing; and it is her visit to Morocco in 1917 that will record more than any of her travel books the very moment before mass tourism changes the place into the object of the tourist gaze, as she gets privileged access to 'unseen' Morocco: 'To see Morocco during the war was therefore to see

---

[6]   Goethe wrote: 'At dawn I saw the first hillside vineyards ... and at last I saw Bolzano, bathed in sunshine ... A balmy air pervaded the whole region' (37).

[7]   As I explained in the general introduction, for John Urry tourist sightseeing is superficial because it focuses on the signs of the typical: 'such as the typical English village, the typical American skyscraper, the typical German beer-garden, the typical French château, and so on. This mode of gazing shows how tourists are in a way semioticians, reading the landscape for signifiers of certain pre-established notions or signs derived from various discourses of travel and tourism ...' (12–13).

[8]   Subsequent page references abbreviated as *WA* in text.

it in the last phase of its curiously abrupt transition from remoteness and danger to security and accessibility; at a moment when its aspect and its customs were still almost unaffected by European influences' (*In Morocco*, 23).[9] But her account will not be immune from the very mindset that underpins western colonialism – and in what follows I shall examine the descriptive and representational values that both unconsciously and also quite intentionally reproduce and legitimize French imperialism and its orientalist ideology.

Reading Wharton's travel writing makes it quite clear that imperialism is cultural as well as political. The process of westernization may be lamented by travellers in search of the Ur-culture of indigenous places, but its legacy is still with us today – in the language, education, dress-codes and institutions of former colonial places. However, as Hobsbawm has argued, 'new social elites based on education in the western manner' were created, yet native ways were not always affected. Hobsbawm continues, 'the great mass of colonial populations hardly changed their ways of life if they could help it … the most powerful legacy of imperialism was, therefore, an education in western ways for minorities of various kinds … wearing their clothes, adopting their peculiar ideas of time, place, and domestic arrangement' (76–9). Wharton gives us an example of such a western-influenced ruler: 'The Caïd is a great man … Enlightened, cultivated, a friend of the arts, a scholar and diplomatist, he seems, unlike many Orientals, to have selected the best in assimilating European influences' – even though he still keeps black slaves (*IM*, 157). He is also a powerful force in the maintenance of French colonialism in Morocco; and like the monks on Mt Athos he is a keeper of the cultural archive – a masculine agency which Wharton wants to support now (in 1917) even when the monks once refused her entry into their domain (in 1888), as we see in *The Cruise of the Vanadis* (174–5).

Lucas Tromly has argued that in supporting the colonial politics of Morocco Wharton 'takes on a masculine agency', but this is troubled at the point where she is shown the women of the harem and 'she is briefly repositioned from masculinised agent of the Occident to a female victim of the Orient' (241). She is annoyed with the 'languor' and 'apathy' of these 'languid' women who are the victims of a particularly oriental version of patriarchy: 'And all these colourless eventless lives depend on the favour of one fat tyrannical man, bloated with good living and authority, himself almost as inert and sedentary as his women' (*IM*, 152). What at first appears to be a feminist response is complicated by the orientalist discourse of the indolent other even when Wharton desexualizes the essentialist image insisting that 'images of sensual seduction' (151), common to the western archive of orientalism, are far from the reality of the Moroccan harem. It is the Moroccan man who is at fault for being the bearer, in Tromly's words, 'of an *insufficient* masculine masculinity' (246).[10] Crucially, however, it is not

---

[9]   Subsequent references in text to the I.B. Taurus 2006 edition and abbreviated as *IM*. It is a recurrent trope in the travel writing discussed in this study that the object is being glimpsed on the point of its disappearance.

[10]   I would add that trapped women entombed in a ritual empty domesticity is though a key theme in Wharton's fiction, and in her argument for a more active and educated

just passivity but sedentariness that limits femininity. Wharton asks the Sultan's mother whether Moroccan women have any desire to travel, and she says no they are too busy in their household (*IM*, 146–7). And Wharton is immediately impressed by the Sultan's mother because of her authority and apparent influence on her son. She is an active woman, not a passive victim of the Orient: 'Here at last was one woman beyond the trivial dissimulations, the childish cunning, the idle cruelties of the harem' (141). But, of course, as Tromly points out, she is 'in a privileged position within a patriarchal order' (246), like Wharton herself, and also supports French colonial rule: 'All is well with Morocco as long as all is well with France' (*IM*, 141). Tromly sums up his argument about Wharton's values in this travel text:

> Ultimately, *In Morocco* is a disheartening text, both for the racism it demonstrates and because it discourages recent considerations of the plurality of meanings and positions in Orientalist discourse. Despite her cosmopolitanism, privilege, and talent, the only position that seems available to Wharton within her own narrative are those of masculinised European colonial agent and silent subaltern female. (248)

However, without wanting to defend Wharton's position described here, I think we need to acknowledge that first Wharton reproduces a masculine agency in her fiction, too, in the portrayal of female victims of the leisure class in New York or the aristocracy in France;[11] and second her reasons for explicitly supporting French rule in Morocco are colonialist in the sense of keepers of the heritage. Some ruins are blamed on native neglect, as is the case with the Roman remains of Volubilis in Morocco where 'little remains' but a 'fragment of a basilica … part of an arch of triumph … and the fallen columns and architraves which strew the path of Rome across the world' (*IM*, 49). As with the old city of Meknes, the evidence is clear that there is no native interest in preserving cultural heritage – reminding us of Forster's criticism of modern Alexandria. In Morocco it is left to the French colonial administration to do the work of cultural preservation. The 'French Fine Arts' have become 'the custodian of the ruins' (49) – and it is here that we see Wharton's imperialism is cultural as well as political. France – which for Wharton is the epitome of western culture – has a curatorial role in Morocco: Moroccan culture will be saved from the natives. And the travel book, *In Morocco*, is dedicated to the sponsor and supporter of Wharton's 1917 visit, General Lyautey, the French Resident-General. Thus the book is a legitimation of French colonial rule, where imperialism is justified by culture. Chapter VI is a eulogy to

---

femininity – based on the example of her own case. We return to Wharton's critique of femininity later in this chapter.

[11] Pamela Knights suggests we think about Wharton's attitude to her female characters: 'Given the unpleasantness and economic ruthlessness of many of Wharton's female characters, her own identification with a male literary gold standard, and many of her declared reservations about women's capabilities and ambitions, did she even like women?' (*The Cambridge Introduction*, 130).

the General's work as the saviour of Morocco from itself and from the Germans by making it a French protectorate in 1912. Here we see that Wharton is well informed of the politics at the time, despite choosing to read the benign effects of imperialism as predominantly cultural. She is not saying that this is always the case in the French North African colonies; indeed, the examples of Tunisia and Algeria prove otherwise. The 'success' of French rule in Morocco is credited to 'the administrator's genuine sympathy with the traditions, habits and tastes of the people'. Moreover – and this is decisive for Wharton – Lyautey appreciates 'all that was most exquisite and venerable in the Arab art of Morocco' which leads him 'to gather about him a group of archaeologists and artists who were charged with the inspection and preservation of the national monuments and the revival of the languishing native art-industries' (170).

Imperialism is cultural when an educated ruling class come equipped with a clear idea of the relationship between cultural and national identity, as indeed France itself did.[12] We should also be aware that Wharton was resident in France and had become known for her war work (for which she would be honoured by the State) – a context indeed for her comments on French colonial rule in Morocco; and an implicit critique of German imperial ambitions at the time of the Great War. There is, though, an important relationship between culture as aesthetic forms and culture as way of life, social practices and customs. Edward Said drew attention to the principal connection between culture and imperialism as the 'power to narrate, or to block other narratives from forming and emerging' (*Culture and Imperialism*, xiii). And as we can see from this study of travel and modernism, narratives of nations are predicated on cultural superiority and often result in racism and xenophobia. The question is which writers challenge those nationalist views emerging out of nineteenth-century imperialism.[13] In her travel writing Wharton gives priority to the idea of culture as aesthetic forms, and then reads the places she visits through those forms or there remnants. In her fiction, however, she also includes the more ethnographic approach to culture, its social practices, customs and gender relations when writing about the New York 'smart set'. So, whereas Wharton looks for the icons of classical and high culture in Europe and reads the Mediterranean crucible through the literature and travel writing of her predecessors in her travel writing, she produces a more recognizably modernist critique of her home culture in her fiction even when working with a late realism. In the next section of this chapter I want to take the cultural aesthetic of her travel writing further, because for her European classical and high culture is also what is lacking in America – a view she shares with Henry James.

---

[12]   For more on Wharton's attitude to French imperialism in Morocco see Frederick Wegener's article 'Edith Wharton on French Colonial Charities for Women: An Unknown Travel Essay'.

[13]   Said writes of the emergent 'disenchantment' in the novel by the late nineteenth century, and one represented by Conrad and Forster in my study. Said concludes: 'I would like to suggest that many of the most prominent characteristics of modernist culture, which we have tended to derive from purely internal dynamics in Western society and culture, include a response to the external pressures on culture from the *imperium*' (187–8).

The Ideology of the Aesthetic: The Art of Living

In Wharton's travel writing descriptions of place are encoded through art, as we see in the following example:

> For though the town [Lovere], at first sight, is dull and disappointing, yet, taken with its surroundings, it might well form the substructure of one of those Turneresque visions which, in Italy, are perpetually intruding between the most conscientious traveller and the actual surroundings. It is indeed almost impossible to see Italy steadily and see it whole. The onset of impressions and memories is at times so overwhelming that observation is lost in mere sensation. (*WA*, 97)

Indeed, the countryside is a landscape constructed as background or foreground in the western tradition of pictorial art[14] – which seems appropriate for the selected descriptions of Italian architecture and gardens, art and the châteaux of France. However, western classical aesthetic values also intrude in representations of Morocco. The ordinary scene is a composition along classical lines: 'To the Occidental travellers the most vivid impression produced by first contact with the Near East is the surprise of being in a country where the human element increases instead of diminishing the delight of the eye.' The passage continues:

> After all, then, the intimate harmony between nature and architecture and the human body that is revealed in Greek art was not an artist's counsel of perfection but an honest rendering of reality: there were, there still are, privileged scenes where the fall of a greengrocer's draperies or a milkman's cloak or a beggar's rags are part of the composition, distinctly related to it in line and colour, and where the natural unstudied attitudes of the human body are correspondingly harmonious, however humdrum the acts it is engaged in ... Moroccan crowds are always a feast to the eye ... the sense of colour ... (*IM*, 129)

Western conventions of perspective are especially the case with ruins – 'the romantic and ruinous Morocco of yesterday' (*IM*, 11), defined within the orientalist discourse as 'a land of mists and mysteries' (15), where 'everything that the reader of the *Arabian Nights* expects to find is here' (36). And even in the Preface to the 1927 edition, we are told that visiting Morocco is 'still like turning the pages of some illuminated Persian manuscript all embroidered with bright shapes and subtle lines' (16). For Wharton all such places seem alike, differences are collapsed in the universal image of the Orient. Fez 'becomes the Bagdad of Al Raschid'. The signs of the typical are economically presented for the western reader: the 'oriental' signifies 'colour and gaiety' (94), 'the scent of jasmine and rose' but 'all the squalor' too (102); 'veiled women' (83) hennaed (97) and the harem (129ff.); mint tea, couscous (100), the bazaar and the storytellers at Marrakech and the caravans from Timbuktu (111–18); 'slim dancing-boys' and

---

[14]   Claudine Lesage claims that Wharton's descriptive style 'makes one think of painting – of Orientalist painters like Decamps – rather than literature'. Introduction to *The Cruise of the Vanadis*, 24. Even though she is talking about Wharton's travel writing we will see that such aesthetic encoding is also present in her fictional narratives.

the 'swarthy musicians … almost as guileless and happy as the round of angels on the roof of Fra Angelico's Nativity' (120–21); a 'fantastic setting, and the hush of that twilight hour, the vision so like the picture of a "Seraglio Tragedy", some fragment of a Delacroix or Decamps floating up into the drowsy brain' (110), or 'a Claude-like vision' (124) – Wharton's perspective has not changed since her first visit to North Africa in 1888. In *The Cruise of the Vanadis* we read:

> In the Arab quarter [of Tunis] we saw many striking figures – children in bright frocks, with broad gold bracelets, women in white burnouses, with black silk yashmaks over their faces, and strangest of all, the Jewesses with silk turbans over their plaited hair (like 17th century pictures of Judith or Herodias) loose flowing sleeves of embroidered gauze or muslin, and flowered silk dresses with jackets braided with gold. (38)

Just as the signs of the typical characterize the object of the tourist gaze, the semiotics of the Orient is always relocated in the representations of Western art and literature; and western scholarship: the art of the Italian Renaissance is read through Burckhardt, the European Gothic through Ruskin, and Wharton's preference for the Italian Baroque (and the *commedia dell'arte*) against Ruskin.[15]

Wharton's gaze, then, is already filtered through cultivated knowledge, a superior view of the object. And despite her critique of mass tourism, she herself also reproduces a pre-constructed perspective – one that legitimizes the high culture of the west in an unreconstructed cultural imperialism and orientalism (in Said's sense). Moreover, Wharton's cultural imperialism has two sides to it: the one is her framing what she sees in western aesthetics in terms of analogies with actual works of art and in the obsession with order, symmetry and harmony in landscape or townscape; the other side is her desire for preservation of traditional buildings, landscape and art – even ruins which she sees as the natural historical archive, deploring attempts to reconstruct them. Ruins are attractive to her – as they are to Henry James – because they allow imaginative recreation: 'The ruins stand on a hill overgrown with olives and consist of the piers and vaulting of a very old church, covered with a climbing mass of green' (*WA*, 42); 'The lower garden of Caprarola is a mere wreck … Plaster statues in all stages of decay … but the outline of the general plan is not easy to trace … and one must … climb through hanging oak woods to a higher level to gain an idea of what the gardens once were' (*WA*, 62).[16] Wright comments that Wharton, Henry James and others were attracted to landscapes composed of ruins with grazing sheep as it gave the decay a natural

---

[15]   'But the reality of Christian slavery in Africa is brought much closer to us by Goethe's description …' (*CV*, 36). Geneviève Lacambre writes of the Orient 'stretching from Egypt through Palestine to Greece' as the perceived birthplace of Western civilization, 'a region that is part of us and yet not quite part of us' (Preface to *The Orient in Western Art*, 7).

[16]   For further examples of ruins and comment on imaginative reconstruction see *Wharton Abroad*, 73: 'before it was destroyed the three terraces of the Villa Muti must have formed the most enchanting garden in Frascati'; and also 90–91 and 114: 'How much more eloquent these tottering stones tell their story, how much deeper into the past they take us, than the dapper weather-tight castles … on which the arch-restorer has worked his will,

and harmonious setting (*WA*, 67 note 8). In her drive through the war-torn regions of France in 1915, Wharton describes the villages and landscape destroyed by the fighting; and here too the scenes are given perspective through her aestheticizing strategy: 'One can see it so from afar, and through the torn traceries of the ruined church, the eye travels over so lovely a stretch of country! … It was a sunless afternoon, and the picture was all monastic shades of black and white and ashen grey … as the day faded, the church looked like a quiet grave-yard in a battle-field' (*WA*, 140–43). But flowers are growing in the devastation, and ploughshares are getting busy again on the ruined land – all 'signs of returning life', so that 'the war scars seem like traces of a long-past woe'; and from her vantage point Wharton can imagine what a ruined town ('the martyr town') might have looked like before the war, and the destruction from bombardment (151–3).

Edith Wharton prioritizes western high cultural values in her travel writing. In Italy she describes the architecture and the art of the Renaissance and the Baroque, as well as the cultivated harmony between landscape and building that makes place an artwork; indeed, her landscape perspectives are themselves constructed paradigmatically on classical aesthetic principles of proportion, symmetry, and harmony as exemplified in the relationship between villa, garden, and the surrounding landscape. Her description of place is framed by an aestheticizing strategy: 'The harmonizing of wood and garden is one of the characteristic features of the villas at Frascati' (*WA*, 65). The garden-architecture of the Villa Falconieri is described as follows: 'From this shady solitude the wooded slopes of the lower park are reached by a double staircase so simple and majestic in design that it harmonises perfectly with the sylvan wildness which characterises the landscape' (*WA*, 73).

However, we should be quite clear that, for Wharton, the category of the aesthetic has an ideological function as it combines the appreciation of unity and harmony in the artefact – artwork, architecture, garden and landscape – with taste as a bulwark against the perceived vulgarities of the modern world.[17] In this she is working with a residual eighteenth-century idea of manners. The aesthetic is nothing more or less than a paradigm for living. Moreover, the classical conceptions of unity and harmony in the travel writing appear as a compensation for the effects of modernity on the human subject in her fiction. Classical harmony is then taken as a 'fixed principle of civilised life', a sign of taste in design which translates into civic value – exemplified at best for Wharton in the French Academy, and the French National Theatre, stabilizing influences on the national culture and its language that is missing in the US (*French Ways and Their Meaning* in *WA*, 172–4). Indeed, Edith Wharton believed that France was the location of the best in civilized living and high culture. She frequently observes that social life in France, even

---

reducing them to mere museum specimens, archaeological toys, from which all the growths of time have been ruthlessly stripped.' See also 128 and 131.

[17] Walter Pater defined taste as an intellectual not an aesthetic category: 'What is meant by taste is an imperfect intellectual state; it is but a sterile kind of culture. It is … the intellectual manner of perfect culture' (137).

when limited to the class to which she was accustomed, is both mature and itself a work of art: 'the French have ... instinctively applied to living the same rules that they applied to artistic creation' (*WA*, 170). Living is a form of art in old Europe, which it is not in America. In France she sees social harmony in marriage between men and women as 'intelligence of life' and 'the intelligent enjoyment of living' (*A Motor-Flight through France* in *WA*, 116–17). Compared to American women who are 'still in the kindergarten', 'the real Frenchwoman' who is 'the freest and frankest of all', is 'grown-up' (*WA*, 176–7). Wharton blames the limits of life at home on the Puritan heritage: 'The long hypocrisy which Puritan England handed on to America concerning the danger of frank and free social relations between men and women has done more than anything else to retard real civilisation in America' (*WA*, 182).

Carol J. Singley has argued that to help her 'to come to terms with her own expatriation and questions about the preservation and dissemination of cultural value in the early twentieth century' Wharton drew on ideas about nationhood from Ernest Renan – and I would add, even when these very ideas contradicted her early cultural theory, as we saw in the discussion of her first travel writing ('Race, Culture, Nation', 32).[18] Renan refuted the dominant organic theory of national cultural identity rooted in the soul and the race. Instead, he argued that a national identity depends on collective memory; which more recently has been argued by Benedict Anderson as discursively created 'imagined communities' (Singley, 'Race, Culture, Nation', 36).[19] Divorcing nation as a cultural (and arbitrary) entity from nationalism worked well for Wharton because it enabled her to understand her own status as expatriate American living in France. The high cultural ideals of France could be the model for other nations, whether America or Morocco: American materialism could be tempered by French taste; Morocco could learn the value of its own cultural heritage and transcend its tribal squabbles with higher cultural ideals. Of course, Wharton holds elitist views and promotes them in her fiction as well as her travel writing. They are so exclusively Eurocentric, upper class, white and High Culture that, like Henry James, she is even blind to the cultural leadership of the US in modernism (New York, Chicago). Throughout her work she favours the traditions of pre-twentieth century European art and architecture, and a classical aesthetic, which are then translated into contemporary civic values: 'Like many others of her time and background, Wharton so completely identified art with traditional European culture that she was unable to appreciate American art or to respond to modern European art ... she extolled European art of the past ... while she scathingly criticized American aesthetic insensitivity' (Dwight, 182).[20]

---

[18]   It is tempting to speculate that the reason why Wharton never published *The Cruise of the Vanadis* in her lifetime might have been because it reproduced organic theories of culture which would not sit happily with Renan's ideas, which she was now espousing.

[19]   See Benedict Anderson, *Imagined Communities: Reflections on the Origin and Spread of Nationalism*. All the writers in this study are restlessly in search of their own 'imagined communities', each thus incapacitated, for different reasons, from 'coming home'.

[20]   She shares this lack of appreciation of American Modernism with Henry James – see the previous chapter for the discussion of James and modernism.

Aesthetic appreciation confers unity on the perceiving subject because it is an act of reason, a reflective intellectual response prepared for by study and connoisseurship – as we saw in the previous chapter in Henry James's recurrent quest for the picturesque scene. But more than just an intellectual value, the aesthetic crucially has a moral value. As Terry Eagleton put it in *The Ideology of the Aesthetic*: 'The morally virtuous individual lives with the grace and symmetry of an artefact, so that virtue may be known by its irresistible aesthetic appeal' (35). Wharton promotes this ideology of the aesthetic in her travel writing and it is a deeply conservative stance, which, as we will see later, is constantly used as an implicit value-judgement of the characters in her fiction.

When in her travel writing Wharton reads place in terms 'of her own standards of aesthetic beauty and form' (Singley, 'Race, Culture, Nation', 42), her preferences in art are decisive. Although she, like Henry James, began her understanding of European art by reading Ruskin, she moved away from his prioritizing the Gothic to challenge his reading of what he called the 'Grotesque Renaissance', which also included the eighteenth-century Baroque and Rococo represented in artists like Tiepolo.[21] Ruskin (1853) writes of the 'grotesque Renaissance' as producing a 'merely pleasurable excitement' as opposed to the experience of 'sublimity of the highest art'. Grotesque art, by which he means the Baroque and Rococo, is 'inferior' and merely 'ornamental' (Ruskin, *Selected Writings* [Oxford], 66). Ruskin and his followers believed that the frescoes of Tiepolo were 'insincere' and 'too sensual', too 'morally lax' (Zorzi, 213). The highly influential judgments of Sir Joshua Reynolds and John Ruskin were accepted without question by the young Henry James, and Edith Wharton in her formative years. A Tiepolo ceiling in Venice was dismissed by James as 'pompous' in 1872; and he maintained his reservations in later life. In Zorzi's words, 'Tiepolo, with his breezy beauty, his bare-breasted queens and nymphs and goddesses, seems to have been overly joyous and sensuous for James's Puritan imagination' (216). A change in taste, however, came about with the 1896 Tiepolo bicentenary celebrations, and the waning influence of Ruskin. Wharton was affected by the change in attitude to the Baroque, and partly through the impact of late nineteenth-century theories of art-for-art's-sake in Walter Pater, J.A. Symonds and others she developed an interest in Tiepolo.[22]

Despite a shared interest in the romantic sublime, Pater opposed Ruskinian aesthetics which he saw as a continuation of the rational apprehension of the object in recollection, and thus as maintaining the Enlightenment split between thought and feeling, mind and body.[23] Pater instead proposed an impressionist aesthetic

---

[21] In the following discussion I draw on Rosella Mamoli Zorzi's 'Tiepolo, Henry James, and Edith Wharton'.

[22] Walter Pater, *Studies in the History of the Renaissance* (1873). John Addington Symonds, *The History of the Renaissance in Italy* (1875–1886).

[23] Ruskin (1856) defines the sublime effect as follows: 'Anything which elevates the mind is sublime, and elevation of the mind is produced by the contemplation of greatness of any kind; but chiefly, of course, by the greatness of the noble things' (*Selected Writings*

criticism, a subjective approach whereby the perceiving subject is, as Matthew Beaumont explains, 'for a moment completely immersed in the object' in a 'passionate attention to the instant' (xix–xx).[24] For Ruskin art has a moral function and architecture a social function (with the Italian Gothic as paradigmatic). For Pater art is only for art's sake and it enables a return to the vital forces of the senses, 'to burn always with this hard gem-like flame, to maintain this ecstasy' against the forces of habit and stereotype in the modern world (119–20). The purest art form is music, and it has a paradigmatic role in Paterian aesthetics: '*All art constantly aspires towards the condition of music*' (Pater, 124, italics in the original) because it is music which has the 'perfect identification of matter and form' (Pater, 127) – as Forster also appreciated.

Edith Wharton 'is the first American writer to admire Tiepolo and allow all the beauty and joy of his world to enter her imagination' (Zorzi, 217). In the Villa Pisani 'the great central saloon has one of Tiepolo's most riotously splendid ceilings' (*Italian Villas and their Gardens* in *WA*, 83–4). In *Italian Backgrounds*, in deliberate challenge to the 'pseudo-Gothicisms' of Ruskin's Italy, Wharton writes:

> Yet Milan is not dependent on the seasons for this mid-summer magic of light and colour. For dark days it keeps its store of warmth and brightness hidden behind palace walls and in the cold dusk of church and cloister. Summer in all its throbbing heat has been imprisoned by Tiepolo in the great ceiling of the Palazzo Clerici: that revel of gods and demi-gods, and mortals of all lands and races, who advance with linked hands out of the rosy vapours of dawn. Nor are loftier colour-harmonies wanting … (*WA*, 106–7. Also cit. in Zorzi, 218.)

What is interesting is that Wharton is open to an art that Ruskin and his generation dismissed as lacking the aesthetic virtues of classical form and instead giving in to the disorder of merely sensual expression. She sees not only the Gothic and early Renaissance which was the exclusive focus of Ruskin, but also the eighteenth-century Italian Baroque. It is for her the Venice carnival in art – and we could suggest, after Bakhtin, a 'carnivalizing' of the colourless, joyless Puritan-preferred Gothic; and, as Zorzi argues, wholly appropriate to an Edith Wharton who, as we shall see later in more detail, satirized 'the stifling conventions of the New York society' in her best novels, *The House of Mirth*, *The Custom of the Country* and *The*

[Everyman], 111 note b). Turner's method of composition is significant for Ruskin because of 'that vision being composed primarily of the strong memory of the place' after his initial sketches *in situ* (*Selected Writings* [Everyman], 81).

[24] One could suggest a difference between Ruskin and Pater in gender terms: the former insisting on craggy mountains and ravines as the location of the sublime (Ruskin, *Selected Writings* [Everyman], 33), and the manly labour of the medieval stonemason, a pre-capitalist non-alienated labour (*Selected Writings* [Everyman], 195–9. See also the Oxford World's Classic edition of *Selected Writings*, 40ff.); the latter (Pater) insisting on the sensualized object, the physical beauty of the male body celebrated in the Renaissance (Pater, 5) and the 'free play of human affection' in late medieval literature (where he locates the beginnings of the Renaissance) (Pater, 144).

Age of Innocence: 'One seems to sense a sort of personal identification with a world where freedom and enjoyment were celebrated, a world that did not exclude sexual and sensual relationships, a world that the dark and oppressive atmosphere of the Victorian nineteenth century could not tolerate or admire' (Zorzi, 220).[25] Tiepolo's frescoes, in Venice or in Würzburg,[26] represent in sublimated form a *jouissance* of colour and form. They capture the open spaces of the sky on the ceiling; the body and movement on the painted surface, with the effect that the space of the interior of the building is full of life – a spatial joy denied to her female fictional protagonist. Moreover, Wharton reads 'harmony of form and colour' in these frescoes – where others saw decadence, she sees a regenerative art (*WA*, 107).[27] Italian architecture from the sixteenth century onwards was seen as 'examples of degeneracy to a generation bred in the Ruskinian code of art ethics' (*WA*, 76).

A Bakhtian carnivalizing is also what attracts Wharton to the 'grotesque and comic figures of the *Commedia dell'arte*' which decorate villas (*WA*, 83); figures which like those in Rabelais's world challenge the 'classical graces' which 'had taken possession of Northern Europe' in the seventeenth and eighteenth centuries (*WA*, 78) – and, as we will see, in Wharton's world such lively grotesqueries challenge the polite, bourgeois world of manners represented in her New York fiction. Thus on her travels, rather than Switzerland with its 'landscape of a sanatorium prospectus' (*WA*, 88), she is attracted more to the Bergamasque Alps in part for 'its associations with the *commedia dell'arte* and the jolly figures of Harlequin and Brighella' (*WA*, 90).[28] Wharton's attraction to the unsettling and dynamic forms of the Italian Baroque is the other side of her desire for the understated harmonious match between villa, garden and surrounding landscape. It is another of her contradictions to add to that between the (qualified) nomadicism of travel and the sedentariness of the writing-room in the self-designed château.

Travel is regenerative for Edith Wharton. Like the medieval pilgrimage, her spiritual quest, as Schriber has argued, makes 'a destination into an object of desire' (263) – which, as we have seen, is a desire predominantly for the classical

---

[25] Yet as Zorzi points out, in the *tableaux vivants* scene in *The House of Mirth* Lily Bart decides not to go as Tiepolo's Cleopatra but significantly as Reynolds's Mrs Lloyd – a picture 'without distracting accessories' (*The House of Mirth*, 132, cit. in Zorzi, 220).

[26] See Zorzi, 229 note 73: 'Wharton did go to Würzburg, but only later, in Dec. 1909 to see "the longed-for Tiepolos at the Prince Bishop's Palace" as she wrote to Sara Norton on Dec. 2, 1909.'

[27] Zorzi quotes Charles Blanc writing about Tiepolo in *History of Painting* (Paris, 1868) where he insists that, and I paraphrase, the effects are only artifice, a 'degenerate intemperance' where behind the apparently fertile images there are only sterile sentiments and ideas with no meaningful depth. For full quotation in the original see Zorzi, 229 note 74.

[28] We see this rejection of Switzerland as the packaged tourist destination in James and Lawrence too. Wharton uses it as an implicit judgment of characters like Undine Spragg in *The Custom of the Country* when she prefers the fashionable Swiss resort of St Moritz to Ralph Marvell's preference for Italy for their honeymoon – which is where James, Wharton, and Lawrence differ from both Ruskin and Pater for whom the Alpine landscape is the location of the Romantic Sublime itself.

western European High Culture and its history: 'the miraculous sacred object is Europe; the sought-after cure is the discovery of an identity, a history, in the sense of the past that Europe offers' (Schriber, 264–5).[29] It is an identity outside the social and cultural constrictions she describes in the New York novels. Her defiance is to assert the right of a woman of her class and upbringing to travel and to write; to display her intelligence, learning and connoisseurship without apology. Moreover, she chooses to live a divorced and single life amongst like-minded people as an expatriate in France – her imagined community. From this vantage point she can continue to assess American society. Going back home will always remind her why she needs to leave again:

> My first weeks in America are always miserable, because the tastes I am cursed with are all of a kind that cannot be gratified here … my first sight of American streets, my first hearing of American voices, and the wild, dishevelled backwards look of everything when one first comes home! You see, in my heart of hearts, a heart never unbosomed, I feel America … out of sympathy with everything.
> (Letter to Sara Norton, cit. in Schriber, 266)[30]

Homecomings are a common difficulty for the writers in this study. Travel for Wharton is the quest for a new life in Old Europe – a paradoxical liberation from the conventions of gender partly in the spirit of the New Woman, while returning to a 'classical' world which modernism will supersede. But has she not misrecognized the object of displacement by confusing the liberation from the restriction of gender with the ecstatic experience of an art whose representation of femininity is as repressive as drawing-room conventions? Sublimated sensations on first sighting a Tiepolo ceiling seem to blind her to the idealized view of women's bodies available there to the male gaze – and yet in her best novels she produces thoroughgoing critiques of the female object in the sight of the male gaze. Additionally, her attraction to the figures in the *commedia dell'arte* and the theatre of improvisation have only a significance as startling contrast to the calculated manners of the New York set in her novels. The reduction of characters to predictable roles and the comedy to the reiterated simple plots of the Italian *opera buffa* tradition is no substitute for an emancipated theatre. Moreover, there is here a profound contradiction between the crude promiscuous comedy of the *commedia* and the fine aesthetics of High Art and architecture – an aesthetics which Wharton wants to convert into an art of living based on traditional refined taste. As Dale M. Bauer argues, 'For as soon as desire became plural, Wharton saw it as defused, no longer the centrifugal force she expected it to be. Modern culture brought all desires and impulses too promiscuously together, balking her preference for classical values of symmetry and balance' (125).

---

[29]   As explained in the previous chapter, for American travellers Europe was the fount of culture where they should find all that was lacking at home.

[30]   I cannot emphasize enough that Wharton's criticism of America – like Henry James's in *The American Scene* as discussed in the previous chapter – can be challenged for her refusing to give any credit to its leading role in modernism.

The sublimation of desire into the aesthetic – 'a desire for artistic enjoyment' (Dwight, 187) – gives an order to desire: that of the classical principles of proportion, symmetry and harmony; and as we have seen, these principles define what it means to be 'civilized'. Celebrating the joy of perception of the Italian villa and its gardens or the Tiepolo fresco enables Wharton's *jouissance*, which is by definition outside the law of the Father, to have its limits defined. There is, therefore, a correlation between demand and *jouissance* – as I argued in the discussion of Lucy Honeychurch's *jouissance* in Florence in Forster's *A Room with a View* – which demonstrates, as Charles Shepherdson explains 'that the symbolic order, the order of desire, sets a limit to *jouissance*, providing a point of reference, localizing what will otherwise be the overwhelming and sacrificial cycle of *jouissance* and demand. This limit is what Lacan calls the paternal metaphor' (71–2).[31] Thus we might be able to account for Wharton's deeply paradoxical demands for travel while needing the stability of residence in a cultivated place to live and write; for refined taste while enjoying the crude *buffa* humour of the *commedia*; for the classical harmony of the Villa and the carnival of the Baroque, favouring Tiepolo while nevertheless insisting on the moral function of art (Ruskin, Arnold) and not just aestheticism (Pater).

Spatial Practices in Wharton's Fiction

The Uses of Travel

In her fiction Wharton draws on her travels as settings for excursions and episodes, and for encounters with cultural otherness. Like Conrad, Forster, Lawrence and James, she takes her characters abroad to test the limits of their cultural understanding. At worst, we see Americans abroad who have no desire to meet the natives, except occasionally when they are from the same class; indeed, her stories focus exclusively on the leisure class – her class – and travel is used either to expose their ignorance and arrogance, or their appreciation and preference for a European life.

'The Lamp of Psyche' (1895) is an early version of the story of the American couple living in Paris because the husband 'can gratify his tastes much more easily in Europe than in America' (*Collected Stories 1891–1910*, 35).[32] The contrast between America and France is a matter of taste and style – a matter of the decoration of interiors characteristic of much of Wharton's writing: 'Delia … longed with unreasoning intensity to get away from it all; from the dreary house in Mount Vernon Street, with its stencilled hall and hideous drawing-room, its monotonous food in unappetizing profusion' (36). By contrast, her husband's house

---

[31]   In *The Age of Innocence* the kinship rites of the symbolic order make Archer's desire impossible.

[32]   Subsequent page references in text to short stories are to the 2001 The Library of America edition.

in Paris is 'delightful' and 'so framed for a noble leisure'; and it is a life of theatre, art and literature, of 'dreaming hours in galleries and museums', a life of 'delicate enjoyments' as opposed to 'the aesthetic barrenness' of their America (37). The story will turn on a secret about her husband's past; but what is important for us is the location of a superior life of culture in Paris.

Not all Wharton's American characters appreciate France. There is an example of the arrogant American abroad in the early story, 'The Last Asset' (1904). Paul Garnett makes no effort to learn the language properly despite having lived in Paris for many years; the city 'seemed to have made as little impression on him as its speech. He appeared to have no artistic or intellectual curiosities, to remain untouched by the complex appeal of Paris' (603). The pretensions of Mrs Newell in the same story represent another Paris; a place of seasons for the leisured society: 'Mrs. Newell's Paris was non-existent in September. The town was a desert of gaping trippers' (605) – a spatial metaphor that represents her mental mapping of Paris in and out of season. Already we see a difference in reading space: for some it is aesthetic enjoyment of culture, for others the exclusive social occasion – and both are different sides of the leisure class. One asset in the story is Mrs Newell's daughter whom she wants to marry well to improve her own social standing; and here we have an early version of a reiterated Wharton story of the wealthy American marrying into the French aristocracy with all the attendant questions of old family names, and the clash of Catholics and Protestants over divorce – a Jamesian story-paradigm too. The last asset is her estranged husband's money to pay for the arranged marriage and his presence at the wedding to satisfy the public image; and the mother gets her way always. We are left with a Garnett who realizes how the mother has manipulated everyone to secure her social status, including her daughter (but Garnett's sentimental view of the marriage offers a surprisingly tender ending).

The plot of the rich American marrying into the staid French aristocracy recurs in Wharton's fiction because it serves to illustrate certain themes: the international theme of the American abroad and the tensions between old money and new money, European traditions and American modernity, the old world and the new world; the problems of inter-cultural marriage (from an author who knew both cultures from the inside); the question of divorce (a burning issue at the time, and one where Wharton would be able to draw on personal experience); marriage as the only destiny for young women in this society and the implications of women as commodities, as objects of exchange.

The early stories make symbolic capital out of settings – houses, interiors, streets and the countryside that Wharton experienced on her travels and described in her travel writing. Wide Paris boulevards, or quiet old quarters, and traditional interiors also set the scene in the novella, *Madame de Treymes* (1907) for staging a confrontation between the Francophile American John Denham and other expatriate Americans living in Paris out of economic necessity but who 'live in active disapproval of the world about them' (183). Mrs Boykin – a recognizable figure in such stories – unashamedly declares that she and her husband 'so thoroughly disapprove of French society that we have always declined to take any part in it' (185). By contrast, Denham, having made his wealth through hard work and now in the leisure class (173), enjoys the life in Paris preferring it to the 'enlightened ugliness' of 'his own lamentable New York' (165) – and thus reflecting the author's well-known views, which are reinforced further when Denham, strolling in the streets of Paris, ruminates on the greater freedoms given there to the 'contact between the sexes', as if there is a correspondence between the spacious boulevard and the openness towards gender (166–7). The novella thus illustrates Wharton's belief that there was in France a greater harmony in marriage because of the mature relationship between men and women who have an 'intelligent enjoyment of living' (*WA*, 116–17), compared to American women who are not 'grown-up' because they have not been exposed to Europe as a key part of their education, and therefore still suffer from their Puritan formation at home. But of course such views, expressed publicly later during the Great War, are only a partial truth as Wharton demonstrates in her portrayal of American women who marry into the French aristocracy and have to conform to traditional family life which restricts their senses of being. Paris consists not just of wide boulevards but also of quarters that are characterized by an 'almost monastic quiet' (*Madame de Treymes*, 176) and 'old walls on quiet streets' (189).

The problems American women might face marrying into the strict ancestral world of the French aristocracy are dramatized most explicitly in the novel, *The Custom of the Country* (1913). When Undine Spragg becomes the Marquise de Chelles she refuses to conform to the demands of the French family – and I will return to this novel later in the chapter. In *Madame de Treymes* Madame de Malrive, formerly the American Fanny Frisbee, explains the strictures of the French 'family organization' as the reason why, now that her marriage has collapsed, she wishes to keep her son; she does not want him to learn to accept their 'network of prejudices and opinions' (172). She has though become less than an American, and it is her sophisticated French manners that attract the attention of Denham, even when her hybrid character – which has developed an 'exotic enjoyment of Americanism' from a distance (179) – is thrown into stark relief by the 'real thing' (181), Madame de Treymes when she first appears to Denham as 'the slender dark lady loitering negligently in the background' (180).

Thus we can see that from her early fiction Wharton appears to complicate views she held about the superiority of French life and the 'new French Woman'. These views are reiterated in 1919 in 'French Ways and their Meaning' discussed above. What we ought to recognize though is that what appears to be a contradiction may be partly explained by reading views expressed in the fiction as attributed to characters in certain determinate contexts and situations. We would not want to attribute to the author the reductionist differences between America and France proposed in the schema of the natural against the cultural, the innocent against the scheming expressed by some of her characters. And as for clannishness: an overview of Wharton's fiction will show the extent to which New York clans also held sway over 'society' – as we see in *The House of Mirth* and *The Age of Innocence*. It is sometimes indeed the Americans who are the schemers, ruthless in achieving their goals, the new capitalists whose tourist industry is destroying the cultural heritage of Europe. In this narrative, old Europe is being overrun by the New World – a proposition worked through in *The Custom of the Country*.

It seems that travel does not always broaden the mind. Deeply entrenched attitudes ensure an unbridgeable gulf between the cultures. *Madame de Treymes* sets in train a play of differences around the divorce – and the divorce issue recurs in several other fictions. The difficulties of Americans marrying into French aristocratic Catholic families reminds us of Henry James's novel, *The American* (discussed in the previous chapter) – and of course several critics have pointed out Wharton's debt to James in her novella, and to James's travel writing in *A Little Tour of France* in her *A Motor-Flight through France*. Millicent Bell, however, insists that 'her interest in Franco-American cultural comparisons was more objective than his, more a question of the precise observation of real manners' (5).

In *The Reef* the French country residence, Givré seems to come straight out of the travel writing in *A Motor-Flight through France* (1908). In the travel text we read, 'we pushed on, by quiet by-roads and unknown villages, by *manoirs* of grey stone peeping through high thickets of lilac and laburnum, and along shady river-reaches where fishermen dozed in their punts, and cattle in the meadow-grass beneath the willows ...' (*WA*, 114). In the novel, Anna Leath and George Darrow go for a drive, 'motoring, traversing miles of sober-tinted landscape in which, here and there, a scarlet vineyard flamed, clattering through the streets of stony villages, coming out on low slopes above the river, or winding through the pale gold of narrow wood-roads with the blue of clear-cut hills at their end ... Then the motor flew on into the dusk' (*The Reef*, 100). The last trope is a celebration of speed – a 'motor-flight'; and the whole description transforms the gentle pastoralism of the travel writing into a more symptomatic impressionism, a scene out of the French Impressionists, and reiterated in this novel: 'The atmosphere was still and pale. The muffled sunlight gleamed like gold tissue through the grey gauze, and the beech alleys tapered away to a blue haze blent of sky and forest. It was one of those elusive days when the familiar forms of things seem about to dissolve in a prismatic shimmer' (*The Reef*, 131). Like the French Impressionist painting, the sensuousness of the world is not confined to the rural landscape; Darrow's walk through the Paris streets 'was like the unrolling of a vast tapestry from which countless stored fragrances were shaken out' (34); and he looks out of his hotel window 'on the vast light-spangled mass of the city' (46). That other modern city, New York, is also a place for the male flâneur. Ralph Marvell's semi-somnambulant walk from the corner of Wall Street towards Washington Square in *The Custom of the Country* enables a 'hot summer perspective' as his death-driven mood 'intensified his physical perceptions, his sensitiveness to the heat, the noise, the smells of the dishevelled midsummer city' (294).

Descriptive codes are, of course, focalized through characters in narrative fiction, revealing their moods or illusions. A woman on a train racing across America in the story, 'The Journey' 'shrank into her corner and looked out of the window at the flying trees and houses, meaningless hieroglyphs of an endless unrolled papyrus' (72) – as if speed blurs the vision in a complex trope of modernity disintegrating into ancient script, codex dissolving into scroll. In *The Reef* Anna

Leath's first impression of a French château is romantic: 'the serene face of the old house seated in its park among the poplar-bordered meadows of middle France, had seemed, on her first sight of it, to hold out to her a fate as noble and dignified as its own mien' (66). However, over time it becomes 'the very symbol of narrowness and monotony' to her, and finally settling into the place 'where one had one's duties' (66). The disillusion is the fate of American women marrying into the French aristocracy and being obliged to conform to a restrictive way of life. It is a process of disillusion from the romantic to the mundane, which has resonances in other Wharton novels too, like the boredom experienced by Undine Spragg in *The Custom of the Country* on becoming the Marquise de Chelles and having to live in the rural seclusion of the family château. Her ambitions will not allow her to suffer such a life for long.

Leisure-Class Femininity and the Specularized Public Space

Wharton gives the issue of disillusion a precise spatial dimension. The interior of the house – in France or America – is sometimes a silent tomb where the woman feels buried alive; the garden or surrounding woodland places of harmony and liberation. In *The House of Mirth* Lily Bart gets some relief in the form of 'physical stimulus' outside the repressive social space of the drawing-room: 'the challenge of the crisp cold and hard exercise, the responsive thrill of her body to the influences of the winter woods' (112).[33] But her spatial practice becomes ever more limited in a novel where the social world is described as a 'gilded cage' (*HM*, 55), and where her aunt, Mrs Peniston's house (where she is living until later in the novel) is to her 'as dreary as a tomb' so that she feels 'buried alive in the stifling limits of Mrs Peniston's existence' (99); and despite a trip abroad to Monte Carlo with the smart New York set there will be no enlargement of the spaces of being: she is snubbed and gets into debt and is reduced to living in smaller spaces, in 'the solitude of her room' (286).

The trope of life as journey that will end in tragedy structures the plot of *The House of Mirth* (1905).[34] As Pamela Knights explains, the female protagonist Lily Bart is 'that socially ambiguous figure, the orphan and poor relation whose journey could end in a grand settlement and fortune, or in isolation and penury ... she is desultory and drifting in a space between trains on a journey between other people's country houses' (*HM*, Everyman's Library, xv). Her principal asset is her appearance; but she also needs to be seen in the right places and with the right people. Before she is finally banished from the public space she is always consciously on display, staging her appearance. The Opera House, like Fifth

---

[33]   References in text abbreviated as *HM* are to the Oxford World's Classics edition edited by Martha Banta (1999) unless otherwise indicated.

[34]   We already saw the trope of life as a journey used by Forster in his novel *The Longest Journey* where the force of expectations and desire lead to disappointment, and in the character of Leonard Bast in *Howards End* result in tragedy. Indeed, what Bast's case has in common with Lily Bart's is the 'abyss' of poverty that awaits them.

Avenue, is the place to be seen – a social space also used in other Wharton novels. The importance of being in the sight of the gaze is clear from the first scene where she is quite deliberately placed as the object of the male gaze. Lori Merish writes about the way fashion has a destabilizing effect on the female subject in this novel: 'This instability is especially apparent in the system of fashion, a symbolic structure that historically has entangled signs of liberation and oppression – of feminine pleasure and autonomy, and masculine power and domination – within the image of the fashionable female body' (322).[35] The novel begins: 'Selden paused in surprise. In the afternoon rush of the Grand Central Station his eyes had been refreshed by the sight of Miss Lily Bart' (*HM*, 5).[36] Like other women of her class 'she had been brought up to be ornamental' (289), so as to secure her value as a commodity in the marriage market, or once married to display her husband's wealth in the form of the latest Paris fashion. Her commodity value is explicit from the start of the novel. 'The beautiful Miss Bart', as Merish explains, 'occupies the increasingly specularized and "feminized" space of the commodity in late nineteenth-century culture – a space organized, Wharton indicates, by male economic power and male desire' (Merish, 326).[37] Lily Bart, like Undine Spragg in *The Custom of the Country*, is expensive – her dress bills alone would require a wealthy husband.

Edith Wharton illustrates here Thorstein Veblen's theory of 'conspicuous consumption'. Veblen argued that in the new wealthy leisure class 'visible success becomes an end in itself sought for its own utility as a basis of esteem' (*The Theory of the Leisure Class*, 16). The beautiful, fashionable woman acts as a trophy for the successful man; a trophy to be displayed on the right public occasion (Veblen, 21). The wives and daughters of successful men must be conspicuous in their leisure; and once Lily Bart has to work for a living – which she is unqualified to do by her upbringing[38] – she can no longer belong to the leisure class. In the novel, Rosedale speaks for the class, when he says, 'the idea of your having to work – it's preposterous' (*HM*, 290). But already 29 and still not married, and more or less disinherited by her aunt and snubbed by her class, Lily Bart has no choice but to work for a living. She will not survive this fall from grace.

---

[35]   Roland Barthes wrote about fashion as a semiotic construction in *The Fashion System* (London: University of California Press, 1990. First published 1967).

[36]   'As an observer, Selden shapes Lily to his own interests, and his view of her becomes one element in what destroys her. Here, however, it is difficult for us not to see Lily as he sees her, as an expensive and polished work of art, a product of social processes Selden cannot quite grasp, because he is another beneficiary.' Pamela Knights, Introduction to *HM* (Everyman's Library), xii.

[37]   The tableaux vivant scene reinforces Lily's status as an object designed for the male gaze and male pleasure; but also as a need she has for being seen to confirm her identity, which makes her identity crisis more acute as she declines towards social invisibility – a point made by Merish (336).

[38]   '… but there was unfortunately no specific head under which the art of saying and doing the right thing could be offered in the market' (*HM*, 261).

Wharton's critique of the leisure class, known from the inside and after having read Veblen and others, focuses on the Woman Question.[39] Lee explains the extent of Wharton's reading to underpin her satire:

> Steeped in Darwin, Spencer and Lamarck, as well as Thorstein Veblen, Wharton demonstrates how 'the power of money' determines 'social credit' and morality, how the old money is complicit with and infected by the influx of the new, how consumption is increasingly linked to display and publicity, and how the role of women is created by, and dependent on, the financial imperatives of this society. (199)

In the terms of the Social Darwinism popular at the time, Lily does not survive in the scheme of the survival of the fittest where Undine Spragg in *The Custom of the Country* does. Lily Bart tells Selden that without a decent enough place to retreat to 'a miserable thing it is to be a woman' (*HM*, 8).

Undine Spragg does not need anywhere to retreat to. She manages her life better than Lily Bart. As marriage is destiny she actively pursues her man – or men in this case, as she becomes a serial spouse, working the system and the wealth of the men to ensure her marriages and divorces when required in her journey of upward social mobility. She has no moral scruples; and we do not get to sympathize with her, as Wharton skilfully engineers a distance to her female protagonist through irony: 'Undine was fiercely independent and yet passionately imitative. She wanted to surprise everyone by her dash and originality, but could not help modelling herself on the last person she met, and the confusion of ideals thus produced caused her much perturbation when she had to choose between two courses' (*The Custom of the Country*, 13).[40] Undine prepares her public appearances carefully in front of the mirror to be as conspicuously glamorous as possible, and times her entrances to perfection. Like the author she is full of drive and determination – but she does not share her author's cultural interests.[41] Clearly 'she was going to know the right people at last – she was going to get what she wanted' (20). But, in answer to Freud's question, 'what does woman want?' ('*Was will das Weib?*'), Undine exclaims: 'I want what the others want' (*CC*, 64).[42] The process of desiring the other's desire begins with wanting to be seen – in the

---

[39]   Veblen also discusses the Woman Question. See Veblen, 229ff. Adorno comments: 'one might reach the conclusion that women have escaped the sphere of production only to be absorbed more entirely by the sphere of consumption, to be captivated by the immediacy of the commodity world no less than men are transfixed by the immediacy of profit. Women mirror the injustice masculine society has inflicted on them – they become increasingly like commodities' (*Prisms*, 82).

[40]   Subsequent page references abbreviated as *CC* in text.

[41]   'Undine's lack of culture shows up at its worst, of course, in Paris' (Lee, 430). 'Undine herself is utterly without aesthetic sensibilities, and for Wharton this is an unpardonable sin' (Showalter, 94).

[42]   'This powerful narrative has a relentless theme. The words wanting, getting, having, are repeated over and over' (Lee, 428).

right place at the right occasion and in the right company. Wanting to be seen always implies wanting to be admired for her appearance, a conspicuous and calculated display of the female subject as ornament-for-the-gaze. It does not go unnoticed (by Ralph Marvell) that her vanity and the 'instinct of adapting herself to whatever company she was in, of copying "the others" in speech and gesture as closely as she reflected them in dress' will not save her from the exposure of her ignorance (100) – and it seems her relationships do disintegrate once they get beyond first impressions.

Wharton invites us to read Undine as a case history, first perhaps through 'all her floating desires',[43] and second as the glittering surface without depth: 'and she herself was the core of that vast illumination, the sentient throbbing surface which gathered all the shafts of light at its centre' (*CC*, 39). The motif of a play of surfaces that recurs through the novel is later summed up by Charles Bowen as he thinks of 'the layers on layers of unsubstantialness, on which the seemingly solid scene before him rested'; of 'human nature's passion for the factitious, its incorrigible habit of imitating the imitation'; of the 'reverent faith in the reality of the sham they had created' (171). This reads like proto-postmodernism, like the now seminal Baudrillardian conceptualization of the real as simulation or simulacra – a world of shiny surfaces without depth.[44] The solid French Marquis on the brink of becoming Undine's next husband does not want his future wife to be part of this Bohemia of glittering surfaces. Bowen assures him that she would be 'safe', because 'Nothing ever goes on! Nothing that ever happens here is real' (*CC*, 172).

Wharton offers us another reading of the American leisure-class world in this novel. She returns to the discourse of anthropology and Social Darwinism first seen in *The House of Mirth*, and takes the critique much further. Ralph Marvell thinks of the older New York generation as the 'aborigines' who are a dying species 'doomed to rapid extinction' by the 'invading race', old money threatened by new money, traditional ways by the new ways of the leisure class. Ironically, Ralph himself will not survive despite trying to play the games of a ruthless business world – ironically not just because he is aware of the superficial values of the business culture, but because his desire to be a writer (on his honeymoon in Italy his artistic sensibility is inspired – like the author) is thwarted by the very world he wants to reject.[45] He fails as a writer and as a businessman. However, the novel ends on a note of possible hope as his son Paul it seems could form a

---

[43]   Near the end of the novel we read, 'She had everything she wanted, but she still felt, at times, that there were other things she might want if she knew about them' (*CC*, 370). It is the object once seen that creates the desire.

[44]   Jean Baudrillard, *Simulacres et Simulations* (Paris: Editions Galilées, 1981). 'Simulacra and Simulations' (part translation) in Mark Poster, ed. *Jean Baudrillard: Selected Writings* (Cambridge: Polity, 1992). One could say of Undine what Pamela Knights says of Lily Bart: 'Fashioned as pure ornament, pure surface, her "fastidiousness" (a word much repeated) marks her distance from sexual desire.' *HM* (Everyman Library edition), xxiii.

[45]   Cecilia Tichi calls Ralph 'an Emerson manqué'. See 'Emerson, Darwin, and *The Custom of the Country*' in Singley, *A Historical Guide*, 102.

partnership with business (with his new step-father, Elmer Moffatt) to sponsor his artistic ambitions. The implications of the novel's title are played out in an anthropological discourse of 'clans' (*CC*, 19), the 'immemorial love-dance' (45); of 'the march of civilization' and the 'rites and customs' (50–51) of its natives, like the interplay of glances and gazes at the opera (41ff.) where the subject is in the 'range of the exploring opera glasses' (234), or a genre of speech which consists of 'the full and elaborate vocabulary of evasion' (273) – a speech style in James's writing too; and of Undine's instinct to adapt in order survive (although Ralph sees this part of her character as a weakness, a lack of depth). Ralph is also aware that he had to learn to 'adapt himself to the narrow compass of her experience' (92) after he realizes on their honeymoon in Italy Undine does not share his interests in nature or art; and after she has left him 'he had gradually adapted himself to the new order of things ... his boy and his book' (265). The story then shifts to France where Undine's next husband expects her to conform to the French aristocratic customs, the 'complicated code of family prejudices and traditions' (302). But she has no interest in dynastic history nor has she the sense of tradition expected in the noble French family. Life for her is lived in the present where she can satisfy her desire for 'change and excitement' as a 'fast' American instead of being 'shut up' in Saint Désert (323). The customs of the countries, France and America, are played out in an opposition of wants and expectations, tradition and modernity, sedentariness and rootlessness, within a narrow class range – the old French aristocracy and the new American leisure class. Undine Spragg will soon move on, not wanting to align herself with a tribe facing extinction, but to return to the new breed of modern Americans who are best suited to modernity where money can buy anything and history and family origins count for little or can be invented – as Elmer Moffatt will prove. Theirs will be a marriage of the opportunists, even when it will not last.

The spatial practices for women in the American leisure class limit their sense of being, whether trapped in the domestic sphere or in their performance in the public sphere, which is 'specularized' – that is subject to visibility and to the (male) gaze women are on display. There seems no escape from the social expectations of gender even when travelling.

Conspicuous Travel

'Wharton would always travel in style' (Lee, 82) – and so do her fictional characters. There are echoes in both *The House of Mirth* and *The Custom of the Country* of her Mediterranean cruise on the luxury steam-yacht, the Vanadis. After crossing the Atlantic Lily Bart is a guest on the yacht, the Sabrina. On a quiet morning she 'leaned over the side, giving herself up to the leisurely enjoyment of the spectacle before her', and what she sees as she looks across the water to the shore establishes the location of luxury tourism on the French Riviera: 'hotels and villas flashed from the greyish verdure of olive and eucalyptus; and the background of bare and finely-pencilled mountains quivered in a pale intensity of light'. She had been on the yacht with her New York set for two months, sailed around Sicily, had spent time ashore in Cannes, Nice and also in the casino in Monte Carlo – all the watering-places of the wealthy tourists; and although the cruise itself 'charmed her as a romantic adventure', it is Cannes and Nice that had 'really given her more pleasure' because in such places she can once again be on display as the 'beautiful Miss Bart'. The whole trip abroad at first helps her forget her problems, 'placing the Atlantic between herself and her obligations' (*HM*, 91–2). But things are about to get worse, as Selden tries to warn her (204), and the fabricated scandal will precipitate her fall from grace.

In *The Custom of the Country* Undine Spragg is invited on a cruise on Van Degen's steam-yacht, the Sorceress (106). Scandal is not an issue for her; her promiscuity is without scruples as she is cultivating a relationship that could lead to her next marriage (but Van Degen does not play her game for long). She also gets invited to go with him motoring in France, 'down to Aix ... and perhaps take a dip into Italy ... As far as Venice, anyhow; and then in August there's Trouville ... There's an awfully jolly crowd there – and the motoring's ripping in Normandy' (184). Wharton mocks both the speech and the mentality of the wealthy leisure-class with the time and the money to travel about by car (a luxury in those days which Wharton herself experienced); and to the places of leisure tourism like Trouville – and we know that Undine is only interested in those places, like St Moritz, where they can be conspicuous in their wealth and leisure. Later Van Degen charters another yacht, the Semantic, and it is made quite clear that the 'American set' abroad do not, as a matter of principle, 'care much about meeting foreigners' (220). They are 'westward-bound nomads' for the season in Paris 'before hurrying back to inaugurate the New York season' (221). Undine is only travelling to be seen with the right people in the right places: 'She might have attached herself to some migratory group winged for Italy or Egypt; but the prospect of travel did not in itself appeal to her, and she was doubtful of its social benefit. She lacked the adventurous curiosity which seeks its occasion in the unknown' (226–7). When her doctor sends her to a 'small quiet place on the Riviera' for her health where 'everyone went to bed at nine' she has to struggle not run away – because here she is as inconspicuous as the place is dull. To distract herself from her boredom she recalls her romantic flight with Peter van Degen: 'she had gone away with him, and had lived with him for two months', when she was allowed to 'buy everything she wanted' (229). Now she feels in 'exile in the wilderness' (231). Once returned to New York she will need to get back into the 'social frame' and has 'a defiant desire to make herself seen' (234), which as we know means going to the opera.

Wharton makes it very clear how important being conspicuous is to the leisure-class, but only in the right place and with the right people – like the *Promenade des Anglais* in Nice (*CC*, 248) or Paris in the spring (251), which enables Undine to be 'rendered visible' (256). However, she will become invisible again for a while after her marriage into the French aristocracy, incarcerated at Saint Désert, another exile in the wilderness – as Wharton plays the motif of being out of sight against being seen in public, of exile and in the social frame for Undine, her most gregarious character. However, once married to Elmer Moffatt she seems to be continually travelling. Now based in 'one of the new quarters of Paris ... [t]hey were always coming and going; during the two years since their marriage they had been perpetually dashing over to New York and back, or rushing down to Rome' (361) – and Wharton indicates her attitude once again through the speech mimicry of free indirect, or direct discourse: '*dashing* over to New York', like Van Degen's '*take a dip* into Italy' and 'there's *an awfully jolly crowd* there – and the motoring's *ripping* in Normandy' (my emphasis).

Conspicuous travel, like the places visited, is satirized within a scheme of values established in Wharton's travel writing; a scheme which includes the opposition between travel and tourism, places of cultural, historical and aesthetic value and those fashionable watering-places for the rich.[46] Wharton also travelled in some luxury,[47] and lived either in her Paris or Riviera residences as her income from her writing or inheritance permitted. She did, though, insist that the wealthy classes should be responsible for the arts and the cultural heritage: 'Leisure, itself the creation of wealth, is incessantly engaged in transmuting wealth into beauty by secreting the surplus energy which flowers in great architecture, great painting, and great literature. Only in the atmosphere thus engendered floats that impalpable dust of ideas that is the real culture' ('The Great American Novel' [1927], rept. in Wegener, *Uncollected*, 156).[48] Conspicuous travel is thus, for Wharton, not an end in itself, because the values it represents are undermined by the destinations preferred, the lack of high cultural interests, and the way in which the leisure-classes take their inviolable world with them, and are immune to any influence from the foreign culture – indeed where the transport and the places they stay are custom-made just for them: the first-class cabins in trans-Atlantic liners, private yachts, luxury hotels and casinos.

The Nomadic and the Sedentary

'America's sedentary days are long since past.' (Wharton, 'The Great American Novel' in Wegener, *Uncollected*, 156)

As to travel – had not Raymond and his wife been to Egypt and Asia Minor on their wedding-journey? Such reckless enterprise was unheard of in the annals of the house! Had they not spent days and days in the saddle, and slept in tents among the Arabs? ... No-one in the family had ever taken so-long a wedding-journey ... Since wedding-journeys were the fashion, they had taken them; but who had ever heard of travelling afterward? What could be the possible

---

[46] Hermione Lee tells us that Wharton 'was determined to be more than an amateur tourist. Her "travel-fever" was not born of mere restlessness or indulgence. She dedicated herself to the study of European culture through twenty years of reading and travelling' (85–6). None of her fictional characters can match their author in this respect.

[47] Wharton's 'servanted' travel contrasts markedly with D.H. Lawrence's 'difficult' travel.

[48] One might speculate that Undine Spragg incorporates a certain fear on Wharton's part that her travels too might be a form of self-aggrandizement.

object of leaving one's family, one's habits, one's friends? It was natural that the Americans, who had no homes, who were born and died in hotels, should have contracted nomadic habits; but the new Marquise de Chelles was no longer an American, and she had Saint Désert and the Hôtel de Chelles to live in, as generations of ladies of her name had done before her. (*The Custom of the Country*, 320–21)

In this key passage in *The Custom of the Country* Wharton reiterates the opposition between the nomadic and the sedentary that formed an underlying tension in her own life, and one worked through in the travel writing. She was an energetic traveller and also had designs on houses, interiors and gardens: contrary impulses of the nomad and the settler – the American expatriate writer finding a house of her own in France to write fiction about the repressive side of the sedentary life especially for women who find themselves encaged in the domestic sphere; and the woman (Wharton herself) in flight from the marriage-destiny of women of her class. Comparing her travel writing and her fiction reveals this tension between travel and residence, mobility and stillness, the contrary impulses in 'incessant travel and … her cultivation of homes, gardens, and habits of writing' (Singley, *A Historical Guide*, 13). In the novel *The Custom of the Country*, the two sides of Wharton are divided into the America nomad, a product of the growing rootlessness of modernity, and the sedentary French aristocracy prefigured in the de Chelles family and their two residences, the country seat and the town house. Raymond de Chelles, Undine Spragg's second husband, has been talked into an extravagant honeymoon seen here as an American desire for travel; but the price for it is that his wife has to become 'un-American' and accept the long noble French family tradition of living at Saint Désert, the name being of course appropriate for the promise of a barren existence in the wilderness of rural France, an existence which the socialite American woman will not be able to tolerate.

Nothing could be further from the buzz of American modernity than the quiet sedate French Château. It is the location of a cultural difference, but one that will obscure any facile hierarchy of values that we would expect if we read the novel through Wharton's *French Ways and their Meaning*. Here French life is no recommendation for the American woman, despite its display of art and taste. As Stephen Orgel claims: 'The intellectual independence of French women does not liberate them from stifling marriages and tedious, pointless social chores, it only enables them to accept the inevitability of these arrangements' (xxiii). The Marquise de Chelles is expected to give up her exciting life for the traditional life at the Château where 'the ladies of the line of Chelles had always sat at their needle-work on the terrace' (*CC*, 322). When she is told that, typical for an American, she appears 'to live on change and excitement' (323), we know this to be true. But she will not be tied down, and her marriage will disintegrate through 'mutual incomprehension' (342). Undine Spragg's restlessness, however, is not a sign of her openness to European travel. On her first honeymoon, she is soon bored by the Italy that her husband, Ralph Marvell (and the author) prefers. She prefers the greater social life of Rome, or fashionable St Moritz to his intoxicating Italian landscapes; he likes 'travelling by slow stages' to appreciate the 'heady fragrances' and 'new colours' (87), getting inspiration for his poetry (89).[49] But he has to give in to her demand for more excitement; to go to Switzerland (91), that 'watering-place world' characterized by cheap amusement in Ralph's opinion (99–100) – and we know from Wharton's travel writing the choice of destinations indicates the difference between travel and tourism. It is Ralph, the poet and traveller, who will not survive in the world of this satirical novel, a victim of the ruthless exploitative business ethos of modern American capitalism, including its marriage market.

In *The Reef* the sedentary wife is contrasted with the younger female lover who is a restless traveller – the narrative begins with delayed departure for France at Dover and a chance meeting between Sophy Viner and George Darrow who will become lovers in transit. At the end of a complex story of indecision, postponement and sexual jealousy, Anna Leath is in Paris looking for Sophy Viner and finds herself in the dingy Hôtel Chicago with Sophy's sister who tells her that, 'Sophy's gone to India ... restless – always was – and she's taken it into her head she'd rather travel' (*The Reef*, 290) – and the novel ends in what Pamela Knights describes as 'the vast pink display of decadence in the modern Hôtel Chicago', another impressionist moment. But this final image is of a world 'without categories or repressions', yet one that offers 'no sense of liberation' for Anna (*Cambridge Introduction*, 89).[50] Clearly, the spatial practices that limit women's sense of being are also signified in the decadent boudoir, or in travelling with the awful Mrs Murrett to overcome restlessness.

The Metaphor of Travel in The Age of Innocence

In *The House of Mirth*, a principal trope is life itself as a journey. In *The Custom of the Country* Ralph, now free from Undine Spragg and seeing the ironies of his situation, reflects on 'the distance he had travelled, the extent to which he had renewed himself' (*CC*, 271). Newbolt Archer in *The Age of Innocence* (1920) acknowledges in the end that he has not travelled 'the distance that the world has travelled' (247) because he could not take any risks, and this left him drifting within the safe zone of his marriage. The trope of 'drifting' has a negative connotation for Wharton, because to drift is to go with the current and not to steer life determinedly towards the fulfilment of desire. As we have seen, she celebrates speed in her motor-flights, and also captures images of modern transport like the speeding train in *The House of Mirth*. The novel begins at Grand Central Station where we see Lily Bart for the first time through Selden's eyes, 'a figure to arrest even the suburban traveller rushing to his last train' (*HM*, 5); and the trope of the

---

[49]   This reads like Ruskin (1856) on travel: 'hence, to any person who has all his senses about him, a quiet walk along no more than ten or twelve miles of road a day, is the most amusing of all travelling; and all travelling becomes dull in exact proportion to its rapidity. Going by railroad I do not consider as travelling at all ...' *Selected Writings* (Everyman), 146–7 note f.

[50]   The decadent indolence described here reminds us of Wharton's reaction to the Moroccan harem discussed above.

speed of life extends this image of modernity into life in the metropolis. Later in the novel we read: 'Lily had the odd sense of having been caught up into the crowd as carelessly as a passenger is gathered in by an express train.' The text continues: 'The train, meanwhile, had scarcely slackened speed – life whizzed on with a deafening rattle and roar' (227). What is interesting in this extension of speed into a trope for life itself is that an ambivalence to modernity emerges, and it is almost as if Wharton is siding with the awful Mrs Peniston for whom 'the modern fastness appeared synonymous with immorality' (125). Moreover, we know from the travel writing and elsewhere in the fiction that Wharton's preferences are for the quiet country residence, where at best harmony is achieved between house, garden and the surrounding landscape (her description of the classic Italian villa) – motor-flights notwithstanding. American modernity is seen at its most tasteless, by contrast, in 'the world of the fashionable New York Hotel – a world over-heated, over-upholstered, and over-fitted with mechanical appliances for the gratification of fantastic requirements, while the comforts of the civilized life were as unattainable as in a desert' (266). Wharton – like the other writers in this study – extends the motif of the mechanical into modern life as 'the ever-revolving wheels of the great social machine', which reduces people to being dull and insignificant (256). Lily Bart expresses her own frustration at being a victim of this world: 'I was just a screw or a cog in the great machine I called life ... What can one do when one finds out that one only fits into one hole?' (300). Finally, we are left with the ultra-modernist image of the men and women she knew 'like atoms whirling away from each other in some wild centrifugal dance' (311) – a trope that looks forward to the excesses of Vorticism (1914) just like the dehumanizing machine will return in Fritz Lang's seminal modernist film *Metropolis* (1926). Wharton echoes a common critique of urban modernity at the time. Georg Simmel's paper 'The Metropolis and Mental Life' (1903) describes the modern individual in the city as 'reduced to a negligible quality', becoming 'a single cog as over against the vast overwhelming organization of things and forces' (rept. in Kolocotroni, et al., eds, 59).[51]

In Edith Wharton's writing to 'travel' is to see the world differently, and to escape from the mundane, material existence of society to 'the republic of the spirit' (Banta, Introduction to *HM*, viii). Travelling to Europe, or returning from Europe, should enable critical perspectives that serve to challenge the symbolic order that circumscribes gender – and as we have seen, most of her leisure-class travellers fail in these terms. In Wharton's novel *The Age of Innocence*, Ellen Olenska has been transformed by marriage to a Polish Count and once back in New York is a disruptive presence because 'completely Europeanised': 'I'm afraid Ellen's ideas are not at all like ours', exclaims Mrs Welland (102);[52] and it is the old New Yorker generation who are most condemning of difference, whether it is in dress code or the state of being separated from the husband when staying married

---

[51]   Ruskin already wrote about the process of the dehumanization of labour in modern capitalism, as men become like 'cog-wheels' as the 'operative' is degraded 'into a machine'. *Selected Writings* (Everyman), 196–7; or in the Oxford World's Classics edition, 40–42.

[52]   Subsequent page references abbreviated as *AI* in text.

is the destiny of all women – in this small world such a woman as the Countess Olenska is perceived as a threat to the kinship system because she is a floating signifier, an object of desire outside the rules of arranged marriages. Indeed, she is constructed as a disruptive force by the ruling New York Matriarchy;[53] and constructed as a romantic object of desire by the young Newland Archer whose conventionality is thrown into disarray by her. We only fully understand the force of his misrecognition retrospectively in the last chapter (set about 26 years later). For here we see that although he, as a young man, is critical of his wife, May, for not being interested in travel,[54] it is he who cannot take the metaphorical journey to a new state of being that would be needed to spend his life with Ellen. By the end of the novel Archer has not travelled 'the distance that the world has travelled' (*AI*, 247) because he remains within the safe zone of 'all his inherited ideas about marriage' (136), even when at first the prospect of marriage seemed to him not 'the safe anchorage he had been taught to think, but a voyage on unchartered seas'. It is the Countess Olenska who 'had stirred up old settled convictions and set them drifting dangerously through his mind' (30). The trope of 'drifting' once again signifies the extent of the disturbance to the otherwise stable and predictable life: Archer is driven to take risks and to play the very game of adultery that he publicly denounces (213–14). The brief encounter with the love object on a secret assignation is the only journey he will go on with her: on the paddle boat which his desire-driven imaginary will read as if 'they were starting on some long voyage from which they might never return' (166) – a wish-fulfilling fantasy spiced by the fear of 'unexpected encounters' that would give them away to public scandal (167). The whole scene, like much of the novel, is focalized through his romantic imaginary and the melodrama is an ironic commentary by the author on his delusional state. Travel for Archer is escape by eloping with Ellen; travel is for him the promise of illicit sex: 'In that train he intended to join her, and travel with her to Washington, or as much farther as she was willing to go. His own fancy inclined to Japan. At any rate she would understand at once that, wherever she went, he was going' (213). He can only wonder at Ellen's state of mind. Wharton, though, will make it quite clear that she can only lose, like all women in her fiction who dare to break the rules. The only choice left to her is to leave by herself, and leave Archer to his marriage and the child that May is expecting. He will, though, have a final chance to decide for Ellen when he goes with his son to Paris, years later and after May has died and the children are grown up. But at the end we are told that 'Archer had lost the habit of travel' (246); and this statement takes on greater significance when once arrived at Ellen's apartment he cannot take the last step and meet her: 'Archer remained motionless, gazing at the upper windows as if the end of their pilgrimage had been attained.' (253) After the long absence of

---

[53] 'The ability to silence dissent is a communal power, and New York silences whatever it designates "unpleasant": scandal, authentic suffering, anything "foreign", any harbinger of change ... Like silencing, ignoring is not the absence of actions or speech but their active suppression and denial' (Elby, 96–7).

[54] '... in reality travelling interested her even less than he had expected' (*AI*, 136).

the intervening years, and being 'enclosed ... in the warm shelter of habit' (225), he admits to himself that his desire belongs only in the realm of the imaginary: sitting on a bench, 'he tried to see the persons already in the room ... "It's more real to me here than if I went up," he suddenly heard himself say; and the fear lest that last shadow of reality should lose its edge kept him rooted to his seat as the minutes succeeded each other' (254).

By the end of the novel Archer is the same age as the author; but he has not taken the journey she has from the conventional life of old New York to the expatriate and richer life in Paris; and it is as if Wharton has the shutters closed on her male protagonist, left outside because he could never make the move that his younger self seemed to desire – and because he finally realizes, as Stephen Orgel puts it, 'the degree to which he has been managed throughout, not only by May, but by the family as a whole' (xvii). I would add that he has also been 'managed' by Ellen (she is always in control of their encounters, and seems to have been waiting for him at the end) and of course by the author who carefully structures the course of his desire by implicitly allowing us to see his self-delusion and inaction. Newland Archer's limitations, then, are marked by his not being able to travel both literally and figuratively.[55]

In *The Age of Innocence* Wharton uses the idea of travel – after her own experience of travel and travel writing – as a metaphor to frame the desires and delusions of Newland Archer for whom marriage at first seems 'a voyage on the unchartered seas' (30), and for whom travel is a metaphor for the ability to break away from the safety and the limits of the conventional life, that 'awfully safe place' (52) – a recurrent theme in Wharton's fiction, and one derived from her own life. Yet, the end of Wharton's journey like that of her character, Ellen Olenska, is to find a place to settle down, to live the life that she cannot live in New York. But Paris after the war becomes more and more like New York as modernity changes the pace and style of life – and this change is represented in the last chapter of *The Age of Innocence*. Wharton captures modernity in a modernist trope: 'Nothing could more clearly give the measure of the distance that the world had travelled. People nowadays were too busy – busy with reforms and "movements"', with fads and fetishes and frivolities – to bother much about their neighbours. And of what account was anybody's past, in the huge kaleidoscope where all the social atoms spun around the same plane' (247–8). In a novel once again written, like *House of Mirth* and *The Custom of the Country* before it, under the sign of Darwin and the new interest in ethnology and anthropology – the sciences of travel in the imperial age which enable the study of the customs and rites of cultures, even of the New York smart set[56] – it is indeed interesting that Wharton chooses to end it under the sign of the new physics ('where all the social atoms spun around the same plane').

---

[55]   Not being able to travel abroad is also a limitation for Rickie Elliot in Forster's *The Longest Journey*, as we saw in Chapter 2.

[56]   'In reality they all lived in a kind of hieroglyphic world, where the real thing was never said or done or even thought, but only represented by a set of arbitrary signs ... quite as, in the books on Primitive Man that people of advanced culture were beginning to read, the savage bride is dragged with shrieks from her parents' tent' (*AI*, 32).

These may be marked as Archer's thoughts, who now feels 'shy, old-fashioned, inadequate' (*AI*, 249), but they also belong to Wharton's ambivalence about modernity – an ambivalence that will have her move out of the metropolis and into the countryside while enjoying the speed of modern technology: the car, and the long-distance phone call, 'electric lighting and five-day Atlantic voyages' (245).[57]

Conclusion

In *The Age of Innocence* Wharton, living in France since 1910, looks back from the aftermath of the Great War to the time of her parents' generation in Old New York of the 1870s, and the sense of loss is a common one after 'death had undone so many' – there is some similarity here with Virginia Woolf's elegy to her parents in *To the Lighthouse* (1927). But Wharton's ending the novel in the early twentieth century gives us a strong sense of history, and of 'the pressures of change' (Pamela Knights, 'Forms of Disembodiment', 23). I suggest that she was taking stock, seeing how far she had travelled; and even when she also, like Newland Archer, may not have travelled the distance that the world had travelled, she had come a long way as a writer and expatriate securing a world of letters and the ideal place for her to write. Hermione Lee tells us: 'Between 1897 and 1937 Wharton published at least one book almost every year of her life … In almost every one of them there is a cultural comparison or conflict, a journey or displacement, a sharp eye cast across national characteristics' (8).

As we have seen in this chapter, travel was the guiding principle in Wharton's life and a key structure in her narrative fiction; and, as in the other chapters of this study, travel and storytelling are closely connected: there are travellers' stories and stories of travel. However, Wharton uses the metaphor of travel to explain reading and writing too. She once wrote that the 'mechanical reader' is 'like a tourist who drives from one "sight" to another without looking at anything that is not set down in Baedeker' ('The Vice of Reading' [1903], rept. in Wegener, *Uncollected*, 101). Real reading, Wharton is saying, is a journey of discovery. In her essay on 'The Great American Novel' Wharton argued that the tendency in American literature had been towards an inward-looking provincialism, developing 'in inverse ratio to the growth of modern travelling facilities'. Yet, a migratory folk by origin and history, Americans, 'have never been sedentary except when it was difficult to get about. Old New York and old New England (owing to this difficulty) sat chiefly at home …'; but 'in those steamless and wireless days Poe was letting his fiery fancy range over all heaven and earth, Melville was situating his tales in the tropics, and Hawthorne colouring his with the prismatic hues of a largely imaginary historic past' (Wegener, *Uncollected*, 156). Modernity has made Americans mobile and

---

[57] Wharton wrote to Bernard Berenson in 1920: 'Paris is simply awful – a kind of continuous earth-quake of motor-busses, trams, lorries, taxis & other howling & swooping & colliding engines, with hundreds & thousands of US citizens rushing about in them & tumbling out of them at one's door' (cit. in Lee, 503).

global and the American abroad has become the topic of novels – as Wharton
and James have demonstrated: 'It is not intended to suggest that the wandering
or expatriate American is the only fit theme for fiction, but that he is peculiarly
typical for modern America'; and 'the nomadic habits of modern life' (Wegener,
Uncollected, 157) have expanded the field of writing to include the attempts to
understand foreign cultures, which for Wharton as for James means Europe and
largely France and Italy.

It is important, though, to notice that travel is a metaphor for states of being
as Edith Wharton, taking herself as exemplary, judges the limits of women (and
men) – in the drawing room or the harem – by whether they are able to travel
and to encounter the cultural other. 'The passive daughters of Morocco' (*In
Morocco*, 158) are only different in kind to the New York women of her novels
waiting to be married off to wealth or already 'suffocating in unsatisfactory
marriages' (Banta, 'Wharton's Women' in Singley, 70). Travel writing is a form of
self-discovery for Wharton, as she writes her way out of the world represented in
her fiction – the world in which she grew up.[58]

Place also serves the recurrent theme of gender. The house or rooms and
interiors generally are often forms of entrapment for Wharton's women, just as the
public space limits their mobility and their sense of being in the sight of the strict
gaze of the conventional. Dress codes and fashion are also forms of entrapment for
the female body, not just in their design but as part of a culture of public display for
a class of women for whom marriage is their exclusive destiny. Merish argues that
the commodification of the feminine in Wharton's writing is 'depicted as endemic
to modernity' (339). In this respect, Social Darwinism is expressed in the generic
principles of literary naturalism. Characters have to struggle with, or succumb
to the forces of determinism: the pressures of family and social conformity are
widespread – and not just for the female characters as the case of Newland Archer
demonstrates. Fashion is another form of determinate pressure; Lily Bart and
Undine Spragg have large bills for their Parisian dresses. The emergent consumer
culture creates a new desire, the desire for commodities – and one reading of
both Lily and Undine is that their desire is displaced onto objects of consumption
rendering them less interested in sexual relations; this is complicated by their
being themselves objects of male desire or female envy.

In *The House of Mirth* Lily Bart sums up Wharton's critique of the state
of women in contemporary New York: 'What a miserable thing it is to be a
woman' (8). The novel represents the very reason for Wharton's need to travel.
Lawrence Selden asks Lily Bart, 'but the being tied down: the routine – don't you
ever want to get away, to see new places and people?' (13) – a routine described as
an entrapment where a woman is 'subdued to the conventions of the drawing-room'
(14). Marriage is destiny for the daughters of this society; marrying for money is
'to soar into that empyrean of security where creditors cannot penetrate' (49) – the

---

[58] Schriber's argument in 'Edith Wharton and Travel Writing as Self-Discovery', 257–67.

novel playing out these propositions into a modern, post-Darwinian ironic version of the novel of manners.

Wharton was critical of modern sexuality because, instead of liberating women at last from being objects of exchange in the marriage market place, it commodified them even more into misdirected objects of desire without passion and genuine emancipation. She preferred the freedoms of the New Woman without the sexual proclivities and the promiscuity of the 'flapper'.[59] The trapped women in her fiction are not much better off than the Moroccan women she sees in the harem: passive, languid, and apathetic, these are women whose femininity is caged (*In Morocco*, 139) as they live in a 'stagnant domesticity' with an 'atmosphere of sensuality without seduction' (152–3).[60] Moreover, like Forster, Lawrence and James, Wharton's critique of gender and sexuality spills over into the form of the novel by undermining the closure of the conventional marriage plot, and thus questioning the domestic destiny of women.

I have discussed the distinction she draws in her travel writing between tourism and travel; and this she shares with the other writers in this study. The first Americans abroad, by necessity, were from the leisure class, and as we have seen in this chapter Wharton's satires are focused on their limitations – often defined as their lack of culture. Wharton also belonged to this class, and although she is unapologetic about the narrow class limits of her writing, she is quite clear about the responsibility of the class: that it should use its means to transmute 'wealth into beauty' to maintain what she calls 'the real culture' ('The Great American Novel' in Wegener, *Uncollected*, 156). Thus the leisure class should be the keepers of the culture – and her fiction presents us with many examples of characters from this class who are, in these terms, irresponsible. Moreover, when we read the fiction through the travel writing we soon become aware of the importance of the aesthetic as an ultimate and transcendent value. The ideology of the aesthetic promoted in her travel writing is a deeply conservative stance that is constantly being undermined in her fiction by those characters who lack the required values, but who are implicitly judged for their lack of taste even in the places they choose to visit abroad. In Eagleton's words, moral imperatives 'infiltrate the very textures of lived experience as tact or know-how, intuitive good sense or inbred decorum' (*The Ideology of the Aesthetic*, 41). In her fiction such manners are also used for repressive purposes. Moreover, art has been commodified by the marketplace and landscape by tourism. If for Wharton the harmony in art or nature is a model for social harmony, for civilization itself, then classical Culture is the highest form of civilization.

As this chapter has argued, place in Wharton's travel writing, and in her fiction – whether in North Africa, Europe or America – is not so much geographic as 'sites

---

[59]   The flapper as 'the figure of misdirected or wanton passion' is the early twentieth-century version of the Victorian female hysteric. See Dale M. Bauer, 'Wharton's "Others"', 138.

[60]   The critique of the harem also resorts to the orientalist lexicon that we see elsewhere in the travel book on Morocco, a key signifier being: 'indolent' (36, 123, 135 and 150).

of contrasting aesthetic value' (Bentley, 163). The aesthetic takes precedence over the psychological, the sexual or the political. Indeed, characters are implicitly judged by their art knowledge: Undine Spragg is the most philistine; Elmer Moffatt given his capitalist credentials surprisingly becomes a major art collector with an expert sense; and Newland Archer shares his art education with the author priding himself 'on his knowledge of Italian art' having read Ruskin, Symonds and 'a wonderful new volume called "The Renaissance" by Walter Pater' (*AI*, 49).[61]

A sign of civilized ways is the Opera House, which, like the secular university, chamber music and widespread literacy would enable a high literary culture. The Western European idea of 'Culture' has dominated what constitutes a minority elite culture and what being civilized means since the Enlightenment – individual or institutional interest in ethnic cultures notwithstanding. However, in *The House of Mirth*, *The Age of Innocence* and other novels, the Opera House is the location of social distinction and ritual where the ruling classes are on display; Wharton observes the ceremony like an ethnographic study of the rites of the tribe. Framed in a modernist irony, she shows us that it is the occasion of being seen at the opera that takes precedence over the art of opera itself.

Despite her well-known rejection of experimental modernism, Edith Wharton occupies the ground between realism and modernism. It is a transitional space of writing where naturalism enables a determinist narrative structure; where restrictive character point of view or free indirect discourse enable a limited narrative perspective and an implicit irony; and where the problems of the human subject combined with a questioning of the real and a critique of modernity all signal a set of modernist concerns shared with other writers at the time; while all the while working within the long tradition of the novel of manners and the ambient social conditions of the characters fundamental to nineteenth-century realism. Like T.S. Eliot, Wharton firmly believed in neo-classical aesthetic values, in the need for stable structures as a bulwark against the disintegration of culture, as we see at best in the classical harmony of the Italian villa, its gardens and surrounding landscape. And yet, like other writers and artists, she lived a cultured life in Paris with, as Pamela Knights argues 'its possibilities of escape from the constraints and hypocrisy of nineteenth-century polite society' (*Cambridge Introduction*, 27).

Nancy Bentley writes of Wharton's contrary impulses of the nomadic and the sedentary, impulses she plays out in her fiction too. An 'incessant traveller' who designed gardens and interiors and sought 'reflective stillness', for whom 'local motor-flights and transatlantic travel were fundamental conditions of living ... Her taste for speed and travel on the one hand, and the rooted critical focus she achieved in her writing on the other' (Bentley, 147). Herein lies a basic contradiction in Wharton: she is anti-modernist in aesthetics, architecture and the built environment; yet an enthusiast for modernity when it comes in the form of modern transport, technology, speed and 'the romance of the motor car' (cit. by Benstock in Singley, *A Historical Guide*, 36).[62] As Singley argues, Wharton

---

[61]   Pater's book was first published in 1873.

[62]   See *The Reef*, 100–101, for an example of the 'enjoyment' of the speeding car.

'wrote with profound ambivalence about the accelerating speed of cultural change in the twentieth century, fascinated by what technology could accomplish, alarmed at what it might destroy'.[63] Yet, as I hope to have shown in this chapter, travel and place are fundamental to the stories she tells and the production of a critique that, like Henry James, problematizes American cultural identity as a crisis of modernity.

---

[63]   'Race, Culture, Nation', 41.

Conclusion

What insights, then, has this study yielded on travel, modernism and modernity? First and foremost the detailed study of the travel writing and fiction of Conrad, Forster, Lawrence, James and Wharton – as broadly representative of English and American writing of the period – has demonstrated that travel and travel writing had a significant impact on literary modernism. Furthermore, modernism transformed travel writing in formal and thematic ways, because of the emergent changes to ways of seeing and representation, of the consciousness of mobility, of difference and otherness and of the limits of Eurocentricism. My study has shown that the metaphor of travel and the structure of the journey and the insistence of topography have significant presence in late realism and early modernism – in the travel fiction of the selected writers. Moreover, even as fiction and travel writing continue to deploy archetypal codes of narratives as journeys and archetypal forms of storytelling like the odyssey, quest and pilgrimage, the selected writers sometimes subject the archetypes – like the codes of conventional realism – to a modernist deconstruction.[1]

It is as if the novel in the modernist period has returned to its origins in the eighteenth century with travel as its founding paradigm.[2] The English tradition of travel fiction begins with *Robinson Crusoe* (1719), establishing the narrative archetype of shipwreck and survival for a travel-curious public; and *Gulliver's Travels* (1726), a more fanciful invention to satirize the absurdities at home. Fielding, Sterne and Smollett turned the novel into a picaresque romp in and around England. But, as Peter Whitfield claims, the Grand Tour, the principal form of travel in the period, did not produce serious fiction: 'In the world of English narrative realism, it is perhaps surprising that a full-length novel built around the Grand Tour did not emerge from the picaresque school of Fielding, Smollett and company.' By the 1790s the Gothic novel did use foreign settings, but only to reinforce the common belief that abroad was the place for immorality, evil and decadence (Whitfield, 178–9). The belief that abroad is the location of immorality has had a long afterlife, as we saw in Forster's Italian fiction and James's stories set in Italy and France. The nineteenth century saw an explosion of travel writing to correspond with the new scientific interests, archaeology, and imperialism. But despite Kipling's Indian fiction, it was Conrad 'who introduced travel as a symbol or metaphor of shifting identity into the English novel' (Whitfield, 240).

---

[1]   A view supported by Jameson's recent study of realism: 'when the realistic novel begins to discover (or, if you prefer, to construct) altogether new kinds of subjective experiences ... demystification finds itself transformed into defamiliarization and the renewal of perception, a more modernist impulse ...' (*The Antinomies of Realism*, 4–5).

[2]   Alexandra Peat writes that the 'English novelistic tradition ... has always been intertwined with the tropes of travel' (21).

And it is here in Conrad's writing that the difference first emerges between modernist travel writing and modernist travel fiction, and the work of the eighteenth-century predecessors.

The return to the metaphor of travel has historical reasons. The literary modernists were travellers and expatriates, mobile in fact and in imagination, whose crossing of frontiers and encounters with cultural difference lead to the widespread questioning of cultural superiority. Moreover, the new consciousness of 'cultural heterogeneity' (Carr, 74) manifests itself primarily in a subjective response to place and the other, just as the old certainties of the subject and the real were becoming problematic – registered as diversely in Conradian impressionism and Jamesian point of view. As we have seen in this study, travel writing and fiction have shared concerns. Indeed, Paul Bowles – a late American modernist – insisted on the need for the travel writer to have the skills of the novelist: 'It takes a writer with a gift for describing a situation to do this well, which is perhaps the reason why many of the travel books that remain in the memory have been produced by writers expert at the fashioning of novels' (*Travels: Collected Writings*, 240). For Henry James, travel itself was the quest for story, what he called 'the story-seeker's journey' – foreign locations and symbolic topographies, the challenge of otherness, the testing of received views: 'There are places whose very aspect is a story or a song' (*English Hours*, 91). Novelists used travel writing as a form to express these concerns: the anxiety about modernity, whether as mass tourism and the superficiality of the tourist gaze or the commodifications of place, or popular culture, all signifying a loss of value. Even when 'anti-touristic rhetoric' had been a feature of travel writing since at least the late eighteenth century, according to Carl Thompson (*Travel Writing*, 122–3), for the modernists more was at stake. In Helen Carr's words: 'Such dismay at the democratization of travel was widely shared among travel writers, many of whom showed the same suspicion of popular travel that modernists exhibited towards popular culture in general' (79).

The travel fiction of the selected writers, as we have seen in some detail, has focussed on the English or American abroad, raising questions about cultural superiority and the ability to respond positively to the encounter with otherness, even when the limitations of such encounters are preconditioned by narrow class allegiances and gender conventions back home. The travelling modernists were of course conscious of such difficulties as they experienced them themselves. Learning lessons from travel becomes an index of character in their fiction. Travel, while being enabled by modern transport technology and more open borders, seems to have encouraged a critical attitude to modernity understood as Progress, an attitude already emergent in the late nineteenth century.[3] Indeed, the newer ethnology encouraged questions to be posed about national cultural identity, cultural norms and cultural values. Yet it appears that, despite their openness to other cultures, Conrad, Forster, Lawrence, James and Wharton never quite abandoned the idea that the origin and cradle of civilization is the Mediterranean because they all, in

---

[3] 'Possibly the most significant contribution of travel literature at the turn of the century was the discovery of the futility of the idea of progress' (Elsner and Rubiés, 54).

one way or another, look to the past – nostalgically or heuristically – as a bulwark against the perceived depredations of modernity: simply put, the cultures and civilizations of the past are valued over and above the present. Moreover, this attitude is encouraged by travel and expressed in the details of travel writing – the architectural monuments, archaeological sites, and the ancient spirit of place. To reiterate Hutchings: 'seeking a particular place which embodies the past, as a retreat from the present … now presents travel across time, reminding us of the early modern relation between nostalgia as homesickness and travel' (217).

A recurrent trope of travel writing – and one seen in the writers discussed in this study – is the glimpse of the object on the point of its disappearance. Claude Lévi-Strauss wrote: 'I wished I had lived in the days of *real* journeys, when it was still possible to see the full splendour of a spectacle that had not yet been blighted, polluted and spoilt.' He wondered, 'when was the best time to see India?' He comes to the conclusion shared by so many travellers that 'a modern traveller' is 'chasing after the vestiges of a vanished reality' (*Tristes Tropiques*, qtd by Elsner and Rubiés, 6). This attitude to travel has had a long life. Paul Bowles was probably one of the last American writers to see the parts of Morocco still untouched by mass tourism.[4] In the early 1950s he notices that the old city (Medina) of Fez is 'virtually unchanged' (39), and that there are 'whole regions' of Morocco 'unseen by tourists' (68). However, by 1954, Tangier is spoilt by 'motor traffic' (92), and in 1956 Bowles notices that young Moslem men are now wearing 'western dress – blue jeans mostly' (145), as modernity is displacing tradition (304). As a counterweight Bowles travels around the remote regions recording the folk music before it too becomes commodified by the tourist industry (271ff.). And in 1991 Bowles concludes that Tangier – where he lived for many years – is 'a place for tourists' (464).

As this study has argued throughout, the drive to see the real and the preconditions of the traveller or tourist's mindset also affect the attitudes to the cultural realities and the question of cultural difference of the foreign places. To reiterate Homi K. Bhabha's words: 'The subject of the discourse of cultural difference … is constituted through the locus of the Other which suggests both that the object of identification is ambivalent, and, more significantly, that the agency of identification is never pure or holistic but always constituted in a process of substitution, displacement or projection' (*The Location of Culture*, 162). Substitution and displacement are the actions of metaphor and metonymy, the figures of symptom and desire. Thus metonymies of travel map desire, and landscapes are symptomatic locations of the uncanny, or spiritual loss, or a deep sense of belonging. The problem of the real addressed in so many ways in literary modernism is central to all the writers in this study – in travel writing and fiction – and it was still a problem for Paul Bowles, and continues to be so today.[5]

---

    4   *Travels: Collected Writings*. Page references in text.

    5   The problem of the real in the undecided distinction between travel and tourism does not, though, end with Bowles. In a recent novel we read about the problems of trying not to be a tourist: 'At first I was unaware of the presence in Madrid of these subtler, quieter Americans, but as I became one, I began to perceive their numbers … that nothing was

Bearing witness to a vanishing world is an experience common to all the writers of this study – in vestiges of traditional customs and the ruins of ancient places and landscapes, abroad or at home. Forster preferred Classical Alexandria to the modern city, as wonder of the ancient world; Lawrence mythologized the landscapes of southern Italy and Sardinia; James and Wharton preferred Renaissance Italy and classical ruins where stones talk – *saxa loquuntur*. Thinking about the newly excavated site of Troy, Freud wrote: 'the ruined walls are part of the ramparts of a treasure house; the fragments of columns can be filled out into a temple ... [yielding] undreamed-of information about the events of the remote past, to commemorate which these monuments were built' ('The Aetiology of Hysteria' (1896), cit. in Simmons, 155). And Wharton wrote: 'How much more eloquent these tottering stones tell their story' (*Wharton Abroad*, 114). Modern Italy, like New York, for Henry James had become vulgar and tasteless; Italy's Golden Age was 300 years before, and now its relics were being destroyed by modern developments and mass tourism, and the disappointment would be great for him and other Americans on the cultural pilgrimage to Europe (*Italian Hours*, 102).[6]

James's aesthetic preference for the past is expressed in nostalgia for the taste and manners that have disappeared. The civilizations of the past are tied up with the idea of being civilized for James, as well as Forster and Wharton. Like Goethe before him the place that contains the history of Culture is Rome, where, as Bakhtin wrote (in his discussion of Goethe's *Italian Journey*), 'terrestrial space and human history are inseparable from one another'. Rome, for Goethe – and for James too – is that 'great chronotope of *human* history', as David Buchanan puts it (156–7). James had no desire to travel to far-off exotic places because he wanted to be only where fully developed 'moral' culture pertained. Thus he never went to the Far East or the South Pacific because, as Fred Kaplan explains, they 'seemed to him superfluous, experiences without a moral core, useless to him as a writer of fiction' (400). For James the European places draw attention to the lack of history and literature of America: 'it takes a great deal of history to produce a little literature' (cit. by Sears, introduction to *The American Scene*, xvii). For Lawrence, though, it is not just older civilizations in the remote regions of Europe but also in the 'savage' landscapes of New Mexico that contain spiritual truths the so-called advanced cultures have forgotten. Conrad, for his part, believed in older integrities that have given way to an inner emptiness, a darkness and savagery in the heart of the human subject – a diagnosis developed later by Freud in *Civilization and its Discontents* (1930). Reflecting on the slaughter of the Great War and the continual threat of further conflict between the European nations – those indeed that stand for the highest form of Civilization – Freud wrote that because of the 'existence

---

more American, whatever that means, than fleeing the American, whatever that means, and their soft version of self-imposed exile was just another of late empire's packaged tours' (Lerner, 48–9).

[6]   Kasia Boddy writes: 'Many American travellers knew exactly what they were looking for [in Europe], based on the books they had read and the paintings they had seen, and what they wanted was for reality to match up' (Elsner and Rubiés, 239).

of this inclination to aggression ... civilized society is perpetually threatened with disintegration' (*Civilization and its Discontents*, 49). For Conrad the 'devastation' of Western imperialism was visible in Africa; for Forster the failures of the British administration in India had pathological dimensions. The high price paid for civilization, Freud argued, is the demand on repression of the sexual drives which, if not sublimated into higher activities – science or the arts for example – can result in a destructive energy (*Civilization and its Discontents*, 34–5).

The new travel consciousness, therefore, lead to a growing discontent with the apparent superiority of Western Civilization, itself tied in with the awareness of the depredatory effects of modernity. There were two reactions. First, there is the example of Lawrence's primitivism – also seen in his namesake T.E. Lawrence in his romanticizing the Arabian desert – which Whitfield describes as 'pursuing a personal quest away from Englishness towards something that had been lost, something more elemental and physical ... deliberately seeking a level of being untainted by civilization, a primitive energy which he felt was the key to the regeneration of western man, now paralysed, corrupted and alienated from his true being' (Whitfield, 252). And I would add to this sense of primal innocence Conrad's nostalgia for the heroic adventure of Empire stories with their male bonding and uncomplicated storytelling, now displaced by the ironies of modernism. Freud wrote that if 'what we call our civilization is largely responsible for our misery' then one 'astonishing' contention is that 'we should be much happier if we gave it up and returned to primitive conditions' (*Civilization and its Discontents*, 23). Freud thought it was a mistake to believe that primitive peoples and races lead a simple and happy life, and one that was no longer attainable for the superior civilization of Europeans. This view first emerged from the early European voyages of discovery (*Civilization and its Discontents*, 24). The second extreme reaction is to reassert the importance of the classical heritage of European civilization as a bulwark against modernity or primitivism[7] – thus creating a tension in the attitudes of the writers studied. For Henry James and Edith Wharton what is wrong with America is that it is simply not Europe; it lacks Culture, a state exacerbated by modernity in the forms of the new business ethos and the superficial wants of the wealthy leisure class.[8] Once settled in England, James hoped to save western culture from Americanization. Wharton, for her part, called upon wealthy Americans to continue to be the keepers of high culture as responsible patrons, despite the

---

[7]   Freud also defined the highest state of Civilization as its High Cultural and scientific achievements as well its religious systems (31); but also that the 'aesthetic attitude' can be a compensation for the discontents of modern civilization (19).

[8]   Interestingly, Perry Anderson has recently argued that the comparison of America and Europe has been maintained by what he calls the 'European Ideology': 'The self-satisfaction of Europe's elites, and their publicists, has become such that the Union is now widely presented as a paragon for the rest of the world ... the belief, on which much of the current ideology is founded, [is] that within the Atlantic ecumene Europe embodies a higher set of values than the United States, and plays a more inspiring role in the world' (*The New Old World*, xv).

pressures of materialism and the spread of mass culture: 'Leisure, itself a creation of wealth, is incessantly engaged in transmuting wealth into beauty by secreting the surplus energy which flowers in great architecture, great painting, and great literature. Only in the atmosphere thus engendered floats that impalpable dust of ideas which is the real culture' ('The Great American Novel' in Wegener, 156).

Culture as civilization is mapped on the points of the compass. Europe is itself divided between the North and the South – a symbolic orientation for travel writers since at least Goethe: 'we northerners who spend our lives in a drab and ... uglier country where even reflected light is subdued'. In Venice the lagoon bathed in 'brilliant sunshine' was like 'looking at the latest and best painting of the Venetian school' (*Italian Journey*, 94); and on a second visit to Rome Goethe notices once again the difference between Northern and Southern Europe: 'There is a brilliance and at the same time a subtly graded harmony which one can hardly conceive up in the north' (417). The North is the location of rationalism and strict morality, the South of sensuality – an opposition first experienced as dull greyness giving way to bright sunlight; and its classical origins – Greek or Roman (or for D.H. Lawrence, Etruscan) – as the harmony of mind and body. There is a persistent, romanticized desire in all the writers studied to return to an earlier state of civilization which is idealized as authentic being – whether primitivist and ruralist, or refined and classical – and one that modernity and modern industrialization in particular is destroying by what Lawrence called 'the perfect mechanizing of human life' (*Twilight in Italy*, 136). Henry James wrote of the modern metropolis, New York as the 'infernal machine' preferring Philadelphia where 'organic social relations' still pertained (*The American Scene*, 206–9). Both Lawrence and James resort to the opposition that we see in T.S. Eliot (and Spengler) between the mechanical and the organic to explain the destructive changes brought about by modernity.

Travel needed to be regenerative, whether through the joy of the aesthetic or the celebration of other cultures or simply the relief of being away from the narrow life at home. Going to Italy is the fulfilment of a dream, or a pilgrimage. For Edith Wharton travel is analogous to the medieval pilgrimage, a spiritual quest, where the destination is an object of desire that is the Classical, Renaissance and Baroque archive of European Culture as a cure for modern tastelessness and as confirmation of a liberating sense of identity to counter the social and cultural constrictions she describes in the New York novels. For the sublimation of desire into the aesthetic, as form of artistic enjoyment, gives an order to desire through the classical principles of proportion, symmetry and harmony; and these principles define the process of a deeper knowledge of the object, and what it means to be civilized.

Another version of the importance of the aesthetic, but for quite different ideological purpose, is the prioritizing of modernism in the work of Bloch and Adorno against the insistence on realism by Lukàcs. For example, in challenging Lukàcs's accusation that modernism is the expression of decadence Adorno wrote: 'The great works of modernist literature shatter this appearance of subjectivity by setting the individual in his frailty into context, and by grasping that totality in him of which the individual is but a moment and of which he must needs remain ignorant' ('Reconciliation under Duress', 160–61). Terry Eagleton has claimed that

'It is possible to read his [Adorno's] work as a retreat from the nightmare of history into the aesthetic' (*The Ideology of the Aesthetic*, 360). This tendency of the flight from the present into the aesthetic can also be seen in many writers with much more conservative credentials, like the writers in this study. Yet, it is these very principles that make the category of the aesthetic an ideology: 'the very textures of lived experience as tact or know-how, intuitive good sense or inbred decorum' are moral imperatives (Eagleton, 41). The category of the aesthetic is promoted in Forster, James and Wharton's travel writing and it is a deeply conservative stance which acts as an absent moral centre to judge both the characters in their fiction that lack taste or seem unable to enjoy Italy, and the places that lack aesthetic appeal in the fiction and travel writing.

Clearly, T.S. Eliot spoke for a high culturist position of literary modernism, expressed in 'The Waste Land' and his essays about Tradition and Culture – it is one shared by Forster, James and Wharton; but surprisingly also by Lawrence, who begins and ends his life in the Mediterranean cradle: 'How wonderful it must have been to Ulysses to venture into this Mediterranean and open his eyes to all the loveliness of the tall coasts ... There is something eternally morning-glorious about these lands as they rise from the sea. And it is always the Odyssey which comes back to one as one looks at them' (*D.H. Lawrence and Italy*, 318).

T.S. Eliot represented the widespread *Kulturpessimismus* after the Great War, and one popularized by Oswald Spengler's *Decline of the West* (1918), which sets the tone and the discourse for the growing fear that Western Civilization is in terminal decline. I am thinking of Nordau's *Degeneration* (1895), and its ironic uses in Conrad's *The Secret Agent*; but also Veblen's *The Theory of the Leisure Class* (1899) and Masterman's *The Condition of England* (1909), which influenced Wharton's and Forster's fiction, respectively. However, if Eliot proposes himself as one kind of cultural leader, Lawrence proposes a quite different leadership as a way out of the cultural crisis in his 1920's masculinist fiction. Spengler insisted that the old organic relation between man and the land, the race and the soil was now displaced by a nomadic migratory life and a mechanical sense of being – Lawrence adopted a similar discourse, especially in *Twilight in Italy*; and Forster opposing the effects of the machine age tried to recover some sense of the spiritual even when looking to other cultures and religions to counter the materialism of modernity. Eliot also insisted that the best condition of culture was organic; and he continued to maintain this position in *Notes towards the Definition of Culture* (1948). Of the three conditions of culture, the first one 'is organic (not merely planned, but growing) structure, such as will foster the hereditary transmission of culture within a culture' (*Notes towards the Definition of Culture*, 15). Western culture continues to be in decline, but should 'grow again from the soil' once wrested from the clutches of the 'political demagogues' (*Notes*, 19). Later Eliot insisted that the highest culture is the European Christian culture (*Notes*, 33–4), because it maintains unity at the regional and the pan-European levels – 'a homogenous general culture, associated with the traditions of one religion' (66). For Eliot the tradition of Western art and literature has to be saved at all costs from the barbarous effects of modernity in the forms of mass, popular culture.

Henry James claimed that 'it takes an endless amount of history to make even a little tradition' (*The American Scene*, 127). Eliot was less optimistic about the maintenance of High Culture as the transmission of Civilization in the 1920s. 'The Waste Land' expresses that post-war *Kulturpessimismus* in the images of a dead land where nothing grows – like Lawrence's 'Marne country' or 'city of the dead' of war-ruined Europe in the short story 'The Borderline' – and where poetry is reduced to 'A heap of broken images'; and where Tiresias, the surrogate poetic voice of the classical heritage has 'foresuffered all', the poet declaring at the end that 'These fragments I have shored against my ruin' – all those quotations and allusions to the archive of Western Culture forming 'an ideal order' (Eliot, 'Tradition and the Individual Talent' [1919] in Kermode, ed., 38).[9] That archive is what Eliot called Tradition, and he insists, like Forster, James and Wharton, that the writer is responsible for the cultural heritage: '[T]he historical sense ... compels a man to write not merely with his own generation in his bones, but with a feeling that the whole of the literature of Europe from Homer and within it the whole of the literature of his own country has a simultaneous existence and composes a simultaneous order' ('Tradition and the Individual Talent', 38).

However, despite the insistence on tradition as a bulwark against the depredations of modernity, I think what has emerged from this study of travel, modernism and modernity is a greater ambivalence which manifests itself in what Caren Kaplan claims is a tension between progress and tradition: 'modernisms promote innovation and convention, change and stability. In modernity, cultural change is a given. Social theorists such as Marshall Berman have argued that the moderns oscillate between a wholehearted endorsement of change and a deep desire for stability' (*Questions of Travel*, 35). Modernity as change or emancipation is central to the literary modernists, and the selected writers in this study are representational. They challenge the limits of national cultural identity, repressive public morality and censorship, and what it still meant to be respectable; they stand for at least a partial rejection of the imperial gaze; and also the tourist gaze, despite it belonging to the democratization of travel, and whose alternative – the travel gaze – is beyond most people for financial or educational or class reasons.

For modernist travel writers encounters with foreigners or expatriates tests preconceptions. Travel in the modernist era is subject to the pressure of otherness, which demonstrates the undermining of old certainties and the realization of the differences between the cultures; but also sometimes the partial loss of native identities through processes of hybridization as an effect of the globalizing force of modernity – western cultural and social practices, even clothing and manners; and tourist expectations. Travel should be an occasion for cultural exchange; it can enable the realization of a lack at home – a lack on a number of levels: climate, food, sexuality, class and culture.

However, sometimes the perceived freedoms abroad are projections of desire not matched by the realities of the traditional life there. As the chapters of this study have demonstrated, the real Italy, India or New Mexico is never quite

---

9   Quotations from 'The Waste Land' (1922) from *Collected Poems 1909–1962*.

available to the visitor's gaze, whether tourist, traveller or expatriate – whether in the forms of the literary-gaze or the art-gaze of the educated informed traveller, or the superficialities of the tourist gaze. Thus it is that topographical representations map desire and enable symbolic resonances, and cultural geographies give way to aestheticized or commodified landscapes. The object in the field of the gaze is affected by degrees of misrecognition. In both tourism and travel there is a failed encounter with the real.

For Conrad the limits of reading the world are captured in impressionist descriptions, linking problems of knowledge with the difficulties of getting the story told. For James and Wharton, the aesthetic is compensation for the forms of degeneration caused by modernity itself. In James's writing the interplay of inhibited or unreliable perspectives becomes a complex form of storytelling. In his writing there is a growing sophistication in the use of narrative point of view, a play on what is seen and known in a radicalization of perspective that is the novelistic equivalent to the modernist art experiment from Impressionism to Cubism, while also being the expression of a modern psychology. Furthermore, the kinds of representational issues in the modernist novel are present in modernist travel writing – descriptive codes (realist, mythic, romantic, impressionist or expressionist)[10] and narrative codes (departure and arrival, incident and adventure, quest or pilgrimage, sea-journey, train-journey or political history); newer and complex presentation of consciousness, perspective and identity.

If travel exposes characters' prejudices and limitations, there is a constant reference to society as theatre or play in James and Wharton as forces of inauthenticity. The instabilities of character and point of view are necessarily matched by the indeterminacies and inconclusiveness of endings, as we see in many of the novels discussed in this study. Sometimes endings take the form of a refusal of the closure of the conventional marriage plot; a convention most explicitly questioned by E.M. Forster. This refusal also concerned the newer questions of gender and sexuality: Forster's challenge to the heterosexual imperative,[11] or Wharton's critique of the demands on women in the American leisure class.

As we have seen in the chapters of this study, travel and expatriation has led to a greater sensitivity to place. The rootless and exiled artist is a modernist phenomenon. The travel imaginary draws attention to the ways in which identity is tied to place; and belonging is destabilized by travel, and Diasporas, migration and expatriation. The modern traveller has an ambivalent relationship to his or her roots, seen to different degrees in the selected writers. Moreover, living abroad a different relationship emerges with the home culture which is expressed as loss or nostalgia or even resentment – like Conrad's attitudes to Poland and imperial Russia in, for example, *Under Western Eyes* and *The Secret Agent* as well as his memoirs and letters; and James's and Wharton's persistent critique of America. A tension in the lives and works of the literary modernists is caused by the counter-tendencies of the nomadic and the sedentary. The nomadic modern life was now

---

[10] What Jameson has called the 'scenic impulse' (*The Antinomies of Realism*, 11).

[11] See Furbank, vol. 1, 192.

characterized by restlessness, drifting, wanderlust, exile; the sedentary by places to write and imagined communities like Lawrence's 'Rananim'. Wharton is a classic example of these contrary impulses, and ones she plays out in her fiction too: a determined and incessant traveller, but also a designer of her own gardens and interiors who sought the quiet place to write, indulging in the pleasures of 'motor-flights' and transatlantic crossings while laying down roots in France.[12] It seems that once deracinated, these writers could never return to their prior state of homeliness except in childhood memories. All the writers in this study have left home, by choice or necessity; yet they have continued to be concerned about the state of their home cultures, and have sought surrogate places to settle where they would be free from the restraints of home – Lawrence in Taormina or Kiowa Ranch and James in Lamb House, Rye. Homecomings were always difficult and therefore often brief visits. Forster, however, returned to live in England, to find a place in the countryside surrounded with friends. Yet he felt homeless even in old age in his rooms at Kings.[13]

There is a topographical insistence in all the writers studied in this book. Moreover, the relationship between topos and trope is common to their travel writing and travel fiction, as both share the narrative codes of the journey – the voyage, the quest, the pilgrimage, the ordeal, the encounter with the other and the consequent challenge to received views and entrenched senses of identity. Place is memorial and archival – *lieu de mémoire*; places have stories to tell; and if already represented in art and literature they become the object of literary tourism, and as already well-known cultural formations through archaeology and architectural history – Wharton's reading of Ruskin, Lawrence's reading of Mexican native Indian ritual, Forster acquiring knowledge of Hindu religion. But there is also metaphorical and symbolic formations of space and place that enable the representation of landscape and land, whether the Neo-classical picturesque so attractive to Henry James's topographical descriptions or the Romantic Sublime residual in much of the writing of literary modernism, or the pastoral tradition of prioritizing the country over the city, and the orientalist tendencies in representing the exotic; or the mythic analogies that appropriate a foreign land for a home culture – the Promised Land, Utopia, the Cradle of Civilization. There is also 'psychic topography' or symptomatic landscape, a metonymic displacement of unconscious wishes or fears – like Conrad's African forest or Lawrence's Australian Bush.

Clearly, then, for the modernist travel imaginary, represented by the selected writers, the textualizations of space and place challenge the reductive processes of the tourist guidebook and the preconditions of the tourist gaze. As argued in the conclusion to Chapter 4, realism in the novel and the tourism in travel writing share

---

[12]   Nancy Bentley's point in 'Wharton, Travel and Modernity', 147.

[13]   Furbank tells us in *E.M. Forster: A Life vol. 2* that Forster 'began to consider where he might go, when he left Abinger. His first thought was Stevenage, his childhood home and the place where, if anywhere, he could imagine he had roots' (264). In 1948, now nearly 70, he is 'still obsessed by his "homelessness"' (282). But eventually in 1953 he heeded the advice of friends and 'made a formal renunciation of "homes" and "roots in the land"' (288).

the drive for a semiotics of the typical. The tourist gaze is inferior to the scrutiny of the educated traveller just as modernism prioritizes the figurative and symbolic representation over the programmatic transparencies of an older realism. Both modernist travel writing and the modernist novel deconstruct cultural stereotypes. However, the shared descriptive and narrative codes, as well as the styles and registers sometimes blur the distinction between late realism and modernism, travel writing and travel fiction.

In the face of the newer identity problematic that undermined traditional, stable notions of sexuality and gender, Conrad, Forster, Lawrence and James searched for the places where an older masculinity still existed outside the restrictions of social class and bourgeois morality, and before the advent of feminism. Conrad's nostalgia for the days when travel was an ordeal of manliness is matched by Lawrence's quest for cultures where men were at one with land. In his tour of America Henry James sees the loss of a vigorous masculinity as symptomatic of the white race in general; and the new businessman as an inferior character. Forster wanted an England where men could lead a classless, authentic and uninhibited existence. His solution to the present crisis of repression was mythic: a return to the space of the ancient English Greenwood – a solution not too different from Lawrence's gaily dressed dancing men, modelled on the ancient Etruscan culture which he imagines as 'a vivid, life-accepting people, who must have lived with real fullness ... dancing in their coloured wraps ... dancing and fluting along through the little olive trees, out in the fresh day' (*Etruscan Places* in *D.H. Lawrence and Italy*, 365–6). Lawrence's English woodland in *Lady Chatterley's Lover* reminds us of Forster's Greenwood where once 'it was possible to get lost' (Forster, 'Terminal Note' [1969] to *Maurice*, 221).[14] Both writers have nostalgic closing images of an older yeoman Englishman – whether Mellors at the end of *Lady Chatterley*, or Stephan Wonham at the end of Forster's *The Longest Journey* quietly ploughing the land in the idyllic Wiltshire countryside: a tendency towards a utopian vision to counter the depredations of modernity seen in Lawrence's rainbow spanning the cleansed earth; indeed a conservative reaction to the ever-despised industrialization, and one in a tradition reaching back to the Romantics.

Where memorable female characters are rare in Conrad – with the notable exception of Emilia Gould in *Nostromo* – the several female characters in the fiction of Forster, Lawrence and James enable them to address the issues in what was known by the late nineteenth century as 'the Woman Question'. And where there is a certain sympathy for Isabel Archer in *The Portrait of a Lady*, Lucy Honeychurch in *A Room with a View* and Ursula Brangwen in *The Rainbow*, there is less for the more feminist Gudrun Brangwen in *Women in Love*, and the 'dreaming woman' of Lawrence's early novel, *The Trespasser*; he even imagines the extinction of the new woman in 'The Woman who Rode Away'. Wharton's women are mostly trapped in the narrow world they seek to conquer; when they do

---

[14]   Forster wants a place hidden from the condemning collective gaze, thus avoiding 'the eyes that fix you in a formulated phrase' as T.S. Eliot expressed it in 'The Love Song of J. Alfred Prufrock' (1917).

succeed, as in the case of Undine Spragg in *The Custom of the Country*, the author makes sure we understand the character required for that success – a diagnosis of the new American leisure classes straight out of Veblen.

This is well-known terrain in the study of gender and sexuality in literary modernism and late realism. What my study has done is to shift the focus to travel, so that, whereas the male characters could travel with relative ease the female characters could not always escape their chaperoned journeys. Moreover, the focus on place demonstrates the greater entrapment of women in the domestic sphere and the marriage market place – to the extent that for Wharton the wealthy New York hostess and her daughters are no freer than the women in the Moroccan harem. Wharton's women may share the privileges of their author but not her freedoms; but the male characters themselves are not much freer. Newland Archer in *The Age of Innocence* criticizes his wife for not being interested in travel, yet he cannot take the journey to a new state of being. Indeed, he could not even travel 'the distance that the world has travelled.' Travel for the man means eloping with the lover, a promise of illicit sex. But this remains a male fantasy as he settles into his family life, losing 'the habit of travel'. The metaphor of travel signifies a state of being: life as a journey filled with risks that may bring about change is opposed to life at home without adventure but with the safety of the conventional life, that 'awfully safe place' (*The Age of Innocence*, 52). It is an opposition, shared with the other writers in this study, between the limits of home and the liberation abroad, which for so many artists and writers of the period meant Italy. Being there and being able to respond to the best the place has to offer for the frustrated or repressed American or English protagonists is a measure of character. But even when life's journey is set in England, like in Forster's *The Longest Journey* or Lawrence's *The Rainbow*, there will be a measure of disillusion only relieved by the utopian endings.

For in these travel narratives it appears that to journey abroad is 'to touch the coasts of illusion' as Lawrence put it (*Phoenix*, 343). For Conrad, disillusion is caused by heroic expectations in a sceptical and ironic age. Henry James came to believe that a life in Italy or France would leave him in a vacuum, adopting the trappings of a cultivated foreign life without moral responsibilities, having neither an Italian nor a properly American identity, a situation he sought to avoid by settling in England. In her fiction set in France, Wharton seems not as certain of the superiority of French life as she was in *French Ways and their Meaning*. Forster's gay adventures in India or Egypt taught him the difficulties of leading an authentic life in other cultures. It seems travel does not always result in the transcendence of entrenched attitudes that maintain the gulf between the cultures.

The travel imaginary, even when under a modernist revision, will still contain residual archetypal characteristics. An example that has emerged in this study is the attraction of the exotic and the romanticized description of landscape. All the writers in this study belong to one degree or another to the long tradition of representing the Orient in western art. Whether as a product of colonialism, or the romanticized desire, as Geneviève Lacambre puts it, 'to return to the roots of civilization, to a more authentic life far from the fumes of industrial civilization'

(Preface to *The Orient in Western Art*, 8), the Western fascination with the Orient continues well into the twentieth century; it underpins the traveller's expectations, and the set of descriptive codes that derive from western art, what I have called the 'art gaze'.[15] Notwithstanding their claims for a more reflective, profound and authentic response to other cultures – rethinking the terms of difference and otherness – all the writers in this study sometimes suffer from slippages into tourist cliché and kitsch description, just as they sometimes revert to orientalist and racist comment, and the belief in the superiority of European traditional culture. At a time of cultural crisis – the age of modernism – there is a residual conservative mindset despite the radical cultural critique to which they all contributed, as this study has demonstrated in some detail. Yet, finally, taken together, Conrad, Forster, Lawrence, James and Wharton are representative of the ways in which travel became significant for English and American literary modernism, as paradigm and trope and as fundamental to their attitudes to modernity.

---

[15] *The Orient in Western Art* covers pictorial art from the early Renaissance styles of Christian biblical allegory to the Romantic exotic with its erotic implications to the Post-Impressionist abstract art where colour takes priority over the accurate depiction of the real.

Bibliography

Primary Literature

Allison, Alexander W. et al., *The Norton Anthology of Poetry* (New York and London: W.W. Norton & Co., 1970).

Austen, Jane, *Pride and Prejudice* (London: Everyman Library, 1991. First published 1813).

Bowles, Paul, *Travels: Collected Writings, 1950–93* (London: Sort of Books, 2010).

Conrad, Joseph, *Almayer's Folly* (London: Penguin Modern Classics, 1976. First published 1895).

———, 'Autocracy and War' *The North American Review*, 181/1 (July, 1905), 3–55.

———, *Chance* (Oxford: Oxford World's Classics Edition, 2008. First published 1914).

———, *Heart of Darkness* (London: Penguin Classics, 2000. First published 1901).

———, *Heart of Darkness and Other Tales* (Oxford: Oxford World's Classics Edition, 2008).

———, *Last Essays* (London: Dent, 1963. First published 1928).

———, *Lord Jim* (Oxford: Oxford World's Classics Edition, 2008. First published 1900).

———, *The Mirror of the Sea* in *The Mirror of the Sea and A Personal Record* (Oxford: Oxford University Press, 1988. First published 1906).

———, *The Nigger of the 'Narcissus'* (New York: Norton Critical Edition, 1979. First published 1898).

———, *Nostromo* (New York: Everyman's Library, 1992. First published 1904).

———, *An Outcast of the Islands* (Oxford: Oxford World's Classics edition, 2009. First published 1896).

———, *The Secret Agent* (Oxford: Oxford World's Classics, 2008. First published 1907).

———, *Typhoon and Other Tales* (Oxford: Oxford World's Classics Edition, 2008).

Eliot, T.S., *Collected Poems 1909–1962* (London: Faber and Faber, 1963).

Forster, E.M., *Abinger Harvest and England's Pleasant Land* edited by Elizabeth Heine (London: Andre Deutsch, 1996. First published 1936).

———, *Alexandria: A History and a Guide* and *Pharos and Pharillon* with an introduction by Miriam Allott (London: André Deutsch, 2004. First published 1922 and 1923, respectively).

———, *The Hill of Devi* (New York and London: Harcourt Brace Jovanovich, 1985. First published 1953).

————, *Howards End* with an introduction by David Lodge (London: Penguin Classics, 2000. First published 1910).

————, *The Longest Journey* (London: Penguin Classics, 2006. First published 1907).

————, *Maurice* (London: Penguin Classics, 2000. Written 1913–1914).

————, *A Passage to India* (London: Penguin Classics, 2005. First published 1924).

————, *A Room with a View* edited by Oliver Stallybrass (London: Penguin Classics, 2000. First published 1908).

————, *Selected Stories* edited with an introduction and notes by David Leavitt and Mark Mitchell (London: Penguin Classics, 2001).

————, *Two Cheers for Democracy* (London: Edward Arnold 1972. First published 1951).

————, *Where Angels Fear to Tread* with an introduction by Ruth Padel (London: Penguin Classics, 2007. First published 1905).

Goethe, J.W., *Italian Journey* translated by W.H. Auden and Elizabeth Mayer (London: Penguin Classics, 1970. First published 1788).

James, Henry, *The Ambassadors* with an introduction by Adrian Poole (London: Penguin Classics, 2008. First published 1903).

————, *The American* with an introduction by William Spengemann (London: Penguin Classics, 1986. First published 1879).

————, *The American Scene* with an introduction by John F. Sears (London: Penguin Classics, 1994. First published 1907).

————, *Collected Stories vol. 1* (New York: Everyman's Library Edition, 1999).

————, *Collected Stories vol. 2* selected and introduced by John Bailey (New York: Everyman's Library Edition, 1999).

————, *Collected Travel Writings: The Continent* (New York: The Library of America, 1993).

————, *Collected Travel Writings: Great Britain and America* (New York: The Library of America, 1993).

————, *Daisy Miller* with an introduction by David Lodge (London: Penguin Classics, 2007. First published 1878).

————, *French Poets and Novelists* (Leipzig: Bernhardt Tauchnitz, 1883. Reprinted by Elibron Classics, 2006).

————, *Italian Hours* with an introduction by John Auchard (London: Penguin Classics, 1992. First published 1909).

————, *The Portrait of a Lady* (London: Penguin Classics, 2003. First published 1881).

————, 'Travelling Companions' *Atlantic Monthly* (November 1870), 600–614 and (December, 1870), 684–97.

Lawrence, D.H., *Aaron's Rod* edited by Mara Kalnins with an introduction by Steven Vines (London: Penguin, 1995. First published 1922).

————, *Complete Poems* edited by V. De S. Pinto (London: Penguin, 1993).

————, *D.H. Lawrence and Italy* edited by Simonetta de Filippis, Paul Eggert and Mara Kalnins (London: Penguin, 2007).

————, *England, my England and Other Stories* edited by Bruce Steele (Cambridge: Cambridge University Press, 1990).

————, *Kangaroo* edited by Bruce Steele with an introduction by Macdonald Daly (London: Penguin, 1997. First published 1923).

————, *Lady Chatterley's Lover* (London: Penguin, 1994. First published 1928).

————, *The Lost Girl* with an introduction by Richard Aldington (London: Penguin, 1988. First published 1920).

————, *Mornings in Mexico and Other Essays* edited by Virginia Crosswhite Hyde (Cambridge: Cambridge University Press, 2009).

————, *Mr Noon* edited by Lindeth Vasey (Cambridge: Cambridge University Press, 1984).

————, *Phoenix: The Posthumous Papers of D.H. Lawrence* edited by Edward D. McDonald (London: Heinemann, 1967. First published 1936).

————, *Phoenix II: Uncollected, Unpublished and Other Prose Works* (London: Heinemann, 1968).

————, *The Plumed Serpent* (London: Penguin, 1985. First published 1926).

————, *Psychoanalysis and the Unconscious* (London: Penguin, 1971. First published 1921).

————, *The Rainbow* edited by Mark Kinkead-Weekes with an introduction by Anne Fernihough (London: Penguin, 1995. First published 1915).

————, *Reflections on the Death of a Porcupine and Other Essays* edited by Michael Herbert (Cambridge: Cambridge University Press, 1988).

————, *The Selected Letters of D.H. Lawrence* compiled and edited by James T. Boulton (Cambridge: Cambridge University Press, 1996).

————, *Selected Short Stories* edited by Brian Finney (London: Penguin, 1982).

————, *Sons and Lovers* edited with an introduction and notes by Helen Baron and Carl Baron (London: Penguin, 1994. First published 1913).

————, *Studies in Classic American Literature* (London: Penguin, 1977. First published 1923).

————, *The Symbolic Meaning: The Uncollected Versions of 'Studies in Classic American Literature'* edited by Armin Arnold (New York: Viking, 1964).

————, *The Trespasser* edited by Elizabeth Mansfield with an introduction and notes by John Turner (London: Penguin, 1994. First published 1912).

————, *Twilight in Italy and Other Essays* edited by Paul Eggert with an introduction by Stefania Michelucci (London: Penguin, 1997).

————, *Women in Love* edited by David Farmer, Lindeth Vasey and John Worthen (London: Penguin, 1995. First published 1920).

Lerner, Ben, *Leaving the Atocha Station* (Minneapolis: Coffee House Press, 2011).

Mann, Thomas, 'Death in Venice', in *Death in Venice and Other Stories* translated by David Luke (London: Vintage Classics, 1998), 197–267.

Wharton, Edith, *The Age of Innocence* (Oxford: Oxford World's Classic Edition, 2006. First published 1920).

————, *Collected Stories 1891–1910* (New York: The Library of America, 2001).

————, *The Cruise of the Vanadis* with an introduction by Claudine Lesage (London: Bloomsbury, 2004).

————, *The Custom of the Country* with an introduction by Stephen Orgel (Oxford: Oxford World's Classics, 2008. First published 1913).

————, *Edith Wharton Abroad: Selected Travel Writings, 1888–1920* edited by Sarah Bird Wright (New York: St Martin's Griffin, 1996).

————, *The House of Mirth* edited and introduced by Martha Banta (Oxford and New York: Oxford University Press World's Classics, 1999. First published 1905).

————, *The House of Mirth* edited and introduced by Pamela Knights (London and New York: Everyman's Library edition, 1991).

————, *In Morocco* (London and New York: I.B. Taurus, 2006. First published 1920).

————, *Madame de Treymes: Four Short Novels* (London: Virago Press, 2006).

————, *The Reef* (Oxford: Oxford World Classics, 1998. First published 1912).

————, *The Uncollected Critical Writings of Edith Wharton* edited by Frederick Wegener (Princeton, New Jersey: Princeton University Press, 1999. First published 1996).

Woolf, Virginia, *To the Lighthouse* (London: Penguin Classics, 2000. First published 1927).

Secondary Literature

Adair, Gilbert, Introduction to *The Longest Journey* (London: Penguin Classics, 2006. First published 1907), ix–xvi.

Adams, David, *Colonial Odysseys: Empire and Epic in the Modernist Novel* (Ithaca and London: Cornell University Press, 2003).

Adorno, Theodor W., *Prisms* translated by Samuel and Sherry Weber (Cambridge: MIT Press, 1967).

————, 'Reconciliation under Duress' (1961) in *Aesthetics and Politics* edited by Rodney Livingstone, Perry Anderson and Francis Mulhern (London: Verso/ New Left Books, 1977), 151–76.

Anderson, Benedict, *Imagined Communities: Reflections on the Origin and Spread of Nationalism* (London: Verso, 1983).

Anderson, Perry, *The New Old World* (London: Verso, 2009).

Ardis, Ann, 'Hellenism and the Lure of Italy' in *The Cambridge Companion to E.M. Forster* edited by David Bradshaw (Cambridge: Cambridge University Press, 2007), 62–76.

Armstrong, Tim, *Modernism: A Cultural History* (London: Polity, 2005).

Ash, Beth Sharon, 'Frail Vessels and Vast Designs: A Psychoanalytic Portrait of Isabel Archer' in *New Essays on The Portrait of a Lady* edited by Joel Porte (Cambridge: Cambridge University Press, 1999. First published 1990), 123–62.

Auerbach, Erich, *Mimesis: The Representation of Reality in Western Literature* translated by Willard R. Trask (Princeton: Princeton University Press, 1968. First published 1946).

Bailey, Quentin, 'Heroes and Homosexuals: Education and Empire in E.M. Forster' *Twentieth Century Literature* 48/3 (Autumn 2002), 324–47.

Bakhtin, M.M., 'Forms of Time and the Chronotope in the Novel: Notes towards a Historical Poetics' [written 1937–1938] in *The Dialogic Imagination: Four Essays* edited by Michael Holquist (Austin: University of Texas Press, 1994), 84–258.

Bahlke, George W., '"See Naples and Die": Two Heroines' Italian Journeys' in *D.H. Lawrence and Literary Genres* edited by Simonetta de Filippis and Nick Ceramella (Napoli: Loffredo Editore, 2004), 55–66.

Banfield, Ann, *The Phantom Table: Woolf, Fry, Russell and the Epistemology of Modernism* (Cambridge: Cambridge University Press, 2000).

Banta, Martha, 'Men, Women, and the American Way' in *The Cambridge Companion to Henry James* edited by Jonathan Freedman (Cambridge: Cambridge University Press, 2000), 21–39.

———, 'Wharton's Women: In Fashion, In History, Out of Time' in *A Historical Guide to Edith Wharton* edited by Carol J. Singley (New York: Oxford University Press, 2003), 51–87.

Baucom, Ian, *Out of Place: Englishness, Empire, and the Locations of Identity* (Princeton: Princeton University Press, 1999).

Bauer, Dale M., 'Wharton's "Others": Addiction and Intimacy' in *Edith Wharton: A Historical Guide* edited by Carol J. Singley (Oxford: Oxford University Press, 2003), 115–45.

Beer, Janet, *Edith Wharton: Writers and Their Work* (Tavistock: Northcote House, 2002).

Bell, Michael, *D.H. Lawrence: Language and Being* (Cambridge: Cambridge University Press, 1992).

Bell, Millicent, ed., *The Cambridge Companion to Edith Wharton* (Cambridge: Cambridge University Press, 1995).

Benjamin, Walter, *Illuminations* (Glasgow: Fontana, 1970. First published 1955).

Benstock, Shari, 'Edith Wharton, 1862–1937: A Brief Biography' in *A Historical Guide to Edith Wharton* edited by Carol J. Singley (New York: Oxford University Press, 2003), 19–48.

Bentley, Nancy, 'Wharton, Travel, Modernity' in *Edith Wharton: A Historical Guide* edited by Carol J. Singley (Oxford: Oxford University Press, 2003), 147–79.

Berberich, Christine, Neil Campbell and Robert Hudson, eds, *Land and Identity: Theory, Memory, and Practice* (Amsterdam and New York: Rodopi, 2012).

Berthoud, Jacques, 'The Modernization of Sulaco' in *Conrad's Cities* edited by Gene Moore (Amsterdam and Atlanta: Rodopi, 1992), 139–57.

Bhabha, Homi K., *The Location of Culture* (London: Routledge, 1994).

Blair, Sara, *Henry James and the Writing of Race and Nation* (Cambridge: Cambridge University Press, 2009. First published 1996).

Blanchard, Lydia, 'D.H. Lawrence and the "Gentle Reader": The Furious Comedy of *Mr Noon*' in *Lawrence and Comedy* edited by Paul Eggert and John Worthen (Cambridge: Cambridge University Press, 1996), 89–108.

Boddy, Kasia, 'The European Journey in Postwar American Fiction' in *Voyages and Visions: Towards a Cultural History of Travel* edited by Jàs Elsner and Joan-Pau Rubiés, 232–51.

Bongie, Chris, 'A Man of the Last Hour', reprinted in *Joseph Conrad: Longman Critical Reader* edited by Andrew Michael Roberts (London: Longman, 1998), 124–51.

Booth, Howard J., 'Lawrence in Doubt: A Theory of the "Other" and its Collapse' in *Modernism and Empire* edited by Howard J. Booth and Nigel Rigby (Manchester: Manchester University Press, 2000), 197–223.

———, 'Maurice' in *The Cambridge Companion to E.M. Forster* edited by David Bradshaw (Cambridge: Cambridge University Press, 2007), 173–87.

Booth, Howard J. and Nigel Rigby, eds, *Modernism and Empire* (Manchester: Manchester University Press, 2000).

Booth, William, *In Darkest England* (London: Salvation Army, 1900).

Bordo, Jonathan, 'The Keeping Place (Arising from an Incident on the Land)' in *Monuments and Memory, Made and Unmade* edited by Robert S. Nelson and Margaret Olin (Chicago and London: Chicago University Press, 2003), 157–82.

Bradbury, Malcom, 'London 1890–1920' in *Modernism* edited by Malcolm Bradbury and James McFarlane (London: Penguin, 1976), 172–90.

Bradbury, Malcolm and James McFarlane, eds, *Modernism: A Guide to European Literature 1890–1930* (London: Penguin, 1976).

Bradshaw, David, ed., *The Cambridge Companion to E.M. Forster* (Cambridge: Cambridge University Press, 2007).

Brantlinger, Patrick, *Rule of Darkness: British Literature and Imperialism, 1830–1914* (Ithaca and London: Cornell University Press, 1988).

Brendon, Piers, *The Decline and Fall of the British Empire 1781–1997* (London: Jonathan Cape, 2007).

Brennan, Teresa, *History after Lacan* (London: Routledge, 1993).

Brooks, Peter, *Henry James Goes to Paris* (Princeton: Princeton University Press, 2007).

Brown, Keith, ed., *Rethinking Lawrence* (Buckingham: Open University Press, 1990).

Buchanan, David, 'Reading the Other: Bakhtin and the Topography of Arrival in Literature' in *Topodynamics of Arrival: Essays on Self and Pilgrimage* edited by Gert Hofmann and Snježana Zorić (Amsterdam and New York: Rodopi, 2012), 151–67.

Burden, Robert, 'Conrad's Heart of Darkness: The Critique of Imperialism and the Post-Colonial Reader', *L'Epoque Conradienne* 18 (1992), 63–83.

———, 'Home Thoughts from Abroad: Cultural Difference and the Critique of Modernity in D.H. Lawrence's *Twilight in Italy* (1916) and Other Travel Writing' in *Landscape and Englishness* edited by Robert Burden and Stephan Kohl (Amsterdam and New York: Rodopi, 2006), 137–61.

———, 'Parody, Stylization, and Dialogics: A Bakhtinian Reading of *The Lost Girl*' *D.H. Lawrence Review* 30/3 (2002), 25–42.

————, *Radicalizing Lawrence: Critical Interventions in the Reading and Reception of D.H. Lawrence's Narrative Fiction* (Amsterdam: Rodopi, 2000).

Buzard, James, 'Forster's Trespasses: Tourism and Cultural Politics' in *E.M. Forster: Contemporary Critical Essays* edited by Jeremy Tambling (Basingstoke: Palgrave New Casebooks, 1995), 14–29.

Carr, Helen, 'Modernism and Travel (1880–1940)' in *The Cambridge Companion to Travel Writing* edited by Peter Hulme and Tim Youngs (Cambridge: Cambridge University Press, 2002), 70–86.

Carswell, Catherine, *The Savage Pilgrimage: A Narrative of D.H. Lawrence* (Cambridge: Cambridge University Press, 1981. First published 1932).

Certeau, Michel de, *The Practice of Everyday Life* (Berkeley and London: University of California Press, 1988. First published 1980).

Childs, Peter, *Modernism and the Post-Colonial: Literature and Empire 1885–1930* (London: Continuum, 2007).

Christensen, Timothy, 'Bearing the White Man's Burden: Misrecognition and Cultural Difference in E.M. Forster's *A Passage to India*' *Novel: A Forum for Fiction* 39/2 (Spring 2006), 155–78.

Cushman, Keith and Earl G. Ingersoll, eds, *D.H. Lawrence: New Worlds* (London: Associated University Press, 2003).

Daniels, Stephen and Denis Cosgrove, eds, *The Iconography of Landscape: Essays on the Symbolic Representation, Design and Use of Past Environments* (Cambridge: Cambridge University Press, 2002. First published 1988).

Delany, Paul, '"Islands of Money": Rentier Culture in *Howards End*' in *E.M. Forster: Contemporary Critical Essays* edited by Jeremy Tambling (Basingstoke: Palgrave New Casebooks, 1995), 67–80.

Derrida, Jacques, *Acts of Literature* edited and introduced by Derek Attridge (New York and London: Routledge, 1992).

Dollimore, Jonathan, *Death, Desire and Loss in Western Culture* (London: Allen Lane, 1998).

Dwight, Eleanor, 'Wharton and Art' in *Edith Wharton: A Historical Guide* edited by Carol J. Singley (Oxford: Oxford University Press, 2003), 181–210.

Eagleton, Terry, *The English Novel* (Oxford: Blackwell, 2005).

————, *Exiles and Émigrés* (London: Chatto and Windus, 1970).

————, *The Idea of Culture* (Oxford: Blackwell, 2000).

————, *The Ideology of the Aesthetic* (Oxford: Blackwell, 1990).

Eggert, Paul and John Worthen, eds, *Lawrence and Comedy* (Cambridge: Cambridge University Press, 1996).

Elby, Clare Virginia, 'Silencing Women in Edith Wharton's *The Age of Innocence*' *Colby Quarterly* 28/2 (June 1992), 93–104.

Eliot, T.S., *Notes towards the Definition of Culture* (London: Faber and Faber, 1962. First published 1948).

Ellis, David, *D.H. Lawrence: Dying Game 1922–1930* (Cambridge: Cambridge University Press, 1998).

Ellis, David and Ornella De Zordo, eds, *D.H. Lawrence: Critical Assessments 4 vols* (Mountfield: Helm Information, 1992).

Elsner, Jàs and Joan-Pau Rubiés, eds, *Voyages and Visions: Towards a Cultural History of Travel* (London: Reaktion Books, 1999).

Evans, Anne-Marie, 'Public Space and Spectacle: Female Bodies and Consumerism in Edith Wharton's *The House of Mirth*' in *Inside Out: Women Negotiating, Subverting, Appropriating Public and Private Spaces* edited by Teresa Gómez Reus and Aránzazu Usandizaga (Amsterdam and New York: Rodopi, 2008), 107–23.

Eysteinsson, Astradur, *The Concept of Modernism* (Ithaca and London: Cornell University Press, 1990).

Farley, David G., *Modernist Travel Writing: Intellectuals Abroad* (Columbia and London: University of Missouri Press, 2010).

Fernihough, Anne, ed., *The Cambridge Companion to D.H. Lawrence* (Cambridge: Cambridge University Press, 2001).

———, *D.H. Lawrence: Aesthetics and Ideology* (Oxford: Clarendon, 1993).

Filippis, Simonetta de and Nick Ceramella, eds, *D.H. Lawrence and Literary Genres* (Napoli: Loffredo Editore, 2004).

Fjagesund, Peter, *The Apocalyptic World of D.H. Lawrence* (London and Oslo: Norwegian University Press, 1991).

Foucault, Michel, *Discipline and Punish* (London: Penguin, 1986. First published 1975).

———, 'Questions on Geography' reprinted in *Michel Foucault Power/ Knowledge: Selected Interviews and Other Writings 1972–1977* edited by Colin Gordon (Harlow: Longman, 1980), 63–77.

Freedman, Jonathan, ed., *The Cambridge Companion to Henry James* (Cambridge: Cambridge University Press, 2000).

Freud, Sigmund, *Civilization and its Discontents* (London: Hogarth Press, 1975. First published 1930).

———, 'A Disturbance of Memory on the Acropolis' (1936) in *The Standard Edition of the Complete Psychological Works of Sigmund Freud vol. 22: 1932–1936* translated and edited by James Strachey (1964) (London: Hogarth Press, 1978).

———, 'Delusions and Dreams in Jensen's *Gradiva*' (1917) reprinted in *The Penguin Freud Library vol. 14. Art and Literature* (London: Penguin, 1990), 29–118.

———, *The Ego and the Id* (1923) reprinted in *The Penguin Freud Library vol. 11. On Metapsychology* (London: Penguin, 1984).

Frisby, David, *Fragments of Modernity: Theories of Modernity in the Work of Simmel, Kracauer and Benjamin* (Cambridge: Polity Press, 1985).

Furbank, P.N., *E.M. Forster: A Life. 2 vols* (London: Faber and Faber, 1977).

Fussell, Paul, *Abroad: British Literary Travelling between the Wars* (Oxford: Oxford University Press, 1980).

Gay, Peter, *Freud: A Life for our Time* (London: Max Press, 2006).

———, *Modernism: The Lure of Heresy* (London: Vintage, 2009).

Gikandi, Simon, *Maps of Englishness: Writing Identity in the Culture of Colonialism* (New York: Columbia University Press, 1996).

Giles, Steve, ed., *Theorizing Modernism: Essays in Critical Theory* (London: Routledge, 1993).

Goodyear, Sara Suleri, 'Forster's Imperial Erotic in *E.M. Forster: Contemporary Critical Essays* edited by Jeremy Tambling (Basingstoke: Palgrave New Casebooks, 1995), 151–70.

Hampson, Robert, '"Topographical Mysteries": Conrad and London' in *Conrad's Cities* edited by Gene Moore (Amsterdam and Atlanta: Rodopi, 1992), 159–74.

Harvey, David, *The Condition of Postmodernity: An Enquiry into the Origins of Cultural Change* (Oxford: Blackwell, 1989).

Hay, Eloise Knapp, 'Cities like Whited Sepulchres' in *Conrad's Cities* edited by Gene Moore (Amsterdam and Atlanta: Rodopi, 1992), 125–37.

Head, Dominic, 'Forster and the Short Story' in *The Cambridge Companion to E.M. Forster* edited by David Bradshaw (Cambridge: Cambridge University Press, 2007), 77–91.

Hobsbawm, Eric, *The Age of Empire 1875–1914* (London: Abacus, 2006. First published 1987).

Holderness, Graham, *D.H. Lawrence: History, Ideology and Fiction* (Dublin: Gill and Macmillan, 1982).

Hulme, Peter and Tim Youngs, eds, *The Cambridge Companion to Travel Writing* (Cambridge: Cambridge University Press, 2002).

Hutchings, Peter J., 'Forster, Modernity and Film' in *E.M. Forster: Contemporary Critical Essays* edited by Jeremy Tambling (Basingstoke: Palgrave New Casebooks, 1995), 213–28.

Hyde, G.M., *D.H. Lawrence* (London: Macmillan, 1990).

Inglis, Tony, 'Reading late James' in *The Modern English Novel: The Reader, the Writer and the Work* edited by Gabriel Josipovici (London: Open Books, 1976), 77–94.

Jackson, Dennis, 'Lawrence's Allusive Art in Lady Chatterley's Lover' in *D.H. Lawrence: Critical Assessments* edited by David Ellis and Ornella De Zordo (Mountfield: Helm Information, 1992), vol. 3, 145–70.

Jameson, Fredric, *The Antinomies of Realism* (London: Verso, 2013).

———, *The Political Unconscious: Narrative as a Socially Symbolic Act* (Ithaca and London: Cornell University Press, 1981).

Johnson, Kendall, *Henry James and the Visual* (Cambridge: Cambridge University Press, 2007).

Josipovici, Gabriel, ed., *The Modern English Novel: The Reader, the Writer and the Work* (London: Open Books, 1976).

———, *Whatever Happened to Modernism?* (New Haven and London: Yale University Press, 2010).

Kaplan, Caren, *Questions of Travel: Postmodern Discourses of Displacement* (London: Duke University Press, 2005).

Kaplan, Carola, 'Absent Father, Passive Son: *The Longest Journey*' in *E.M. Forster: Contemporary Critical Essays* edited by Jeremy Tambling (Basingstoke: Palgrave New Casebooks, 1995), 51–66.

Kaplan, Fred, *Henry James: The Imagination of Genius – A Biography* (New York: William Morrow, 1992).

Kermode, Frank, *Concerning E.M. Forster* (London: Weidenfeld and Nicolson, 2009).

———, *Essays on Fiction 1971–1982* (London: Routledge, 1983. First published 1970).

———, *Lawrence* (Glasgow: Fontana, 1973).

———, ed., *Selected Prose of T.S. Eliot* (London and Boston: Faber & Faber, 1975).

Kinkead-Weekes, Mark, *D.H. Lawrence: Triumph to Exile 1912–1922* (Cambridge: Cambridge University Press, 1996).

———, 'Decolonising Imagination: Lawrence in the 1920s' in *The Cambridge Companion to D.H. Lawrence* edited by Ann Fernihough (Cambridge: Cambridge University Press, 2001), 67–85.

Kirchner, Paul, 'Topodialogic Narrative in *Under Western Eyes*' in *Conrad's Cities* edited by Gene Moore (Amsterdam and Atlanta: Rodopi, 1992), 223–54.

Knights, Ben, *Writing Masculinities: Male Narratives in Twentieth-Century Fiction* (London: Macmillan, 1999).

Knights, Pamela, *The Cambridge Introduction to Edith Wharton* (Cambridge: Cambridge University Press, 2009).

———, 'Forms of Disembodiment: The Social Subject in *The Age of Innocence*' in *The Cambridge Companion to Edith Wharton* edited by Millicent Bell (Cambridge: Cambridge University Press, 1995), 20–46.

Kolocotroni, Vassiliki, Jane Goldman and Olga Taxidou, eds, *Modernism: An Anthology of Sources and Documents* (Edinburgh: Edinburgh University Press, 1998).

Lacan, Jacques, *Ecrits: A Selection* translated by Alan Sheridan (London: Routledge, 1995. First published 1966).

———, *Feminine Sexuality: Jacques Lacan and the école freudienne* edited by Juliet Mitchell and Jacqueline Rose (London: Macmillan, 1982. First published 1975).

———, *The Four Fundamental Concepts of Psychoanalysis* (London: Penguin, 1987. First published 1973).

———, *The Seminar Book I* edited by Jacques-Alain Miller and translated with notes by John Forrester (Cambridge: Cambridge University Press, 1988. First published 1975).

———, *The Seminar Book II* edited by Jacques-Alain Miller and translated by Sylvana Tomaselli with notes by John Forrester (Cambridge: Cambridge University Press, 1988. First published 1978).

Larabee, Mark D., 'Joseph Conrad and the Maritime Tradition' in *A Historical Guide to Joseph Conrad* edited by John G. Peters (Oxford: Oxford University Press, 2010), 47–76.

Leavis, F.R., *The Great Tradition* (London: Penguin, 1948).

Lee, Hermione, *Edith Wharton* (London: Vintage Books, 2008).

Lefebvre, Henri, *The Production of Space* (Oxford: Blackwell, 1991. First published 1974).

Lemaire, Gérard-Georges, ed., *The Orient in Western Art* with a preface by Geneviève Lacambre (Paris: Könemann, 2005).

Levenson, Michael, *A Genealogy of Modernism* (Cambridge: Cambridge University Press, 1984).

———, *Modernism* (London: Yale University Press, 2011).

Livingstone, Rodney, Perry Anderson, and Francis Mulhern, eds, *Aesthetics and Politics* (London: Verso/New Left Books, 1977).

Martin, Robert K., 'The Double Structure of *Maurice*' in *E.M. Forster: Contemporary Critical Essays* edited by Jeremy Tambling (Basingstoke: Palgrave New Casebooks, 1995), 100–114.

Masterman, C.F.G., *The Condition of England* edited with an introduction and notes by James T. Boulton (London: Faber and Faber, 1988).

Maves, Carl, *Sensuous Pessimism: Italy in the Work of Henry James* with a foreword by Ian Watt (Bloomington and London: Indiana University Press, 1973).

McClintock, Anne, *Imperial Leather: Race, Gender and Sexuality in the Colonial Conquest* (London: Routledge, 1995).

McLauchlan, Juliet, 'Conrad's "Decivilized" Cities' in *Conrad's Cities* edited by Gene Moore (Amsterdam and Atlanta: Rodopi, 1992), 57–84.

Meissner, Collin, 'Talking about Money: Art and Commerce in America' in *Advances in Henry James Studies* edited by Peter Rawlings (London: Palgrave, 2007), 263–82.

Merish, Lori, 'Engendering Naturalism: Narrative Form and Commodity Spectacle in U.S. Naturalist Fiction' *Novel: A Forum for Fiction* 29/3 (Spring 1996), 319–45.

Michelucci, Stefania, *Space and Place in the Works of D.H. Lawrence* (London: McFarland, 2002).

Moffat, Wendy, *A Great Unrecorded History: A New Life of E.M. Forster* (New York: Farrar, Strauss and Giroux, 2010).

Mongia, Padmini, 'Ghosts of the Gothic: Spectral Woman and Colonized Spaces in *Lord Jim*' in *Joseph Conrad: Longman Critical Reader* edited by Andrew Michael Roberts (London: Longman, 1998), 155–70.

Moore, Gene, ed., *Conrad's Cities* (Amsterdam and Atlanta: Rodopi, 1992).

Morton, H.V., *In Search of England* (London: Methuen, 2000. First published 1927).

Najder, Zdzisław, *Joseph Conrad: A Life* (New York: Camden House, 2007).

Nora, Pierre, ed., *Lieux de mémoire* 3 vols (Paris: Gallimard, 1997).

Nordau, Max, *Degeneration* (London: University of Nebraska Press, 1993. First published 1895).

Nyman, Jopi, *Under English Eyes: Constructions of Europe in Early Twentieth-Century British Fiction* (Amsterdam: Rodopi, 2000).

Parrinder, Patrick, *Nation and Novel: The English Novel from its Origins to the Present Day* (Oxford: Oxford University Press, 2006).

Parry, Benita, 'Problems in Current Theories of Colonial Discourse' *The Oxford Literary Review* 9/1–2 (1987), 27–58.

Pater, Walter, *Studies in the History of the Renaissance* with introduction by Matthew Beaumont (Oxford: Oxford World's Classics, 2010. First published 1873).

Peat, Alexandra, *Travel and Modernist Literature: Sacred and Ethical Journeys* (New York: Routledge, 2011).

Peppis, Paul, 'Forster and England' in Bradshaw, David, ed., *The Cambridge Companion to E.M. Forster* (Cambridge: Cambridge University Press, 2007), 47–61.

Peters, John G., *The Cambridge Introduction to Conrad* (Cambridge: Cambridge University Press, 2006).

———, ed., *A Historical Guide to Joseph Conrad* (Oxford: Oxford University Press, 2010).

Pinkney, Tony, *D.H. Lawrence* (London and New York: Harvester, 1990).

Porte, Joel, ed., *New Essays on The Portrait of a Lady* (Cambridge: Cambridge University Press, 1999. First published 1990).

Porter, Dennis, *Haunted Journeys: Desire and Transgression in European Travel Writing* (Princeton: Princeton University Press, 1991).

Posnock, Ross, 'Henry James, Veblen and Adorno: The Crisis of the Modern Self' *Journal of American Studies* 21 (1987), 31–54.

Pratt, Mary Louise, *Imperial Eyes: Travel Writing and Transculturation* (London: Routledge, 1992).

Punter, David, *Modernity* (London: Palgrave, 2007).

Pykett, Lyn, *Engendering Fictions: The English Novel in the Early Twentieth Century* (London: Arnold, 1995).

Rawlings, Peter, ed., *Advances in Henry James Studies* (London: Palgrave, 2007).

Roberts, Andrew Michael, ed., *Joseph Conrad: Longman Critical Reader* (London: Longman, 1998).

Roberts, Neil, *D.H. Lawrence, Travel and Cultural Difference* (London: Palgrave Macmillan, 2004).

Roy, Ashish, 'Framing the Other: History and Literary Verisimilitude in E.M. Forster's *The Hill of Devi*' *Criticism* 36/2 (Spring 1994), 265–89.

Royle, Nicholas, *The Uncanny* (Manchester: Manchester University Press, 2003).

Ruskin, John, *Selected Writings* edited by Dinah Birch (Oxford: Oxford World's Classics, 2009).

———, *Selected Writings* edited by Philip Davis (London: Everyman, 1995).

Rylance, Rick, 'Lawrence's Politics' in Keith Brown, ed., *Rethinking Lawrence* (Buckingham: Open University Press, 1990), 163–80.

Said, Edward, *Culture and Imperialism* (New York: Alfred A. Knopf, 1993).

———, 'Intellectuals in the Post-colonial World' *Salmagundi* 70–71 (Spring-Summer 1986), 49–74.

———, *Orientalism* (London: Routledge, 1978).

Salmoni, Steven, '"The Very Air we Breathe": The Aesthetics of Experience in Henry James's "From Chambéry to Milan"' *Studies in Travel Writing* 12/3 (November 2008), 230–35.

Scherer Herz, Judith, '*A Room with a View*' in *The Cambridge Companion to E.M. Forster* edited by David Bradshaw (Cambridge: Cambridge University Press, 2007), 138–50.

Schriber, Mary Suzanne, 'Edith Wharton and Travel Writing as Self-Discovery' *American Literature* 59/2 (May 1987), 257–67.

Seshadri-Crooks, Kalpana, *Desiring Whiteness: A Lacanian Analysis of Race* (London and New York: Routledge, 2000).

Shepherdson, Charles, *Vital Signs: Nature, Culture, Psychoanalysis* (London: Routledge, 2000).

Sheppard, Richard, 'The Problematics of European Modernism' in *Theorising Modernism* edited by Steve Giles (London: Routledge, 1993), 1–51.

Showalter, Elaine, '*The Custom of the Country*: Spragg and the Art of the Deal' in *The Cambridge Companion to Edith Wharton* edited by Millicent Bell (Cambridge: Cambridge University Press, 1995), 87–97.

Simmons, Laurence, *Freud's Italian Journey* (Amsterdam and New York: Rodopi, 2006).

Simpson, Hilary, 'Lawrence, Feminism and the War' in *D.H. Lawrence* edited by Peter Widdowson (London: Longman Critical Reader, 1992), 90–102.

Singley, Carol J., ed., *A Historical Guide to Edith Wharton* (Oxford: Oxford University Press, 2003).

———, 'Race, Culture, Nation: Edith Wharton and Ernest Renan' *Twentieth-Century Literature* 49/1 (Spring 2003), 32–45.

Spengler, Oswald, *The Decline of the West: Abridged Edition* translated by Charles Francis Atkinson (Oxford: Oxford University Press, 1991. First published 1918).

Stanley, Henry Morton, *In Darkest Africa: Or, the Quest, Rescue, and Retreat of Emin Pasha, Governor of Equitoria* 2 vols (Santa Barbara, California: The Narrative Press, 2001. First published 1890).

Stape, J.H., ed., *The Cambridge Companion to Joseph Conrad* (Cambridge: Cambridge University Press, 2004. First published 1996).

Stewart, Jack F. 'Expressionism in *The Rainbow*' *Novel* 13/3 (Spring 1980), 298–315.

Stoll, Rae H., '*The Longest Journey*: Language, Desire, History' *E.M. Forster: Contemporary Critical Essays* edited by in Jeremy Tambling (Basingstoke: Palgrave New Casebooks, 1995), 30–50.

Supiot, Alain, 'Spirit of Social Law', *New Left Review* 83 (July–August 2013), 99–113.

Tambling, Jeremy, ed., *E.M. Forster: Contemporary Critical Essays* (Basingstoke: Palgrave New Casebooks, 1995).

Thacker, Andrew, *Moving through Modernity: Space and Geography in Modernism* (Manchester: Manchester University Press, 2003).

Thompson, Carl, *Travel Writing* (London: Routledge, 2011).

Tóibín, Colm, *All a Novelist Needs: Colm Tóibín on Henry James* edited with an introduction by Susan M. Griffin (Baltimore: Johns Hopkins University Press, 2010).

Tracy, Billy T., *D.H. Lawrence and the Literature of Travel* (Ann Arbor: University of Michigan Research Press, 1983).

Tromly, Lucas, '"The Small Talk of the Harem": Discursive Communities and Colonial Silences in Edith Wharton's *In Morocco' Studies in Travel Writing* 13/3 (September 2009), 239–50.

Urry, John, *The Tourist Gaze* (London: Sage, 2006. First published 1990).

Veblen, Thorstein, *The Theory of the Leisure Class* (Oxford: Oxford World's Classics, 2009).

Watson, Nicola J., *The Literary Tourist* (London: Palgrave, 2006).

Watts, Cedric, 'Conrad and the Myth of the Monstrous Town' in *Conrad's Cities* edited by Gene Moore (Amsterdam and Atlanta: Rodopi, 1992), 17–30.

Wegener, Frederick, 'Edith Wharton on French Colonial Charities for Women: An Unknown Travel Essay' *Tulsa Studies in Women's Literature* 17/1 (Spring 1998), 11–21.

Weigle, Marta and Kyle Fiore, *Santa Fe and Taos: The Writer's Era 1916–1941* (Santa Fe: Ancient City Press, 1994. First published 1982).

Weisbuch, Robert, 'James and the Idea of Evil' in *The Cambridge Companion to Henry James* edited by Jonathan Freedman (Cambridge: Cambridge University Press, 2000), 102–19.

White, Andrea, *Joseph Conrad and the Adventure Tradition* (Cambridge: Cambridge University Press, 1993).

Whitfield, Peter, *Travel: A Literary History* (Oxford: The Bodleian Library, 2011).

Widdowson, Peter, ed., *D.H. Lawrence* (London: Longman Critical Reader, 1992).

Williams, Raymond, *Culture and Society* (London: Penguin, 1958).

———, *The English Novel from Dickens to Lawrence* (London: Hogarth Press, 1984).

———, *The Politics of Modernism: Against the New Conformists* (London: Verso, 1989).

Woolf, Virginia, 'Mr. Bennett and Mrs. Brown' *Collected Essays vol. 1* edited by Leonard Woolf (London: Chatto and Windus, 1966. First published 1925), 319–37.

Worthen, John, *D.H. Lawrence and the Idea of the Novel* (London: Macmillan, 1979).

———, *D.H. Lawrence: The Early Years 1885–1912* (Cambridge: Cambridge University Press, 1991).

———, *D.H. Lawrence: The Life of an Outsider* (London: Allen Lane, 2005).

Zorzi, Rosella Mamoli, 'Tiepolo, Henry James, and Edith Wharton' *The Metropolitan Museum Journal* 33 (1998), 211–29.

Index

For Product Safety Concerns and Information please contact our EU representative GPSR@taylorandfrancis.com Taylor & Francis Verlag GmbH, Kaufingerstraße 24, 80331 München, Germany

Printed and bound by CPI Group (UK) Ltd, Croydon, CR0 4YY

01/05/2025

01858410-0001